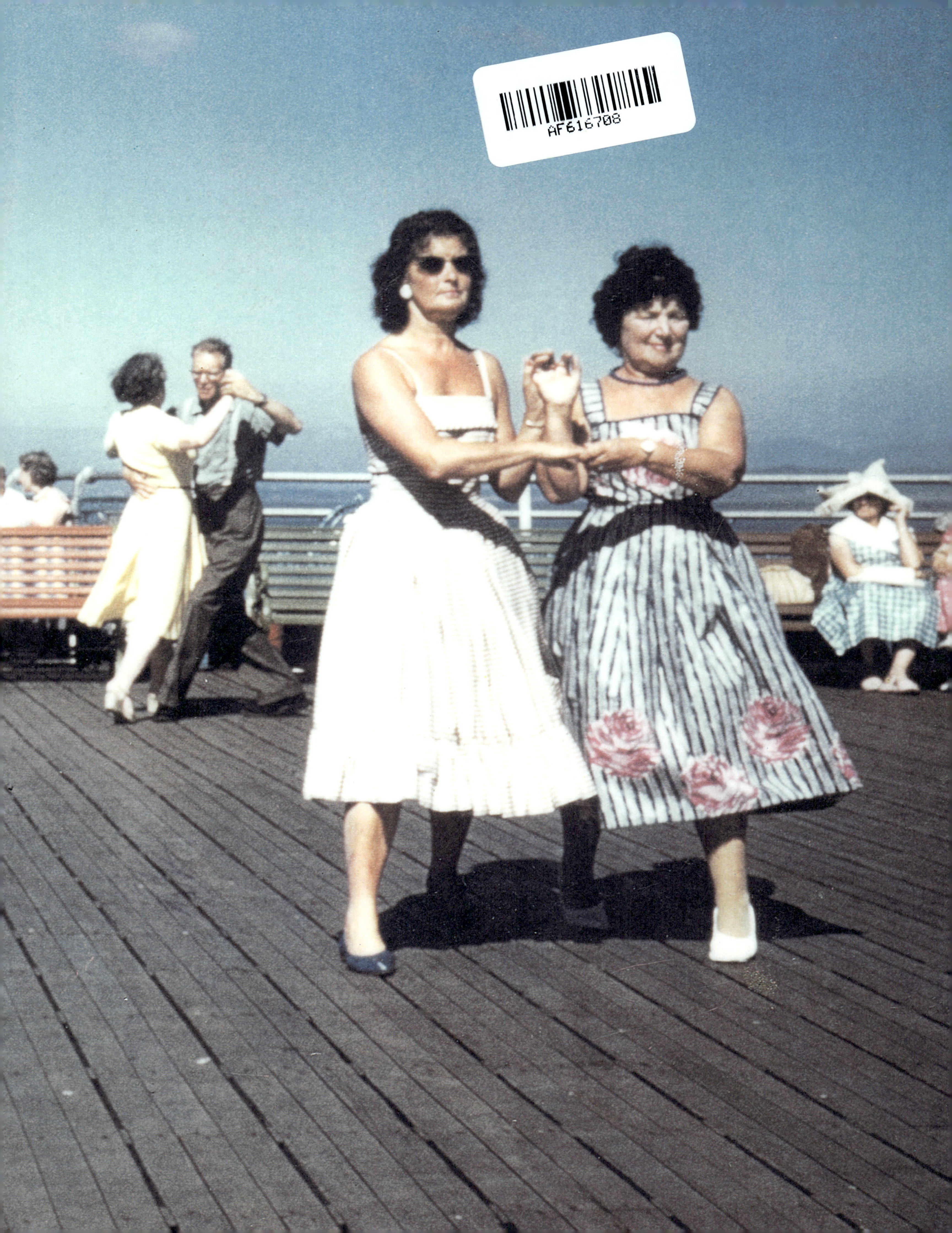

AF616708

Just Above The Mantelpiece

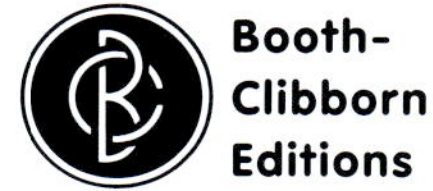

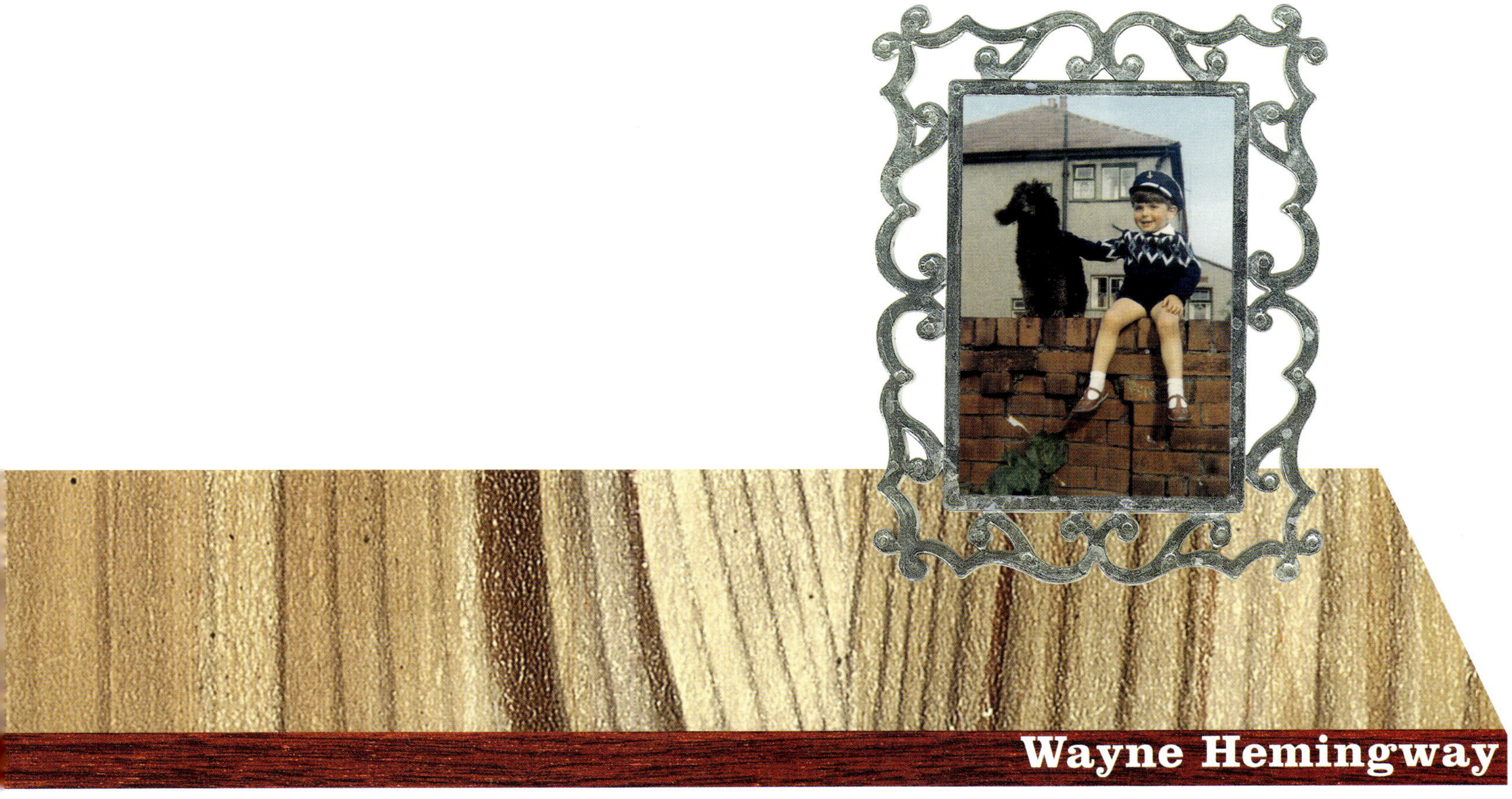

Wayne Hemingway

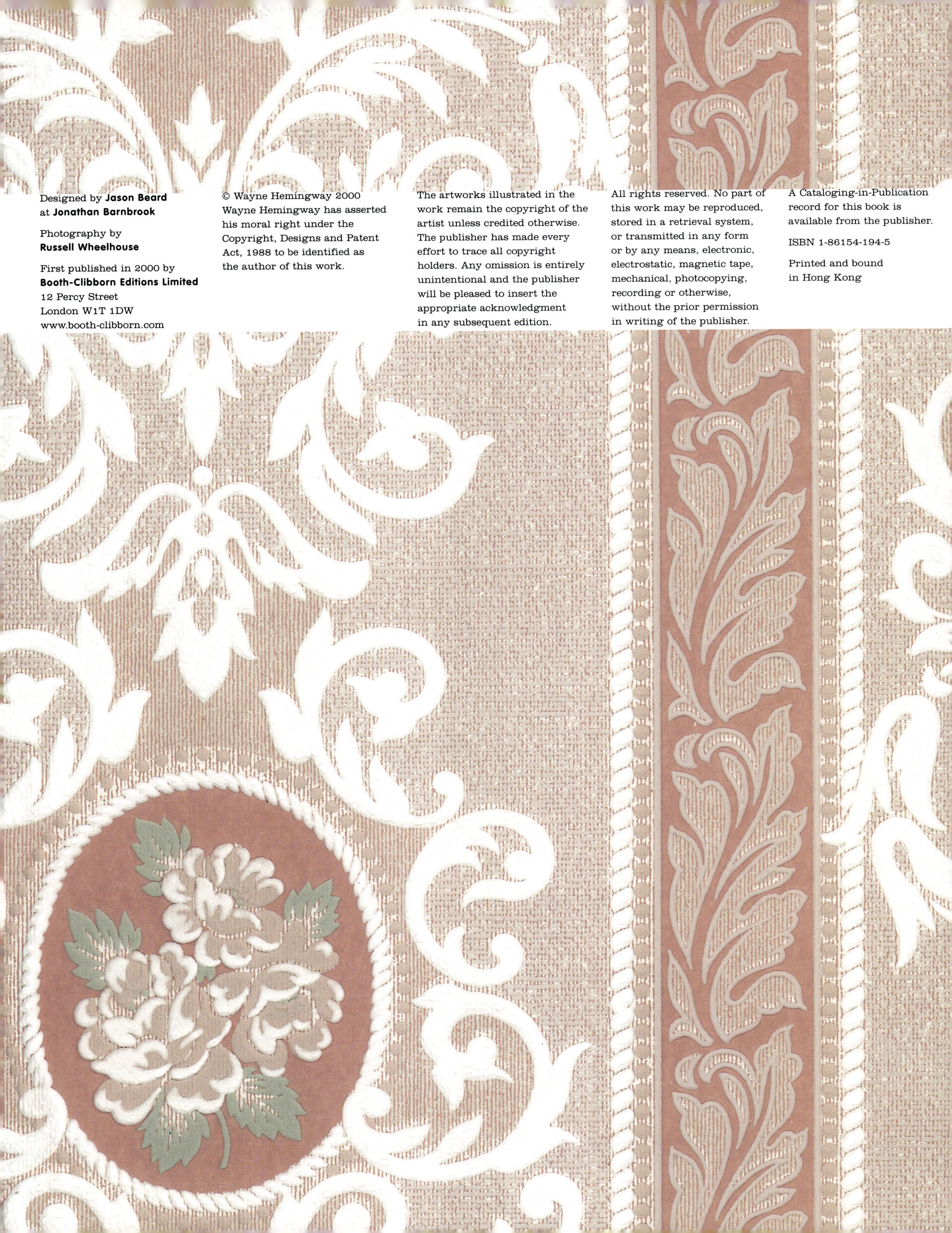

Designed by **Jason Beard**
at **Jonathan Barnbrook**

Photography by
Russell Wheelhouse

First published in 2000 by
Booth-Clibborn Editions Limited
12 Percy Street
London W1T 1DW
www.booth-clibborn.com

© Wayne Hemingway 2000
Wayne Hemingway has asserted his moral right under the Copyright, Designs and Patent Act, 1988 to be identified as the author of this work.

The artworks illustrated in the work remain the copyright of the artist unless credited otherwise. The publisher has made every effort to trace all copyright holders. Any omission is entirely unintentional and the publisher will be pleased to insert the appropriate acknowledgment in any subsequent edition.

All rights reserved. No part of this work may be reproduced, stored in a retrieval system, or transmitted in any form or by any means, electronic, electrostatic, magnetic tape, mechanical, photocopying, recording or otherwise, without the prior permission in writing of the publisher.

A Cataloging-in-Publication record for this book is available from the publisher.

ISBN 1-86154-194-5

Printed and bound
in Hong Kong

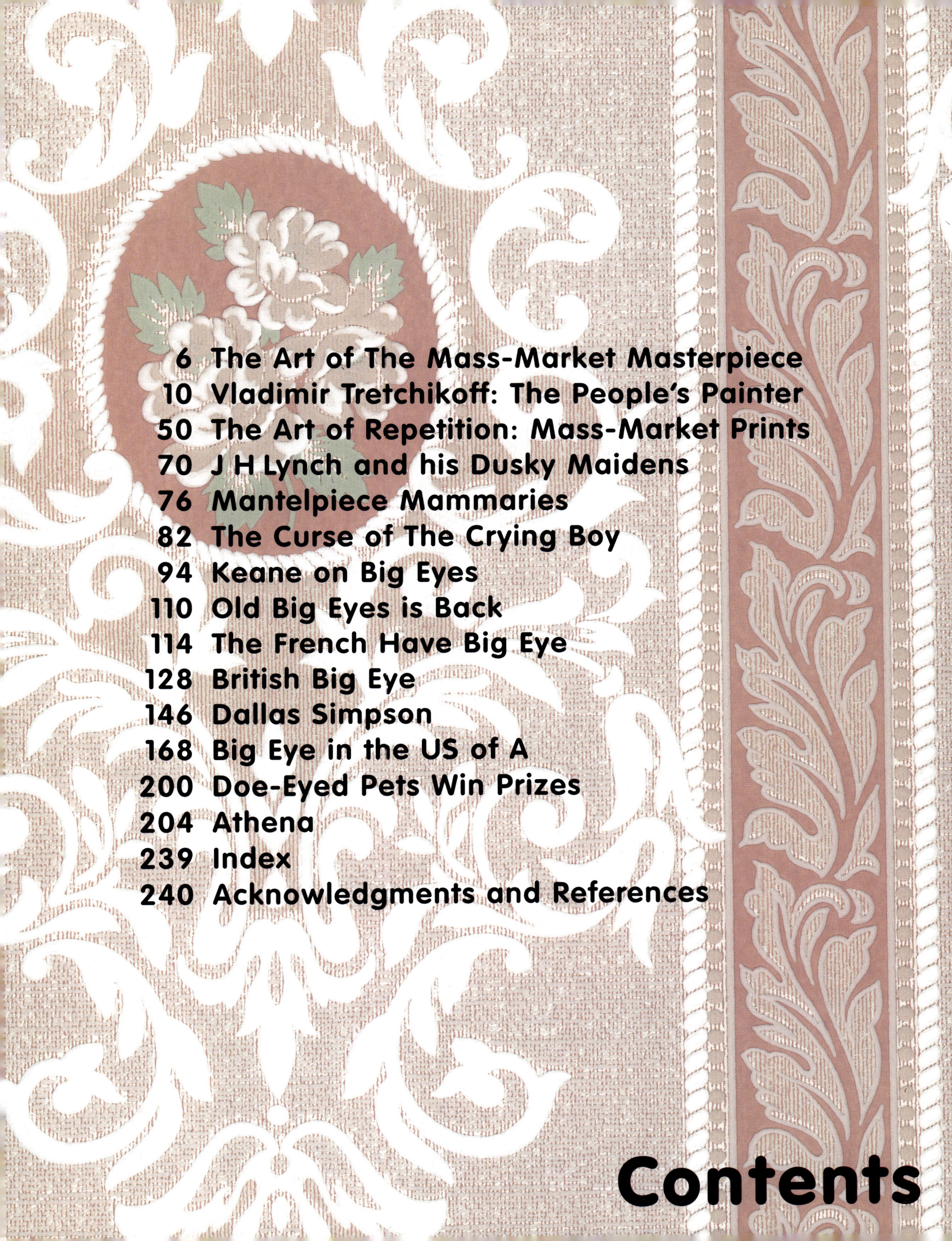

Contents

I was born in 1961 in Morecambe on the north-west coast of England and spent my first seven years in an art gallery: **15 Thirlemere Drive, Morecambe**, the home of my grandmother, Ida Hemingway, an appreciator and collector of mass-market masterpieces. Thirlemere Drive was a special place; a world of windmills, delicate waterfalls and playful gnomes angling for goldfish, coiffured poodles – my Nan had one called Cha-Cha – named after her favourite dance, net curtains, 'no vacancy' signs, antimacassars, Spanish castanets, dolls in national costume, knitted toilet-roll covers, blown-glass animals, fold-out postcards, straw donkeys, leather-covered decanters, velvet bulls, vintage-car ashtrays, snowstorms, and owls made from shells off the beach. Eric Morecambe's mum lived next door and Thora Hird round the corner.

Ida loved her art, but not for her the Mayfair galleries or Sotheby's and Christie's auction rooms. She bought

The Art Of The Mass-Market Masterpiece

through **Freeman's** and **Littlewoods'** catalogues, **Argos**, **Hitchen's** (a more famous Morecambe discount land-mark) and the myriad of promenade gift shops.

Whilst Jackson Pollock, Patrick Caulfield, David Hockney, Andy Warhol, Francis Bacon et al became fat on the lavish purchases of a handful of big spenders and unreasonably wealthy art collectors, and while the middle classes bought David Shepherd's elephants and tigers, Ida and her contemporaries sacrificed the odd fish-and-chip supper for the art of **Idylle**, **Betty Raphael**, **Genet**, **Cominoff**, **Dallas Simpson** and, of course, **Vladimir Tretchikoff**.

The chimney breast over the mantelpiece was the first area of wall to be covered by Ida's art collection. Slowly just about every other wall in the house was transformed into part of the gallery. Unreasonably vibrant-skinned oriental beauties fought for precious wall space with big-eyed animals and even bigger-eyed children (their

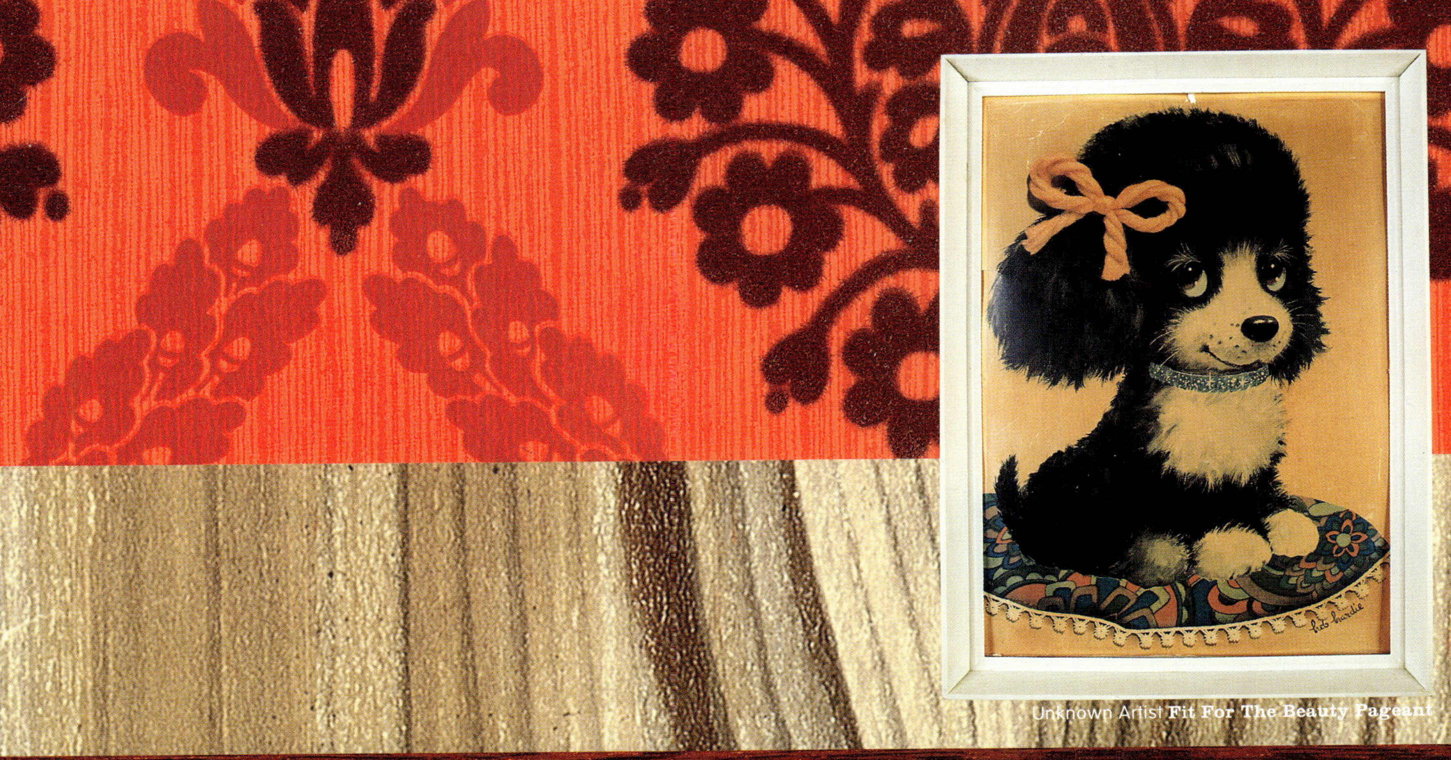

Unknown Artist **Fit For The Beauty Pageant**

big eyes were nothing to do with a night on Class A drugs). Some children clutched teddies, others played instruments, others simply cried. Wild horses running through lakes appeared next to mystical swans with naked Adams and Eves perched on their wings.

When my mother got married in 1968, we moved out of Ida's house into a high-rise in Blackburn, but my mother's skill with pin pictures and her psychedelic posters couldn't replace the Thirlemere Drive Gallery and its regular visitors, the blue-rinse ballroom-dancing 'art' critics who marvelled at Ida's big-eyed boys. **'They look just like little Wayne'**, they would say, time and again.

Thirteen years later I started collecting mass-market art and have never been able to pass a charity shop or thrift store, a jumble or rummage sale, since. I have seen it celebrated in a post-modernist ironic way and I have been saddened by its inclusion in kitsch iconography. Let's not celebrate it for these reasons. Value deserves

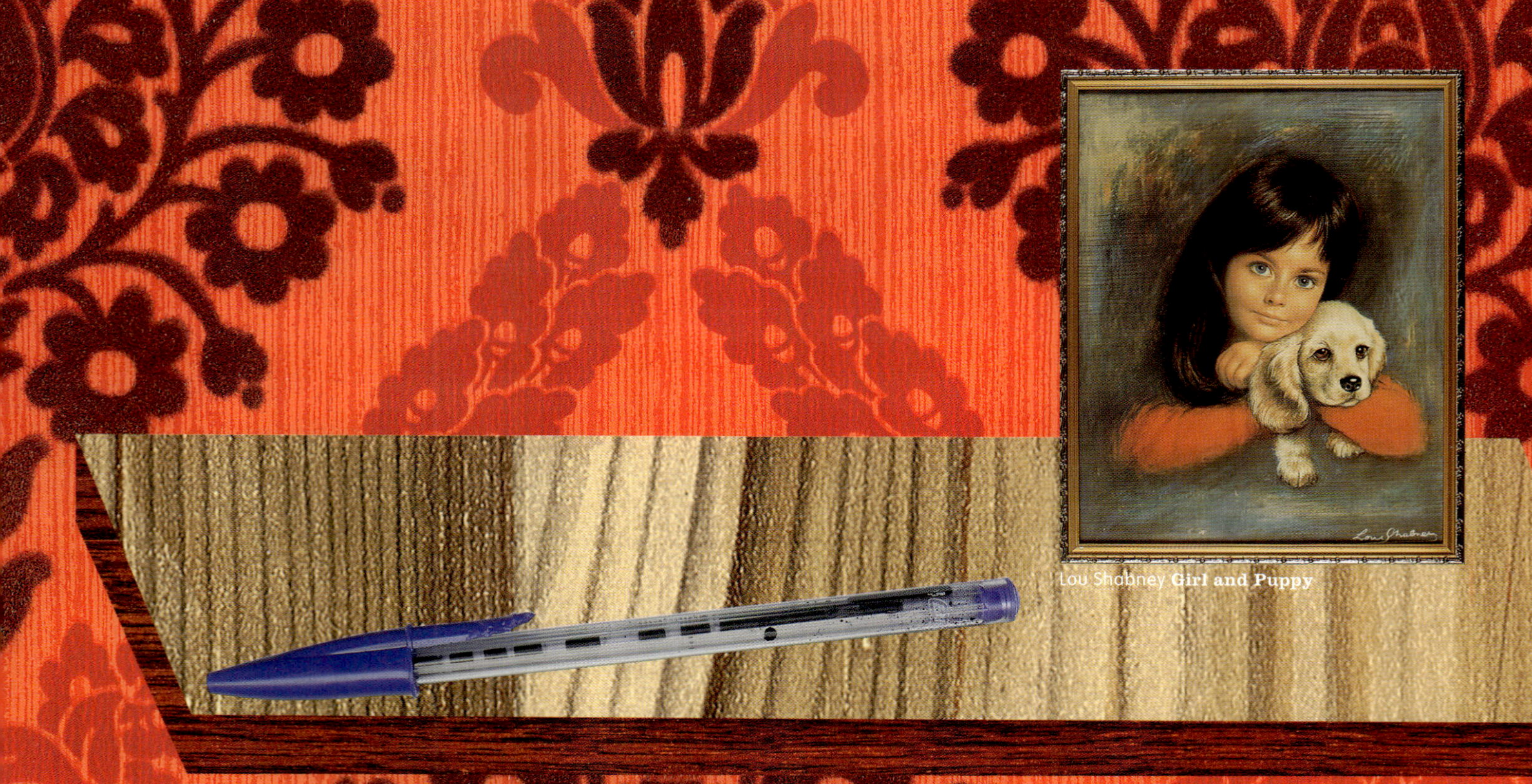

Lou Shabney **Girl and Puppy**

to be restored to a genre derided by certain members of the art elite and respect should be given to artists whose work broadened the horizons of collecting to reach the working classes, making this art form available to a wider public than ever before.

Today we have annual 'Affordable Art Fairs' in London with David Hockney prints selling in their thousands. London's Royal College of Art organizes Absolut Secret, an event where drawings by famous artists such as Chris Offili can be bought for £35. Contemporary Visual Arts magazine annually gives away prints by the likes of Patrick Caulfield and Tracey Emin to its subscribers.

If the mass-market artists of the past had been painting today, then the internet would surely have played its part. As photographer Nick Knight put it in an interview with i-D Magazine, 'art used to be created for a rich elite. Now we are seeing the opposite. Everyone can have access to our ideas – it's what Pop Art should have been.'

Vladimir Tretchikoff was the world's first mass-market artist and his commercial success was an inspiration to many other artists. He was born in the wilds of Siberia, but when aged only four, the 1917 Russian Revolution scattered his family around the globe. They were never reunited. He emigrated to China, was orphaned at 11 and became a professional artist at the age of 13. After moving to Singapore he held his first exhibition, aged 20, became a propaganda artist for British Intelligence and was duly imprisoned in Java. Here he developed his style as a painter of warm colours and exotic subjects.

Tretchikoff eventually settled in South Africa where his work was belittled and heavily criticized in the press for providing what the **Cape Times** called **'cheap sensation for the masses'**. It was here, in exhibitions, that his paintings were even attacked and slashed. **Tretchikoff** himself realised the problem: **'If I were not selling and had received no recognition from the public, these people would never have attacked me – I might even have been considered**

Vladimir Tretchikoff: The People's Painter

a worthy member of their select circle.' Yet in 1953 an exhibition of his work in Cape Town attracted 120,000 visitors and a subsequent exhibition 420,000, a huge number at that time. Invited to North America, he spent five years touring to record crowds in San José, San Francisco, Los Angeles, Dallas, Chicago, Seattle, New York, Montreal and Toronto.

The Seattle Post said: 'A sobering situation has existed on the eighth floor at Frederick and Nelson for the past two weeks. On show in the Little Gallery has been an outstanding display of twenty-five paintings loaned by the San Francisco Museum of Art. This valuable collection represents the work of the greatest names in contemporary painting. But hardly anyone has noticed the display because they've been rushing right past on their way to the Exhibition Hall to see the work of the Russian painter, Vladimir Tretchikoff. This is the kind of situation that could make an artist trade in his brushes for basket-weaving materials.'

In 1960 a London exhibition, held in a specially constructed gallery on **Harrods'** ground floor, broke all records and cemented **Tretchikoff**'s reputation as the best-selling print artist worldwide, beating Picasso – who, it is said, is the only artist to have made more money than **Tretchikoff**.

Tretchikoff, consciously or not, spat in the face of elitism in the art world. Before he decided to mass-produce his prints in 1952, the wealthy would pay significant sums for his originals. Their prices fitted the investment economy of high-brow culture. However, within two years of the paintings being reproduced in print form, **Tretchikoff** became relegated to 'low brow' status. In fact, **Tretchikoff**'s decision to reproduce his prints was arguably one of the most democratic moments in the history of modern art. It transformed the relationship between artist and purchaser to one between artist and a hundred thousand purchasers every time a print was put on sale. Stuart Cloete, in the foreword to the art book **Tretchikoff**,

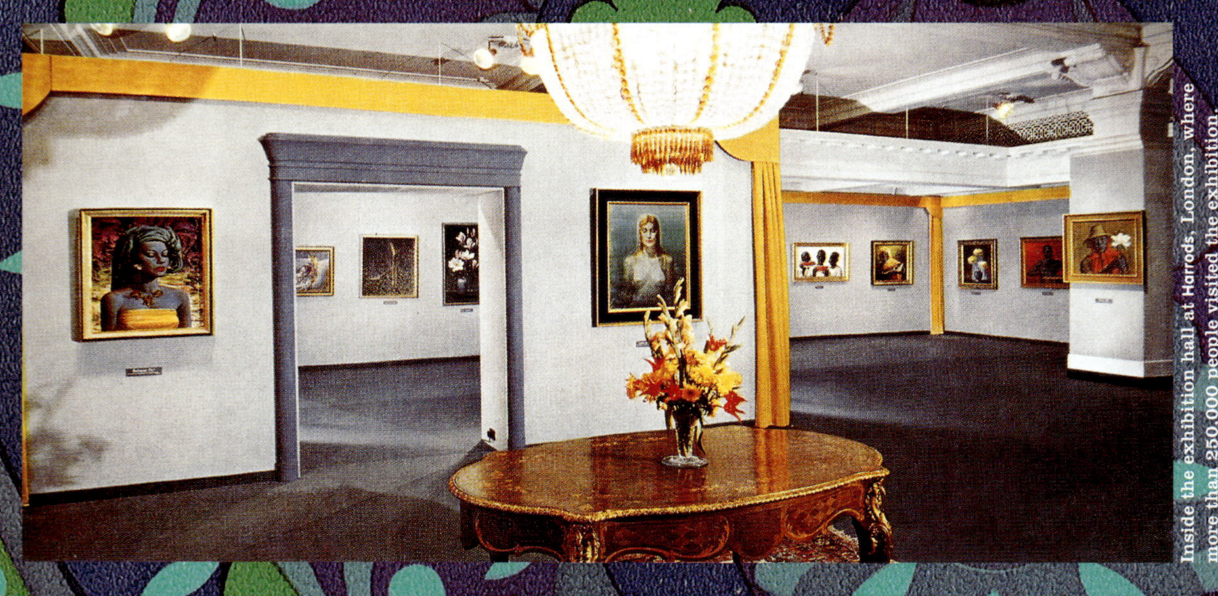

Inside the exhibition hall at Harrods, London, where more than 250,000 people visited the exhibition.

published in 1969, noted: 'The prints [sell] for a few guineas, dollars, francs, marks, escudos, yen, Malay and Hong Kong dollars. This can be no accident ... and ... is unique in the annals of Art. It is this which infuriates his critics who cannot understand his universal appeal.'

Twenty-five years later that elitism, in its turn, has been scorned as a new art-aware, 'no brow' generation buy Tretchikoff prints to prove they do not need highly priced originals to show their taste. These are the same people who would like to own the art of fellow 'no brows' Sarah Lucas, Tracey Emin and Damien Hirst, but who find Tretchikoff an ironic, affordable alternative. Today his work is represented in the Louvre but not in the South African National Gallery.

Tretchikoff's art is full of contradiction and has probably received more praise and criticism than that of any other twentieth-century artist. His public acclaim was first examined in the 1974 BBC documentary *The Green Lady*, directed by Alan Yentob. The programme opens with the then well-known art critic, William Fever, saying, 'Let us examine this painting, which is arguably **the most unpleasant work of art to be published in the 20th century.** You've got **flat form**, hair that is not hair at all but is simply an opaque layer of **dull and insipid** paint. You have shoulders which have **no substance**, you have muzzy line work.'

But the public who bought **Tretchikoff's The Green Lady** from the counter next to the sanitary pads and dental floss at their local chemist thought differently. Mrs Cusack, a cockney equivalent of Morecambe's dancing ladies, told William Fever in the documentary that the painting had **'meaningful beauty', 'soothing and calming qualities'** and **'spiritual meaning'**. Some described 'her', **The Green Lady**, as a goddess and the work as a quasi-religious piece of art. Others talked of **The Green Lady** representing an exotic, far-away country that most people dream of visiting but know they never will.

To **Tretchikoff, The Green Lady** had always been **'a girl he casually glimpsed in a restaurant'** or a **'green-faced girl** with a supernatural gift'. The BBC took him to a séance with a spiritual medium in Marylebone to try to retrace her origins. The transcript from this part of the programme reads:

MEDIUM: Never – never link up again now. In fact I think, quite frankly, the person's not alive. Let's see – oh, I think they were murdered. And that ... I don't know why we should go on but I can tell you I feel I've got to say it to you. I don't know – how long – how long ago since you saw the person?

TRETCHIKOFF: During the war.

MEDIUM: Yes, nine years ago something happened ... not in this life. They had a tragic end, there's a murder and I think you'll find that you're going to be led to the place where it was – somewhere – I think it's New York.

The voice-over commentary then runs: 'Well, we didn't pursue our enquiries any further than that. We never discovered who she was and perhaps she is just an image and never was a person at all.'

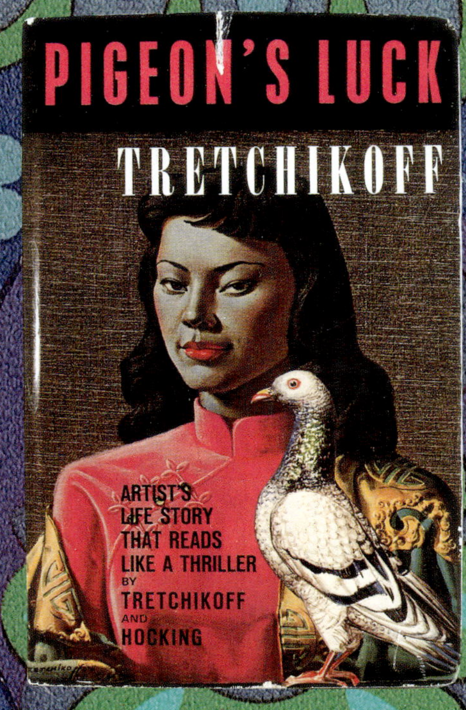

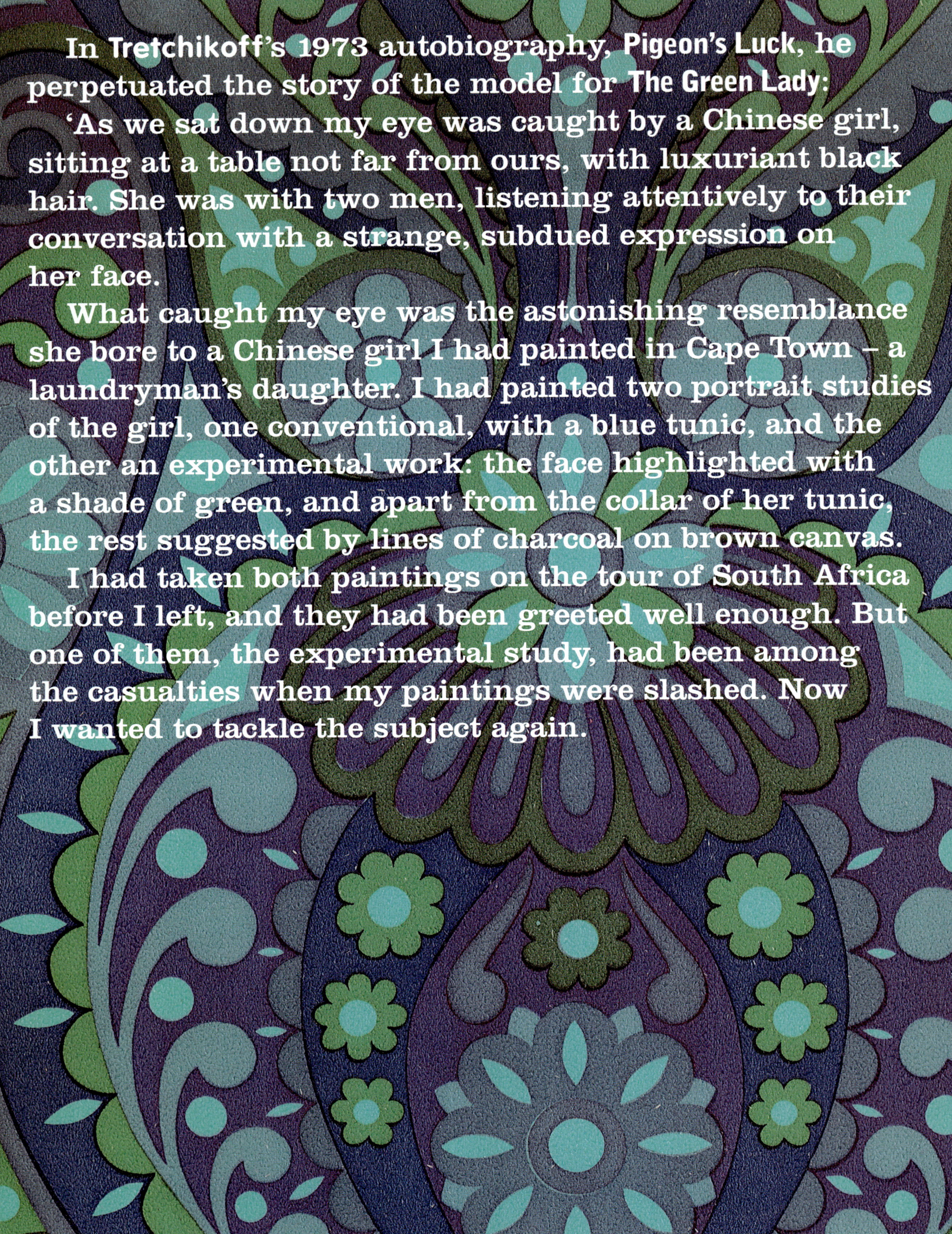

In Tretchikoff's 1973 autobiography, **Pigeon's Luck**, he perpetuated the story of the model for **The Green Lady**:

'As we sat down my eye was caught by a Chinese girl, sitting at a table not far from ours, with luxuriant black hair. She was with two men, listening attentively to their conversation with a strange, subdued expression on her face.

What caught my eye was the astonishing resemblance she bore to a Chinese girl I had painted in Cape Town – a laundryman's daughter. I had painted two portrait studies of the girl, one conventional, with a blue tunic, and the other an experimental work: the face highlighted with a shade of green, and apart from the collar of her tunic, the rest suggested by lines of charcoal on brown canvas.

I had taken both paintings on the tour of South Africa before I left, and they had been greeted well enough. But one of them, the experimental study, had been among the casualties when my paintings were slashed. Now I wanted to tackle the subject again.

Looking at the girl in the restaurant, I was somehow taken right back to my childhood. I felt I knew the girl. Joe was talking to me, but I was not very attentive.

"Hey come down to earth," he said. "Where are you?"

"Actually, in China," I said. "That girl over there took me right back. I would like her as a model."

Joe looked across at her. "I don't think there'll be any problem," said Joe casually. "I know her father.'"

Twenty-four years later, in the 1997 South African documentary **Red Jacket**, the true story of **Tretchikoff**'s long-term love affair with Lenka, the beautiful subject of his art, became public.

Tretchikoff, not unlike **The Beatles**, globally tuned into peoples' artistic senses. In many ways, he achieved everything that Andy Warhol stated he wanted to do but could never achieve because of his coolness. In **The Green Lady**, **Tretchikoff** created an image as recognisable as the **Mona Lisa** and a print that is still one of the the top three best-selling prints ever.

Vladimir Tretchikoff **Miss Wong**

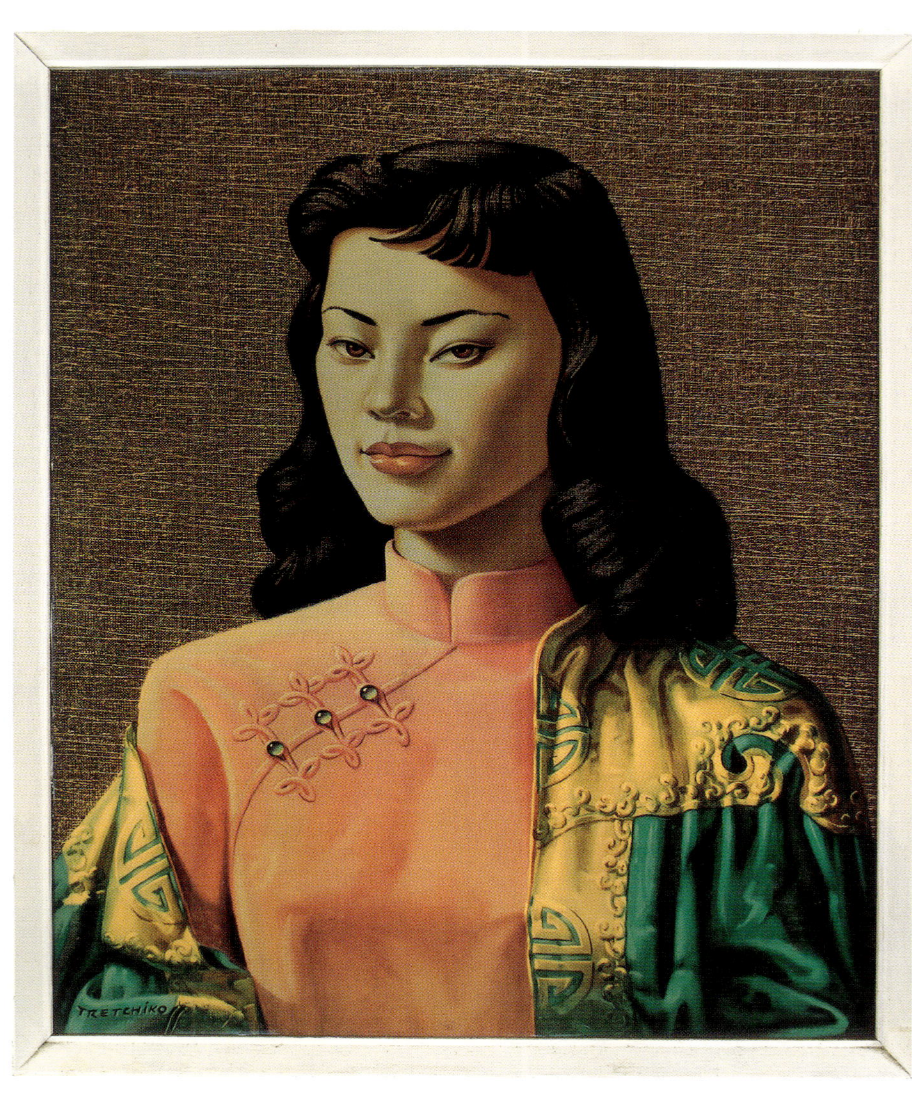

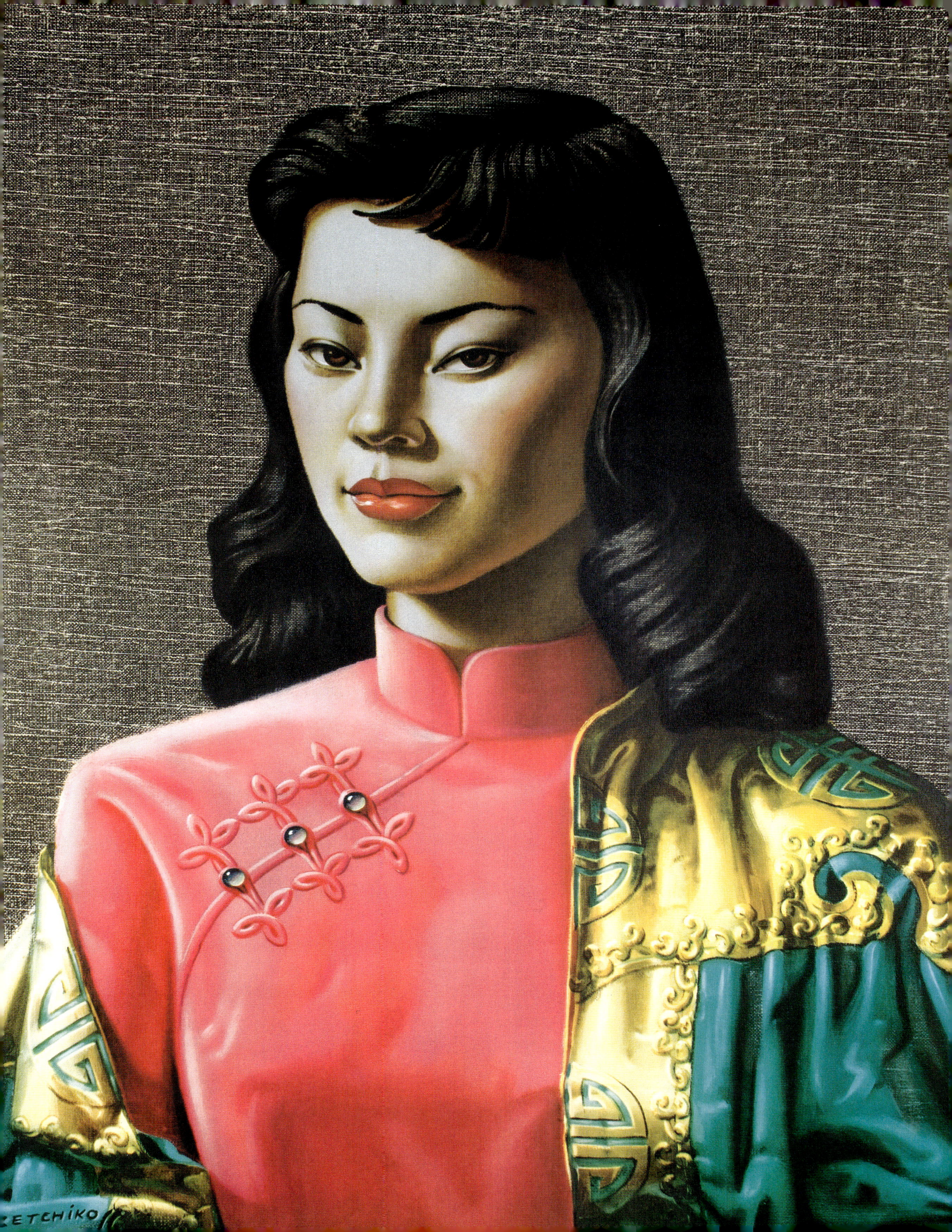

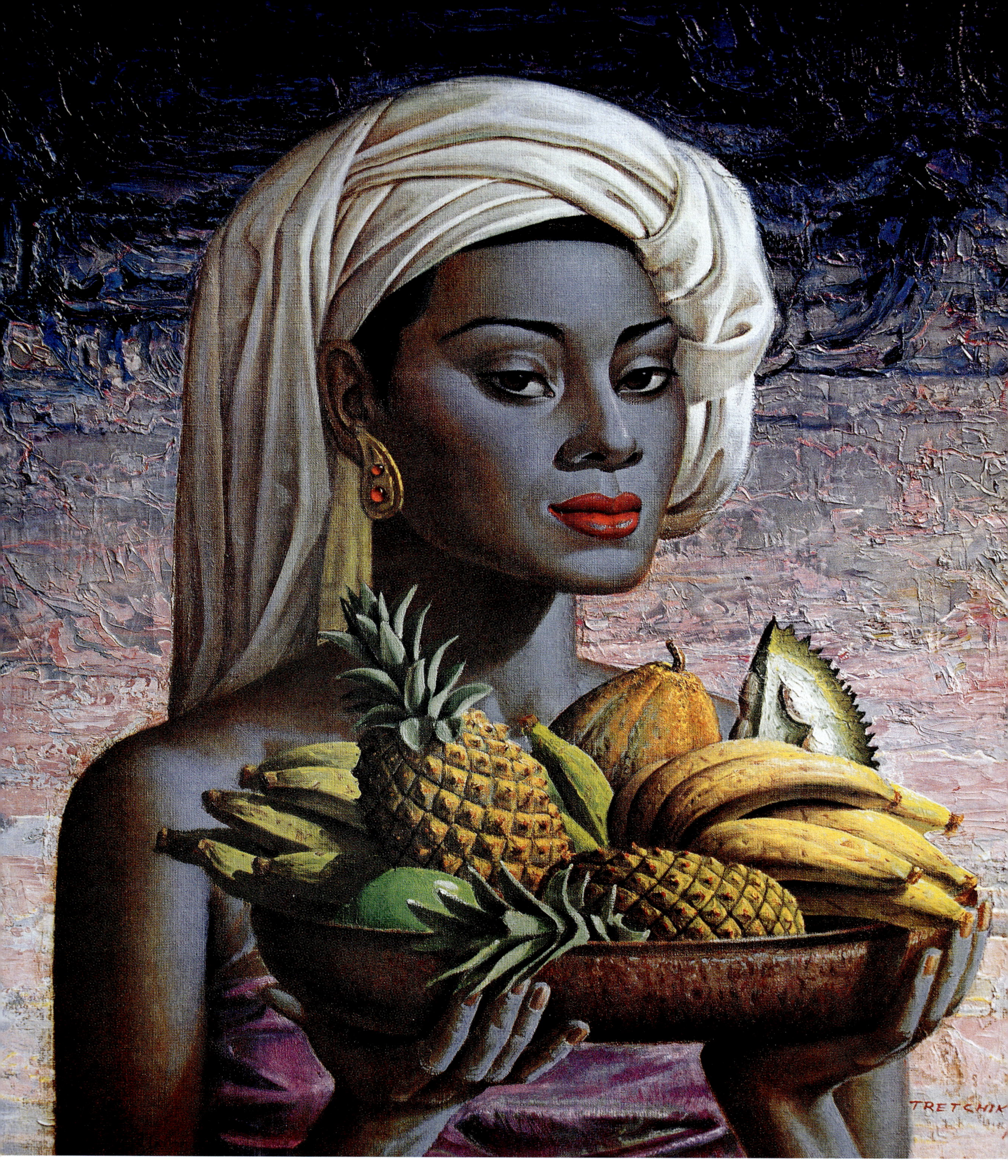

Vladimir Tretchikoff **Fruits of Bali**

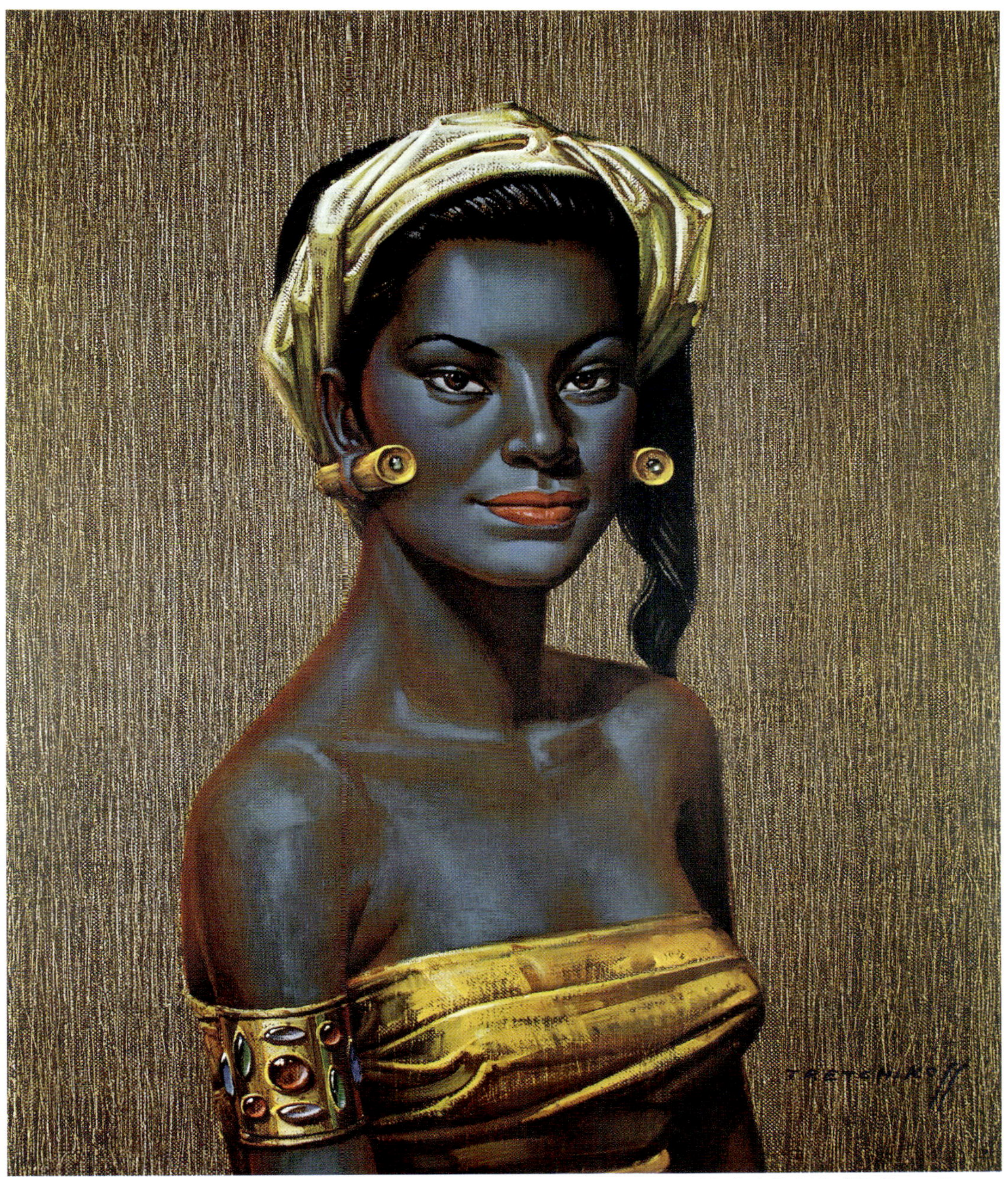

Vladimir Tretchikoff **Balinese Dancer**

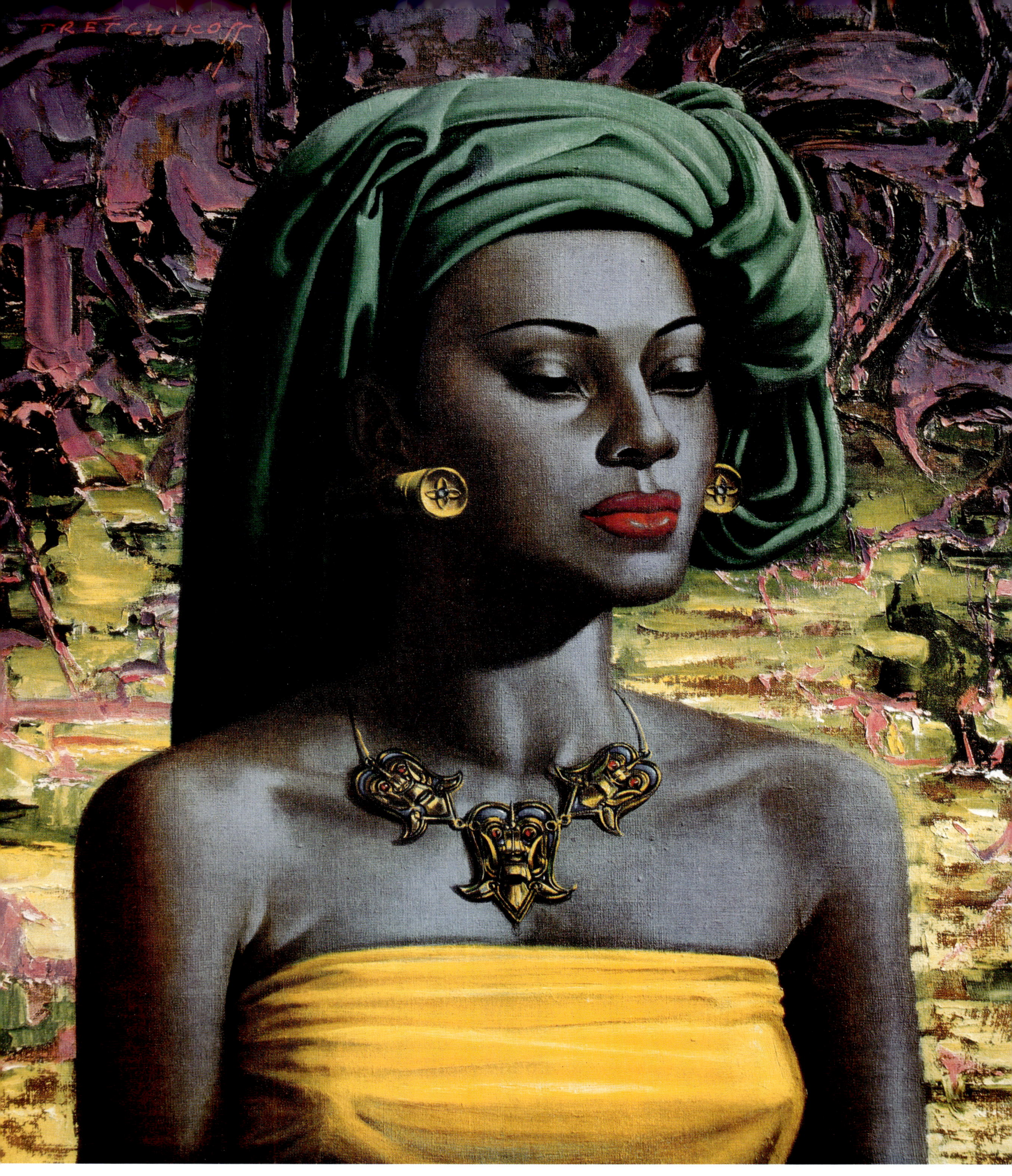

Vladimir Tretchikoff **Balinese Girl**

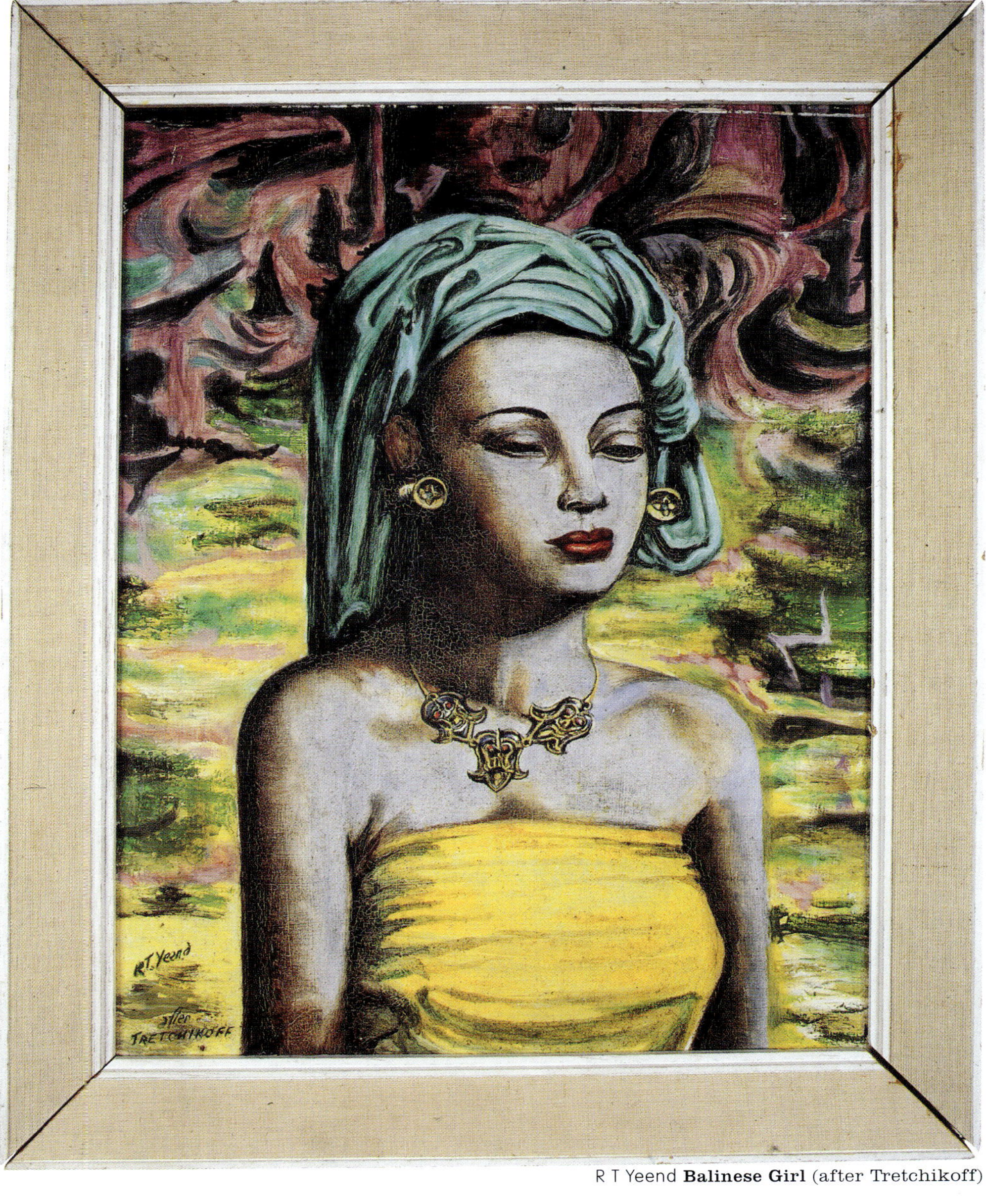

R T Yeend **Balinese Girl** (after Tretchikoff)

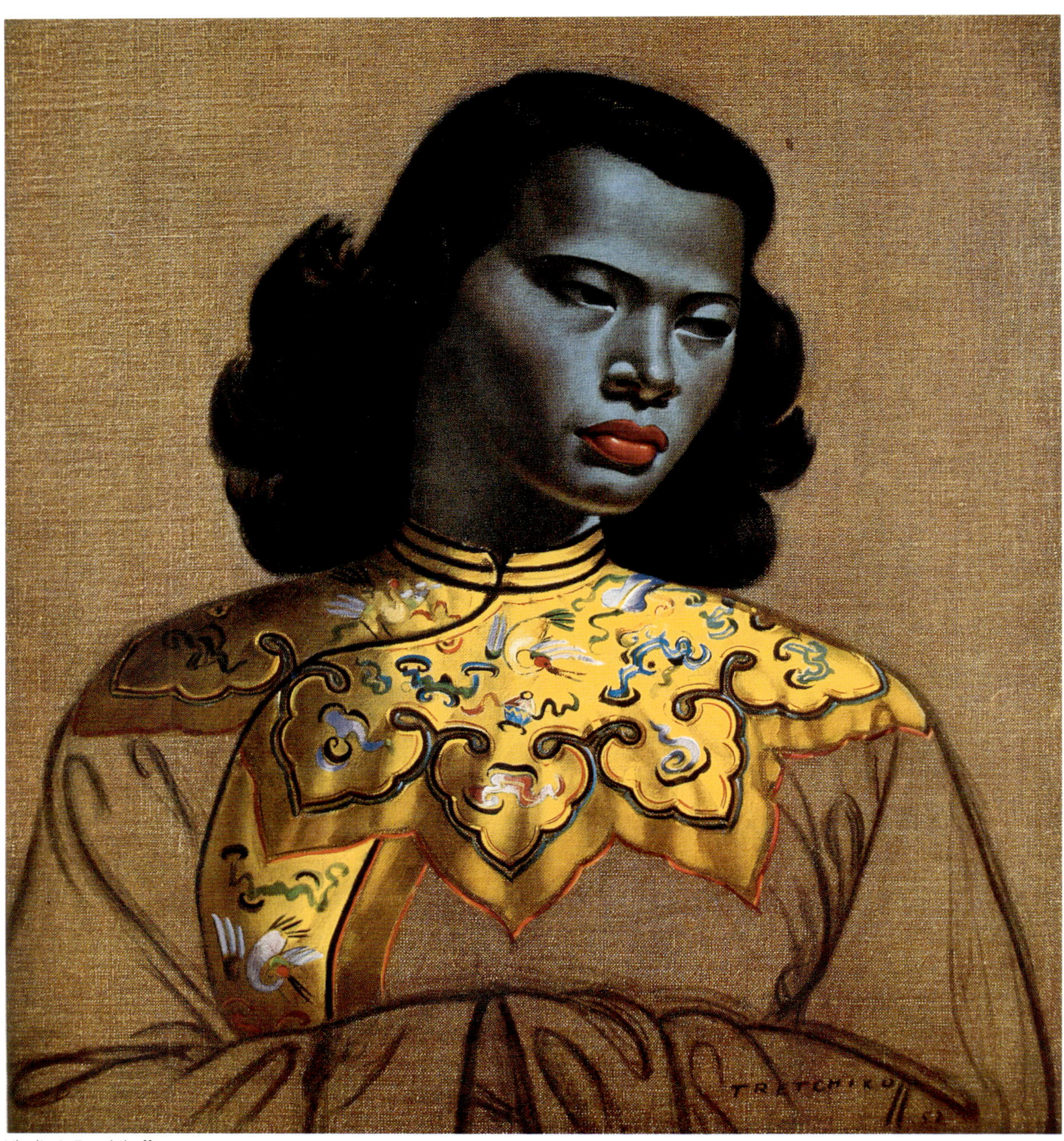

Vladimir Tretchikoff **Chinese Girl**

Vladimir Tretchikoff **Lady of the Orient**

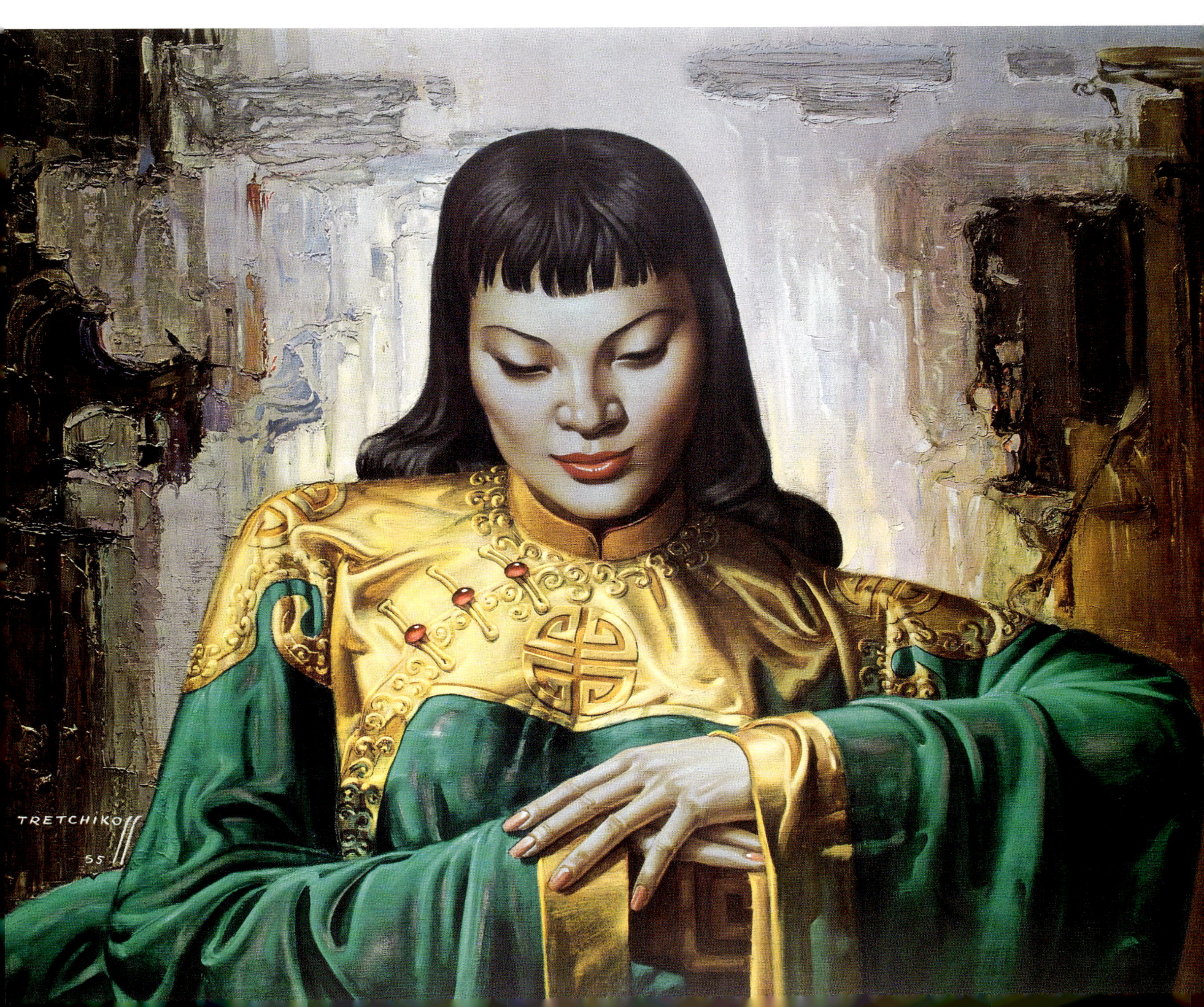

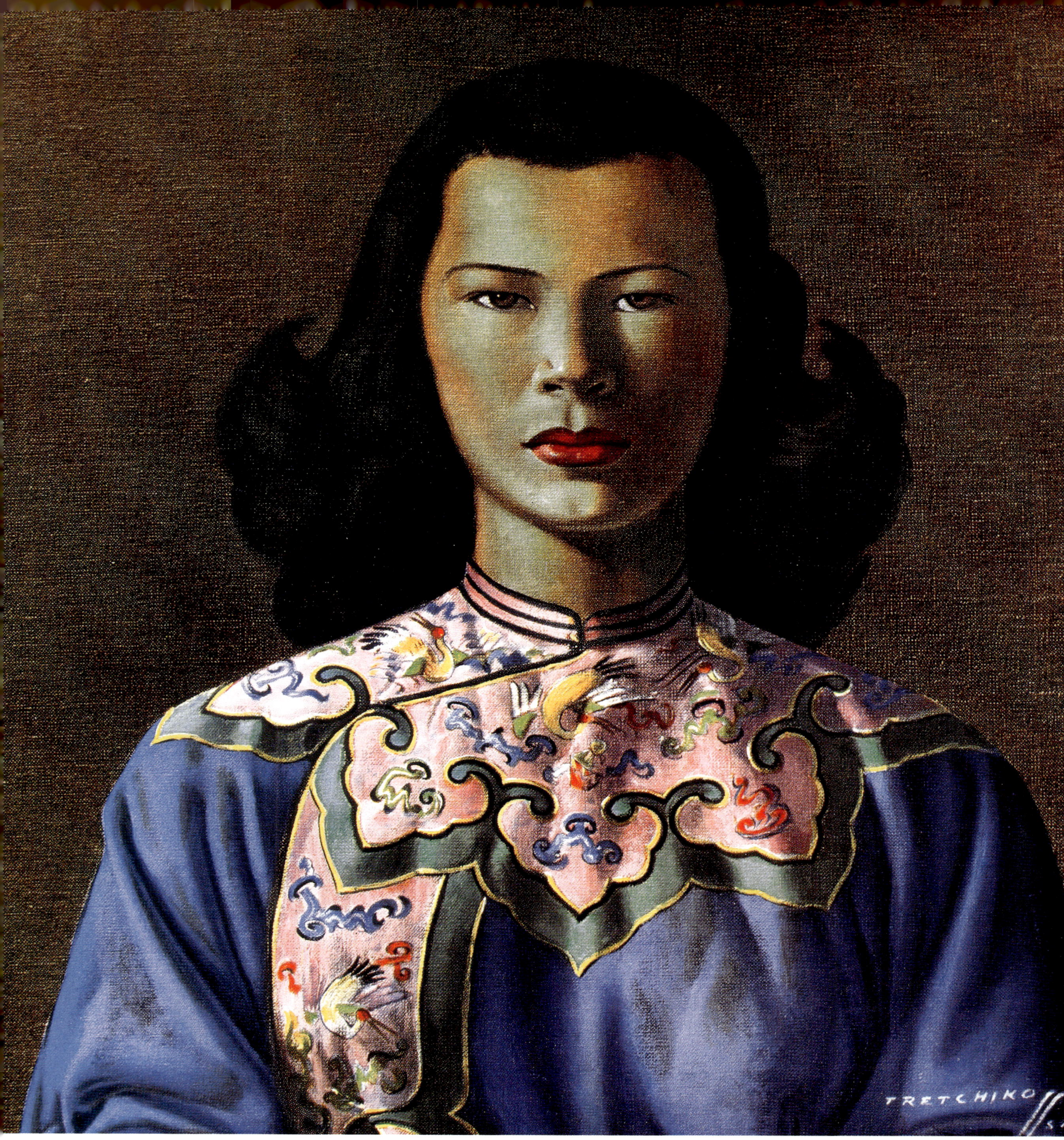

Vladimir Tretchikoff **Chinese Girl** 1952

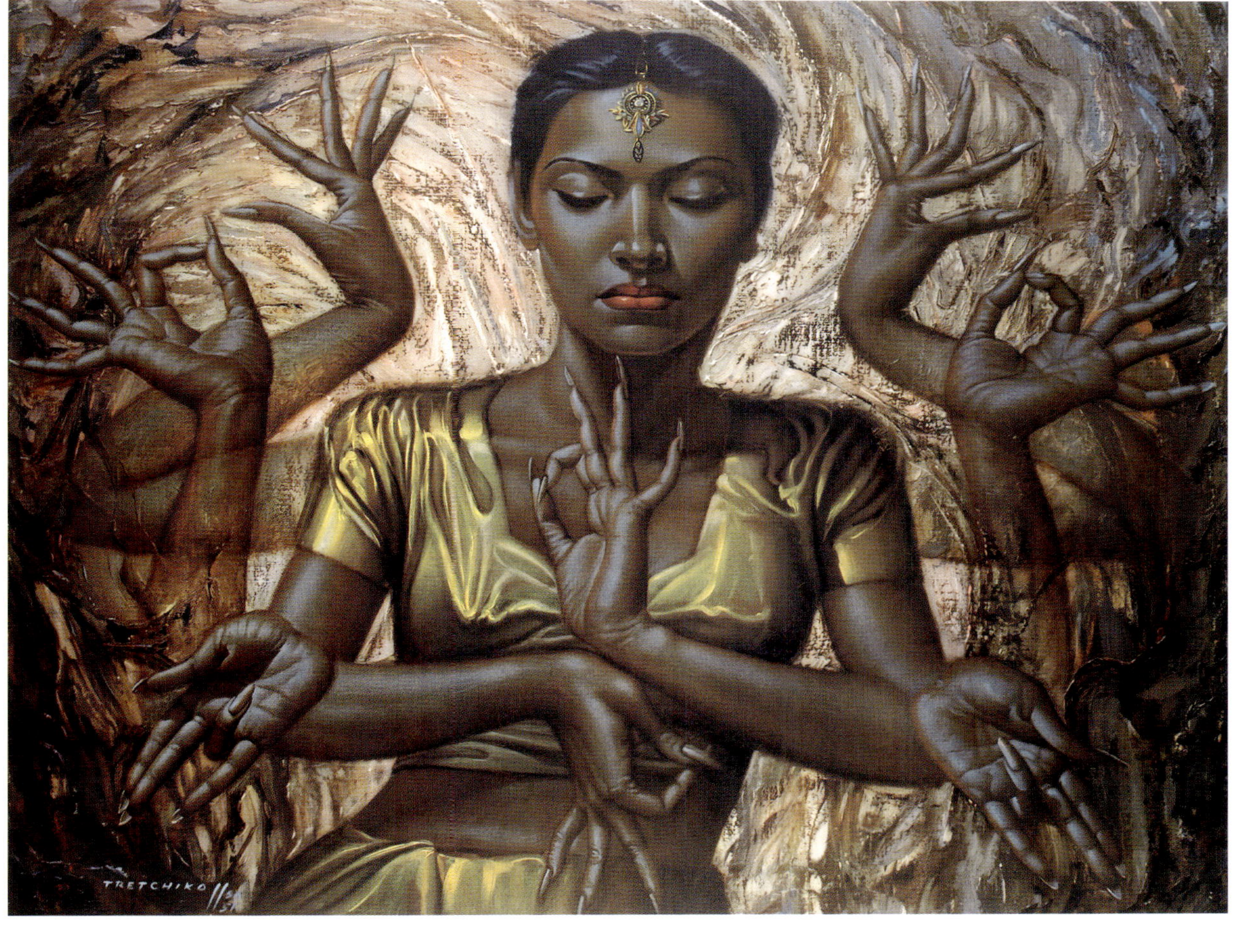

Vladimir Tretchikoff **Hindu Dancer** 1951

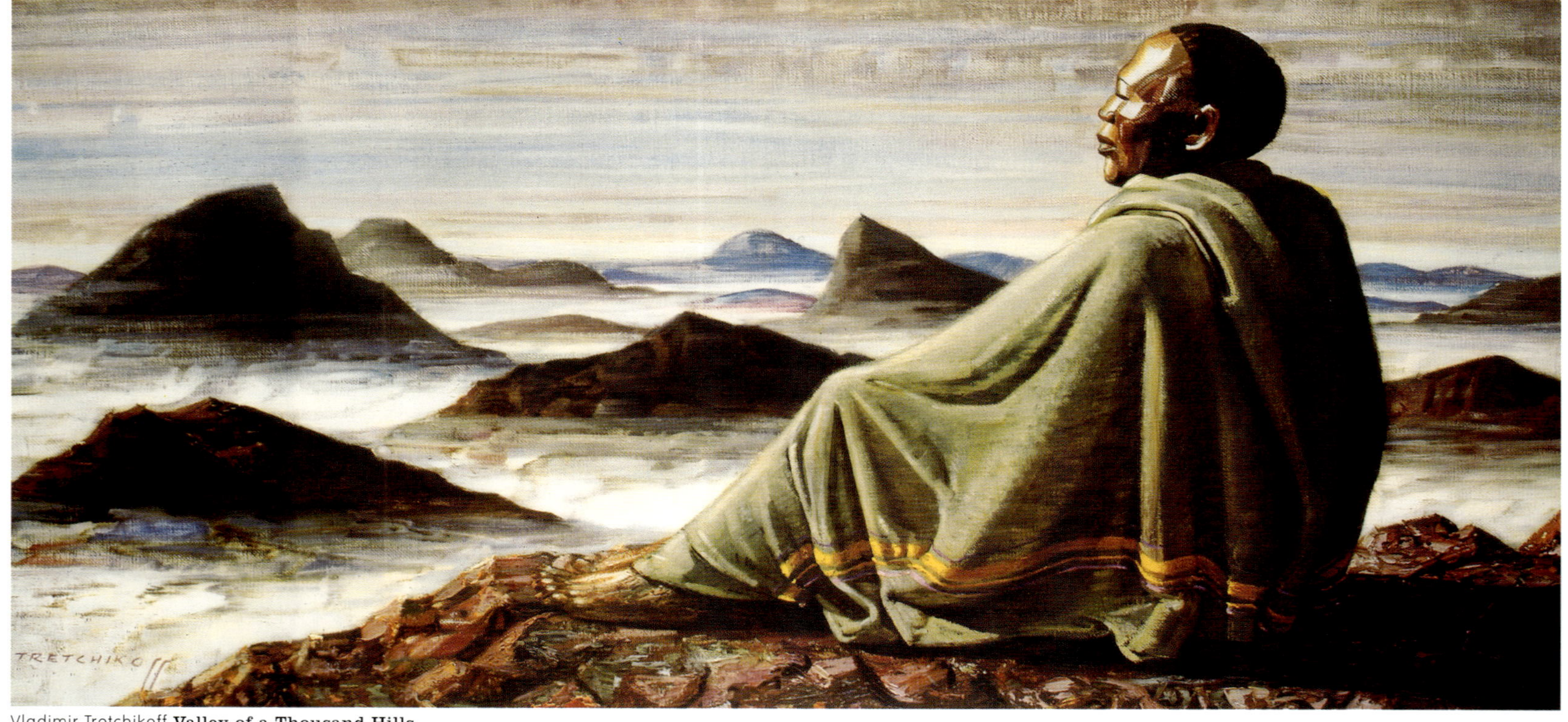

Vladimir Tretchikoff **Valley of a Thousand Hills**

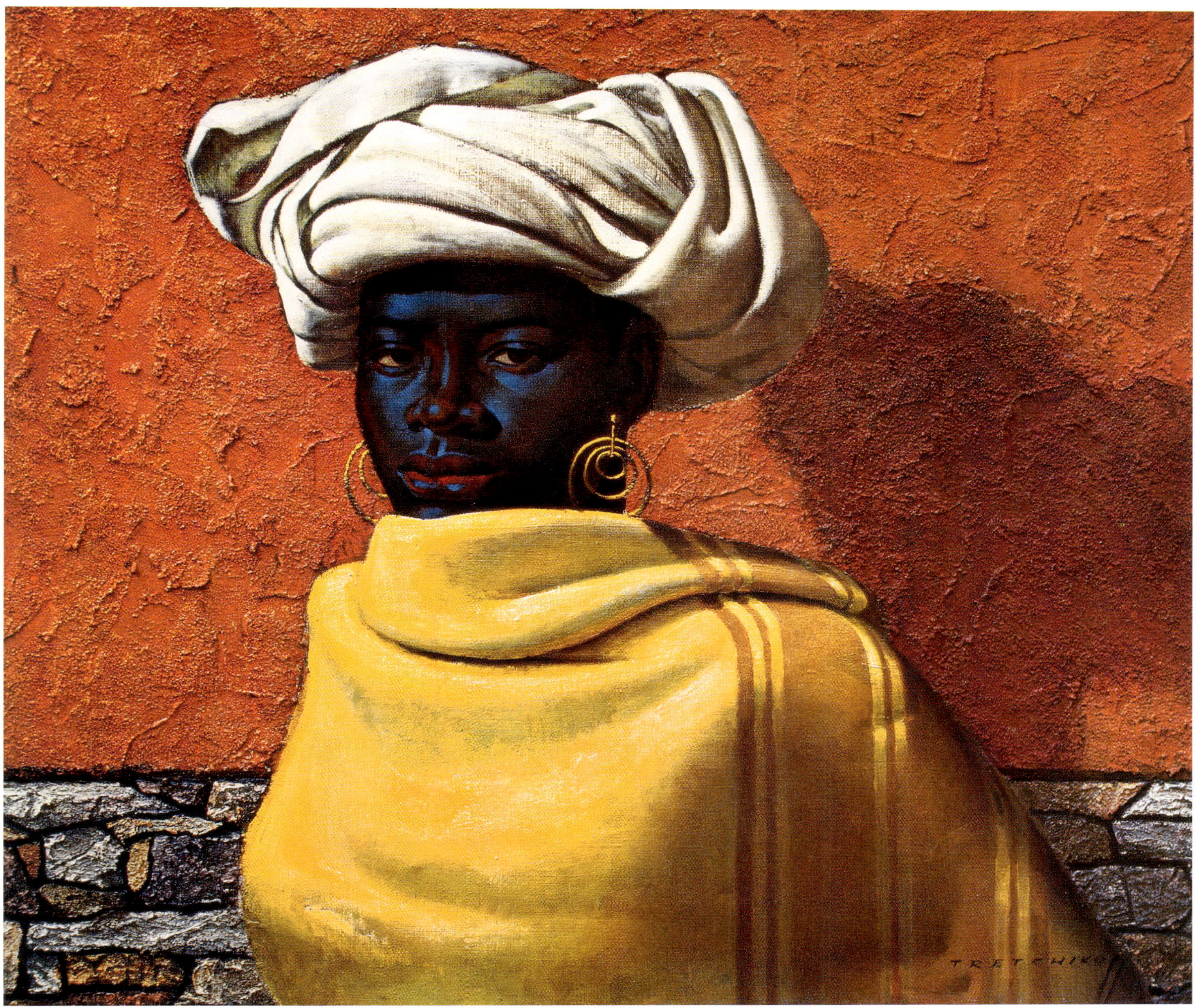

Vladimir Tretchikoff **Swazi Girl**

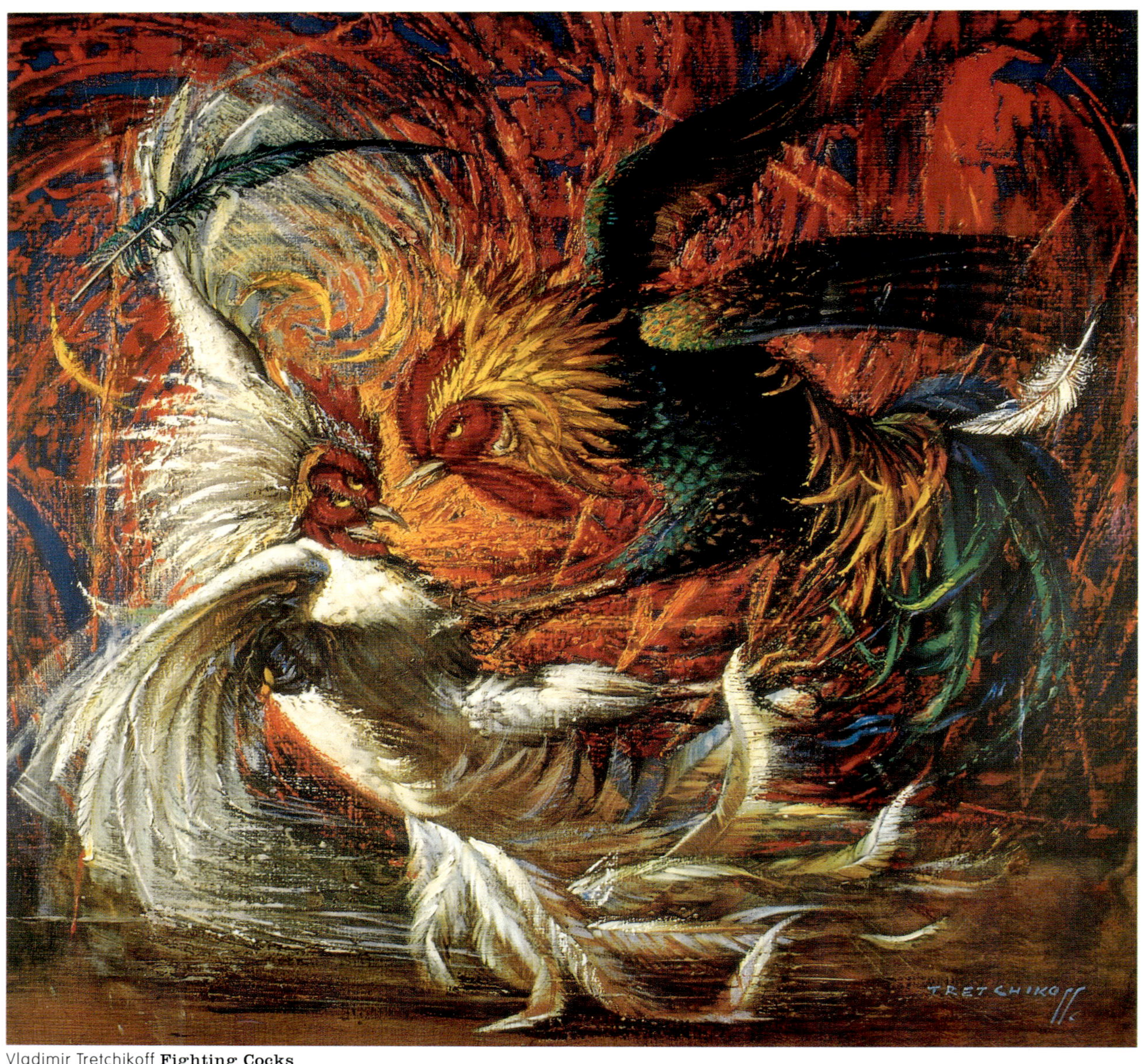

Vladimir Tretchikoff **Fighting Cocks**

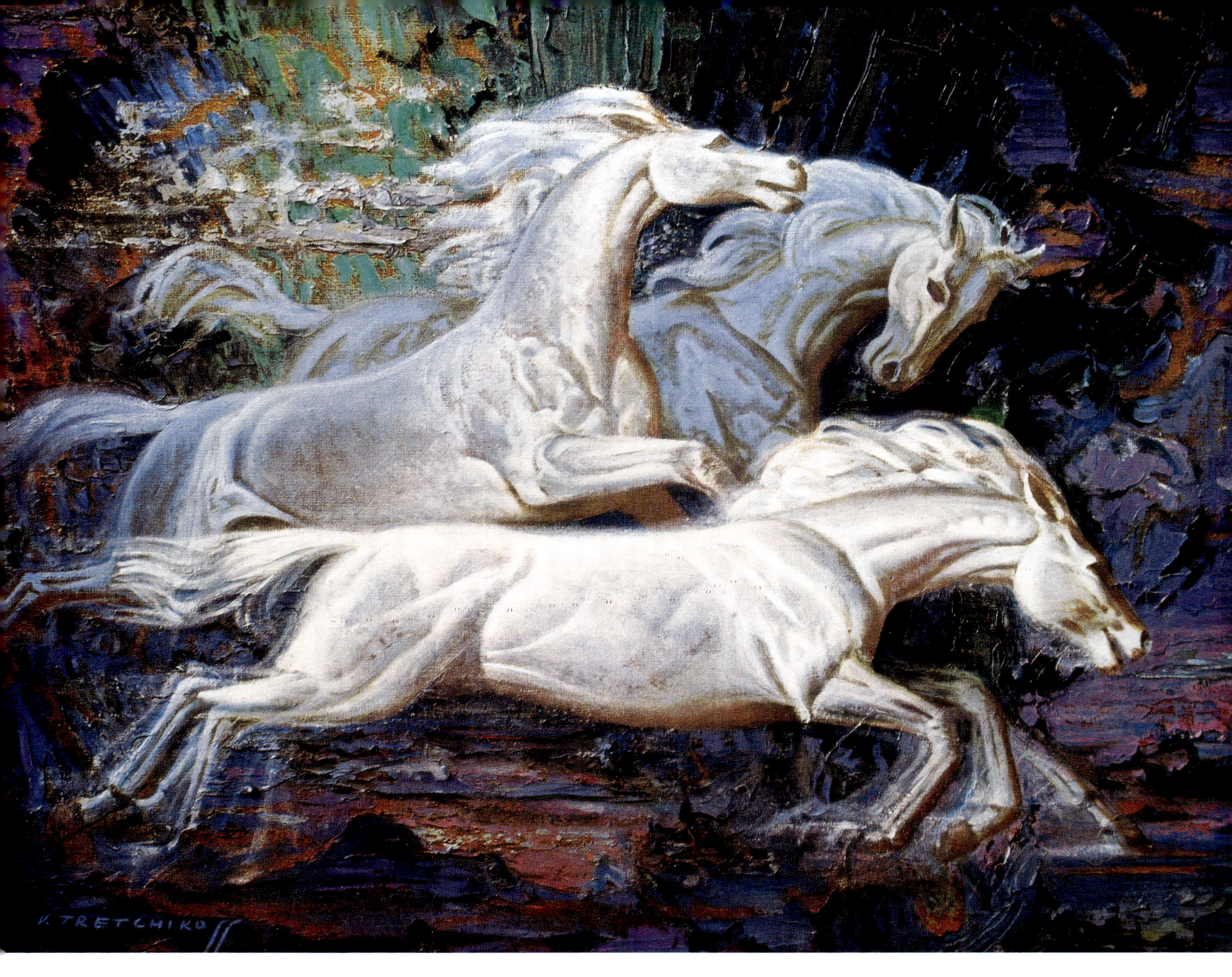

Vladimir Tretchikoff **Wild Horses**

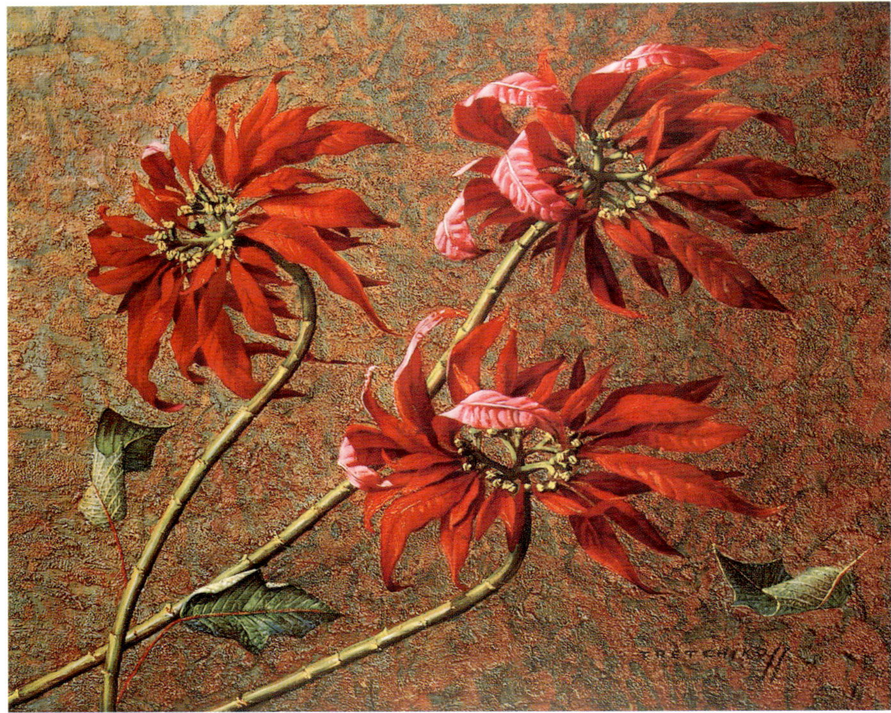

Vladimir Tretchikoff **Windy Day**

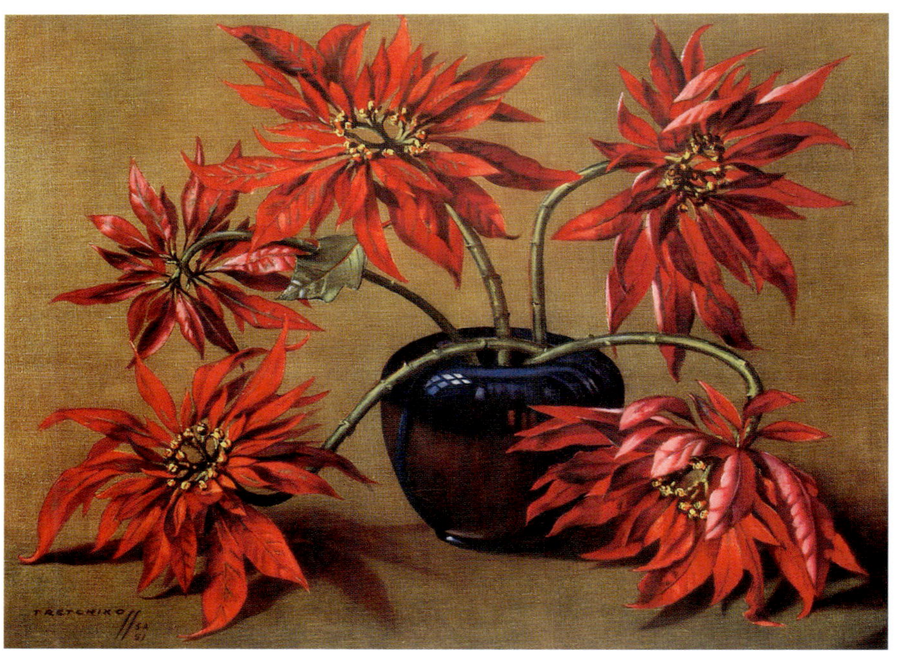

Vladimir Tretchikoff **Poinsettia** 1951

Vladimir Tretchikoff **Weeping Rose** 1949

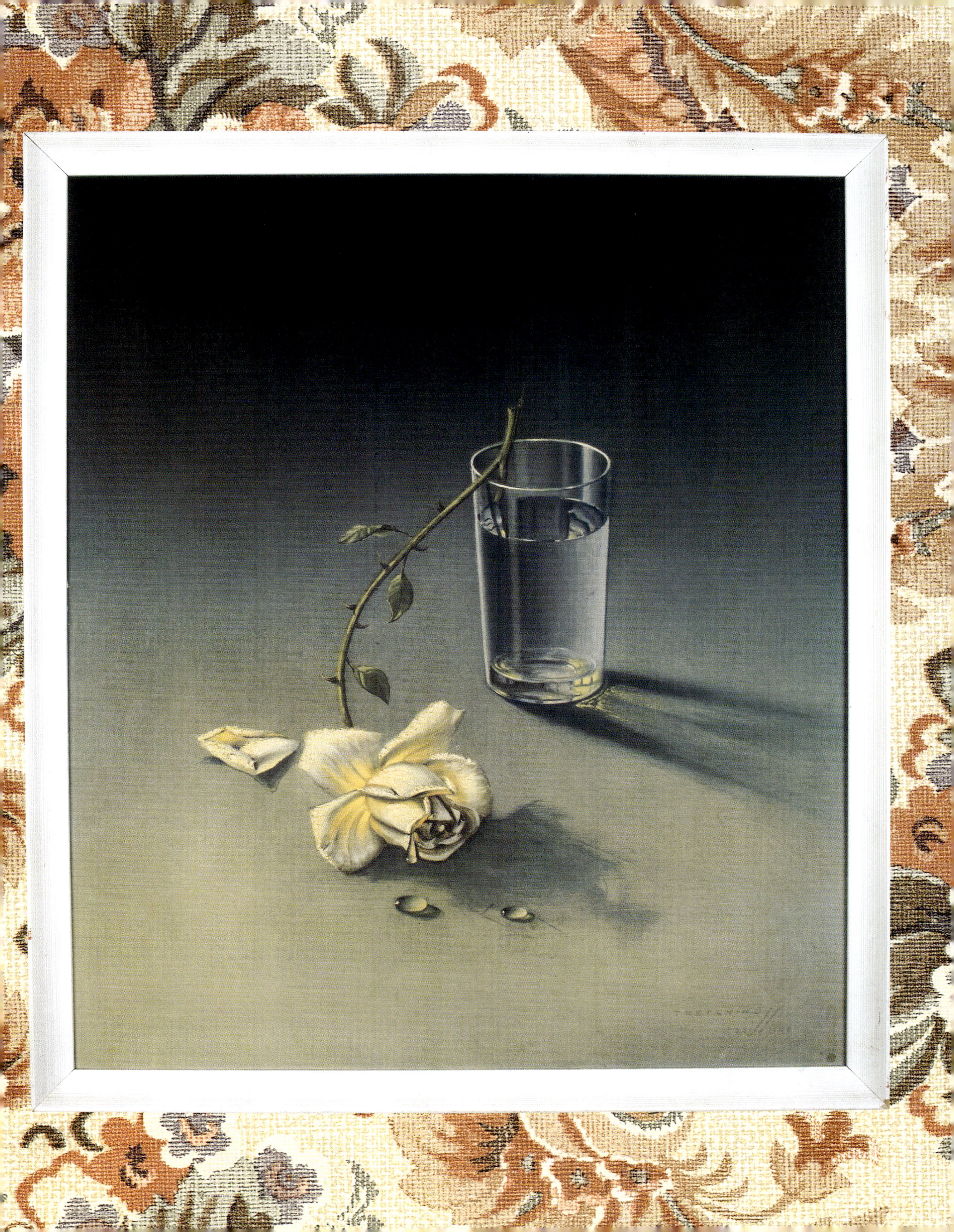

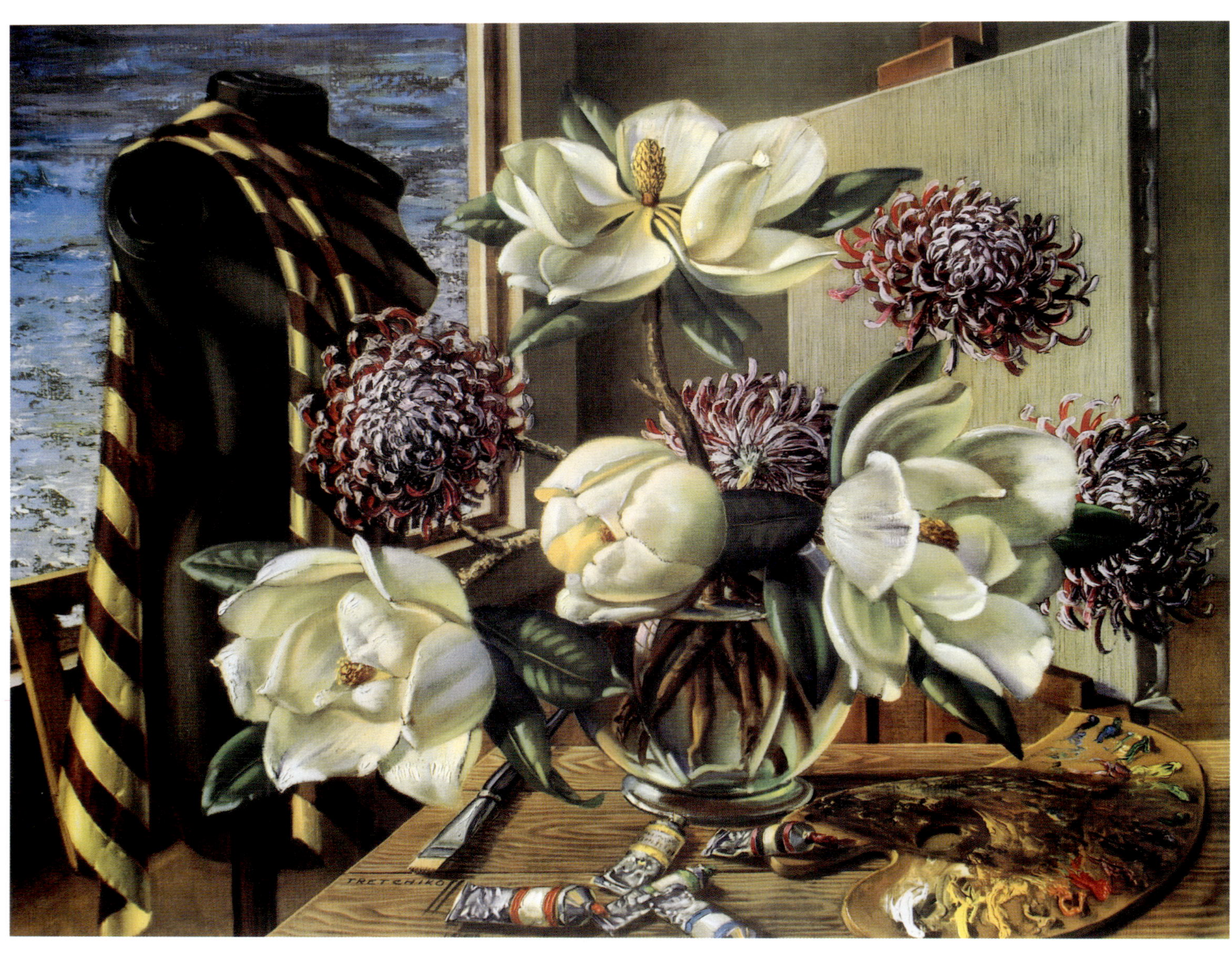

Vladimir Tretchikoff **Silent Models** 1951

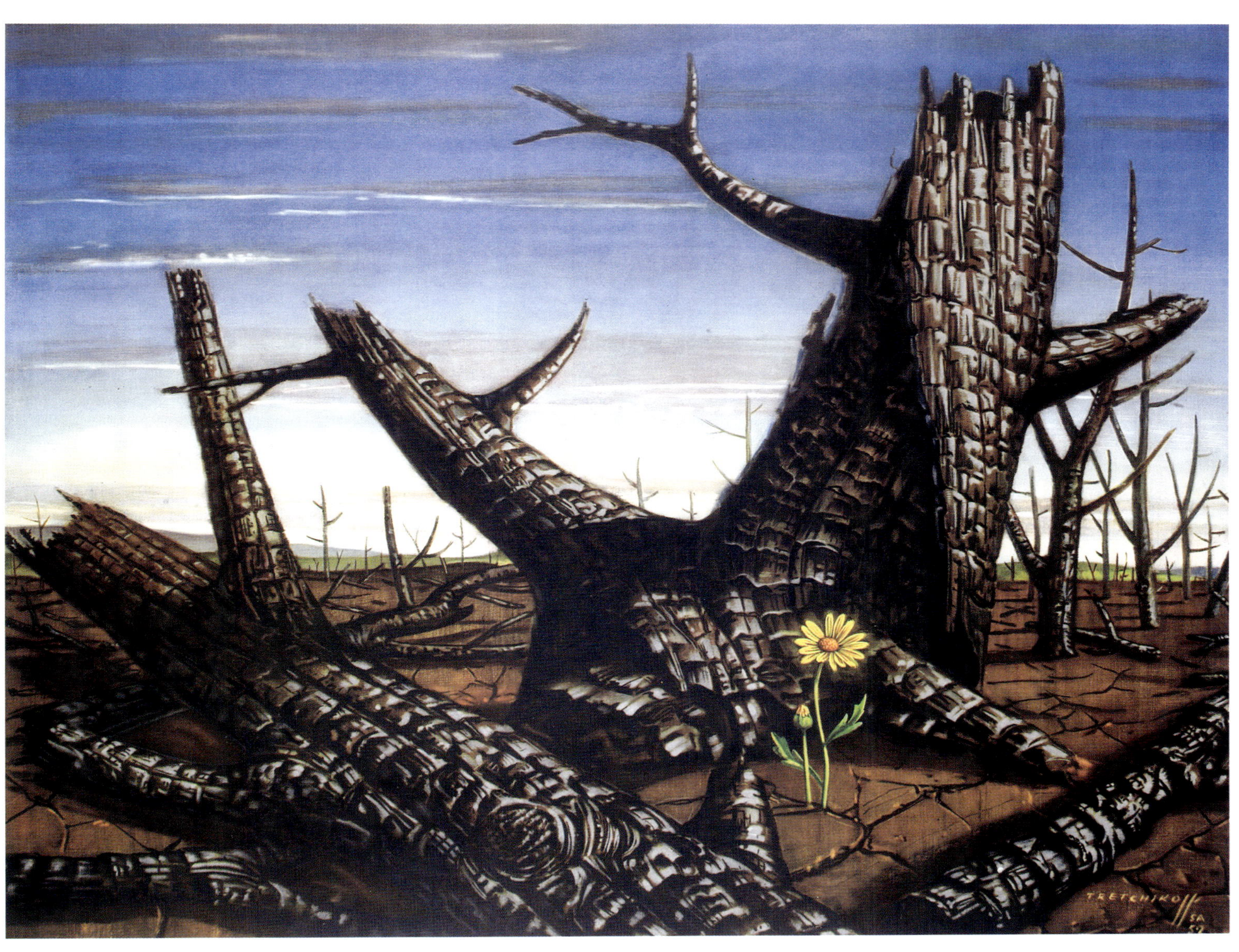

Vladimir Tretchikoff **Spring** 1952

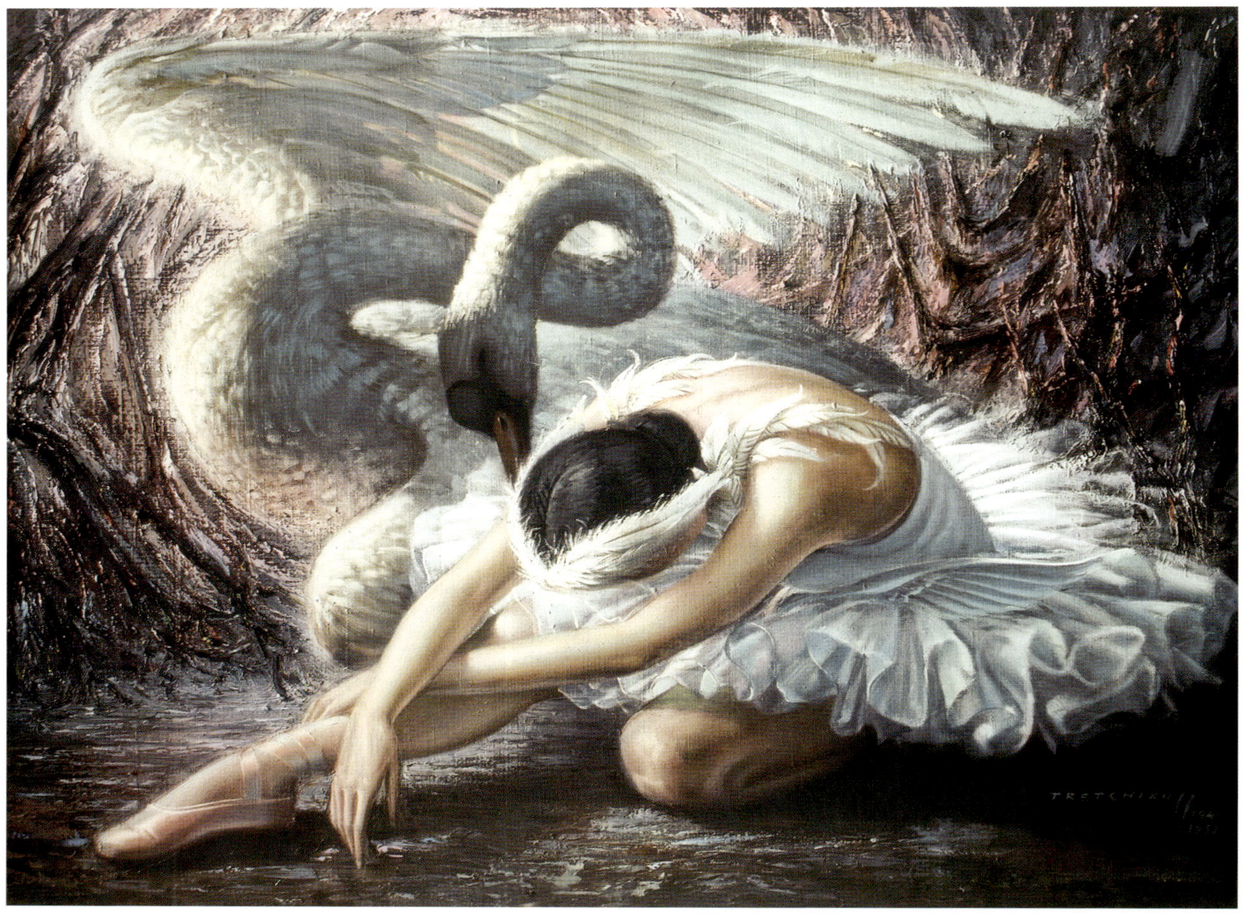

Vladimir Tretchikoff **The Dying Swan** 1951

Vladimir Tretchikoff **Rainy Day**

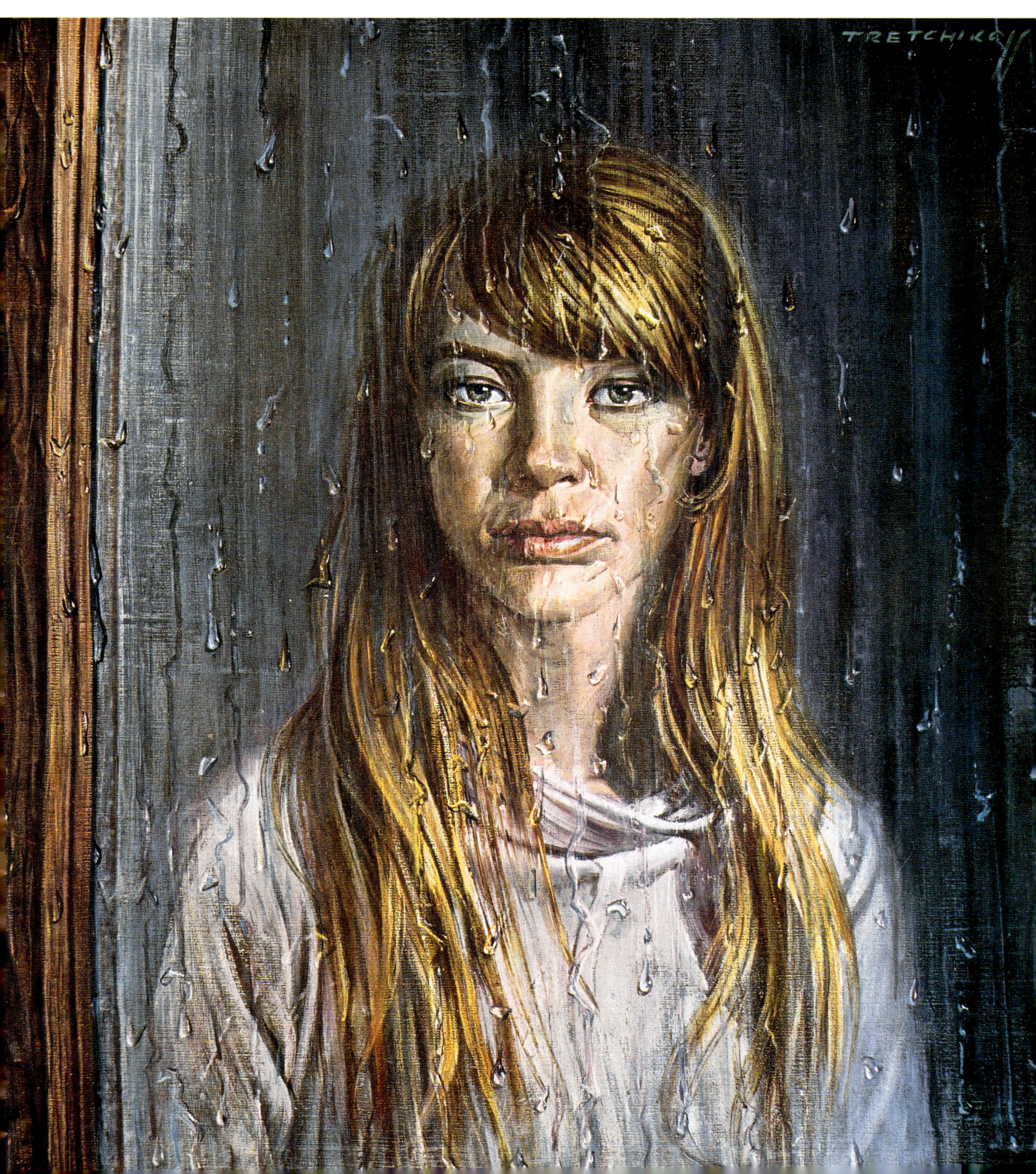

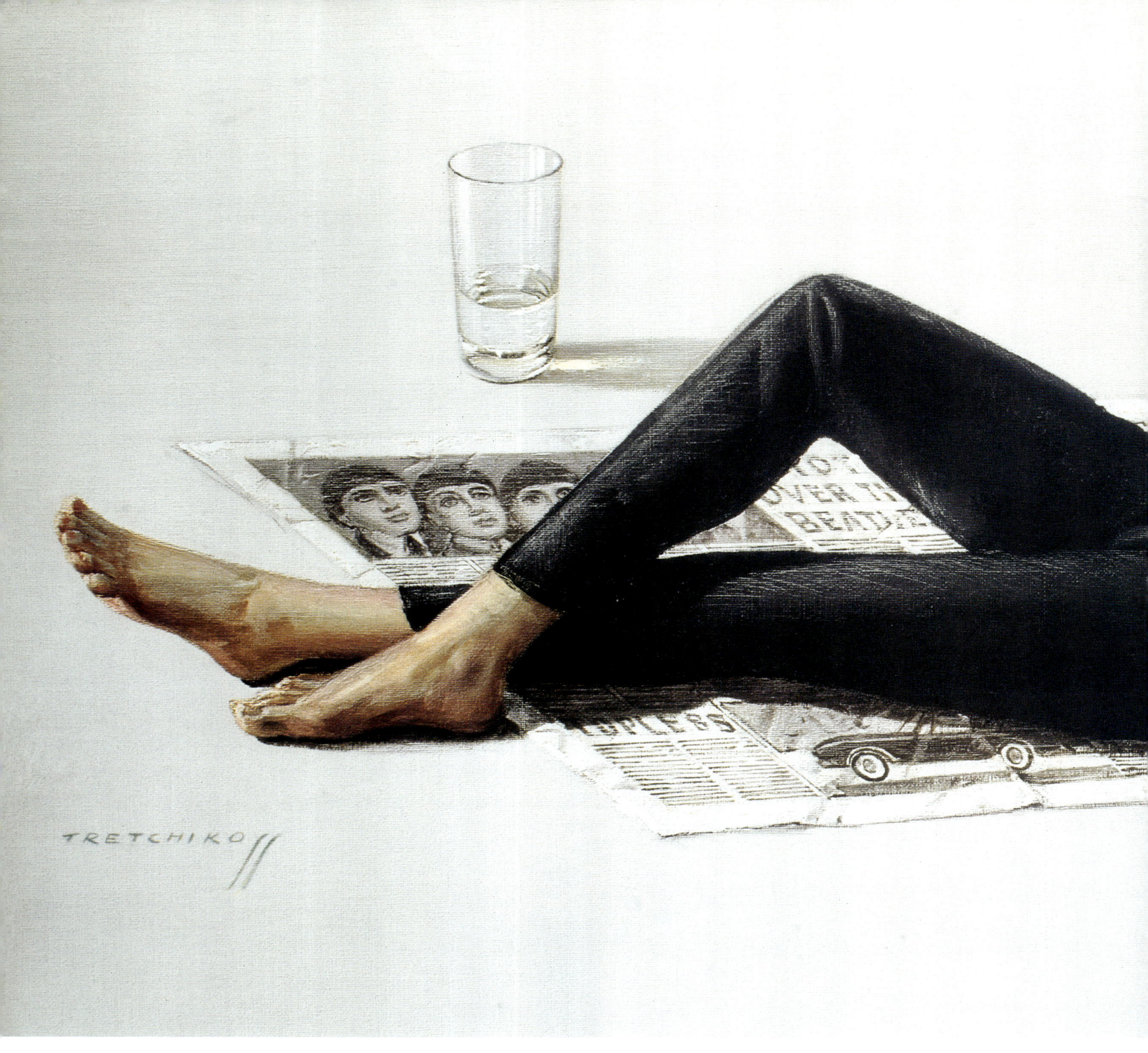

Vladimir Tretchikoff **Erica**

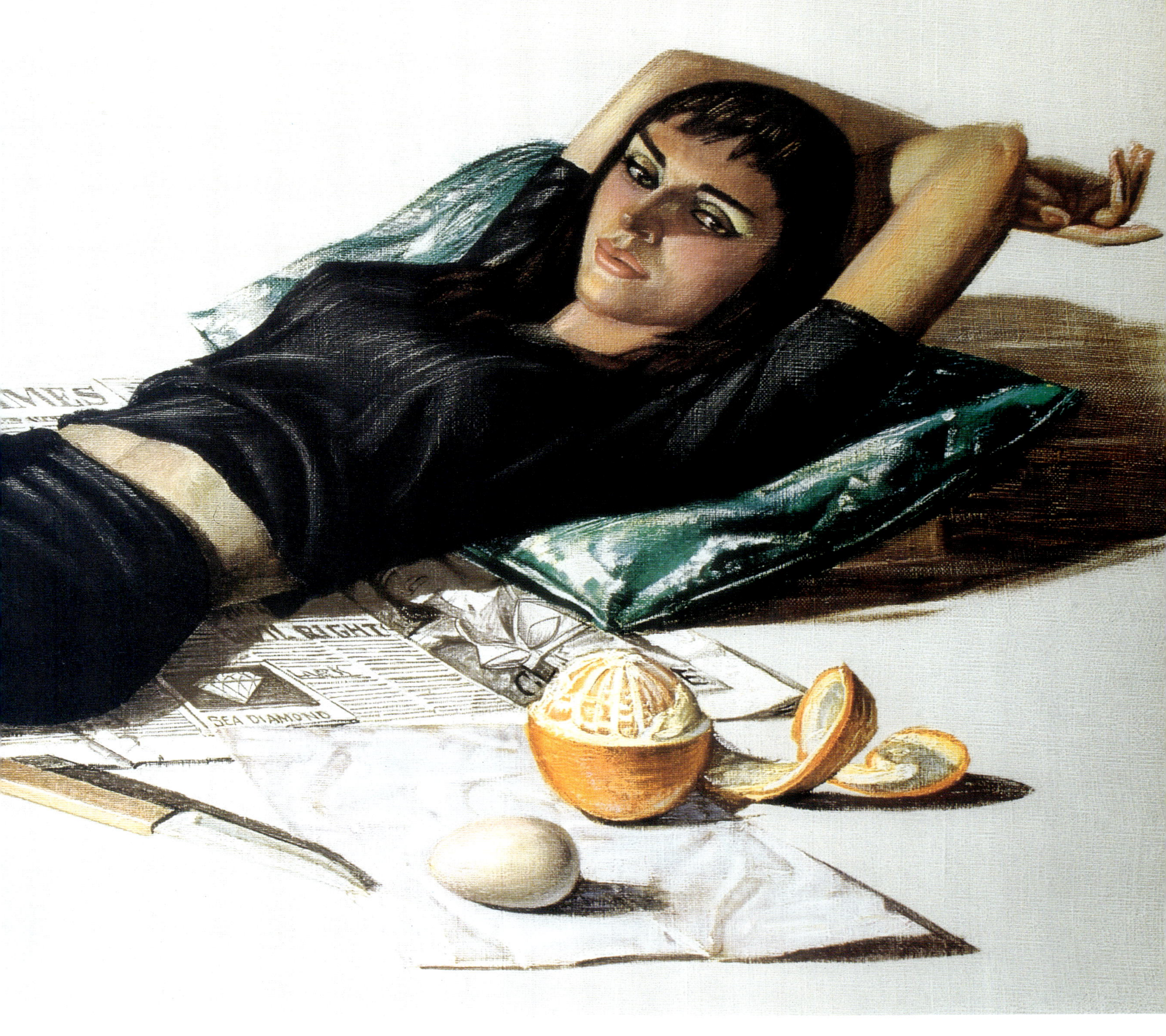
SEA DIAMOND

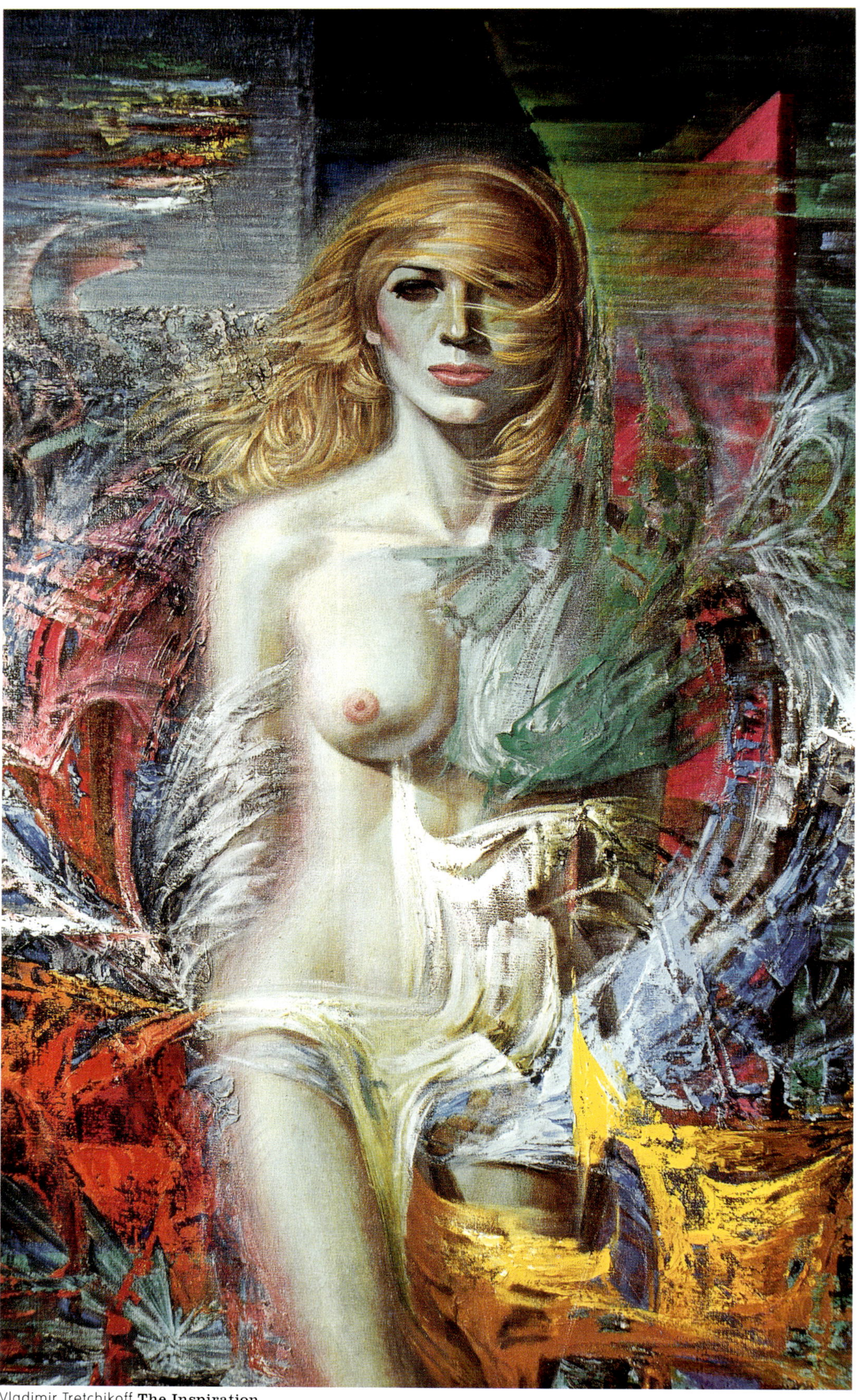

Vladimir Tretchikoff **The Inspiration**

Vladimir Tretchikoff **Venus**

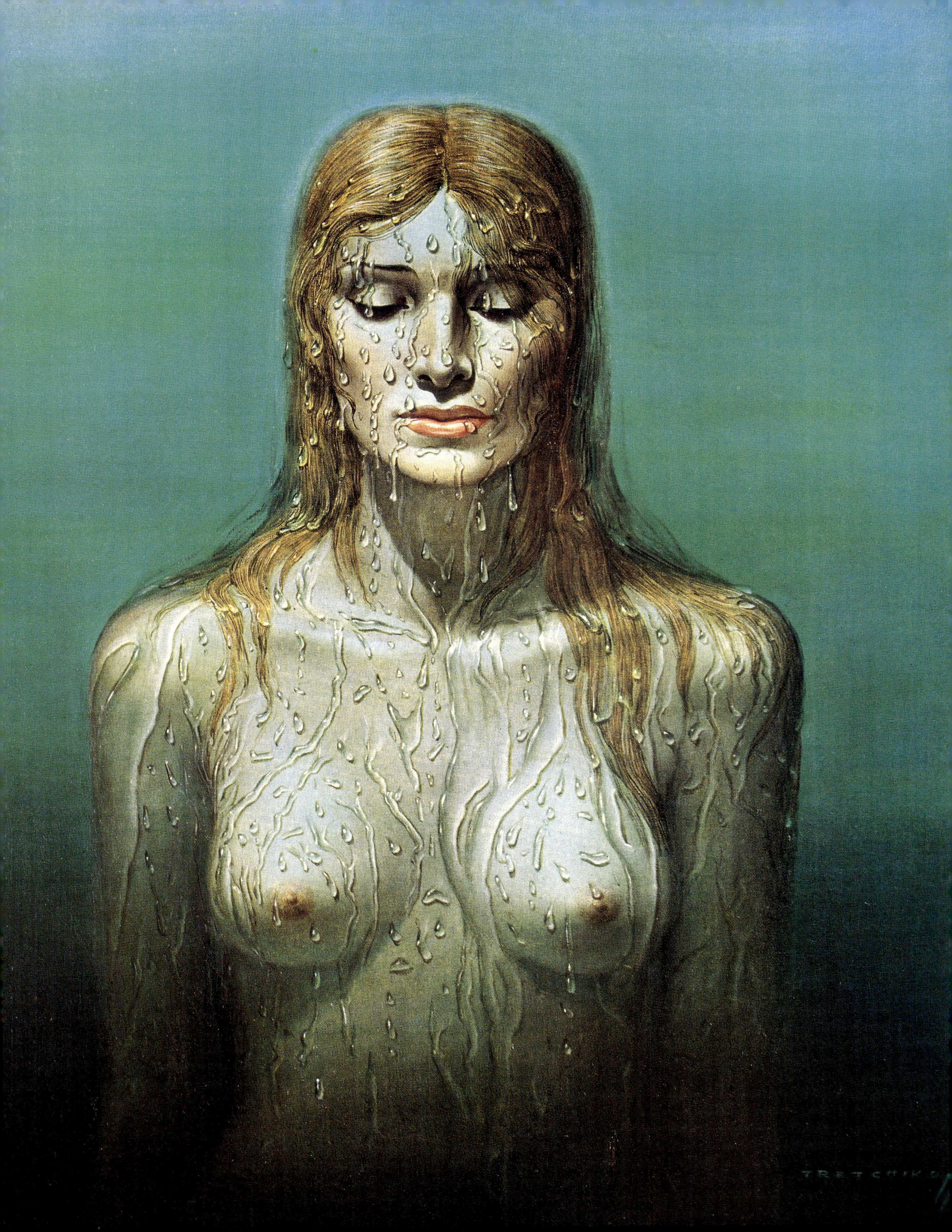
TRETCHIKO

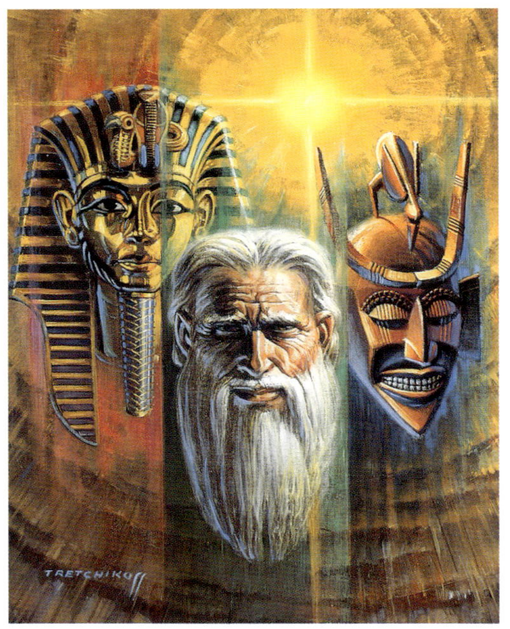

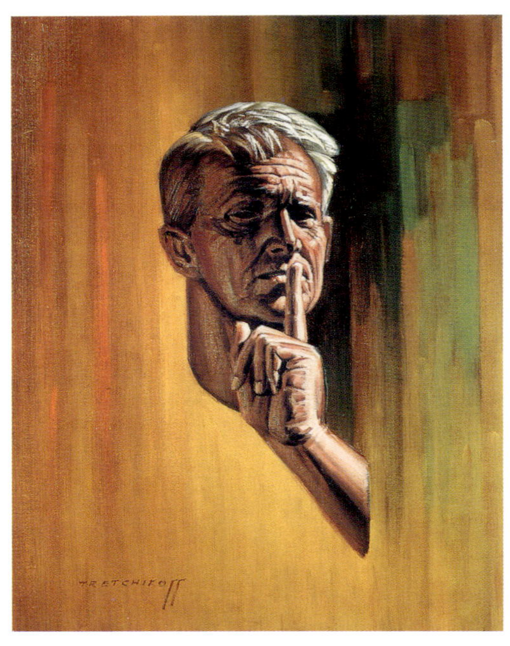

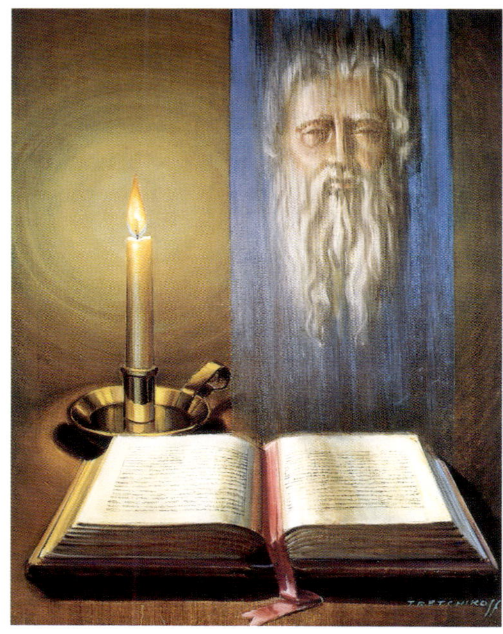

Vladimir Tretchikoff
Ten Commandments No 1. Thou Shalt Have No Other

Vladimir Tretchikoff
Ten Commandments No 3. Take Not the Name of The Lord Thy God in Vain

Vladimir Tretchikoff
Ten Commandments No 4. Remember That Thou Keep Holy the Sabbath Day

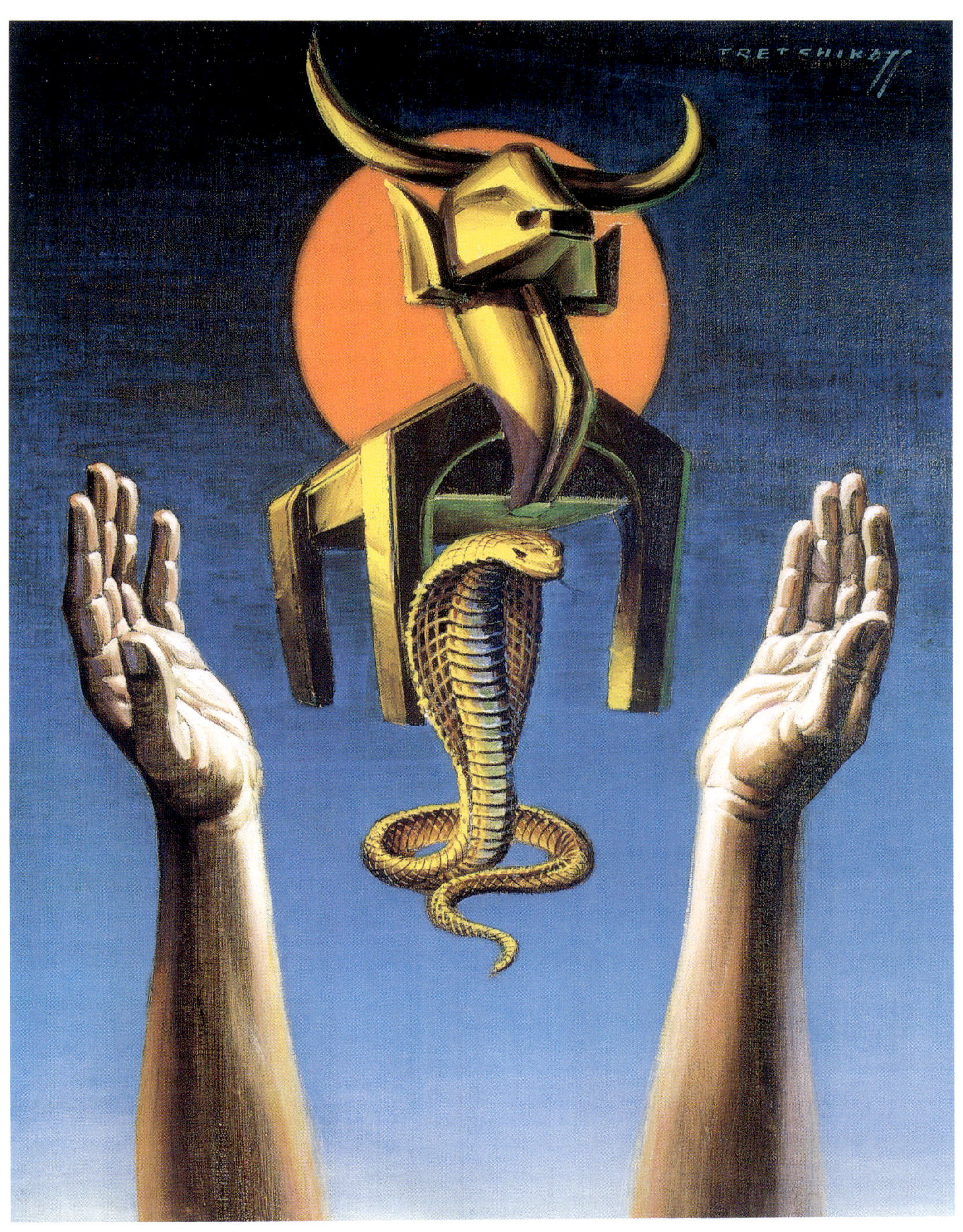

Vladimir Tretchikoff
Ten Commandments No 2. Thou Shalt Not Make Thyself a Graven Thing, To Adore It

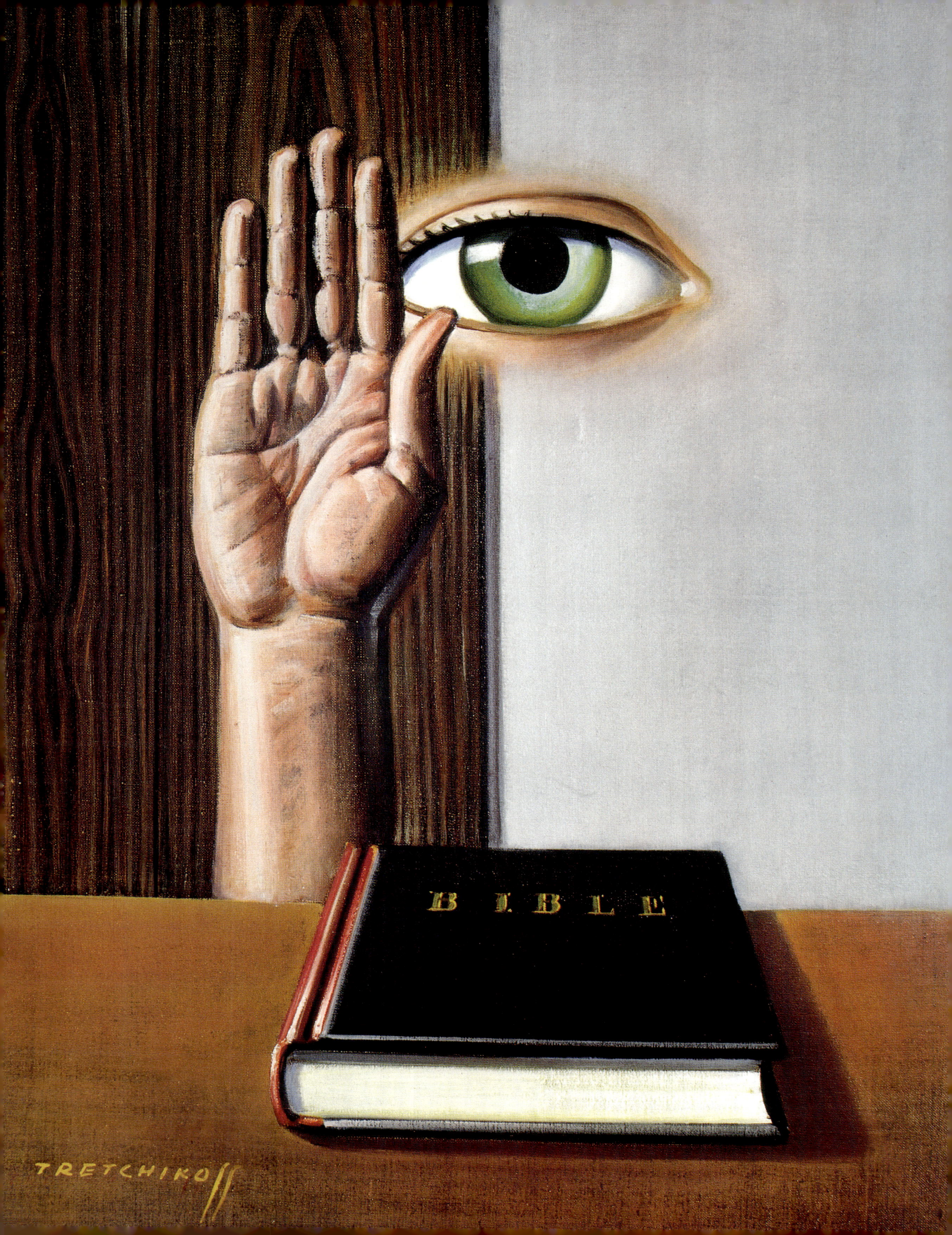

BIBLE
TRETCHIKOFF

Vladimir Tretchikoff
Ten Commandments
No 7. Thou Shalt
Not Steal

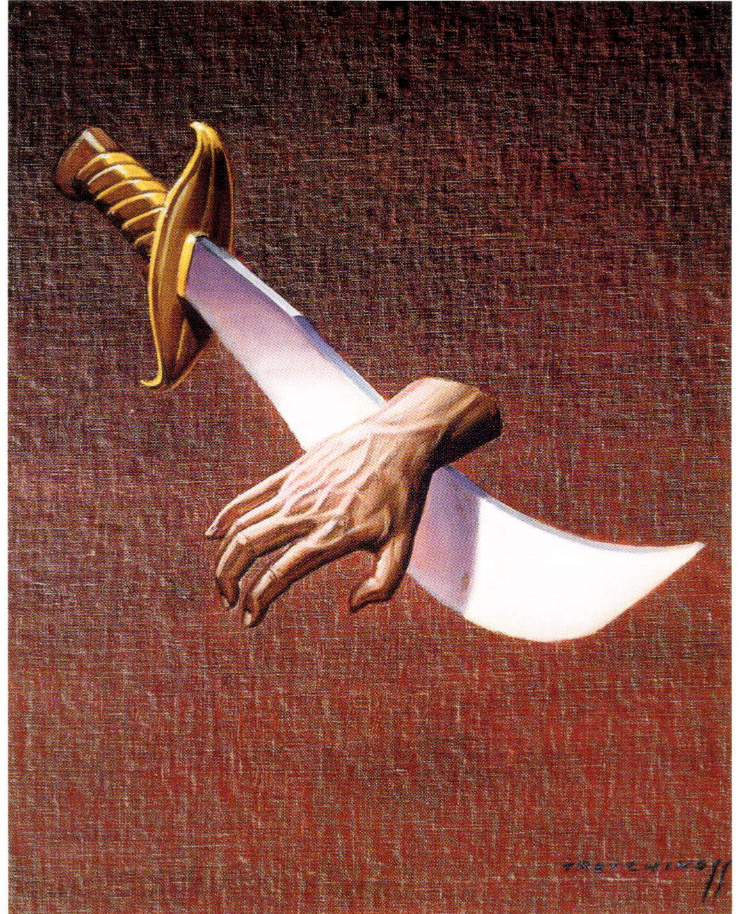

Vladimir Tretchikoff
Ten Commandments
No 5. Honour Thy
Father and Mother

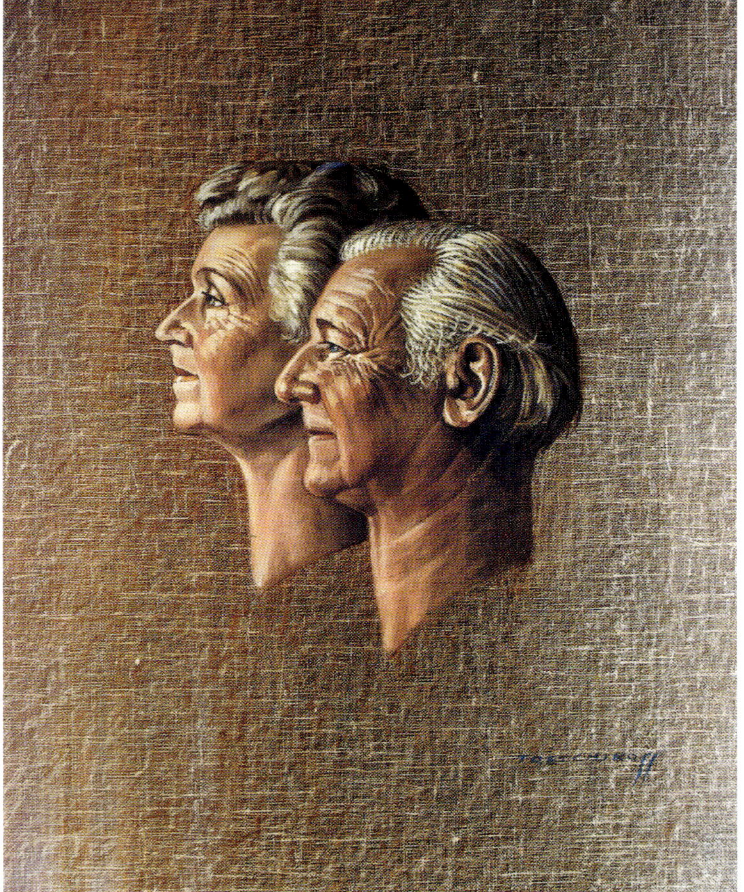

Vladimir Tretchikoff
Ten Commandments
No 8. Thou Shalt Not
Bear False Witness

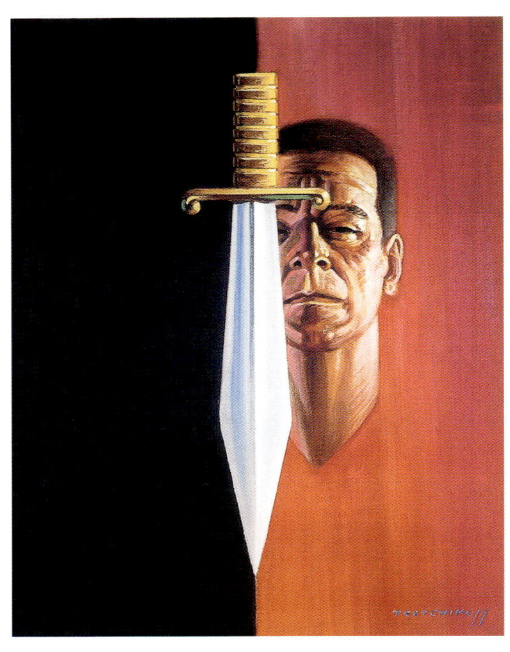

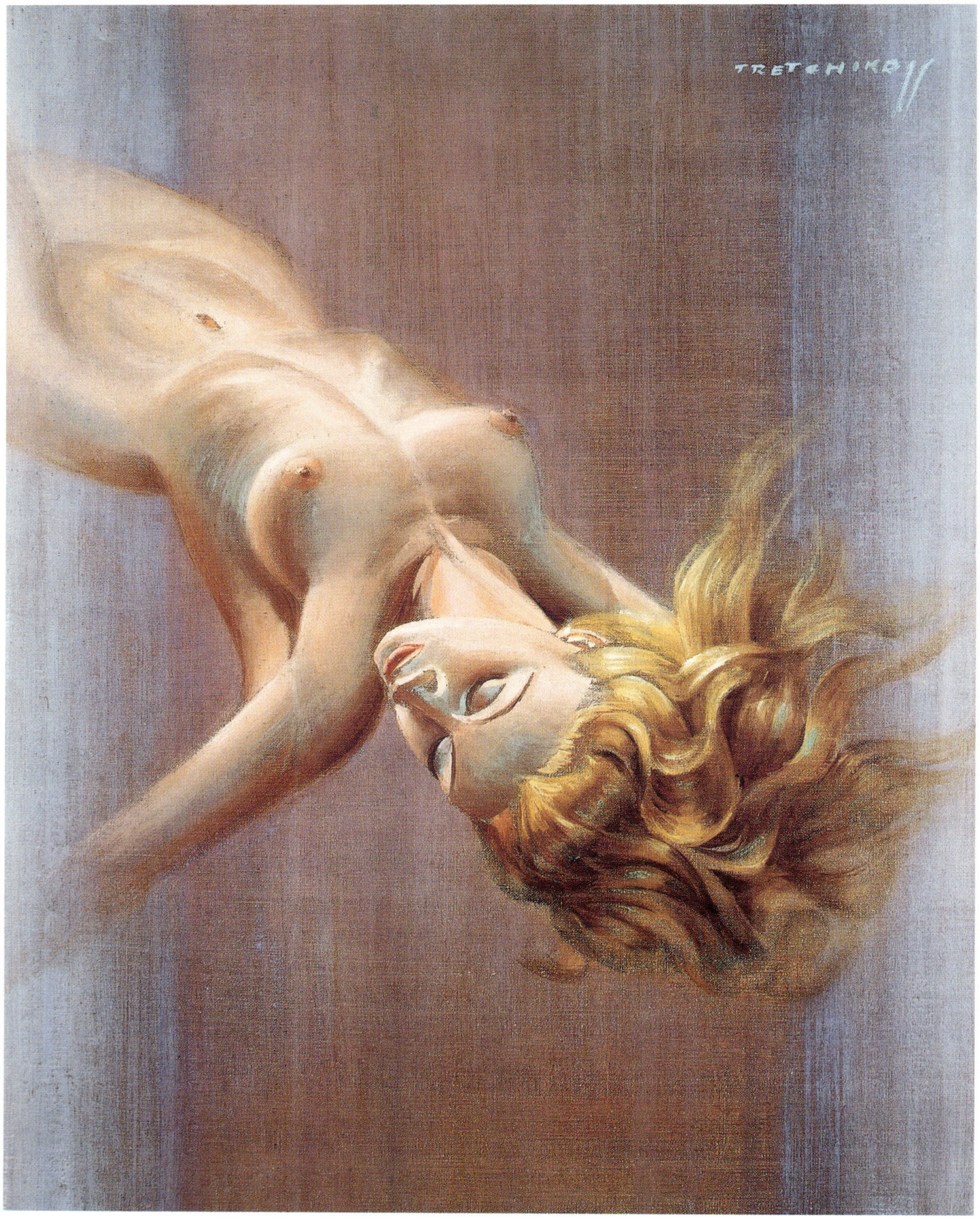

Vladimir Tretchikoff
Ten Commandments No 6. Thou Shalt Not Kill

Vladimir Tretchikoff
Ten Commandments No 9. Thou Shalt Not Commit Adultery

Vladimir Tretchikoff
Ten Commandments No 10. Thou Shalt Not Covet Thy Neighbours Goods

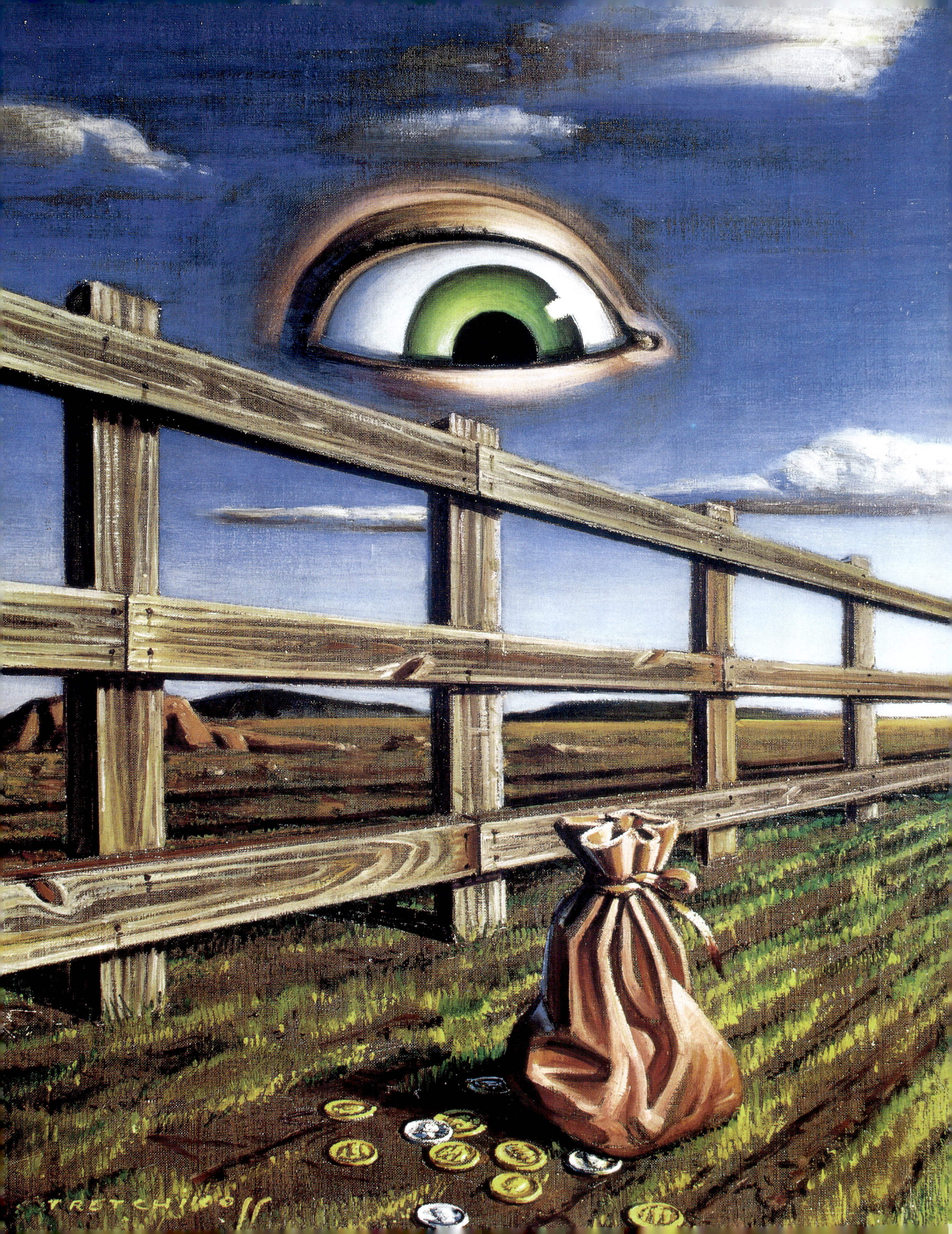

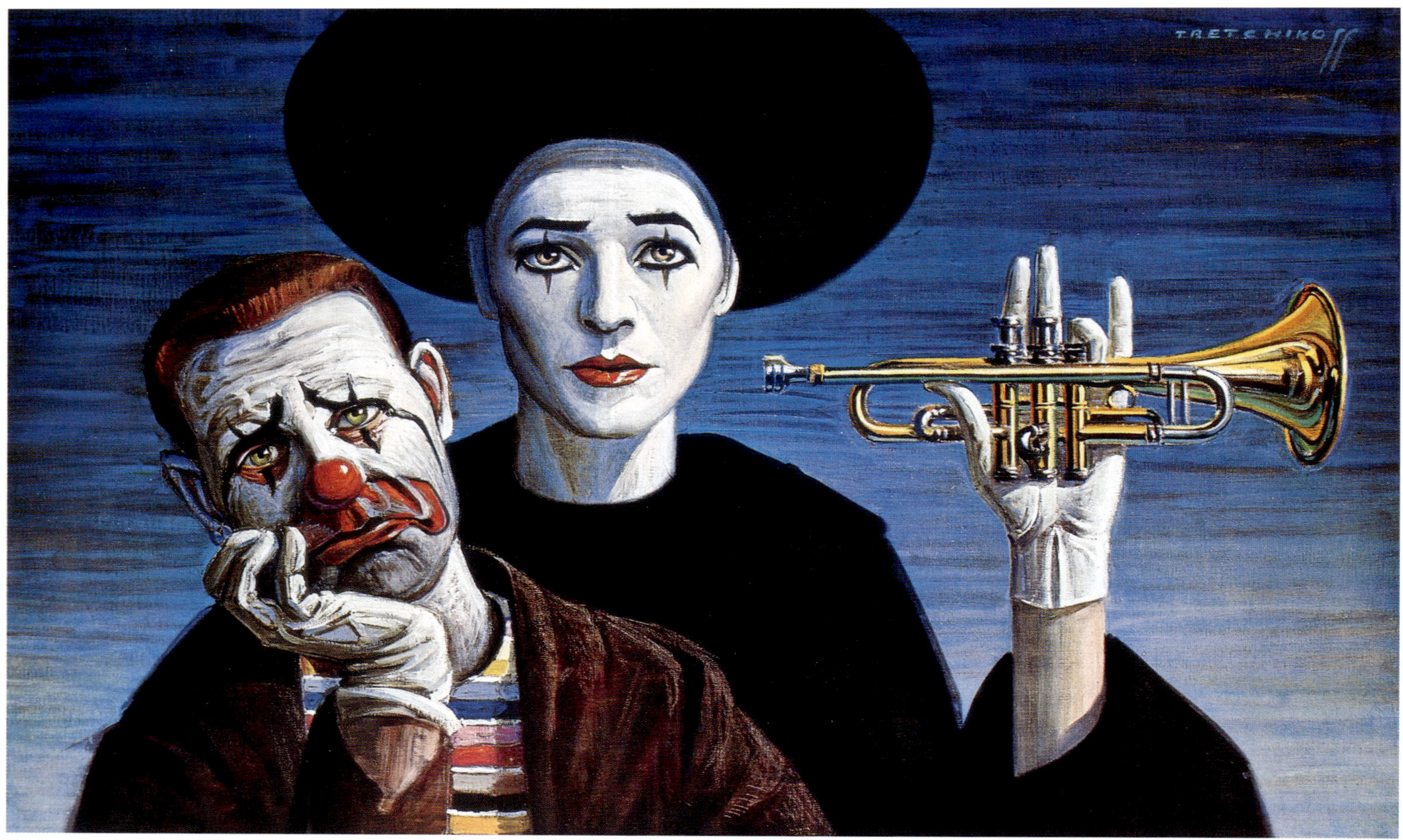

Vladimir Tretchikoff **Clowns**

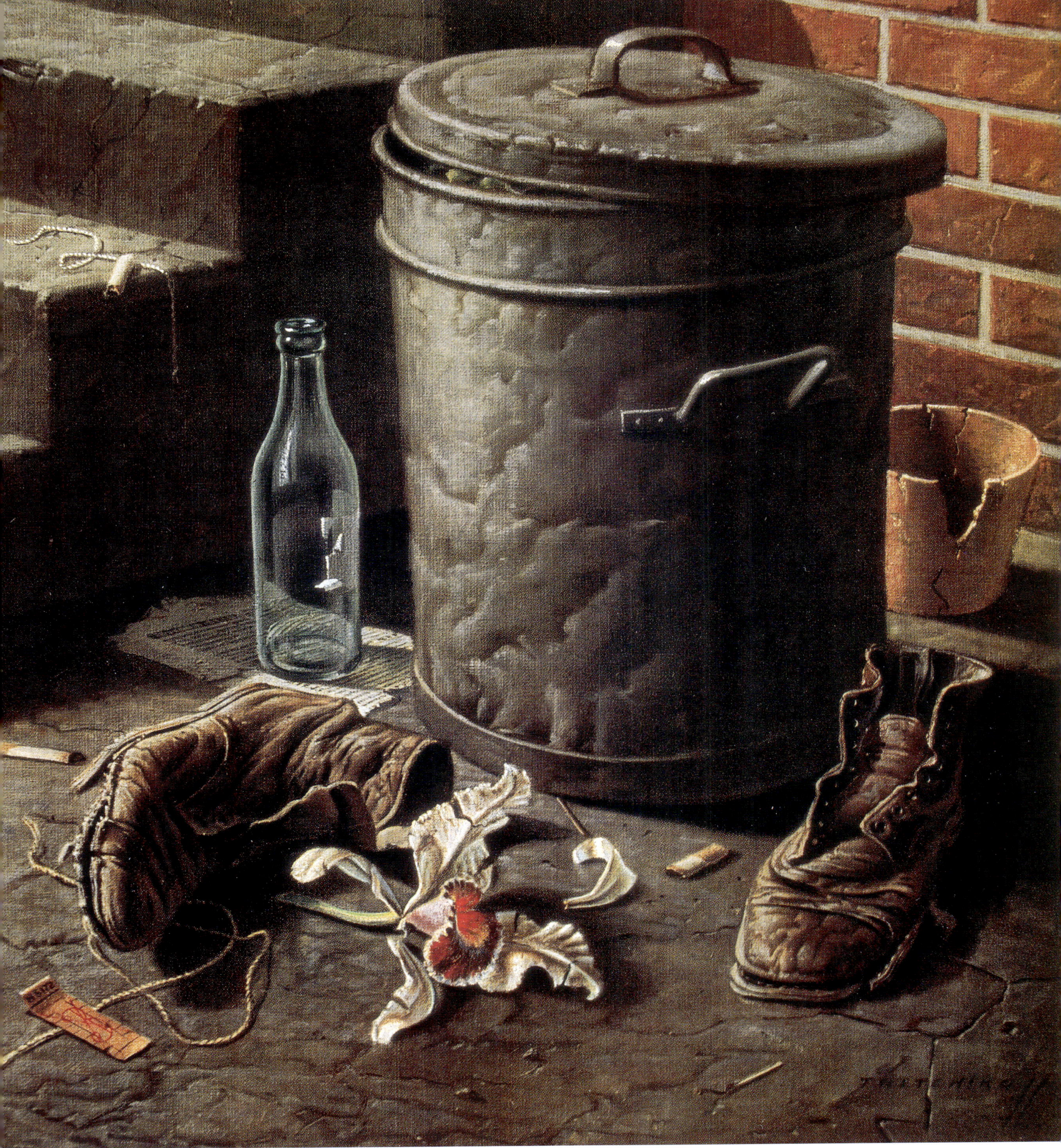

Vladimir Tretchikoff **Journey's End**

The advent of mass-produced prints allowed artists to mine a rich seam. Repetition may have been boring and stifling but it gave them an acceptable living.

Violet Skinner, seemingly inspired by **Tretchikoff's Wild Horses**, painted a series of Galloping Horse prints starting in 1959 with **Mares' Tails in the Sky**. More followed, with **Into the Happy Lands** in 1961, **High Spirits** in 1963 and **The Cooling Stream** in 1967.

Clemente perpetuated his ubiquitous **Red Skirt** from 1956 to 1960, following it up with **La Guitarista, Los Nouillandos** and **The Fire Dance**. This repetition, practiced in order to earn a regular income, was belittled by the critics. But is it any different from the Chapman Brothers' reworking of their child sculptures or Damien Hirst churning out his spin paintings, or indeed Turner, Picasso and Pollock, who were obsessively drawn back to the same genre or subject matter?

Repetition didn't always work for mass-market artists. **Stephen Pearson** created the world's all-time number one best-selling print, **Wings of Love**, which was made famous in the film **Abigail's Party**. With three million copies already sold, it is still selling at a rate of over two hundred per week. Yet curiously **Pearson** had little success with repetition.

The Art of Repetition: Mass-Market Prints

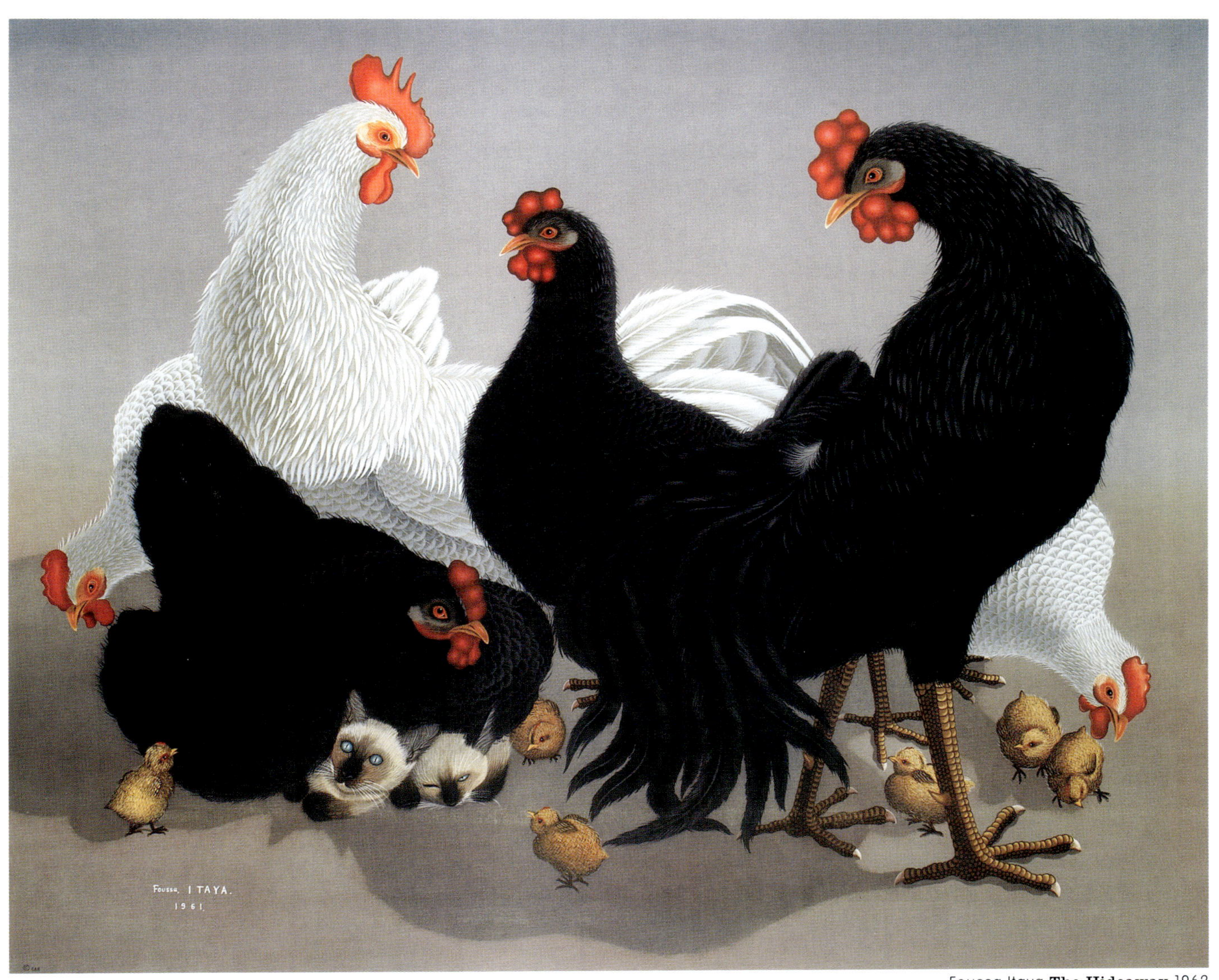

Foussa Itaya **The Hideaway** 1962

F R S Clemente **The Red Strut** 1956

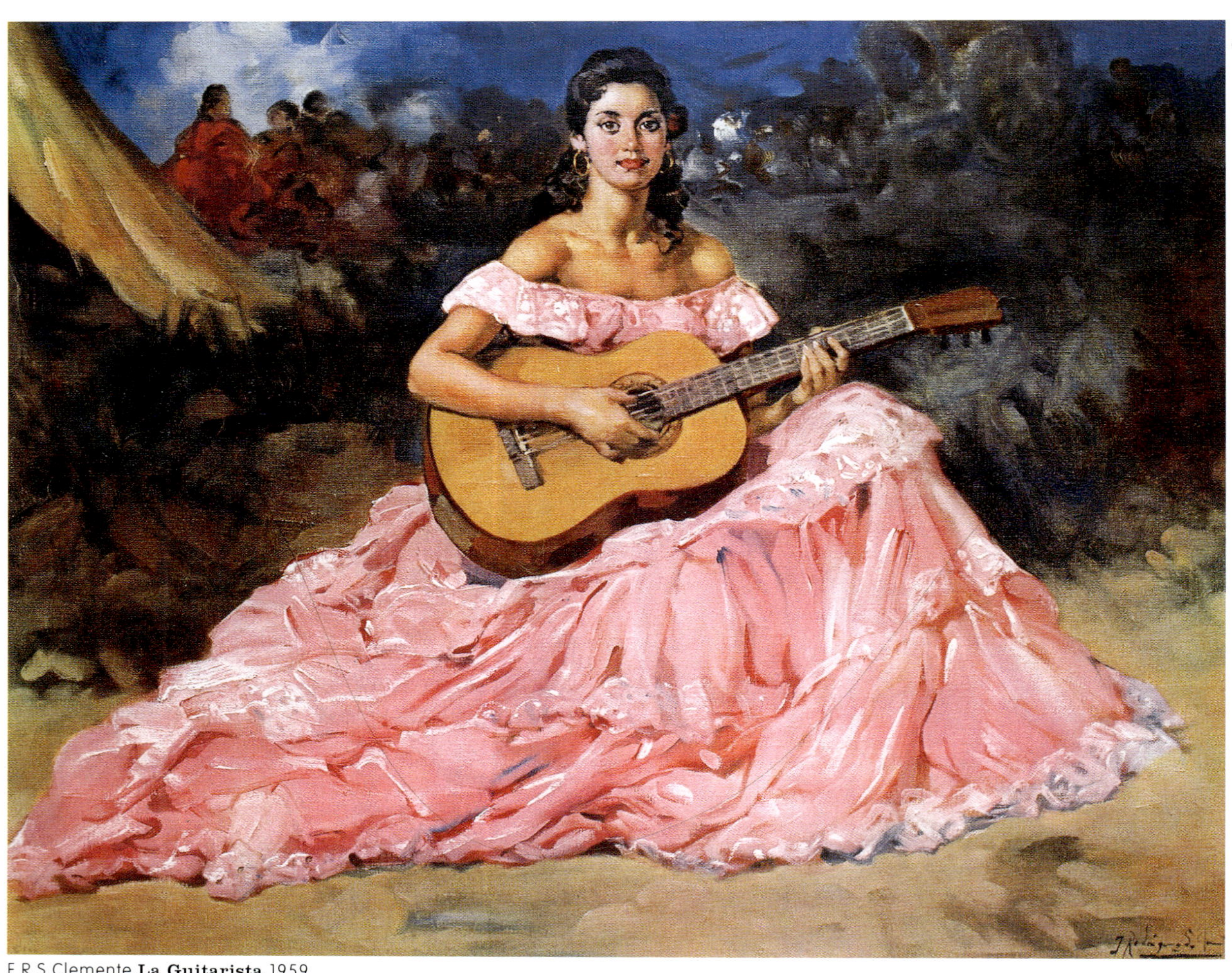

F R S Clemente **La Guitarista** 1959

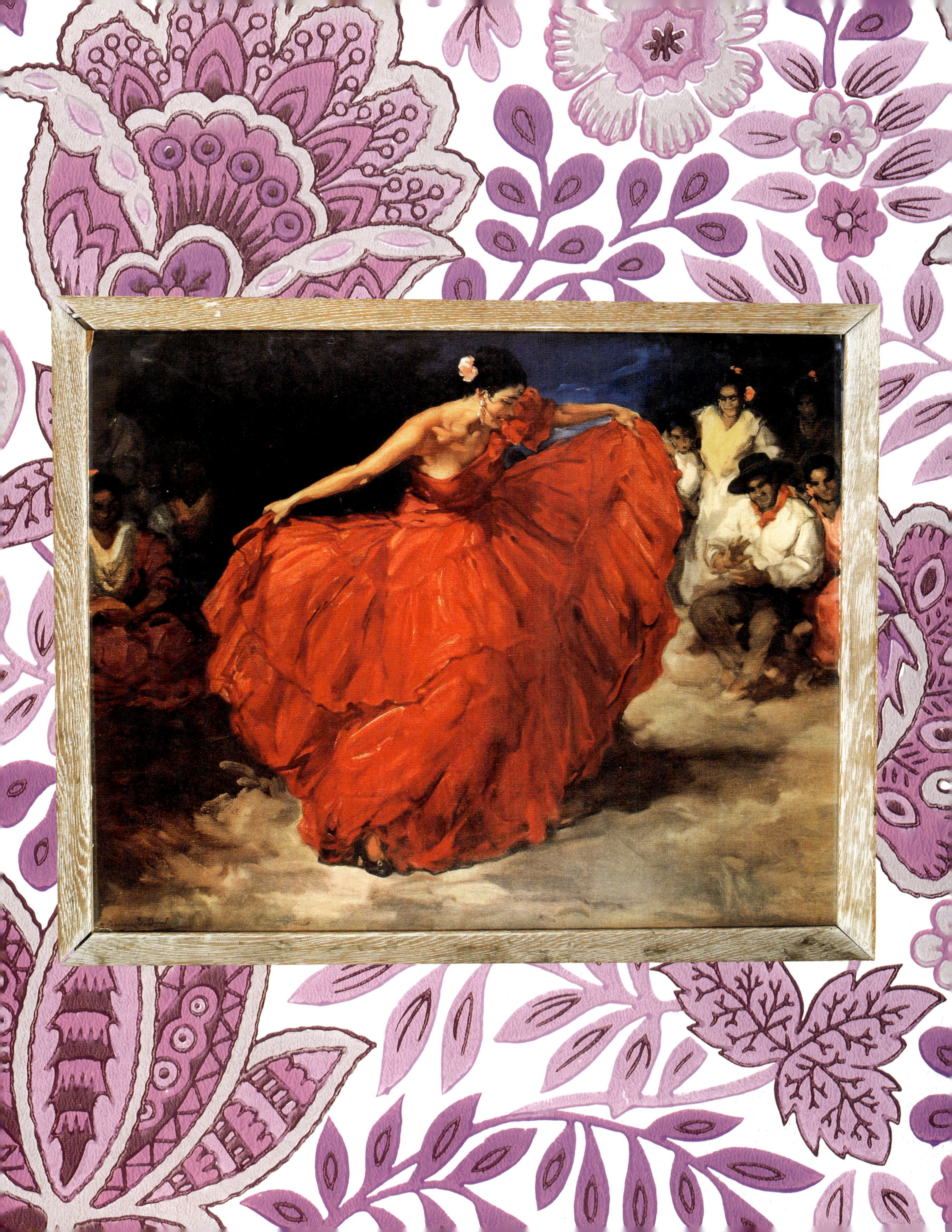

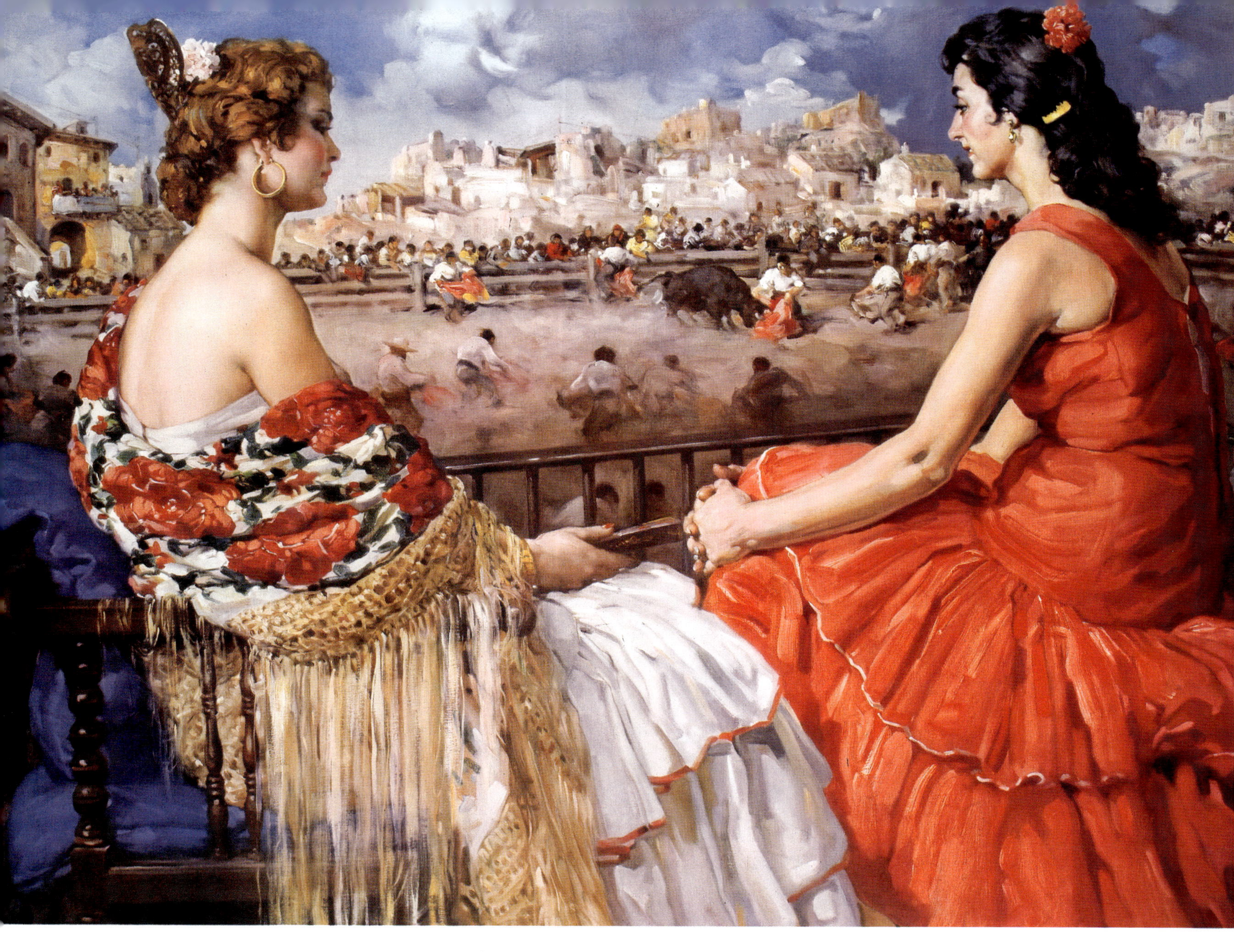

F R S Clemente **Los Nouillandos** 1959

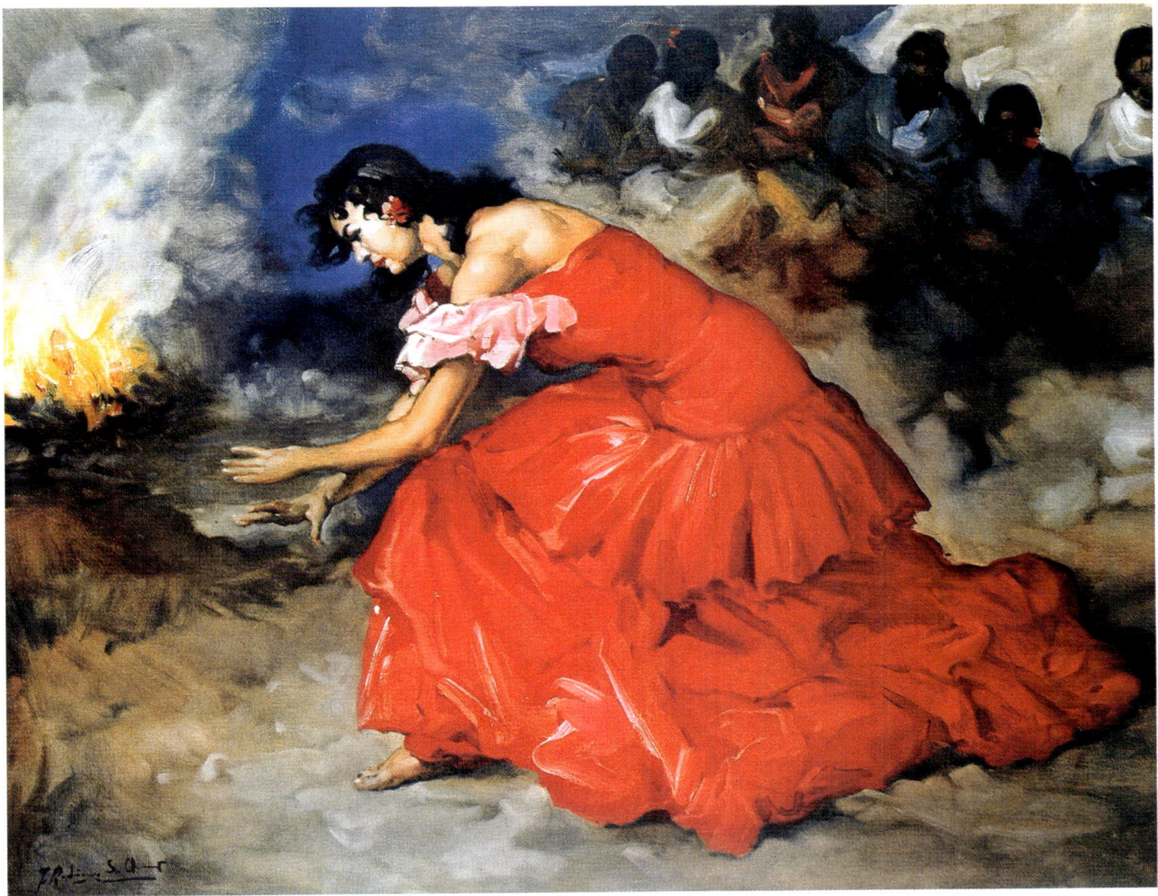

F R S Clemente **The Fire Dance** 1960

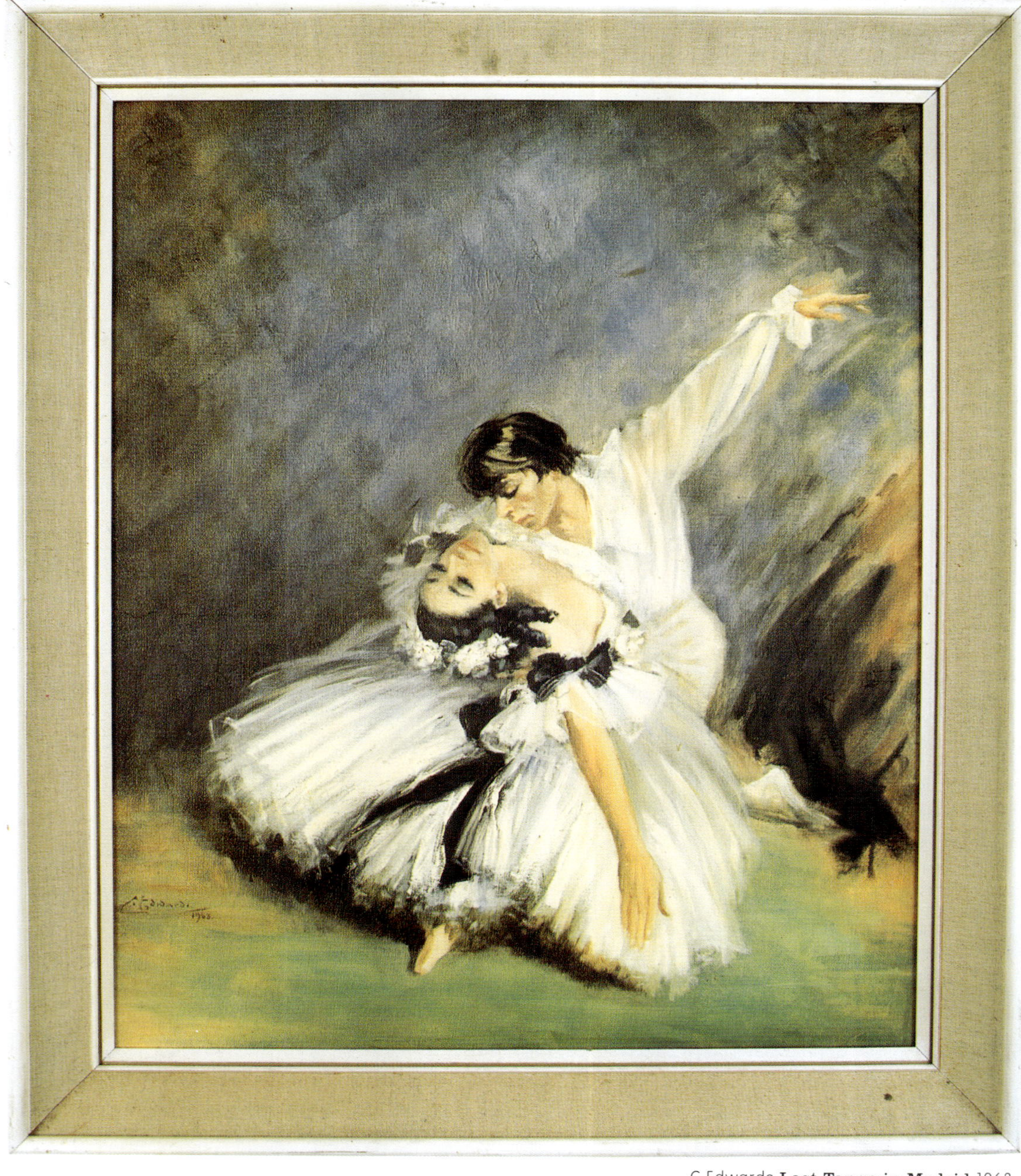

C Edwards **Last Tango in Madrid** 1963

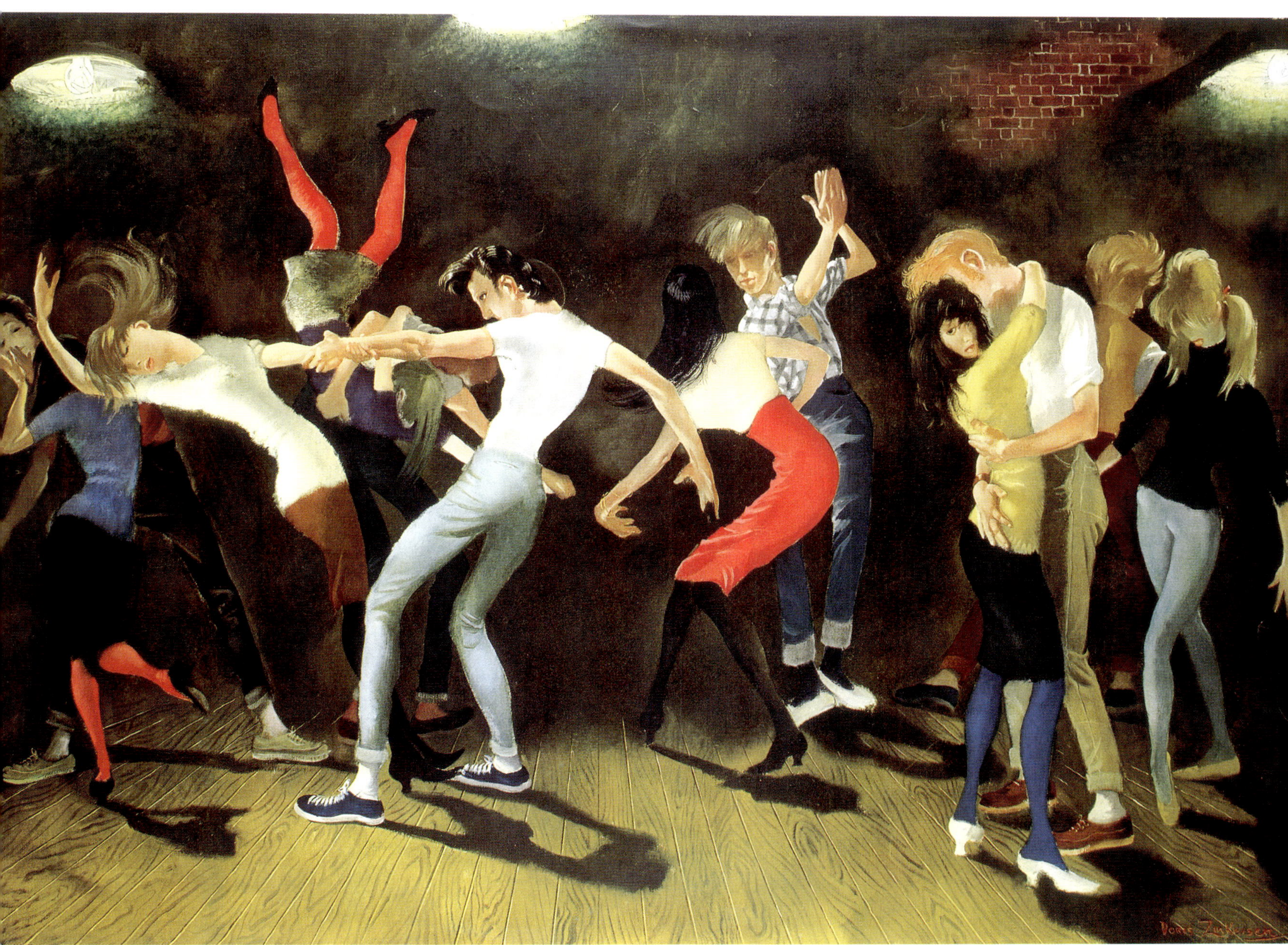

Doris Leireiser **The Rockers** 1963

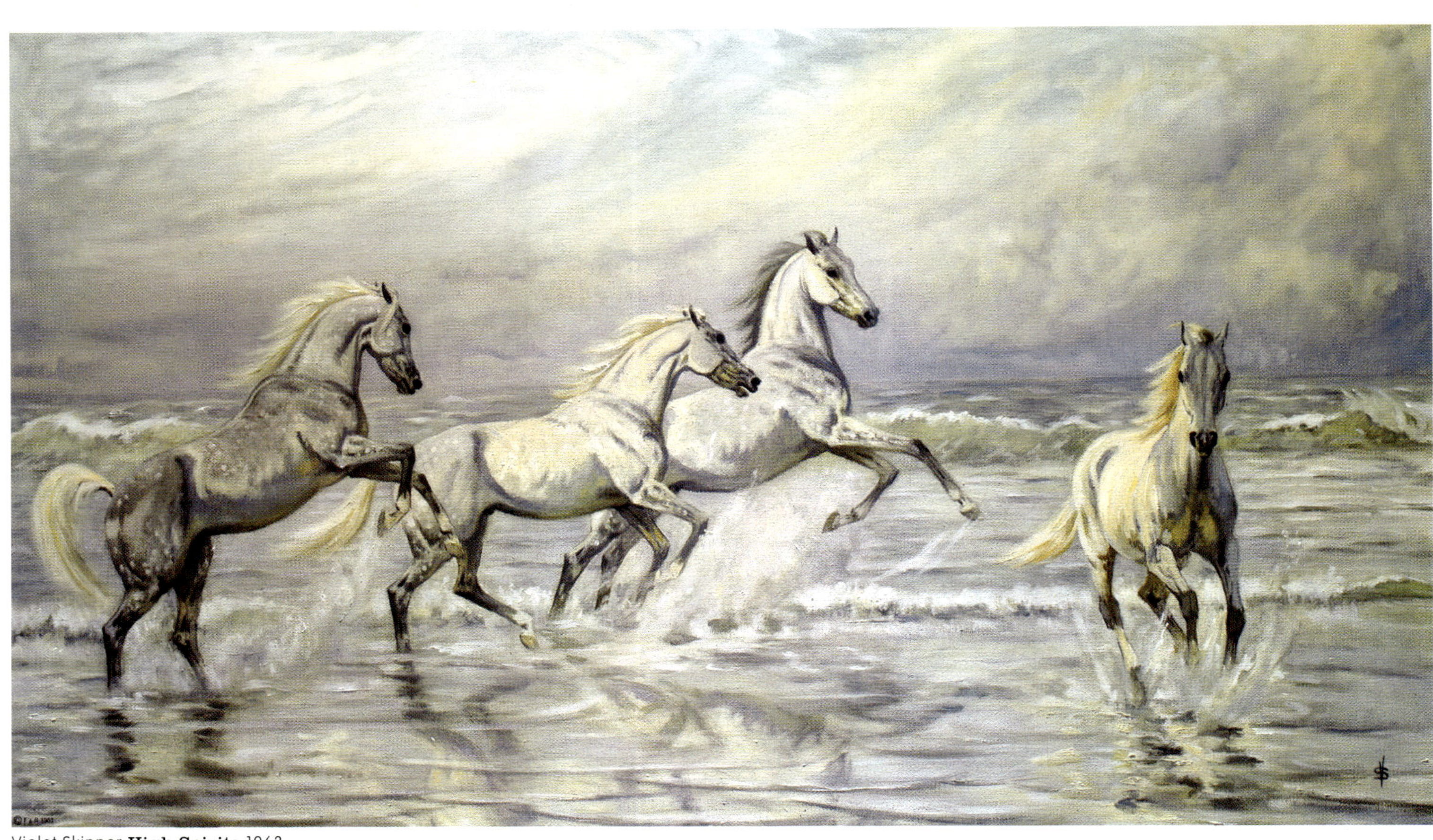

Violet Skinner **High Spirits** 1963

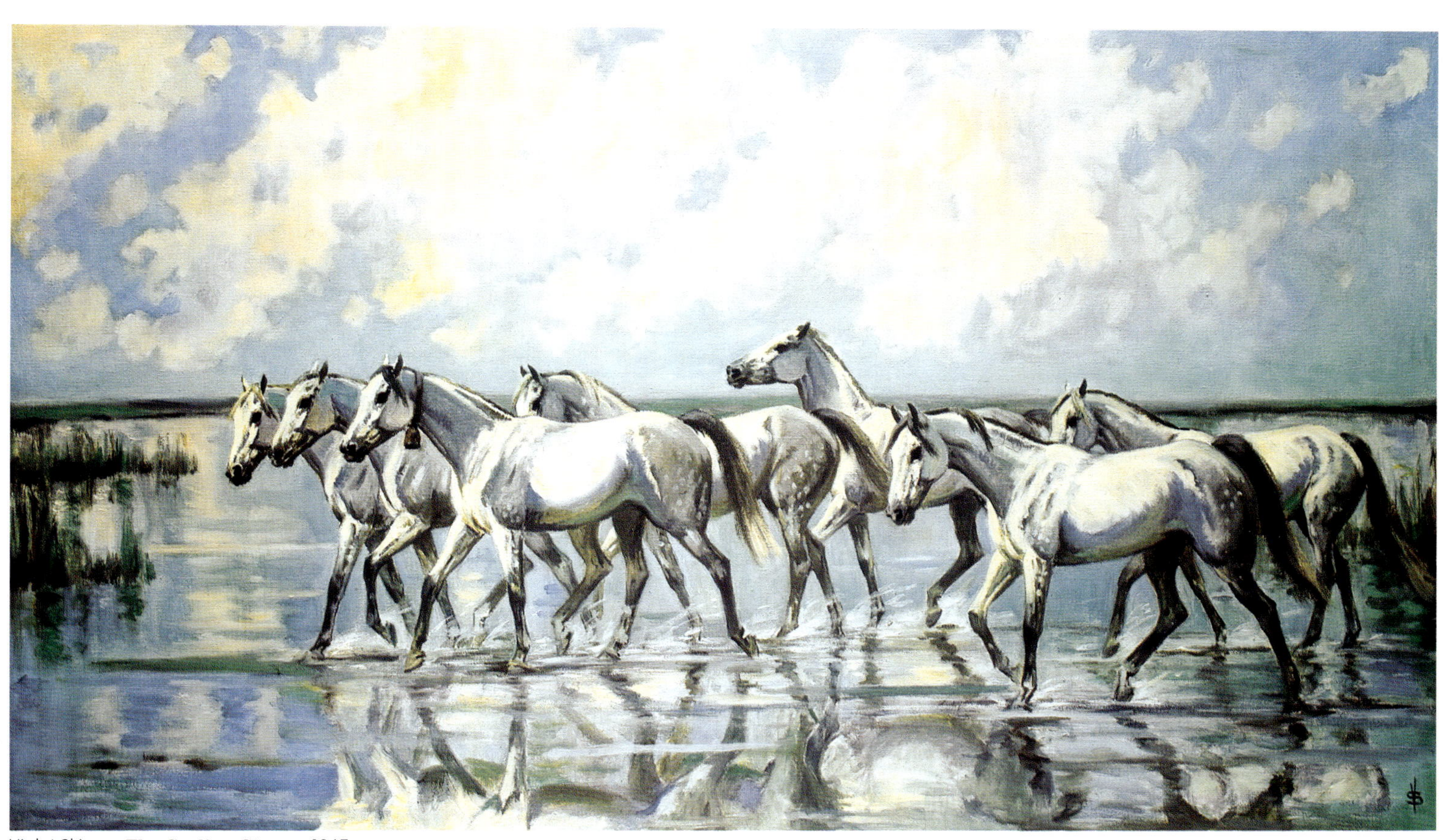

Violet Skinner **The Cooling Stream** 1967

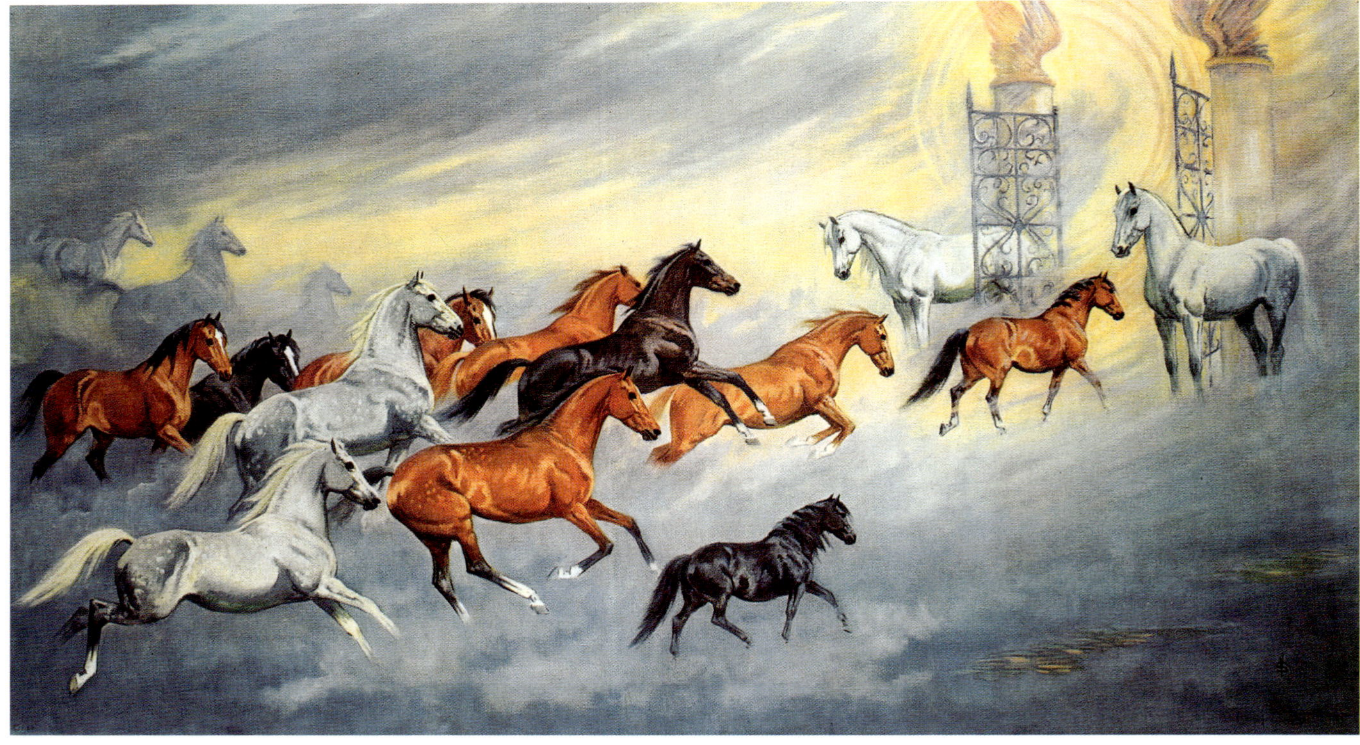

Violet Skinner **Into the Happy Lands** 1961

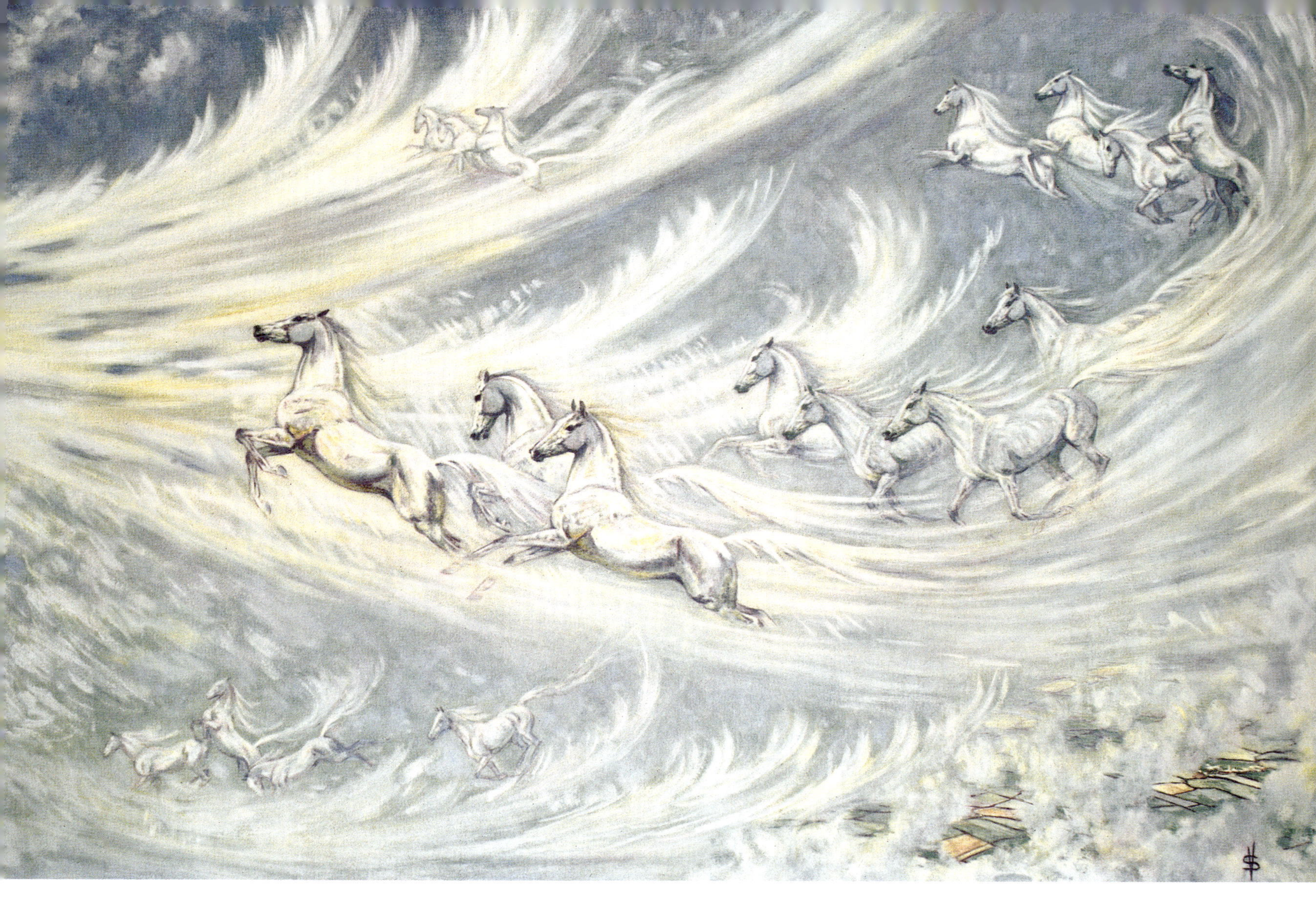

Violet Skinner **Mares' Tails In the Sky**

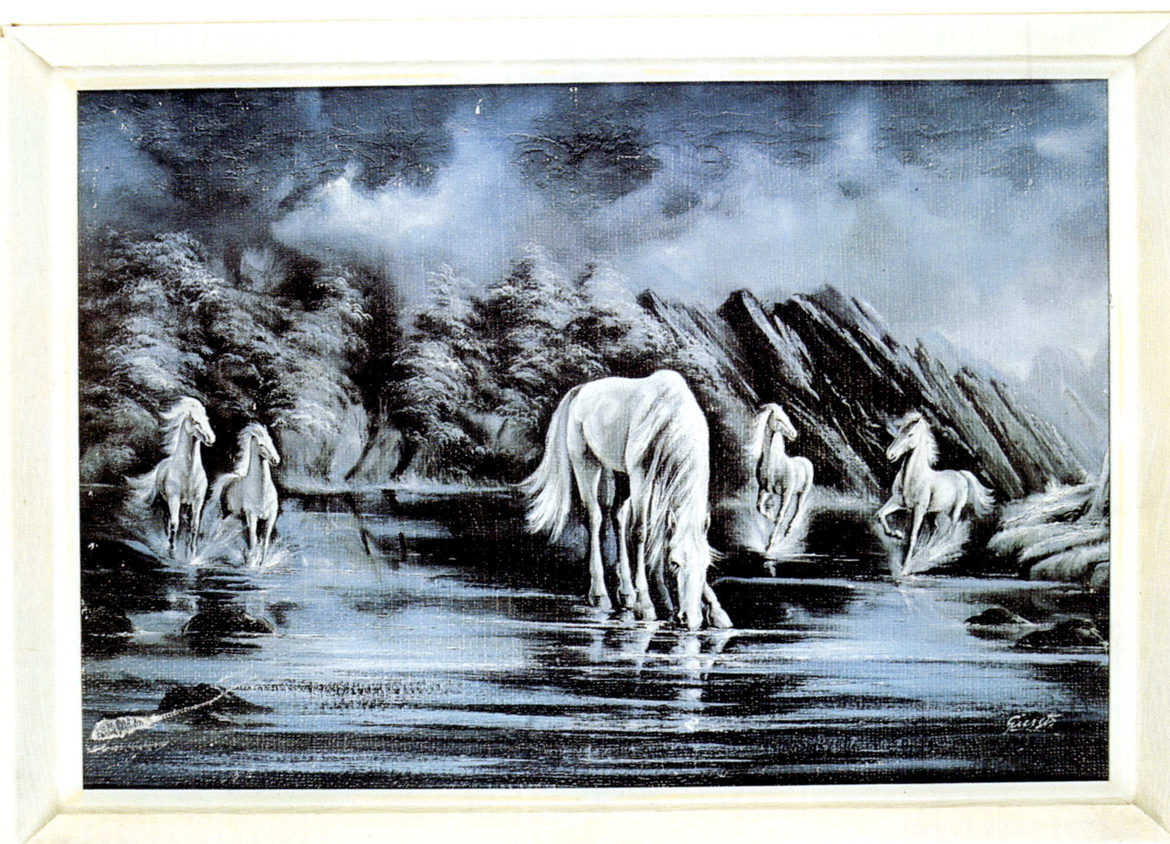

Giusto **White Horses**

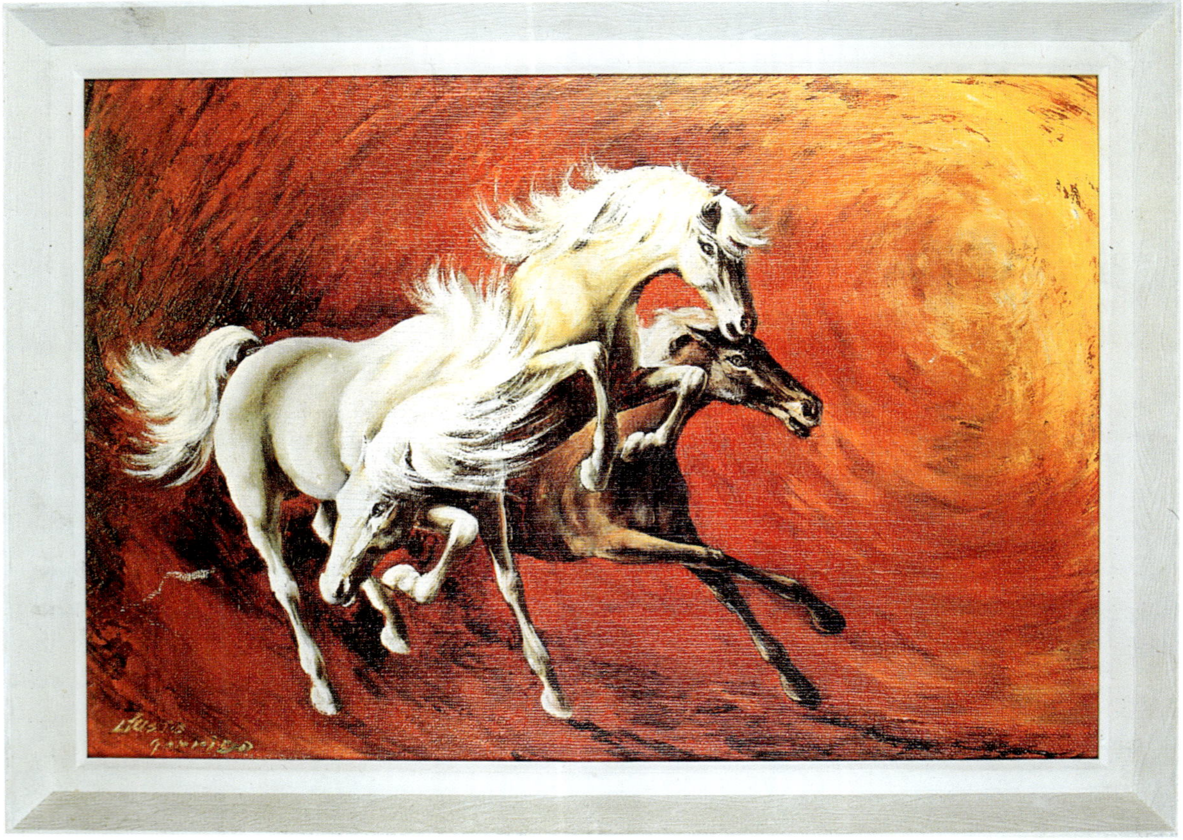

Giusto **Crazy Horses**

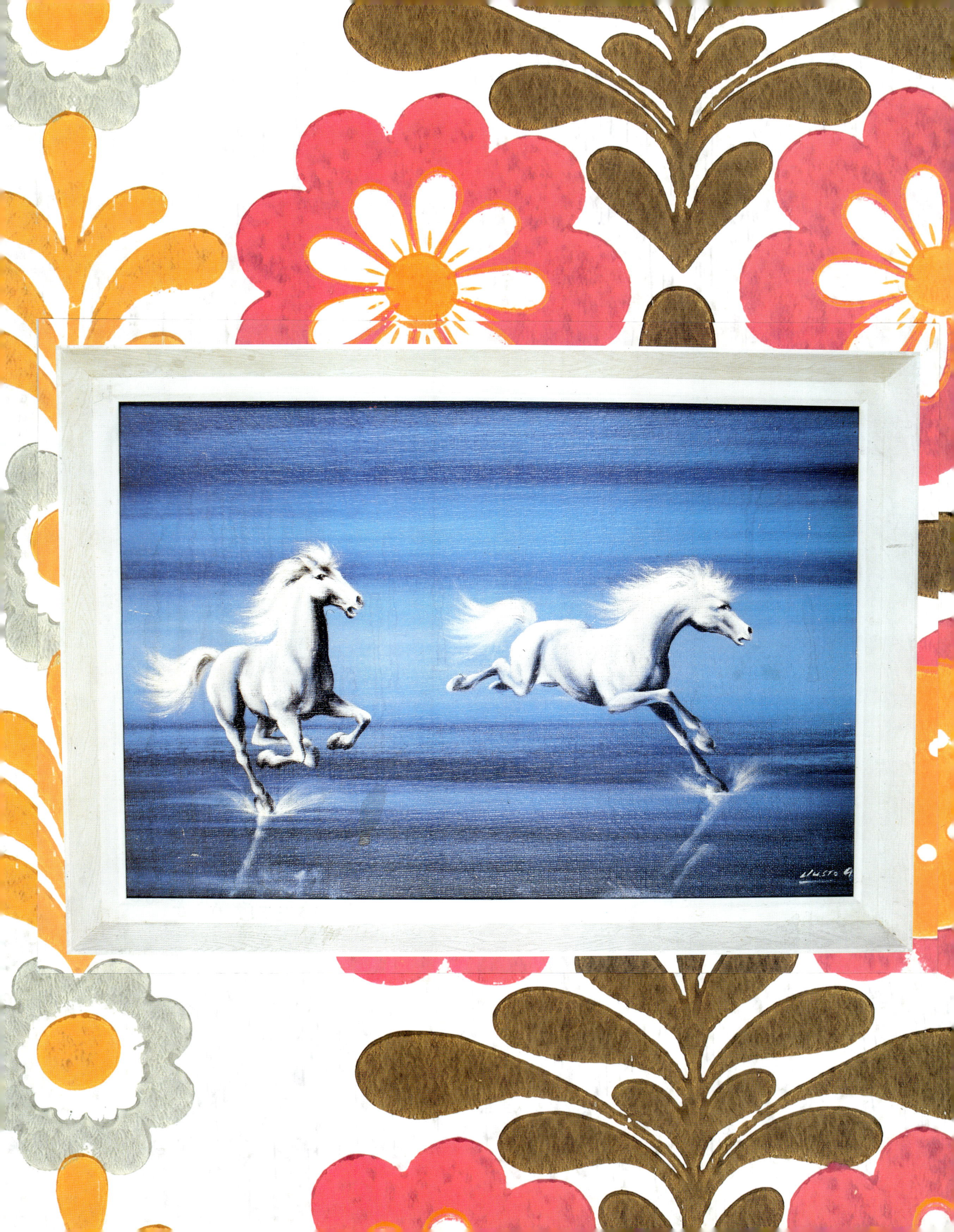

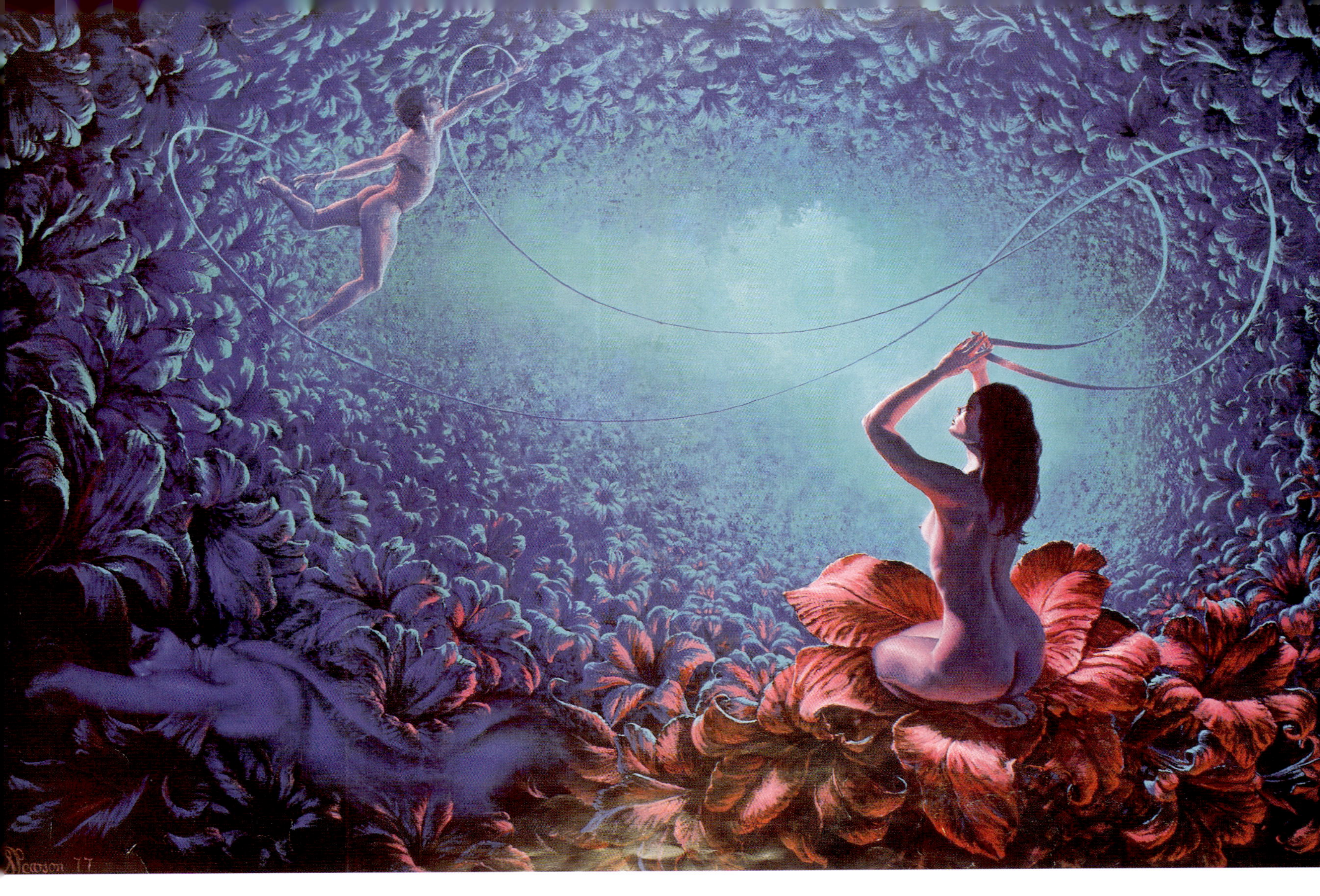

Stephen Pearson **Le Rêve en Bleu** 1977

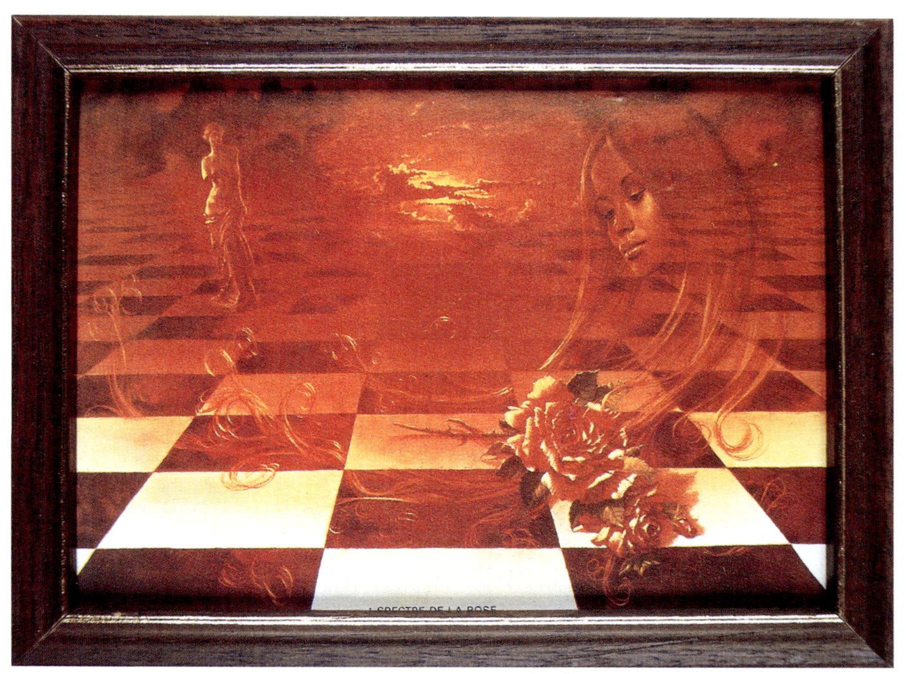

Stephen Pearson **Spectre de la Rose** 1975

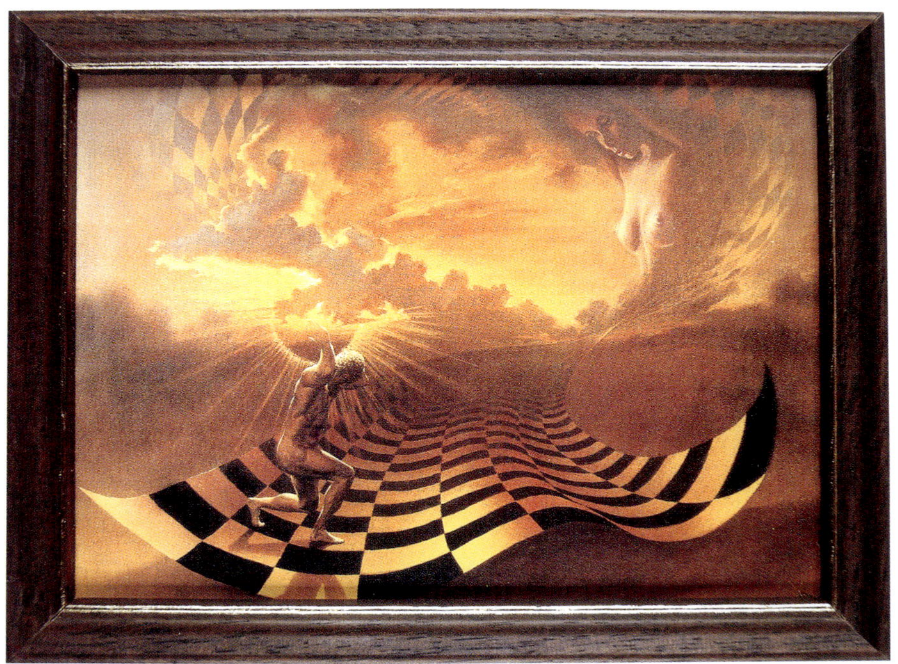

Stephen Pearson **Solar Offering**

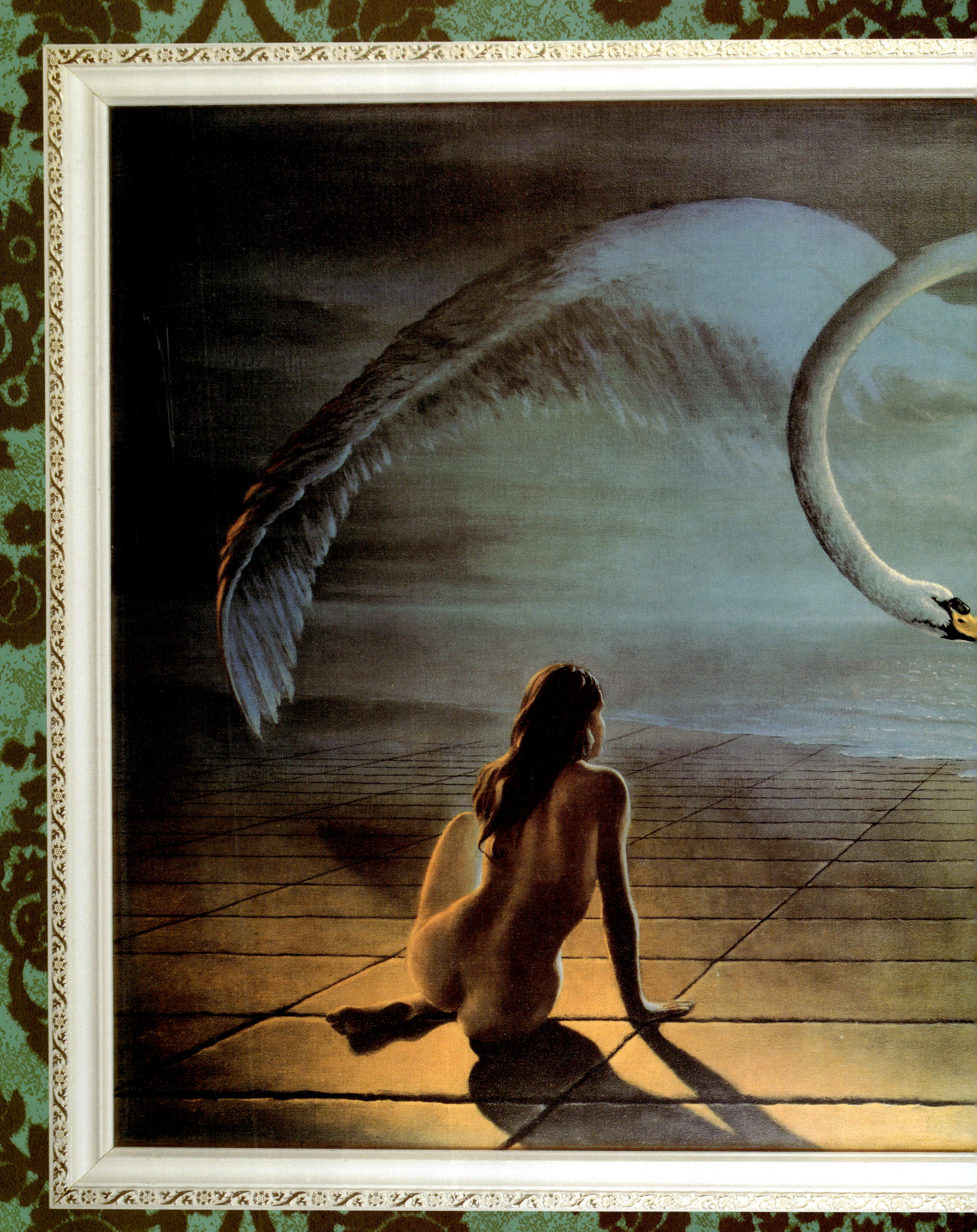

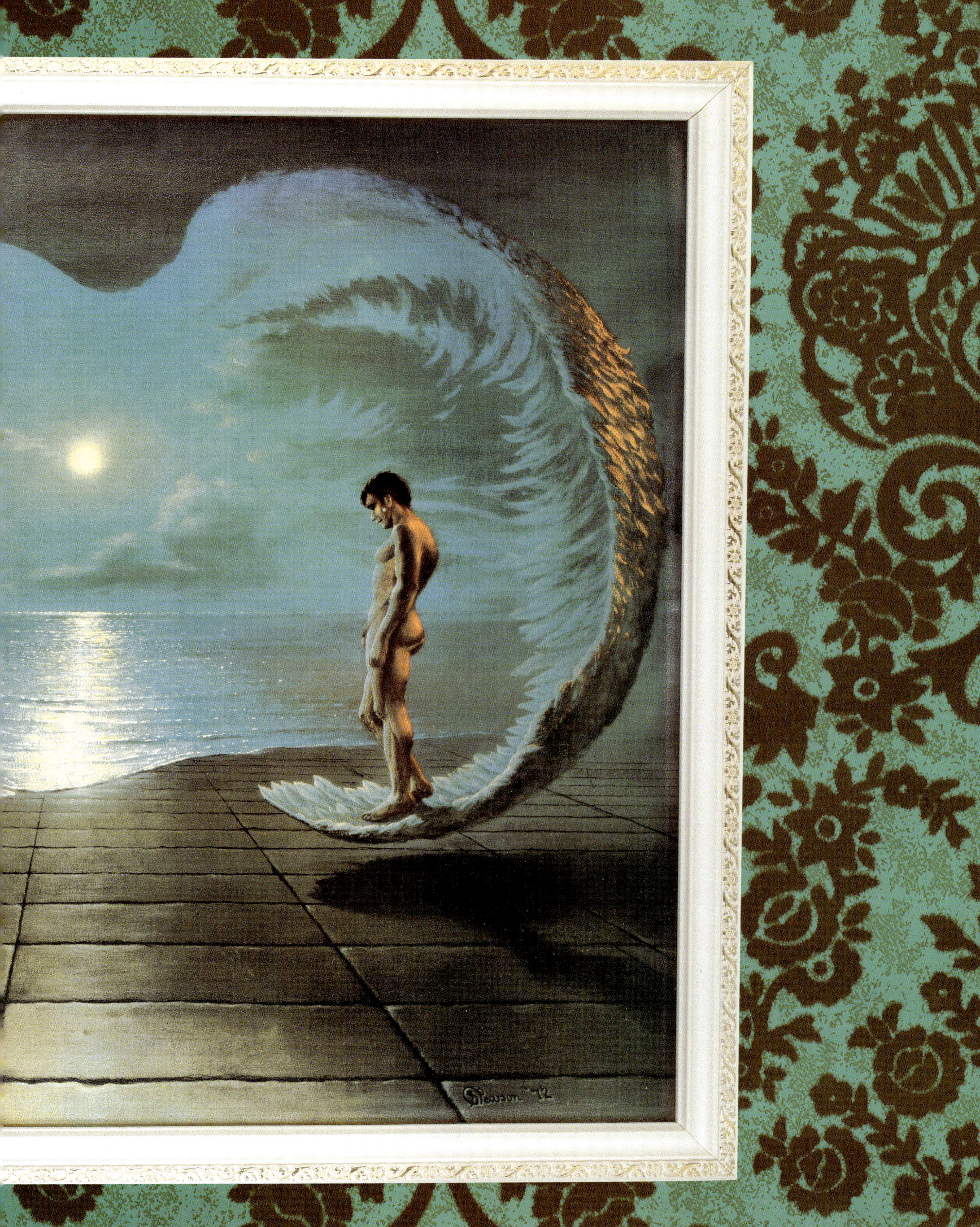
DPearson '72

preceding page: Stephen Pearson **Wings of Love** 1972

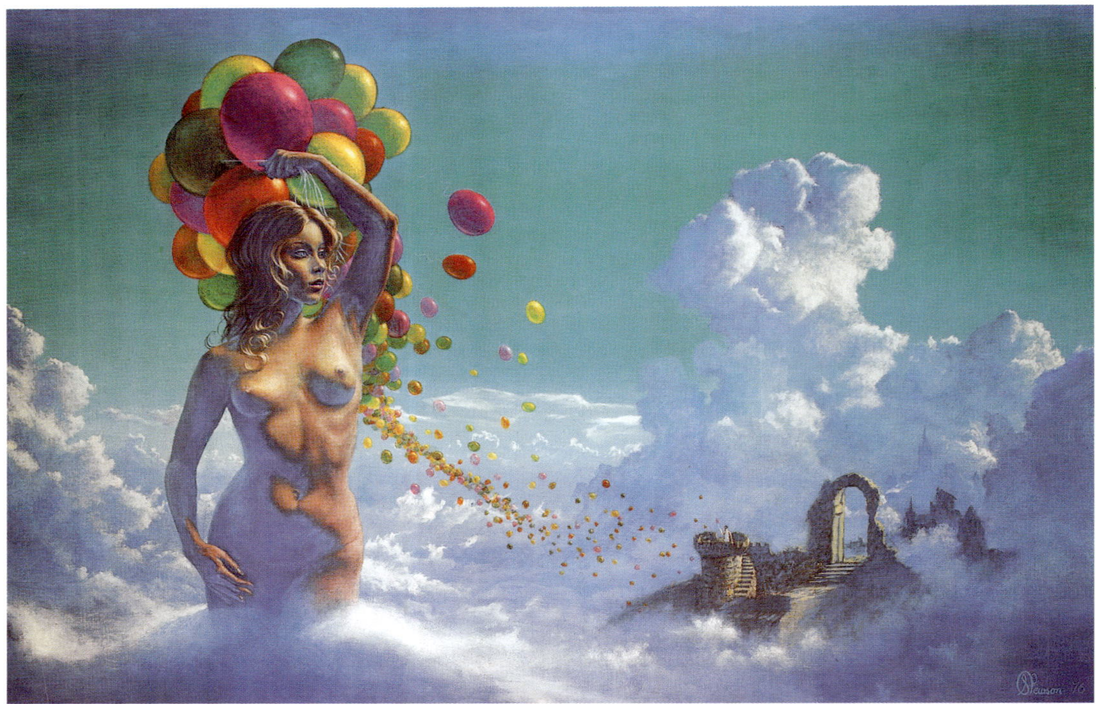

Stephen Pearson **Up, Up and Away** 1976

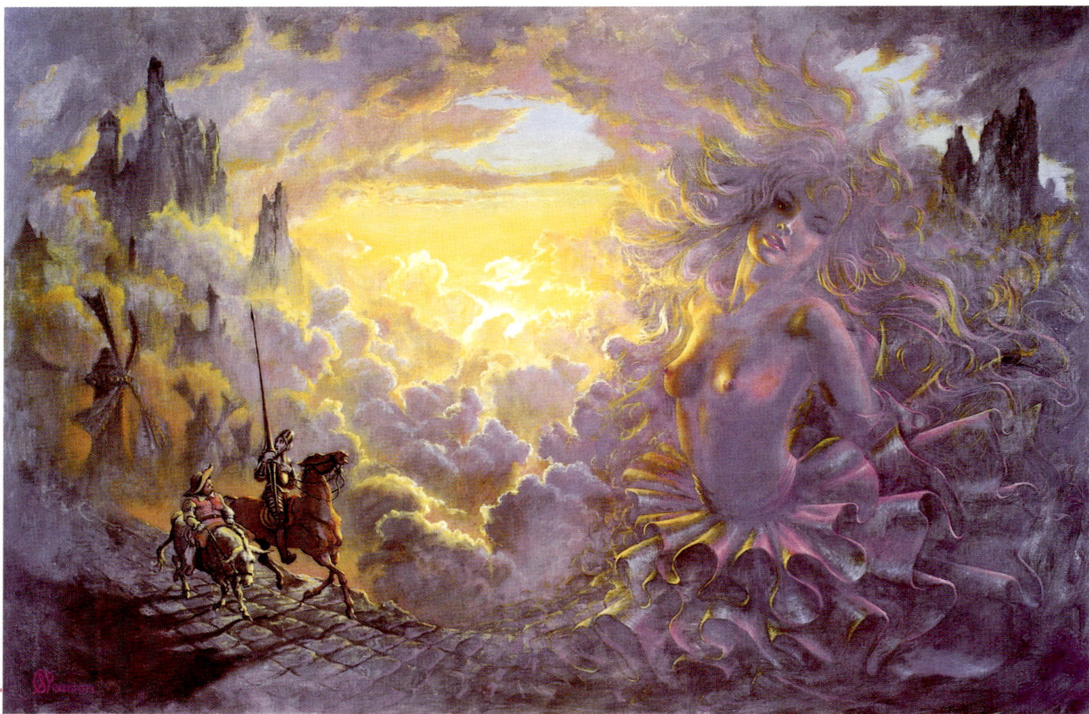

Stephen Pearson **Quixote's Dream** 1975

Stephen Pearson **Stallion** 1978

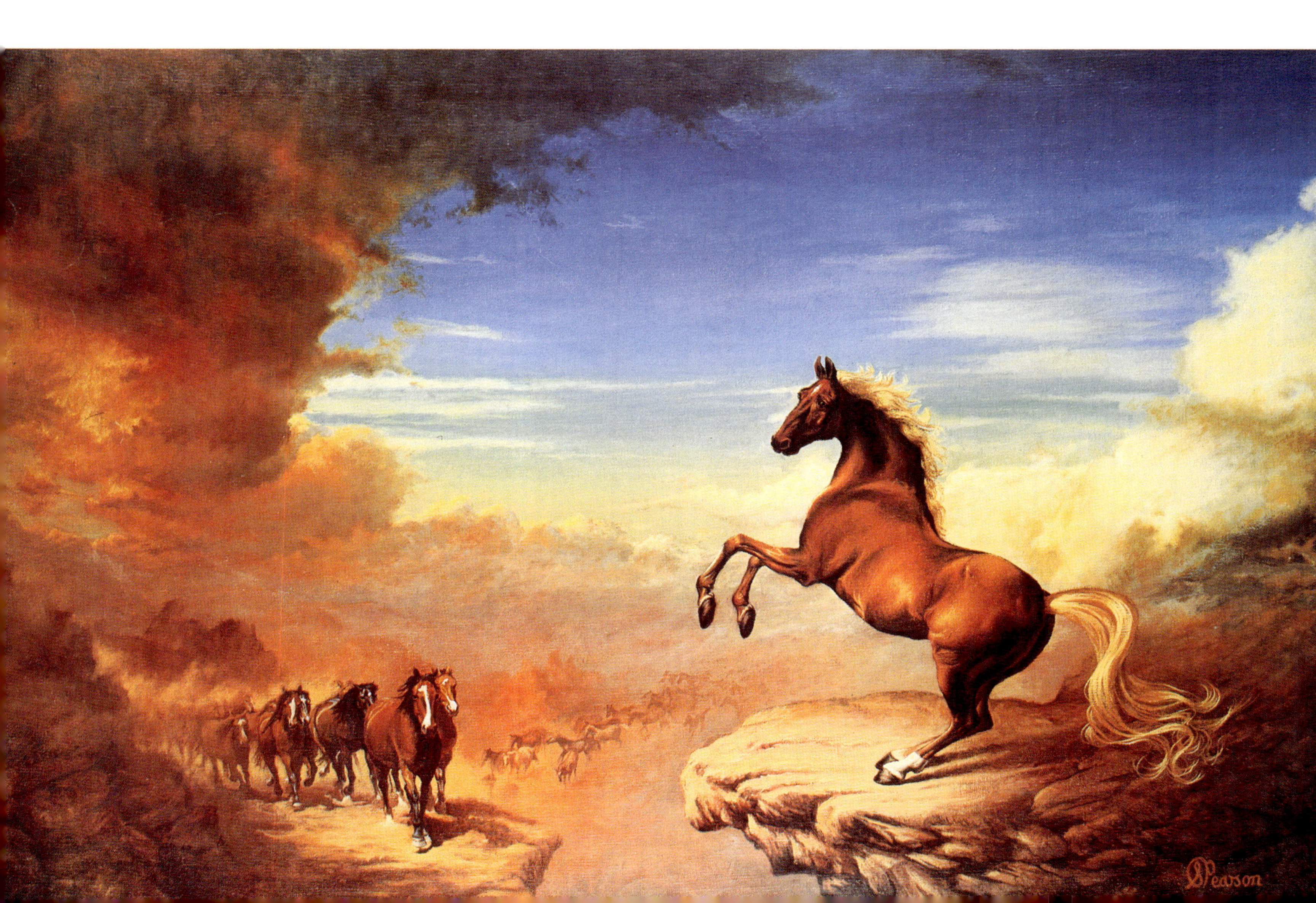

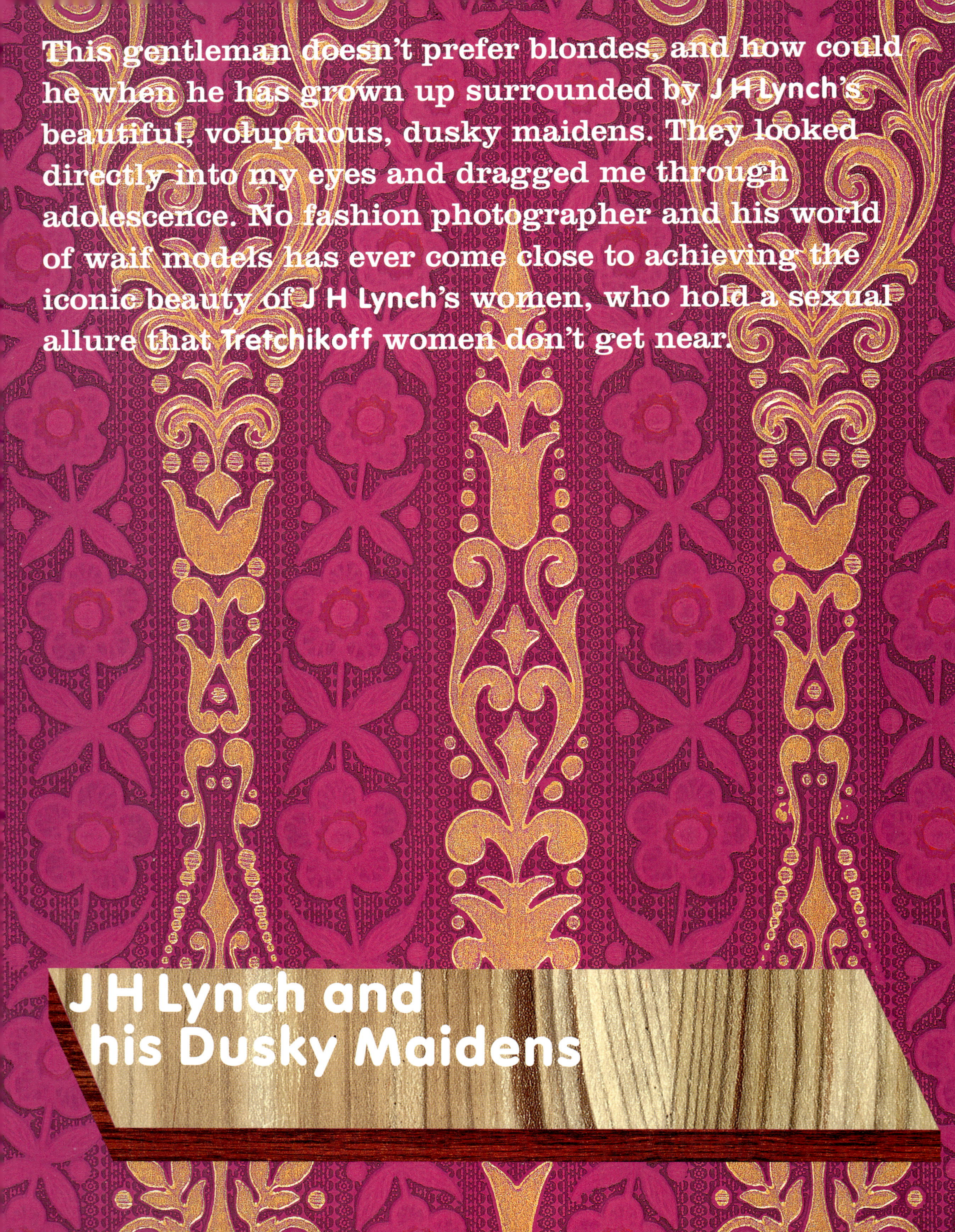

This gentleman doesn't prefer blondes, and how could he when he has grown up surrounded by J H Lynch's beautiful, voluptuous, dusky maidens. They looked directly into my eyes and dragged me through adolescence. No fashion photographer and his world of waif models has ever come close to achieving the iconic beauty of J H Lynch's women, who hold a sexual allure that Tretchikoff women don't get near.

J H Lynch and his Dusky Maidens

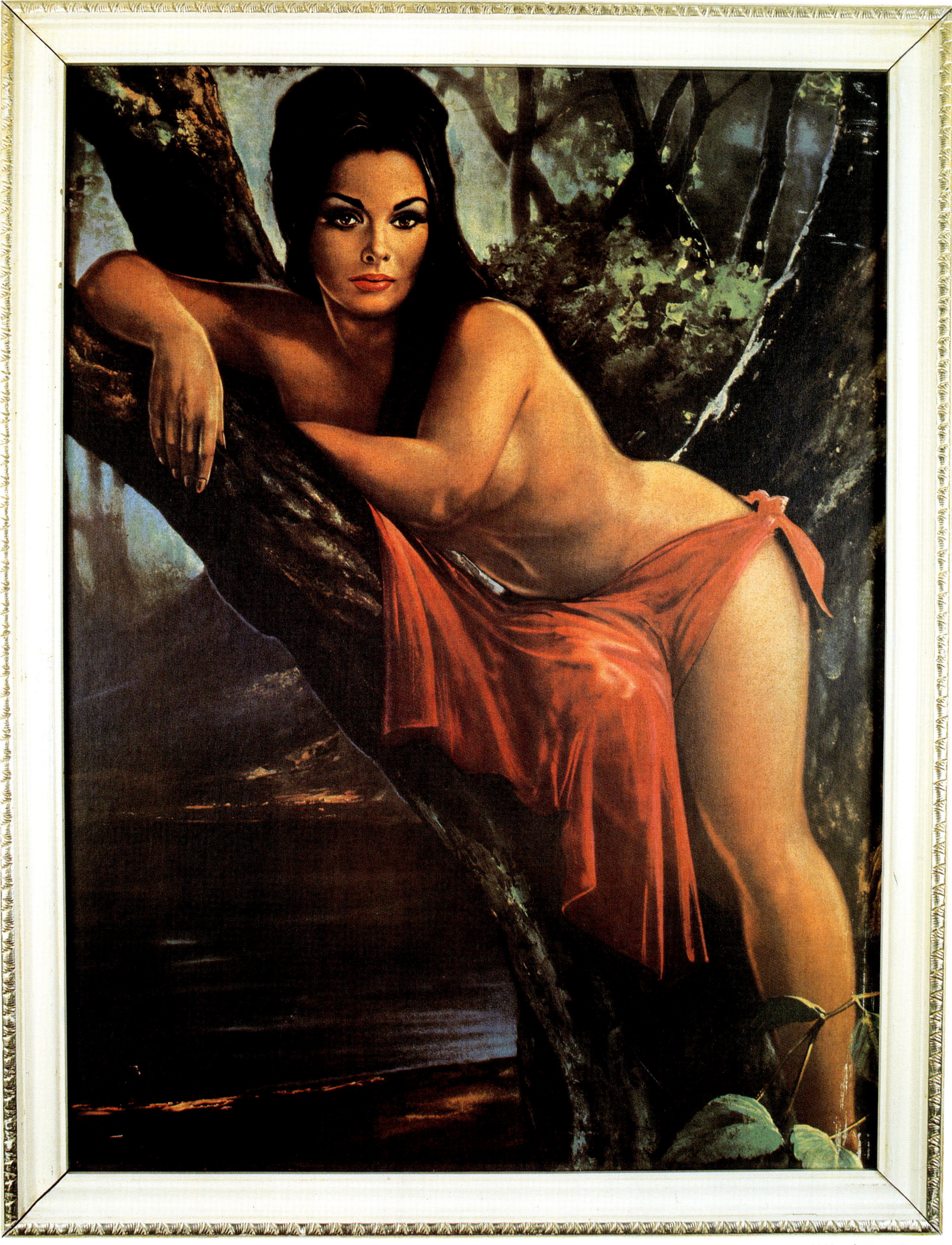

J H Lynch **Tree Woman**

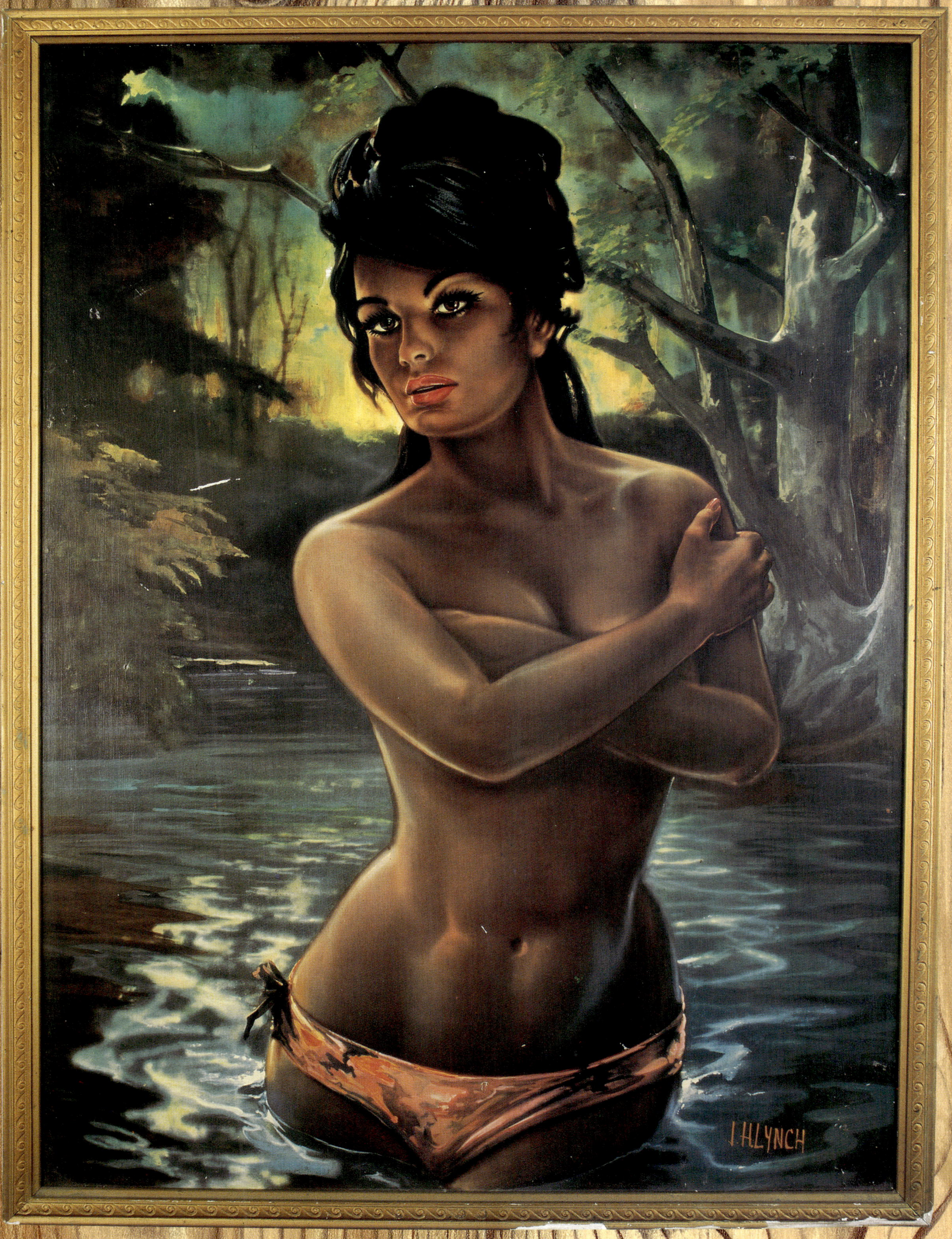
J.H.LYNCH

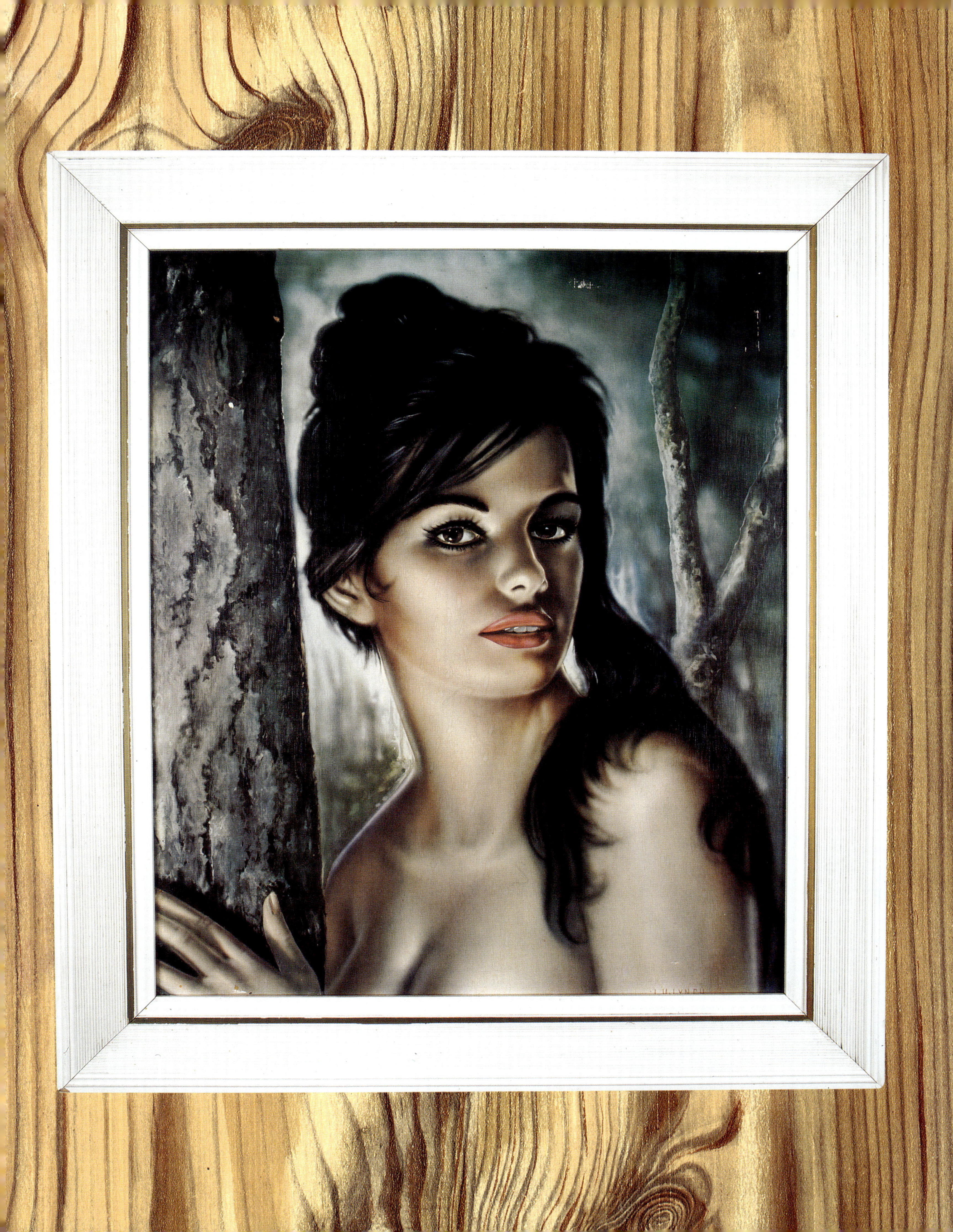

preceding page: J H Lynch **Nymph** 1975; J H Lynch **Tina** 1975

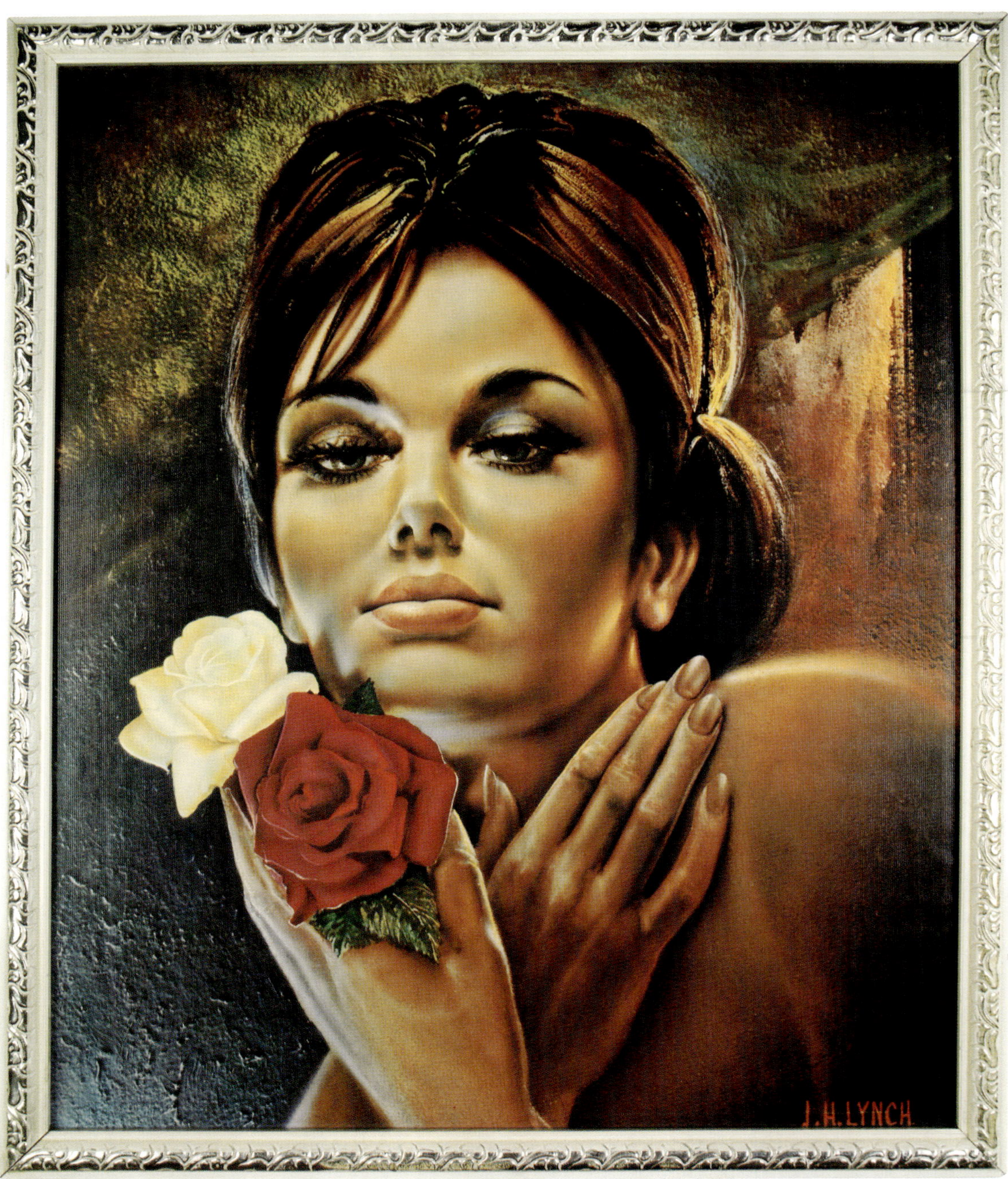

J H Lynch **Rose**

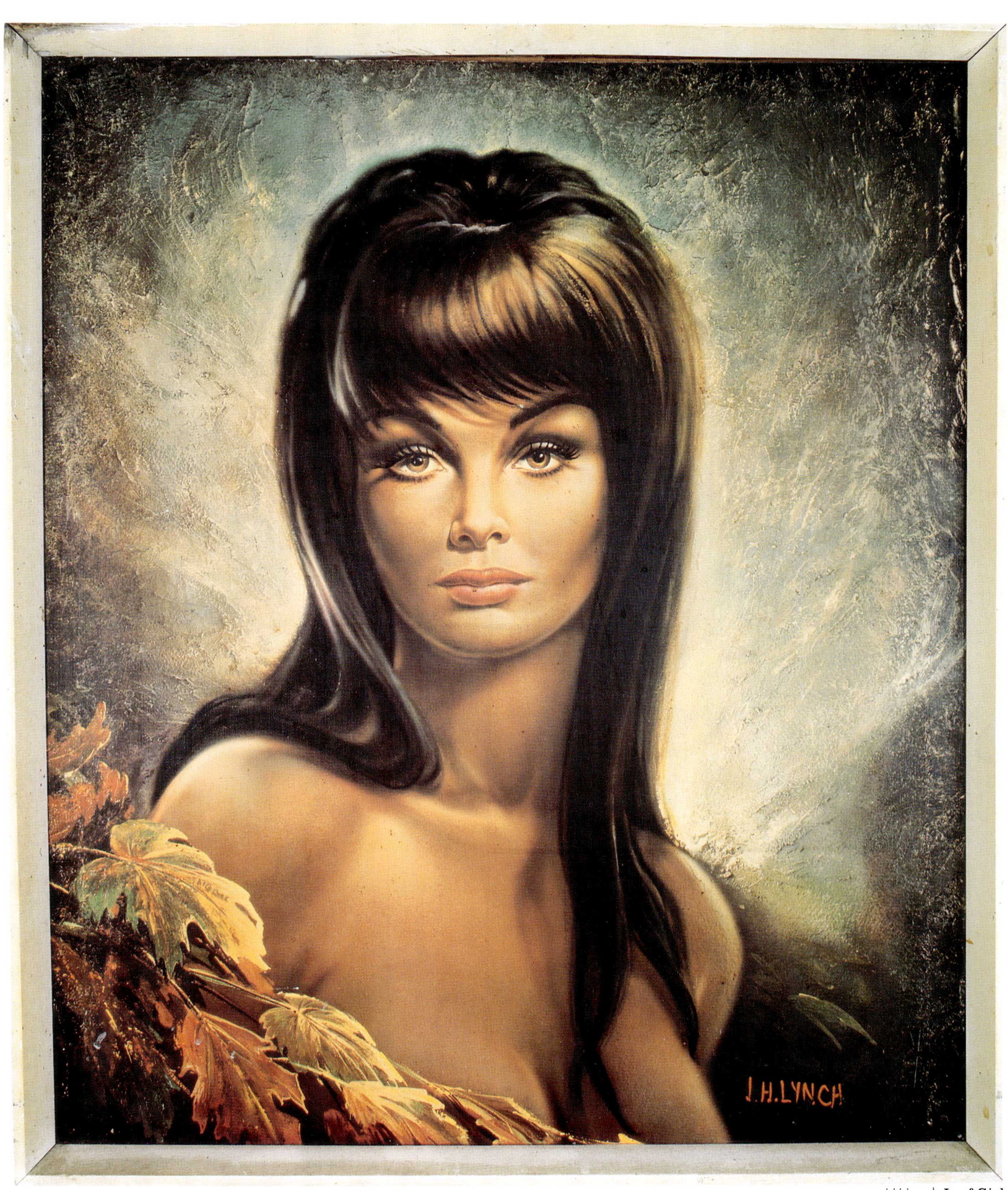

J H Lynch **Leaf Girl**

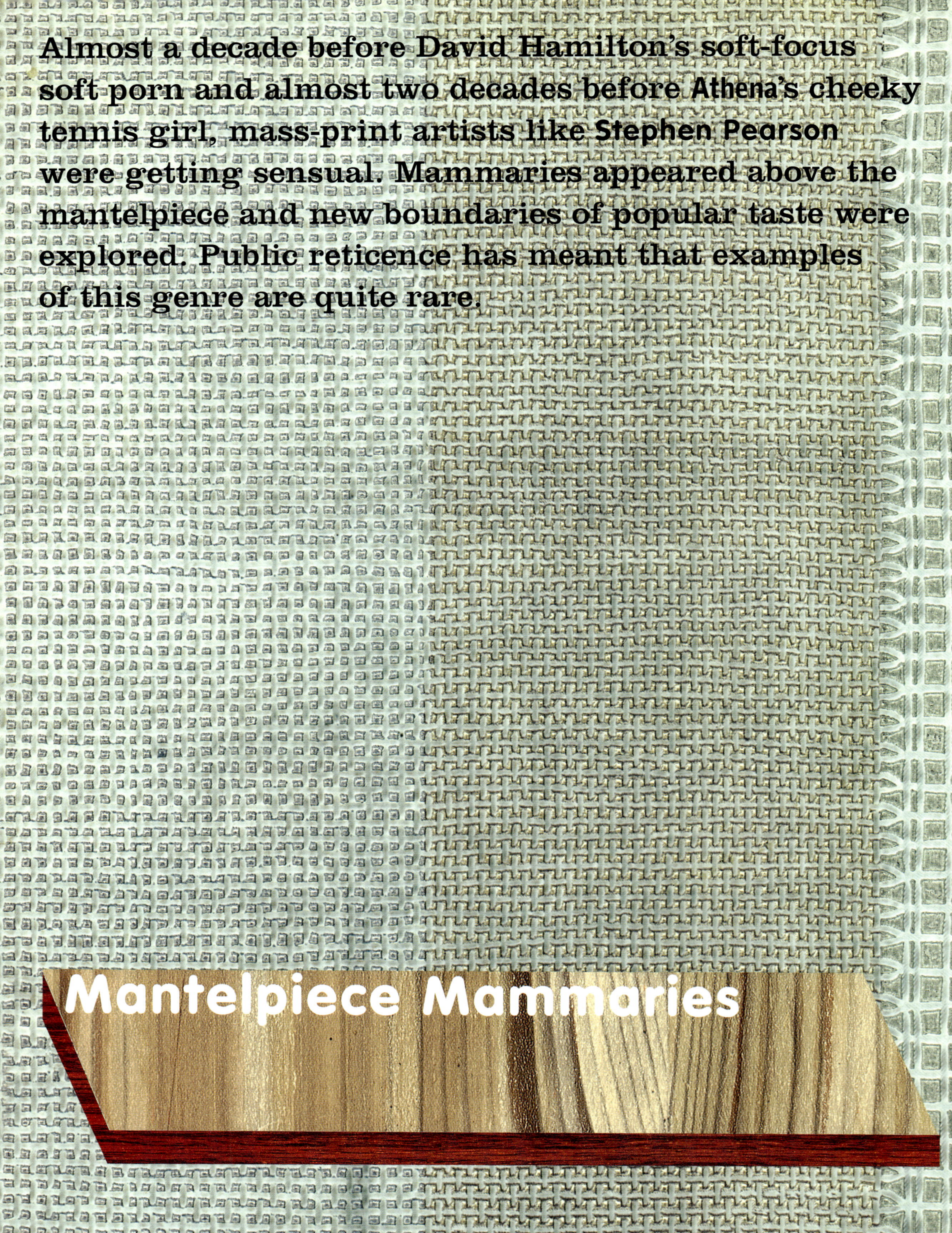

Almost a decade before David Hamilton's soft-focus soft porn and almost two decades before Athena's cheeky tennis girl, mass-print artists like Stephen Pearson were getting sensual. Mammaries appeared above the mantelpiece and new boundaries of popular taste were explored. Public reticence has meant that examples of this genre are quite rare.

Mantelpiece Mammaries

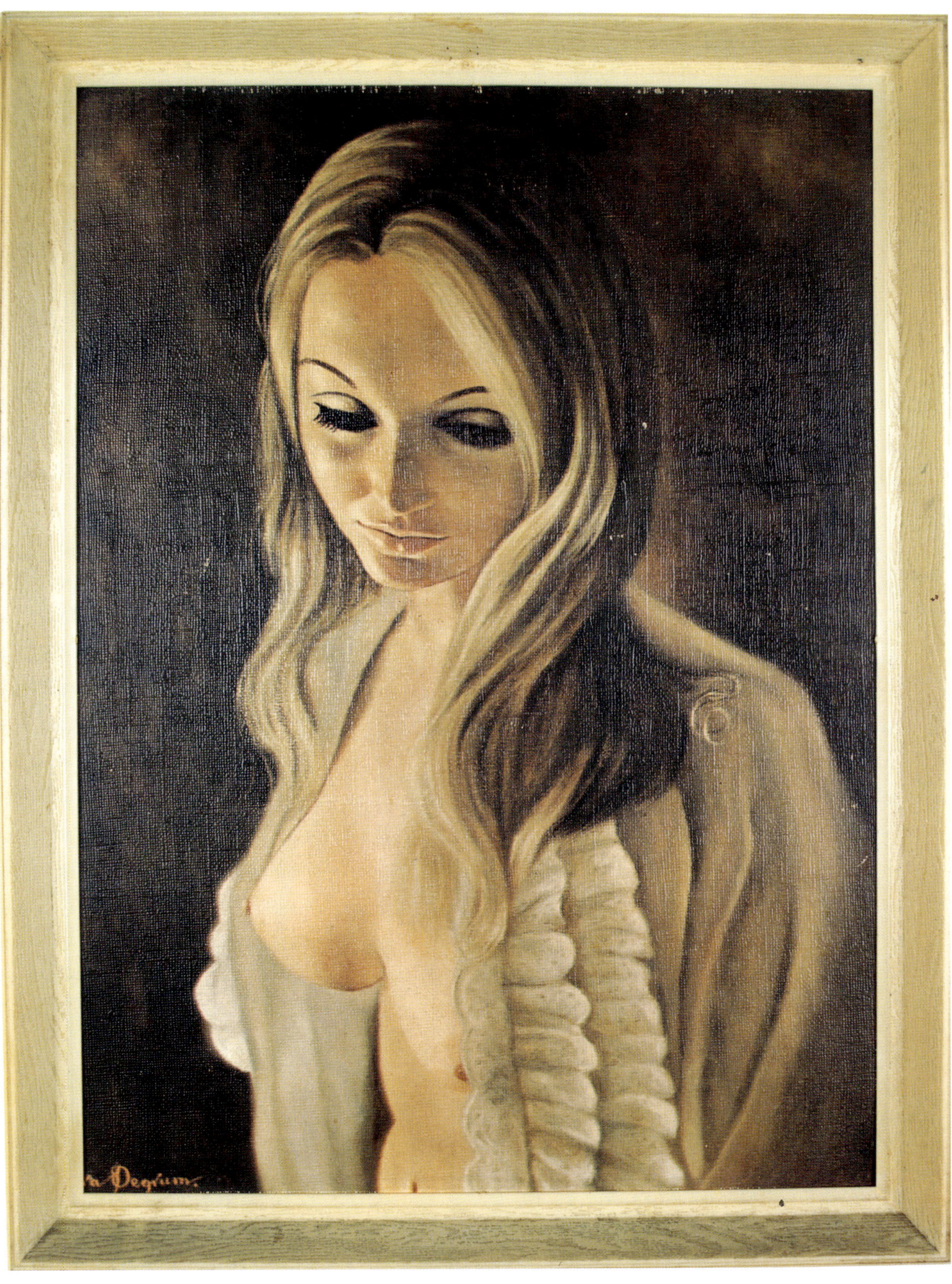

Degrum **Nice Blouse**

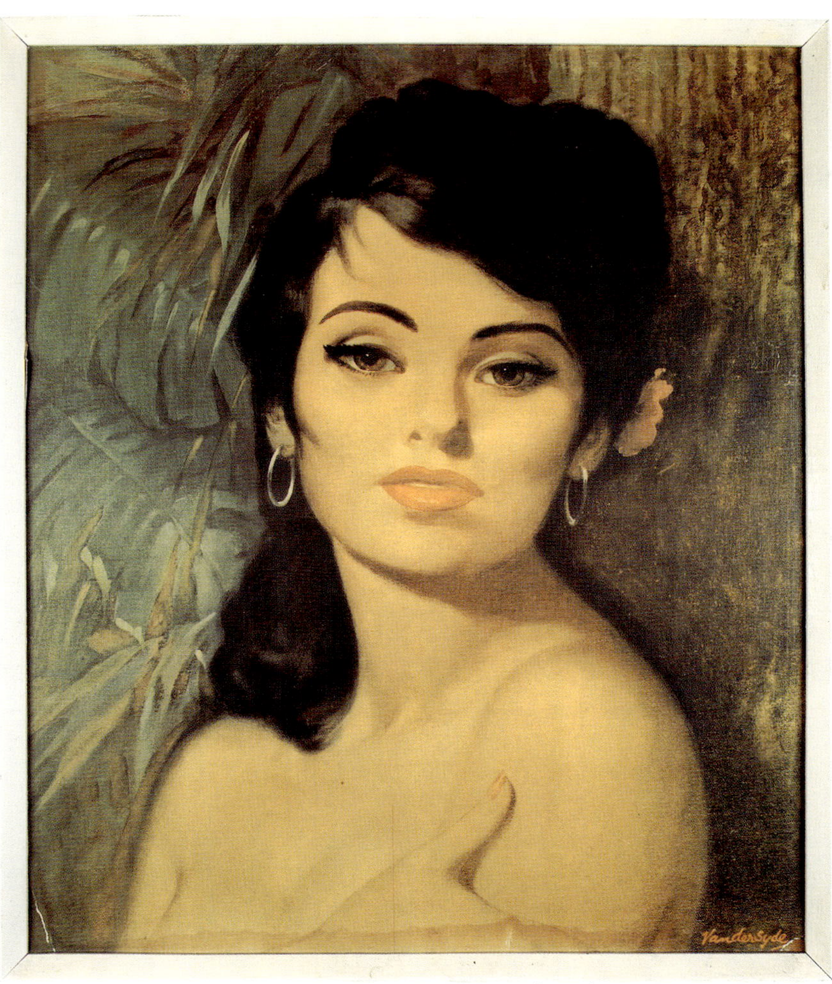

Van der Syde **Big Earring Gypsy Gal**

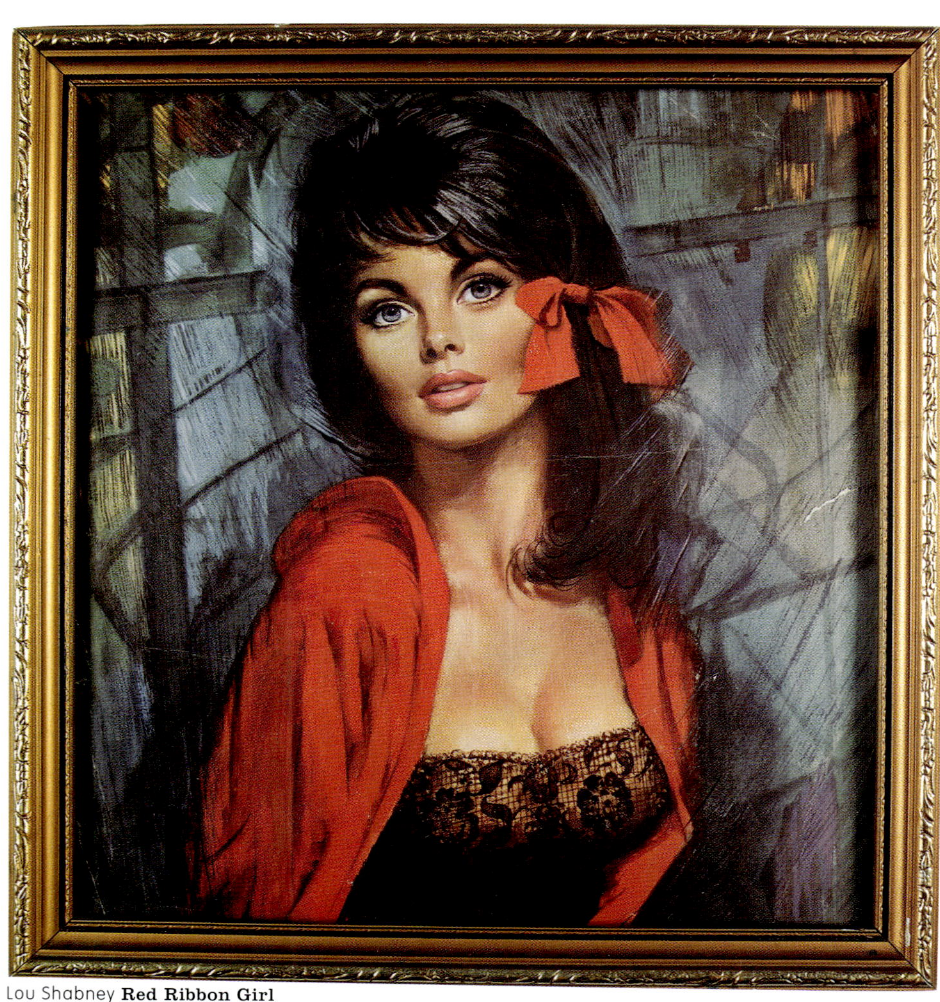

Lou Shabney **Red Ribbon Girl**

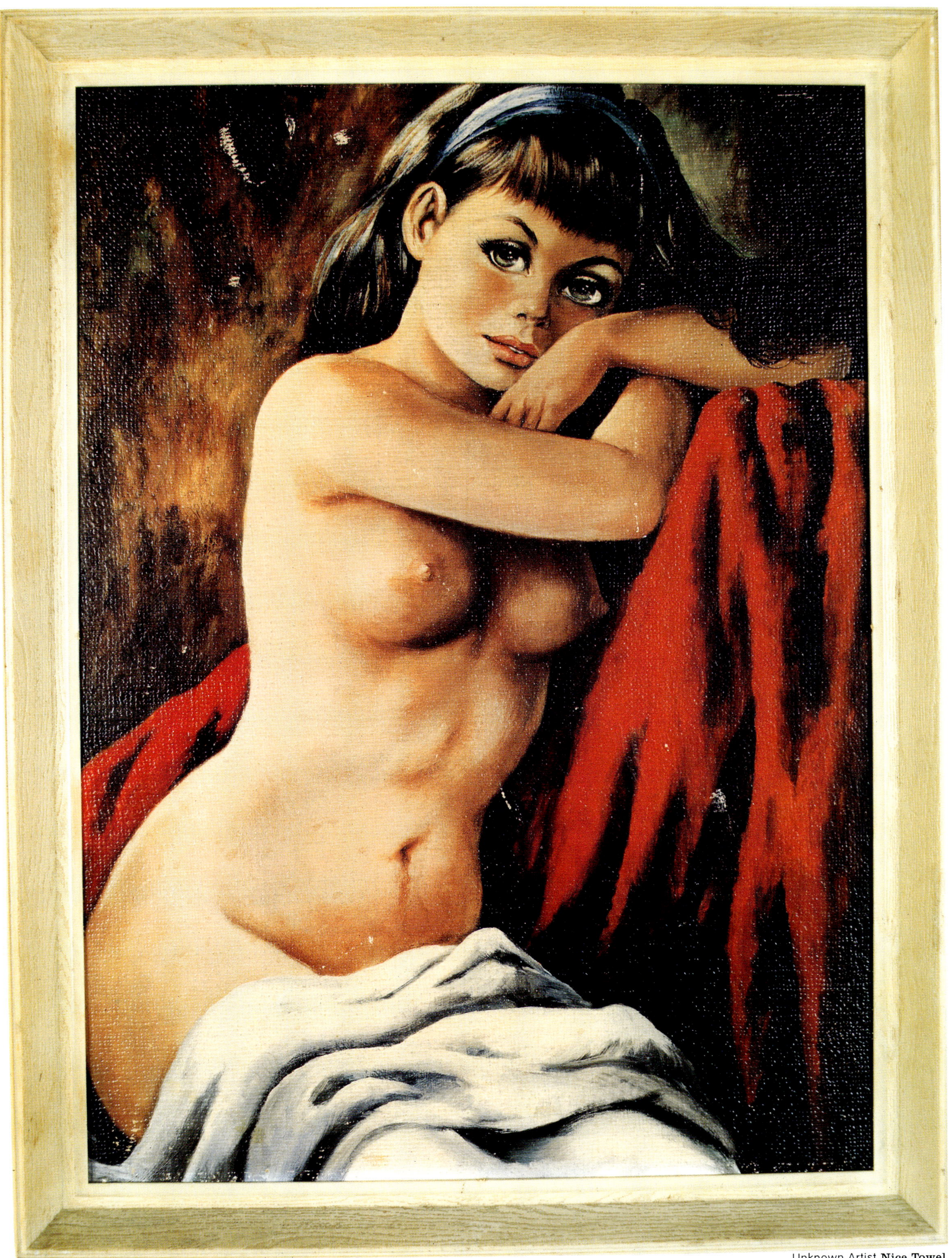

Unknown Artist **Nice Towel**

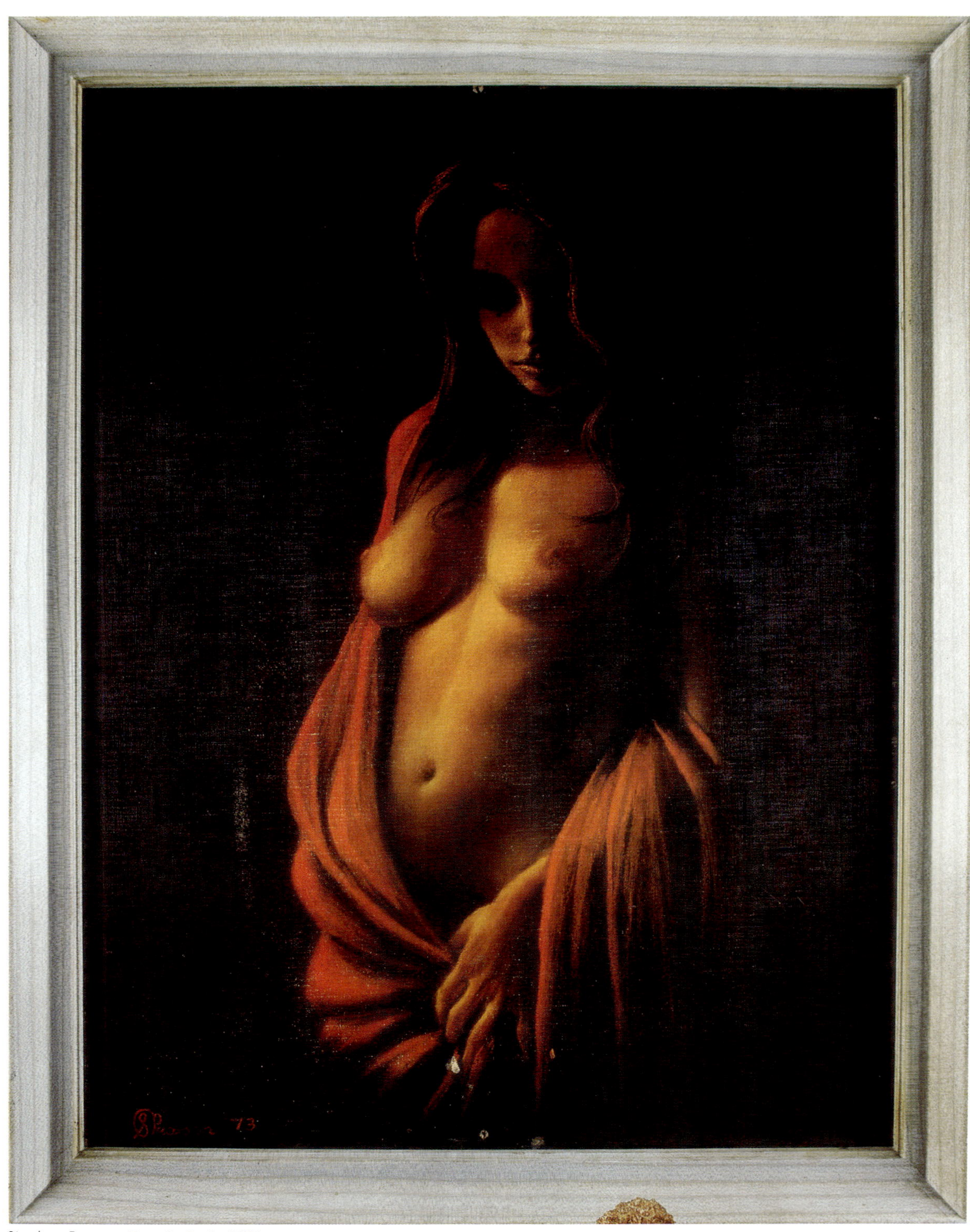

Stephen Pearson **Lovely Lady** 1973

Stephen Pearson **Emanuelle** 1976

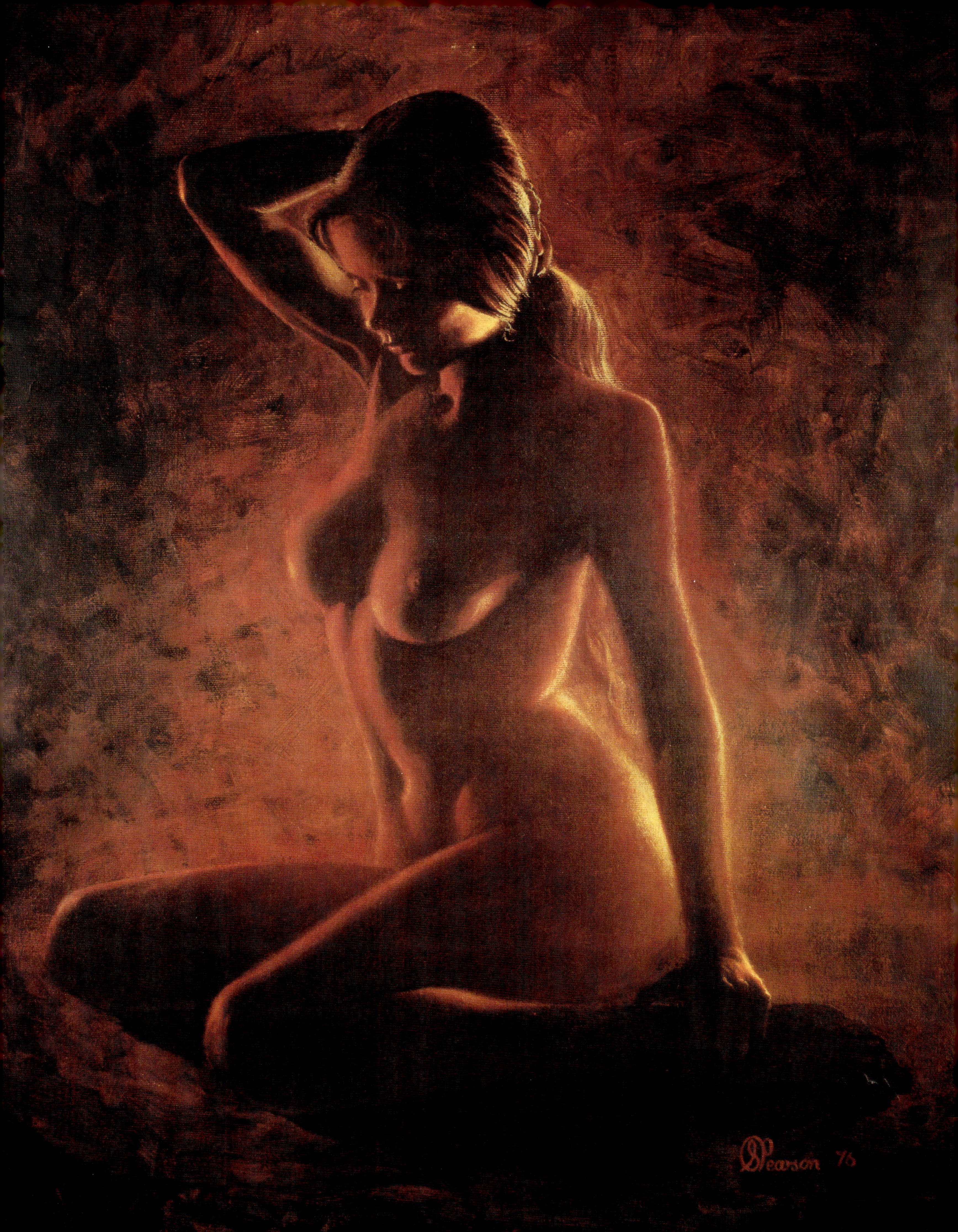
Pearson 76

It is not clear when and who painted the first crying child but mass-market artists such as Dallas Simpson, Anna Zinkeisen and Irene Spencer all grasped the concept that sad eyes cry. I'm not clear why tens of thousands should want something as sorrowful as a child in distress peering down from the living-room wall, but there is no doubting the haunting quality of some of the works. Eventually, however, the 'haunting' was interpreted as a curse. In the early 1980s a series of house fires were attributed to what The Sun called, 'the curse of the Crying Boys'. National panic was fanned by the tabloids. The Sun reported that 'many' homes were destroyed by fire while a Crying Boy picture survived untouched. Some said they had been dogged by ill luck since buying a Crying Boy and in the words of The Sun, 'people who have tried to burn their own prints deliberately have found them indestructible'.

The Sun offered to burn Crying Boys for their readers and they reported the response as follows:

The Curse of The Crying Boy

'Rose Farrington, of Preston, sent us hers saying: **"Since I bought it in 1959 my three sons and my husband have all died. I've often wondered if it had a curse."**

TV presenter Robert Dougall was also happy to dispose of his picture. It was part of the studio set for his show **Years Ahead**... Robert, 71, said: **"We can't risk the curse striking Channel 4."**

Male stripper Big Doofer, who caught fire on stage, claims he is a victim of the jinx. Big Doofer, real name Adrian Martin, is recovering from burns to his face after a fire-eating routine went wrong on stage last week. Adrian, of Rotherham, said: **"It only happened after I taunted my wife's Crying Boy picture about the curse."**

But Angela Barnes, of Clifton, Notts., says there is no trouble when the picture is next to one of a Crying Girl. She said: **"The jinx only strikes when they are separated."**

Dr Peter Baldry, a chemist at London's City University, confessed last night that there is no scientific explanation

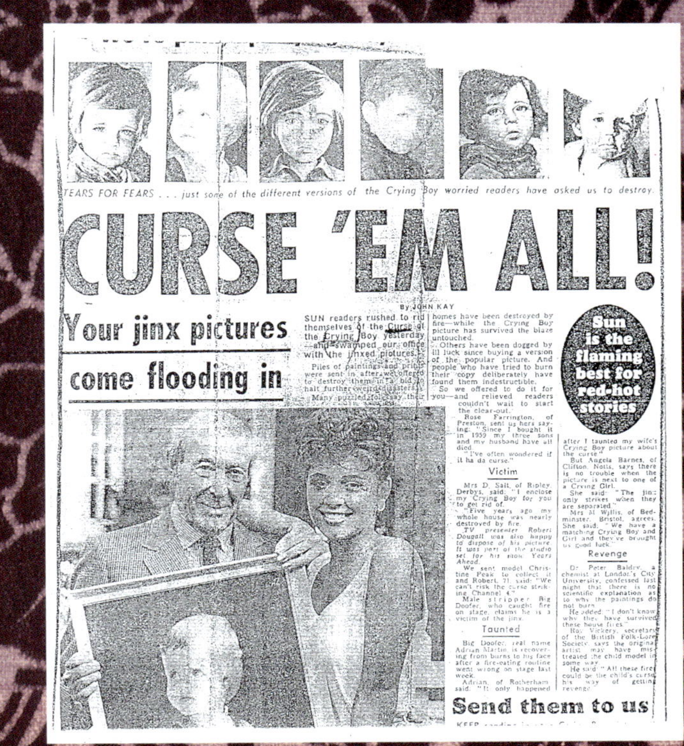

TEARS FOR FEARS . . . just some of the different versions of the Crying Boy worried readers have asked us to destroy.

CURSE 'EM ALL!

Your jinx pictures come flooding in

By JOHN KAY

SUN readers rushed to rid themselves of the Curse of the Crying Boy yesterday—and swamped our office with the jinxed pictures.

Piles of paintings and prints were sent in after we offered to destroy them in a bid to halt further weird disasters.

Many puzzled folk say their homes have been destroyed by fire—while the Crying Boy picture has survived the blaze untouched.

Others have been dogged by ill luck since buying a version of the popular picture. And people who have tried to burn their copy deliberately have found them indestructible.

So we offered to do it for you—and relieved readers couldn't wait to start the clear-out.

Rose Farrington, of Preston, sent us hers saying: "Since I bought it in 1959 my three sons and my husband have all died.

"I've often wondered if it ha da curse."

Victim

Mrs D. Salt, of Ripley, Derbys, said: "I enclose my Crying Boy for you to get rid of.

"Five years ago my whole house was nearly destroyed by fire."

TV presenter Robert Dougall was also happy to dispose of his picture. It was part of the studio set for his show Years Ahead.

We sent model Christine Peak to collect it and Robert, 71, said: "We can't risk the curse striking Channel 4."

Male stripper Big Doofer, who caught fire on stage, claims he is a victim of the jinx.

Taunted

Big Doofer, real name Adrian Martin, is recovering from burns to his face after a fire-eating routine went wrong on stage last week.

Adrian, of Rotherham, said: "It only happened after I taunted my wife's Crying Boy picture about the curse."

But Angela Barnes, of Clifton, Notts, says there is no trouble when the picture is next to one of a Crying Girl.

She said: "The jinx only strikes when they are separated."

Mrs Al Willis, of Bedminster, Bristol, agrees. She said: "We have a matching Crying Boy and Girl and they've brought us good luck."

Revenge

Dr Peter Baldry, a chemist at London's City University, confessed last night that there is no scientific explanation as to why the paintings do not burn.

He added: "I don't know why they have survived these house fires."

Roy Vickery, secretary of the British Folk-Lore Society, says the original artist may have mistreated the child model in some way.

He said: "All these fires could be the child's curse, his way of getting revenge."

Sun is the flaming best for red-hot stories

Send them to us

KEEP ...

Report in The Sun, dated 26 October 1985, on the curse of the Crying Boy.

as to why the paintings do not burn. He added: "I don't know why they have survived these house fires."

Roy Vickery, secretary of the British Folk-Lore Society, says the original artist may have mistreated the child model in some way. He said: "All these fires could be the child's curse, his way of getting revenge."'

Crying Boys are now comparatively rare, except in Tunisia where I recently bought an Arabic Crying Boy at the weekly market in Sousse.

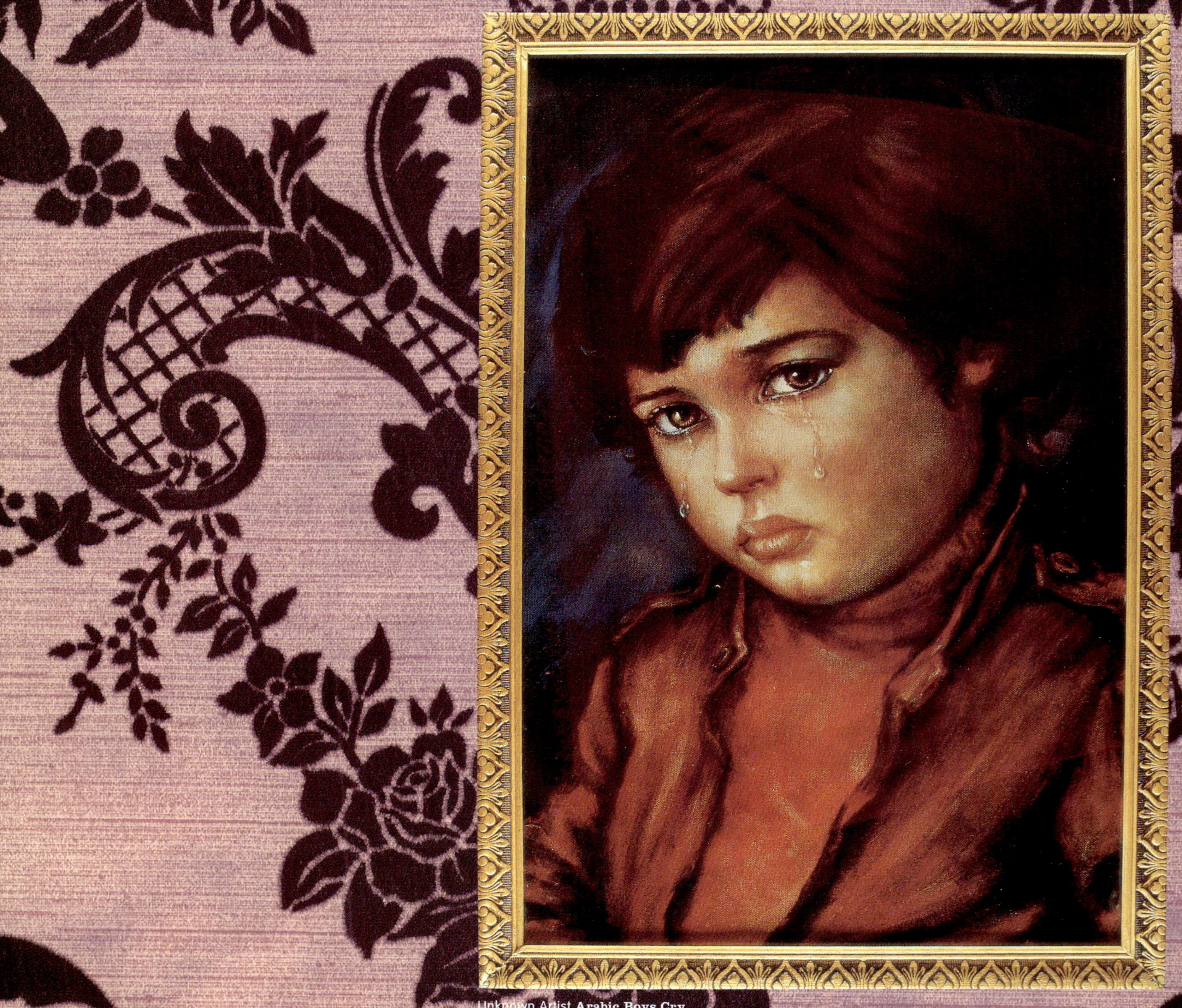

Unknown Artist **Arabic Boys Cry**

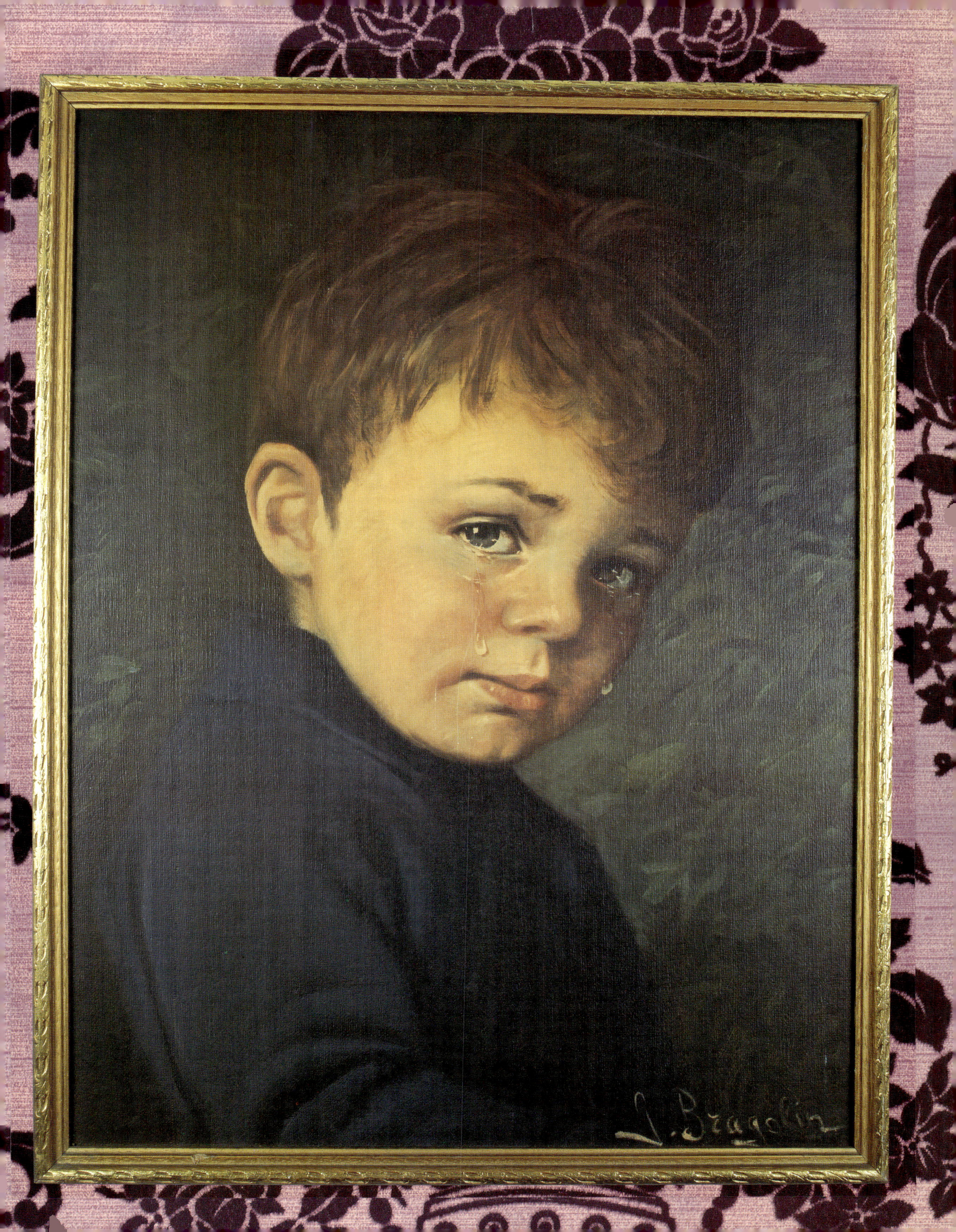

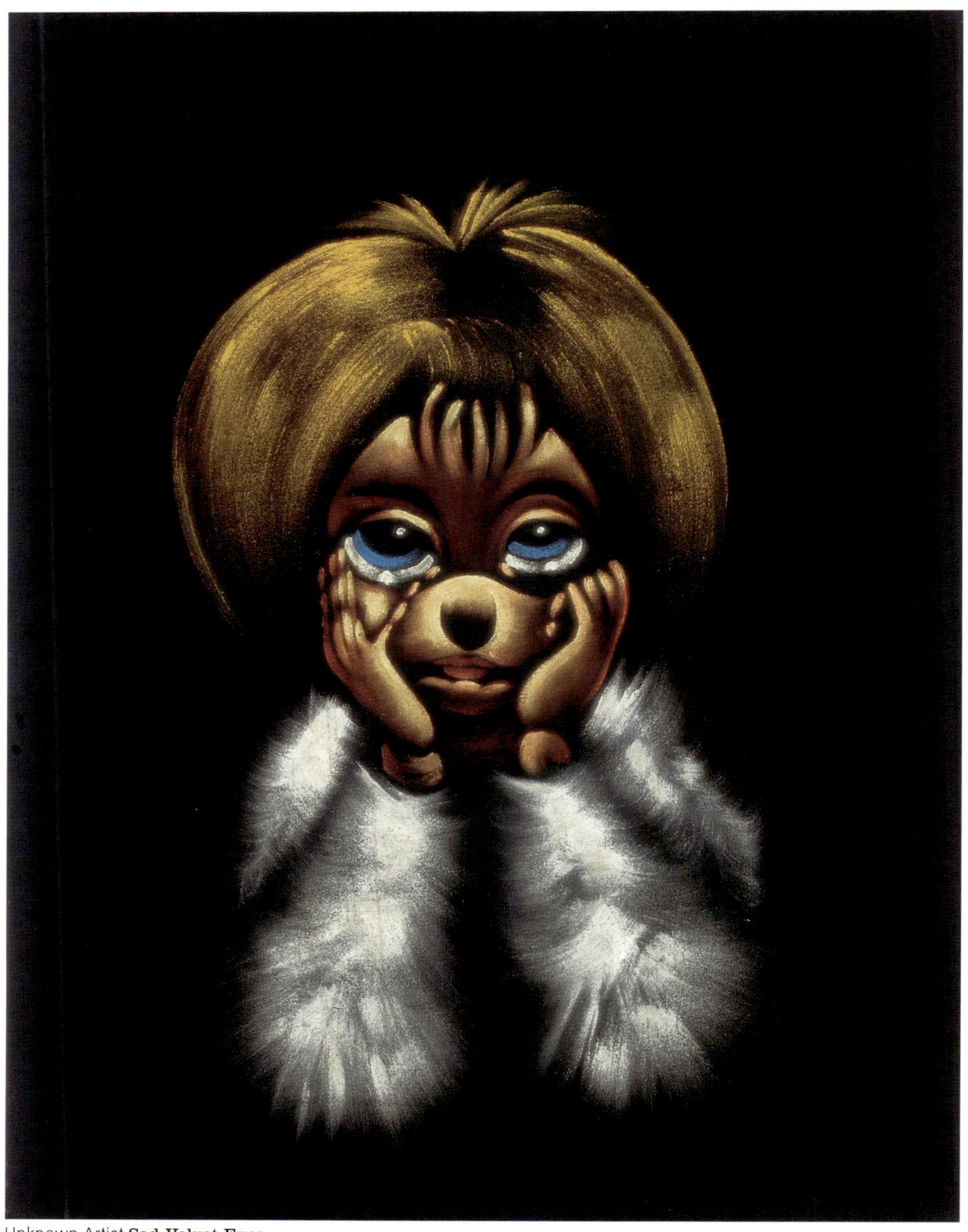

Unknown Artist **Sad Velvet Eyes**

Irene Spencer **The Locket** 1972

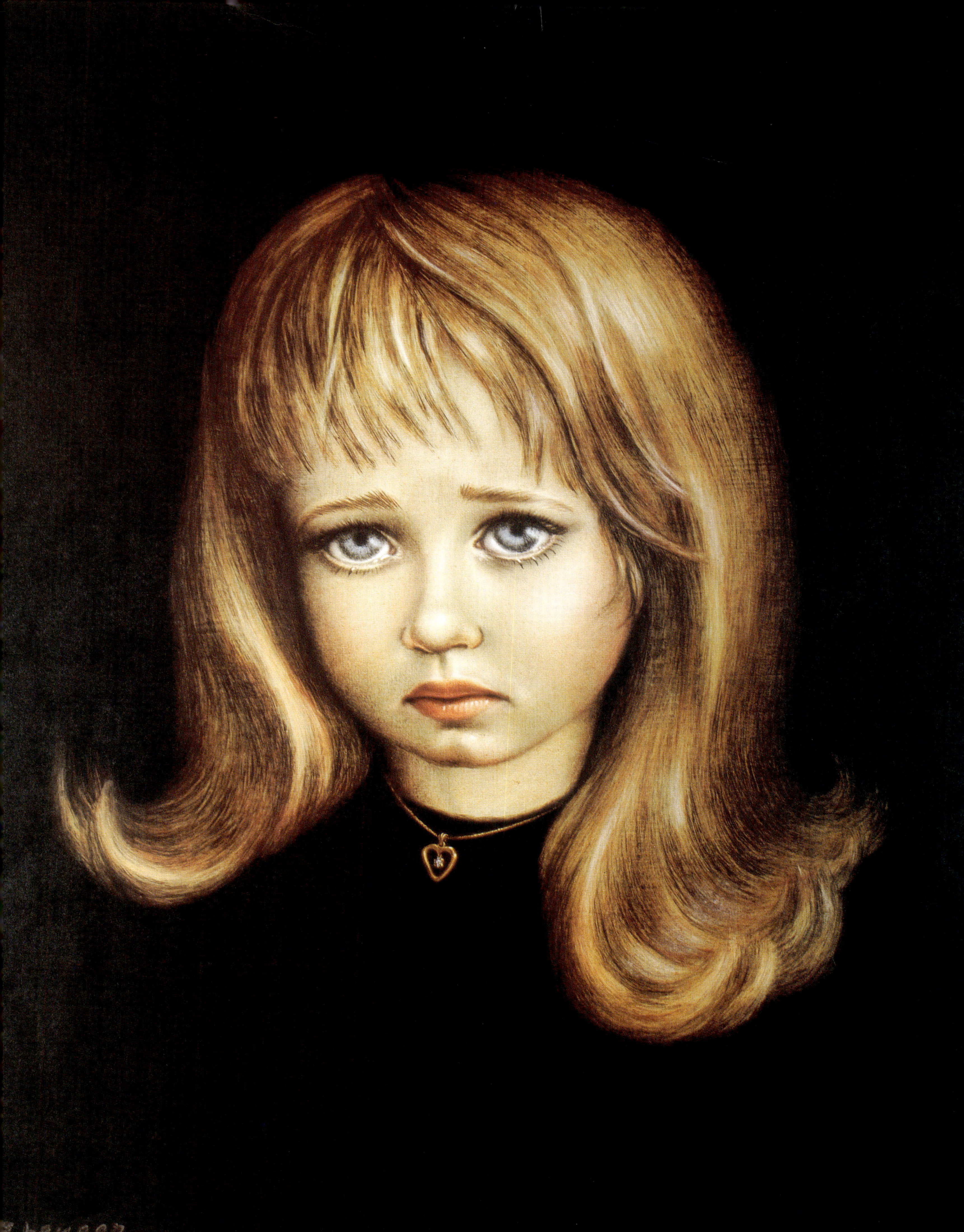
Spencer

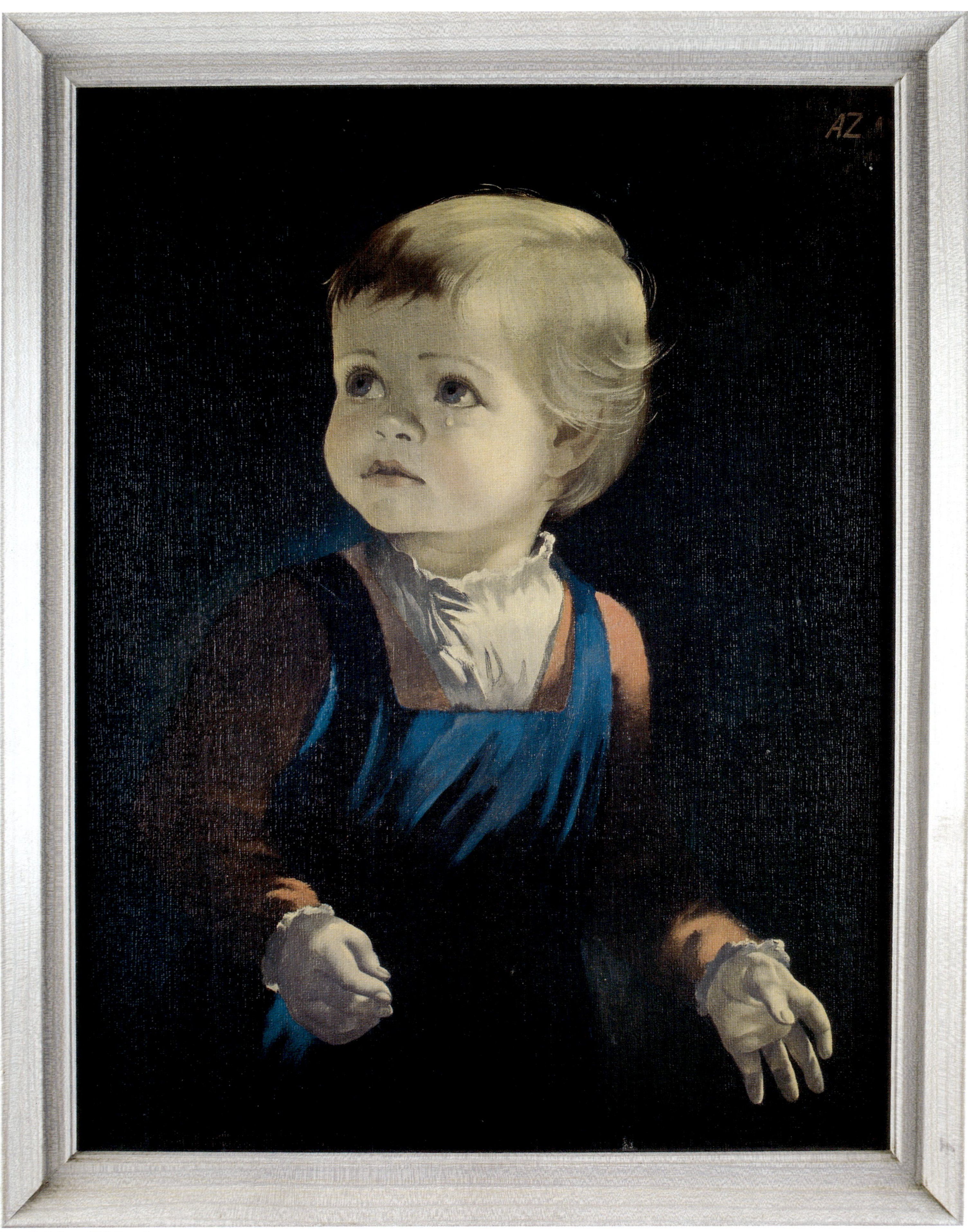

Anna Zinkeisen **Childhood**

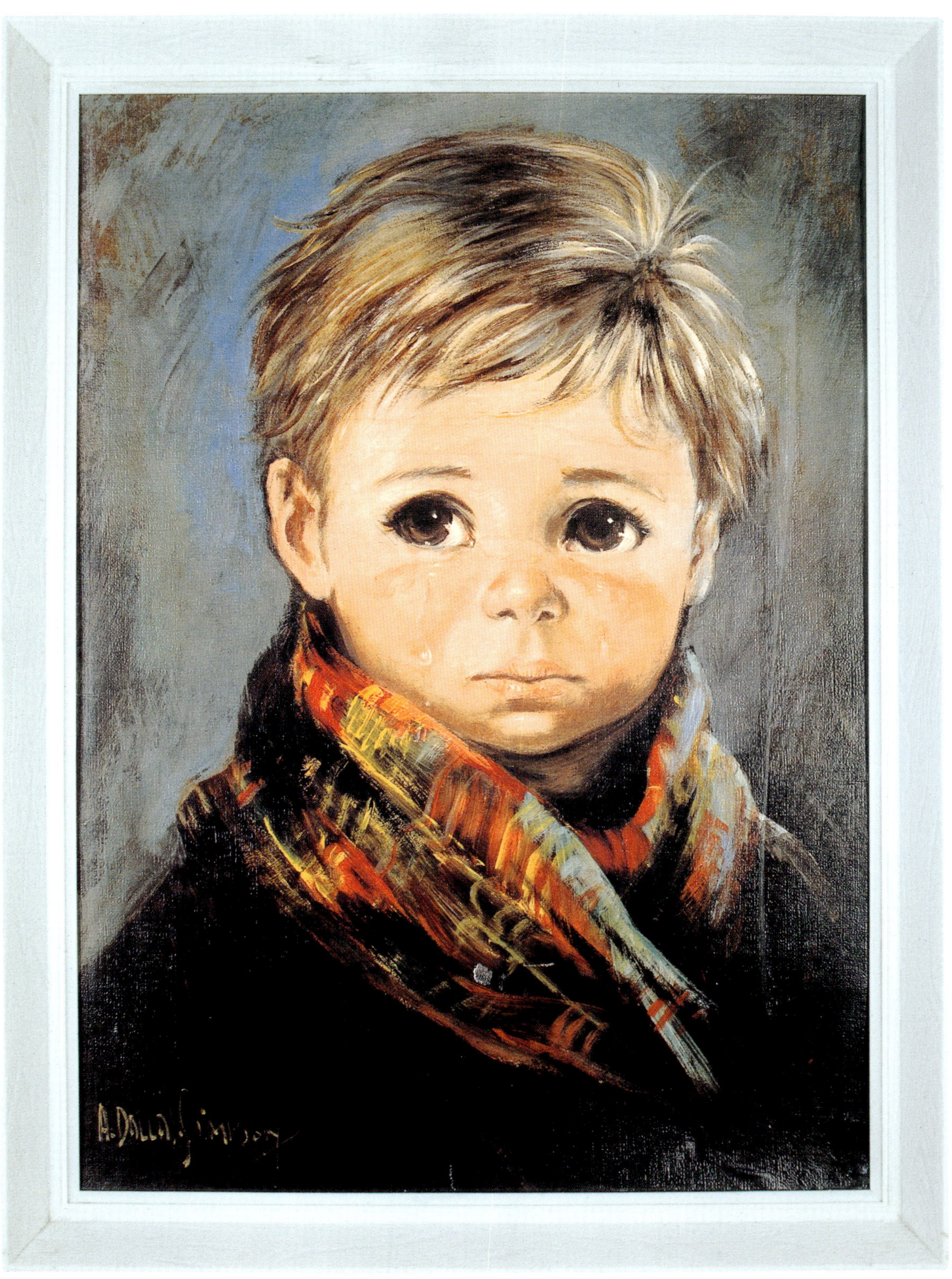

Dallas Simpson **Cold and Upset**

following pages: A D'Argent **Crying Girl**; A D'Argent **Crying Boy**

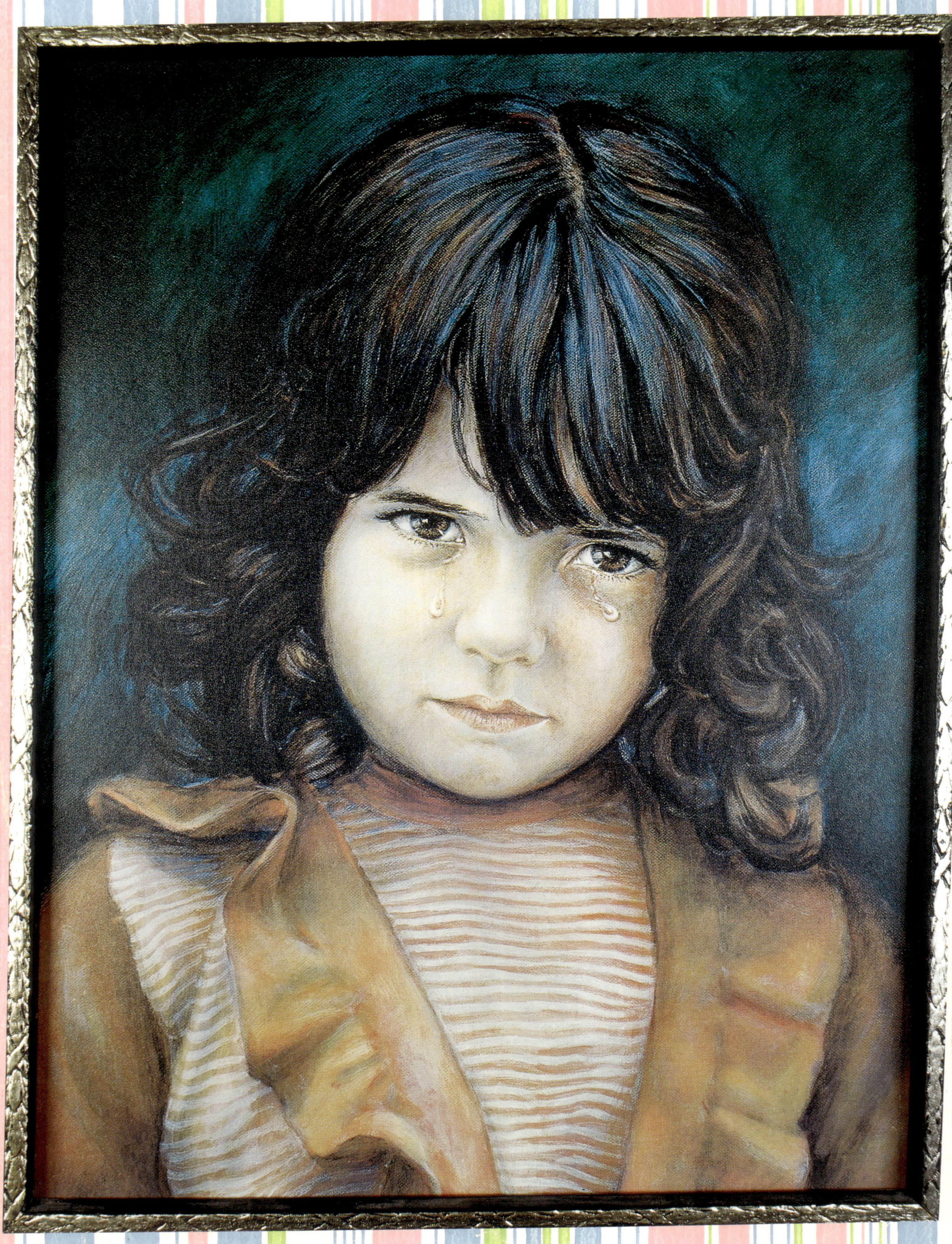

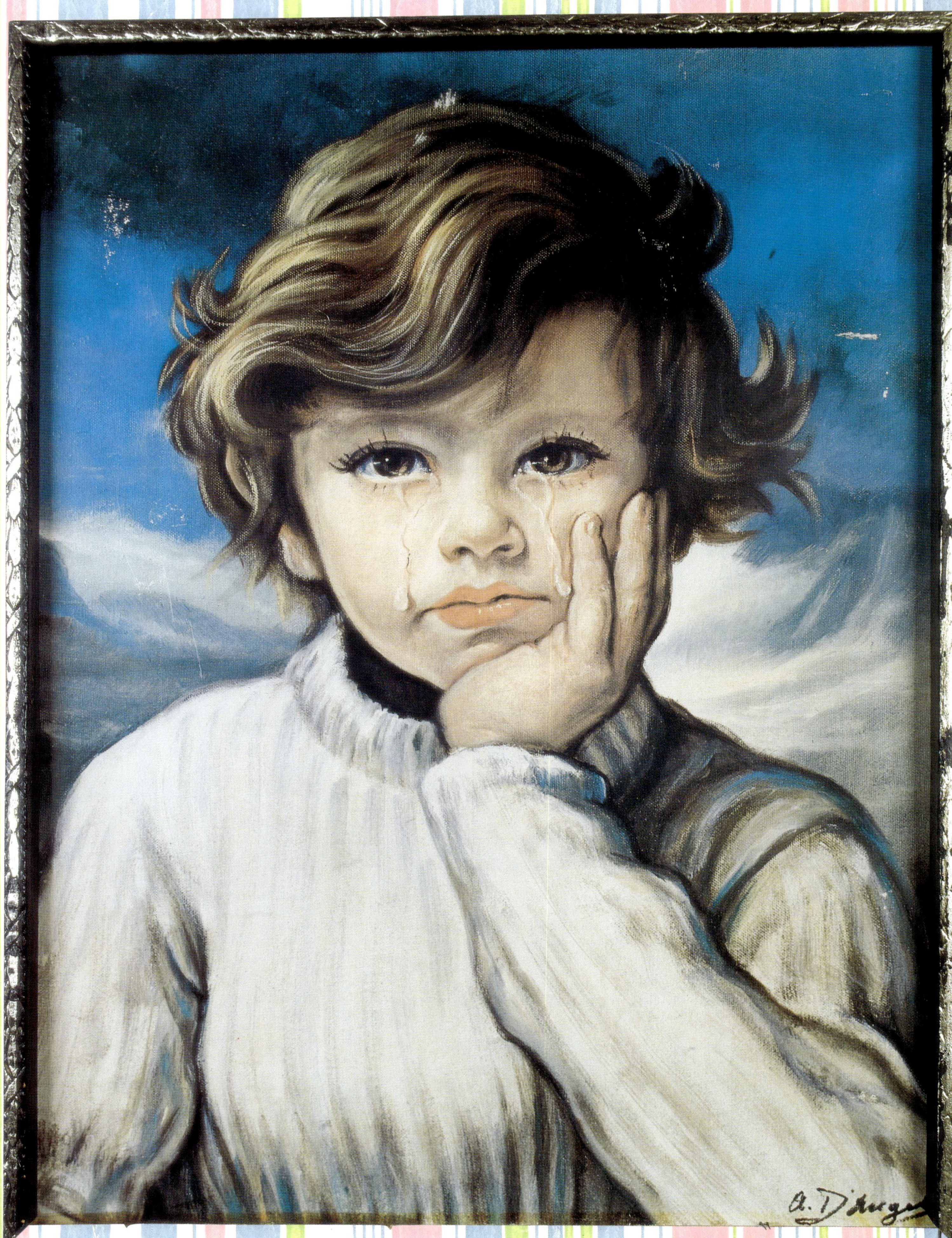

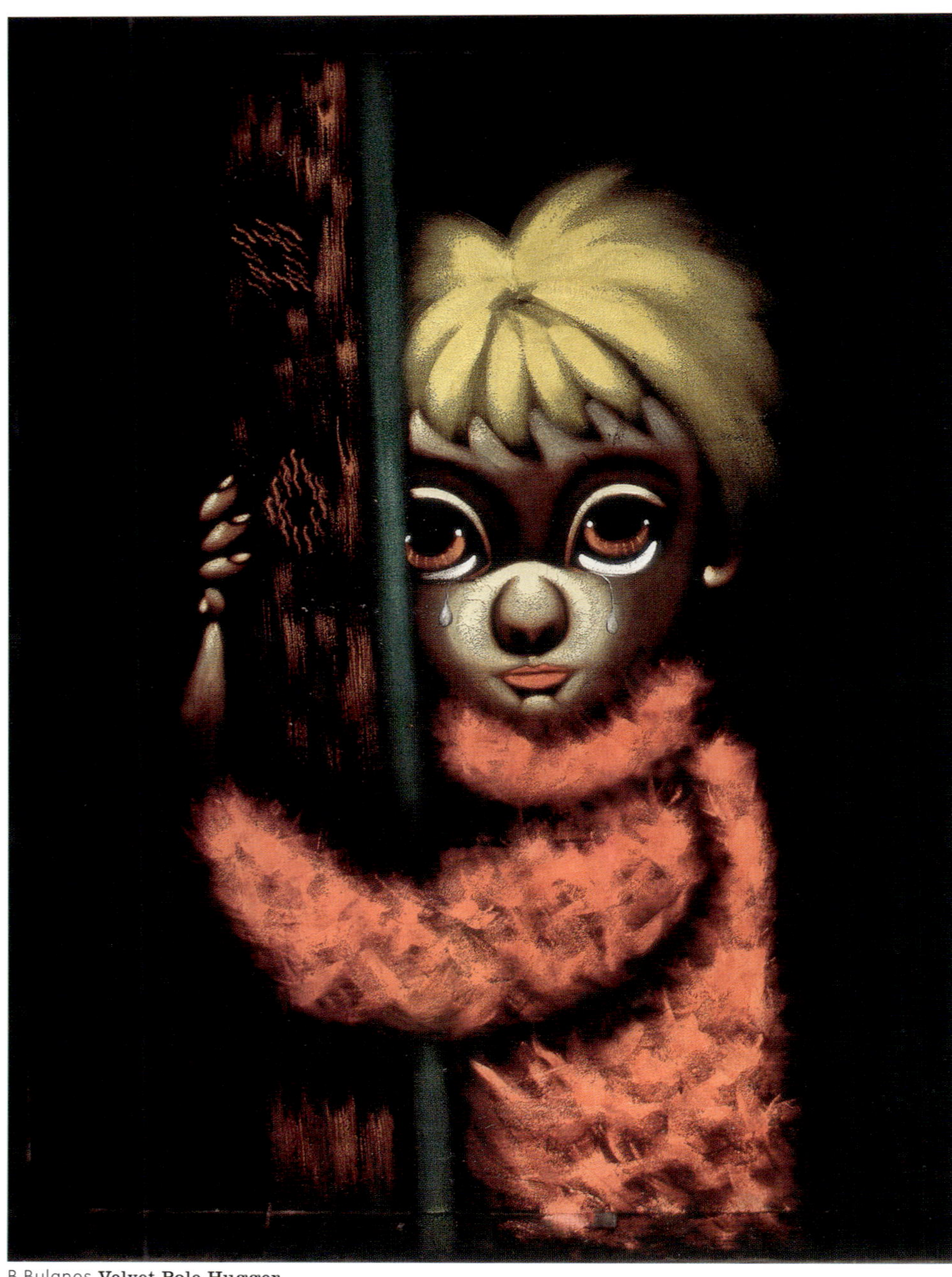

B Bulanos **Velvet Pole Hugger**

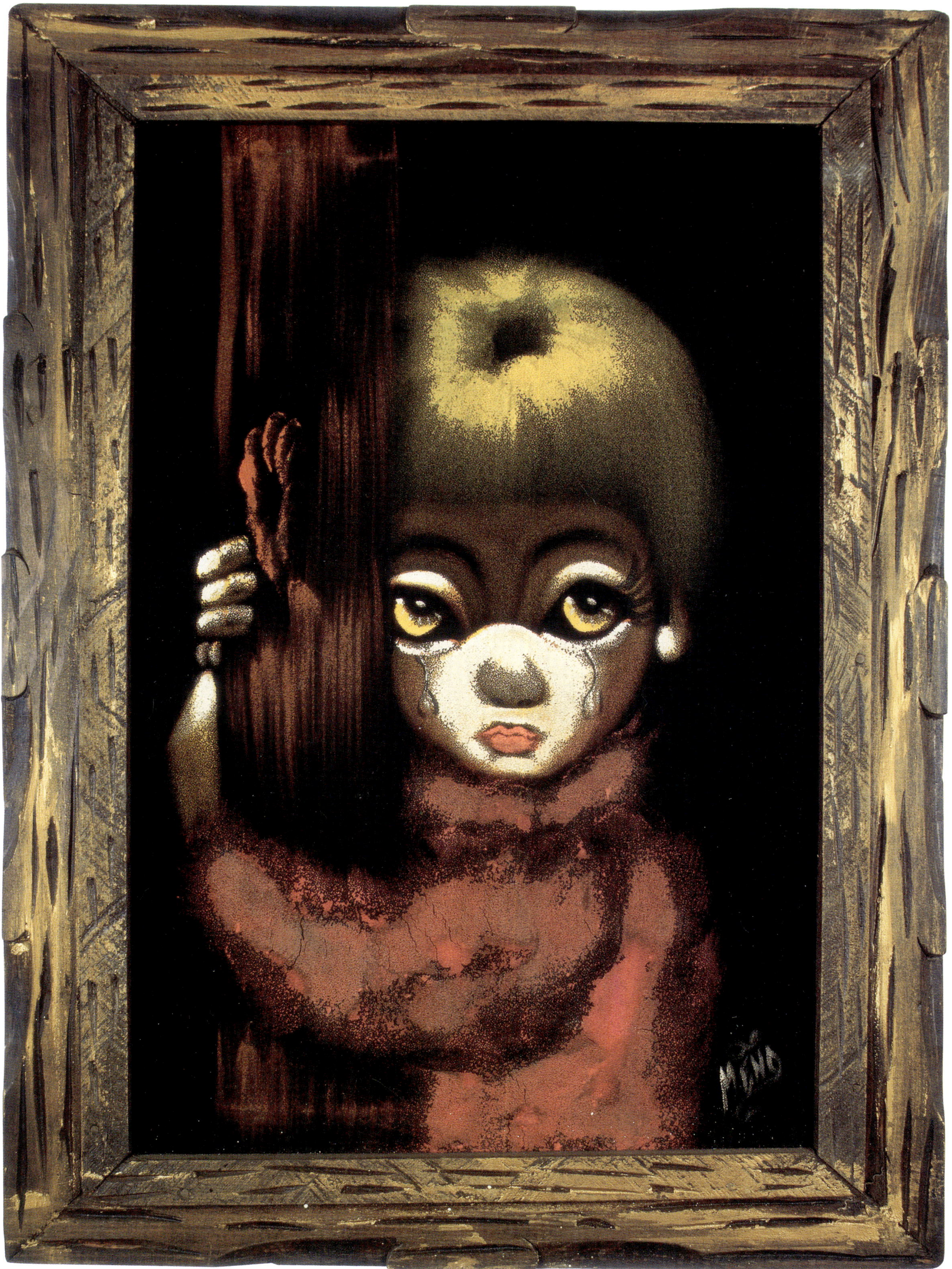

Meno **Velvet Pole Hugger No 2**

When **Margaret Keane** began to paint her portraits of big-eyed children in San Francisco in the 1950s, she and her then husband, **Walter Keane**, were trendy members of the North Beach bohemian scene. **Margaret** had graduated from selling drawings to fellow students at high school to painting portraits of tourists and somehow, later, stars such as Nathalie Wood, Robert Wagner, Joan Crawford, Zsa Zsa Gabor, Jerry Lewis and his family, and Liberace. But it was **Walter** who took credit for some of her early paintings, claiming that the inspiration came from his time in Berlin, where the hungry post-war kids who filled the streets saddened him. He made the unusual move of opening his own gallery and then began mass-marketing Big Eye prints in an entrepreneurial way never experienced before. The art world was horrified and the **Keanes** reviled within it, but the public with unprecedented fervour accepted their art.

Keane On Big Eyes

The Keane relationship broke up in 1965 and Margaret moved to Hawaii. In 1970, in a radio interview, Margaret revealed that it was her and not her then husband who had painted the big-eyed faces. 'I'd have to lock the door of the paint-room,' she later explained. 'He wouldn't allow anyone in. I was like a prisoner.'

She challenged Walter to a public paint-out in San Francisco Park after he told the press she was claiming credit for the paintings because she thought he was dead. When the case came to court the judge ordered them both to paint. Margaret Keane produced a work within an hour while Walter Keane claimed he couldn't paint due to a sore shoulder and hand. Margaret was awarded $4 million but never received anything from her 'destitute' ex-husband. Walter is now in his eighties and happily reels off conspiracy rants about his wife's 'lie of the century'.

Margaret has intimated that a series of unanswered inner questions – why the pain? why the sorrow? why the death? – were reflected in the eyes of her subjects, the sadness seen in her paintings from the early Sixties reflecting her own feelings while she was married to Walter. 'Gradually it dawned on me that I was painting my own inner emotions,' she explained in an interview with the New York Times in 1999. As a devoted Jehovah's Witness, she believes that she has found the answers to these 'whys' in the Bible and that the sad eyes are slowly becoming happier.

After a first revival in the 1970s, early Keane was again in vogue in the late 1990s. Tim Burton, the director, commissioned a Keane portrait of his fiancée Lisa Marie and their dog Poppy. Matthew Sweet, the rock star, is an avid collector. A plethora of websites have sprung up and a Keane can now achieve $200,000 in the Keane Eyes Gallery in San Francisco.

In 1999 the New York Times published a fashion illustration feature in which clothes designed by John Galliano,

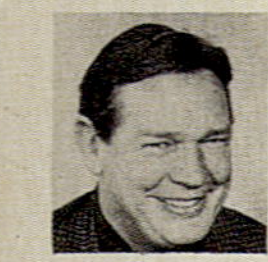

©1961 Walter Keane - All rights reserved From the oil painting "Peace on Earth" by Walter KEANE - Studio at 494 Broadway, San Francisco, and 798 Madison Ave., New York City

STAMP

Printed in U.S.A.

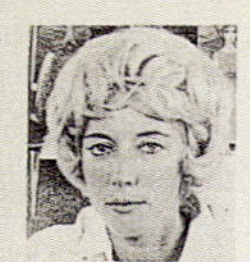

© 1965 Margaret Keané—All rights reserved. From an oil painting "On the Beach at Waikiki" by Margaret Keane—Studio at 494 Broadway, San Francisco.

STAMP

Printed in U.S.A.

Postcards issued in the Sixties to promote Keane paintings.

Oscar de la Renta, Christian Lacroix, Dolce and Gabbana and Gianfranco Ferre were painted onto new **Keane** Big Eye originals. Since then computer-generated wide eyes have found their way into the works of cutting-edge photographers Inez van Lamsweerde, David LaChapelle and Vinoodh Matadin. 'Big Eye', as it is now known, has also become popular with some of the more intelligent members of the rock world. The Eels used Big Eye art for record covers and T-shirts on their **Beautiful Freak** album, single and tour; Blur used abstract Big Eye art on the posters for the single **Coffee and TV**.

Margaret Keane, now 72 and living in the San Francisco Bay area of the United States, is still painting, although in a happier vein. She wrote in 1975, 'I was driven to paint because it was my therapy, escape and relaxation, my life completely revolved around it. I still enjoy it immensely, but the addiction to it and dependency are gone.'

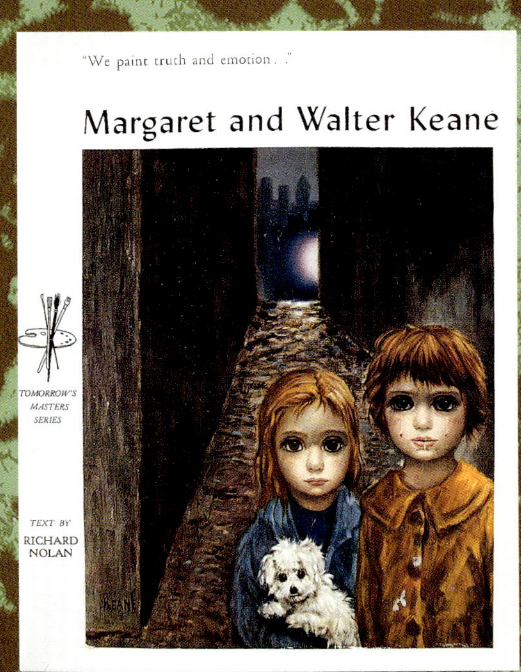

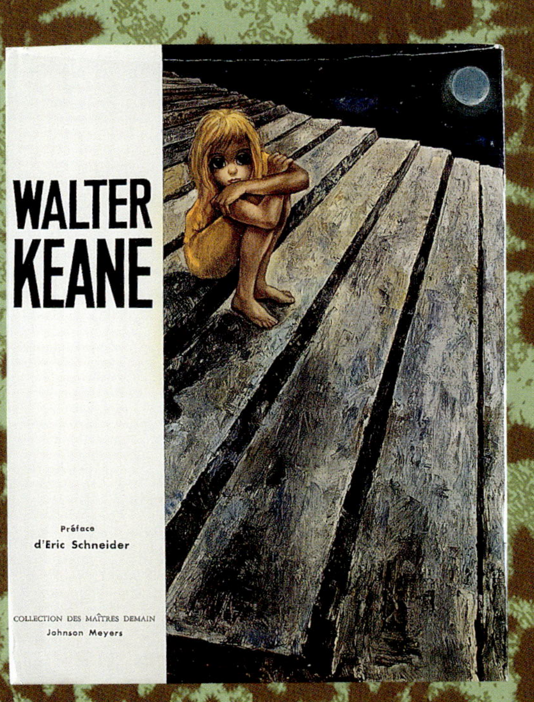

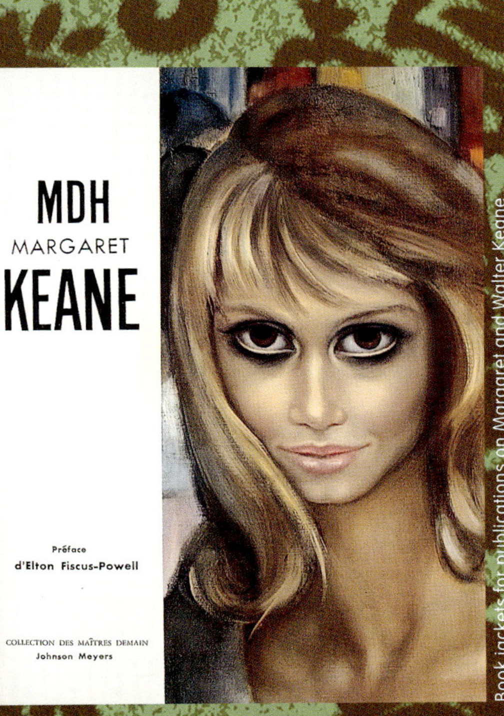

Book jackets for publications on Margaret and Walter Keane.

The **Keane** story serves as a parable of late twentieth-century culture: bohemian artists decide to make money by becoming mass-market, consequently becoming shunned by bohemian society, only to find that over a thirty-year period media coverage of bohemian culture turns it into mass-market art again!

Certainly the painting style originated by **Keane** has permeated the consciousness of literally millions of people. If Pop Art has any link to the concept of popular art, then **Keane** could be as important as Warhol and, as Andy Warhol said to **Life** magazine in 1965: 'I think what Keane has done is just terrific. It has to be good. If it were bad, so many people wouldn't like it.'

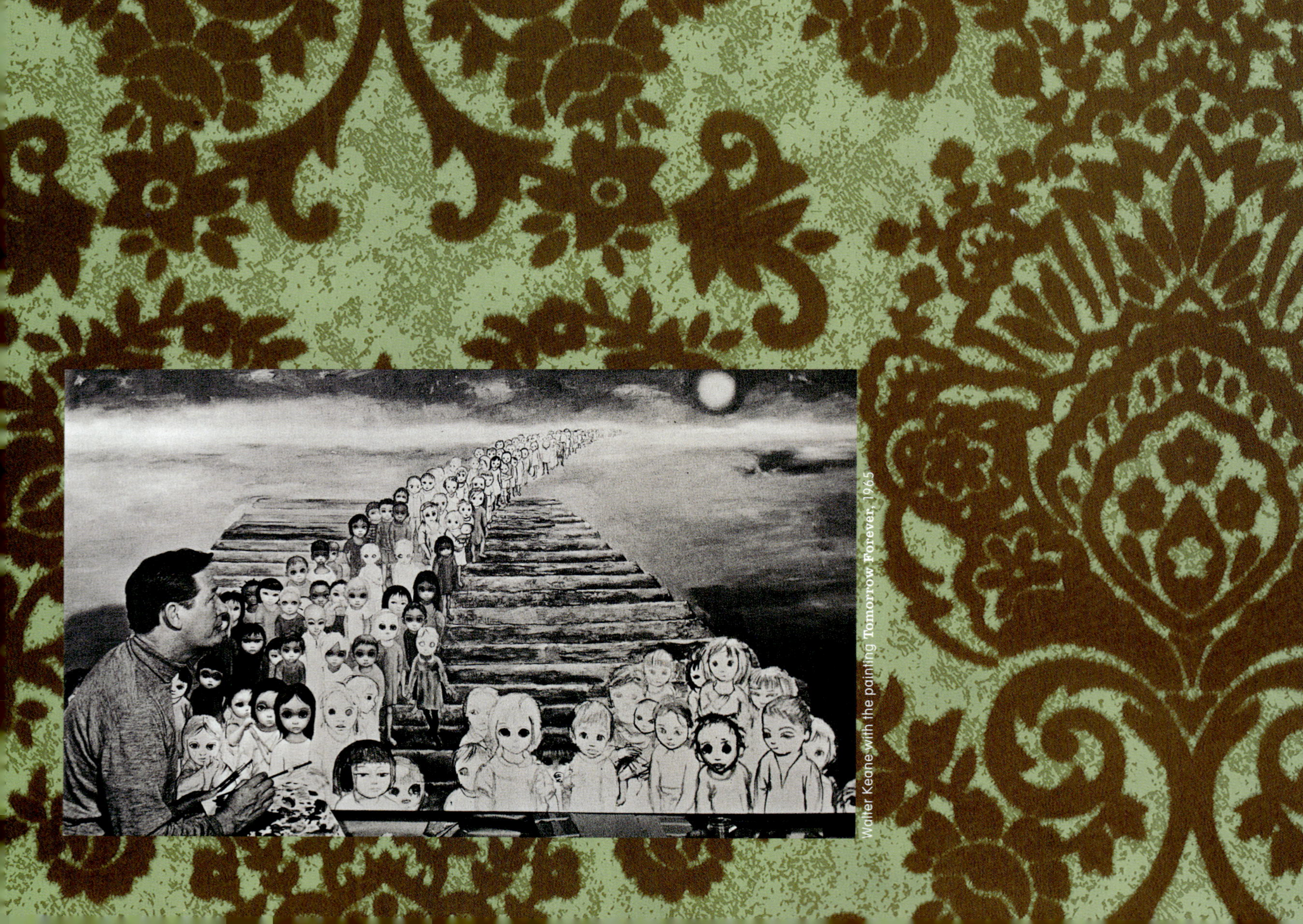

Walter Keane with the painting **Tomorrow Forever**, 1965

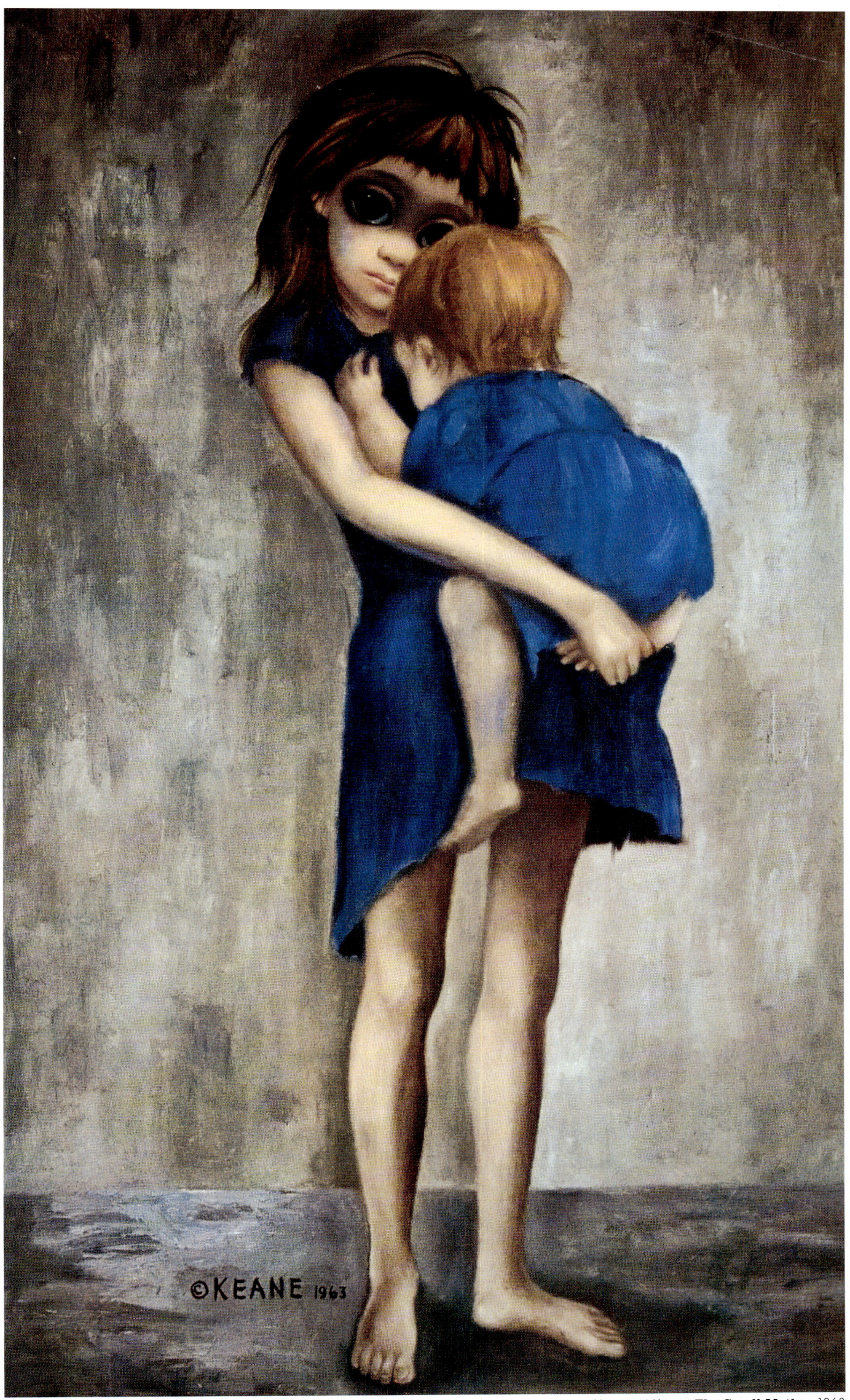

Margaret Keane **The Small Mother** 1963

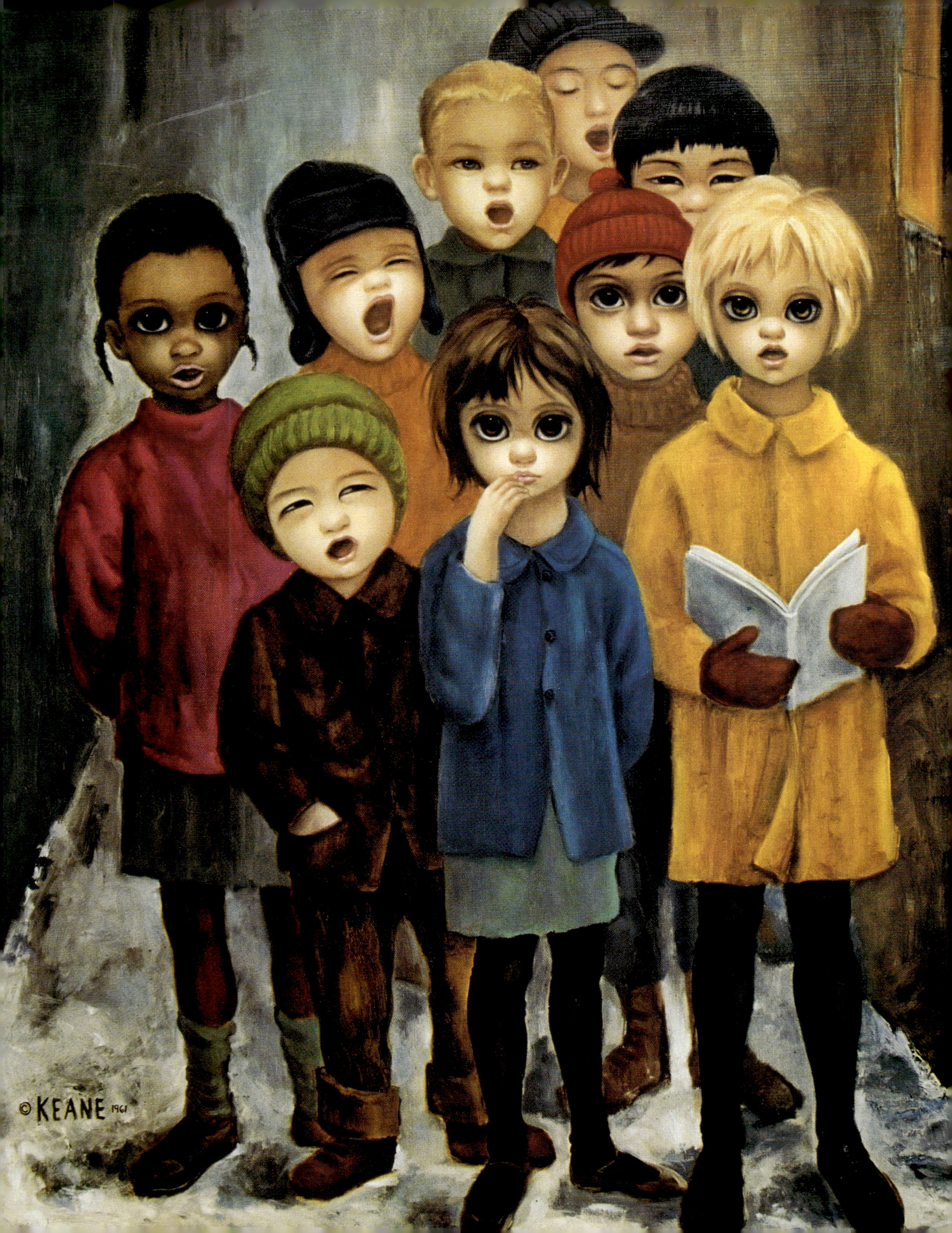
©KEANE 1961

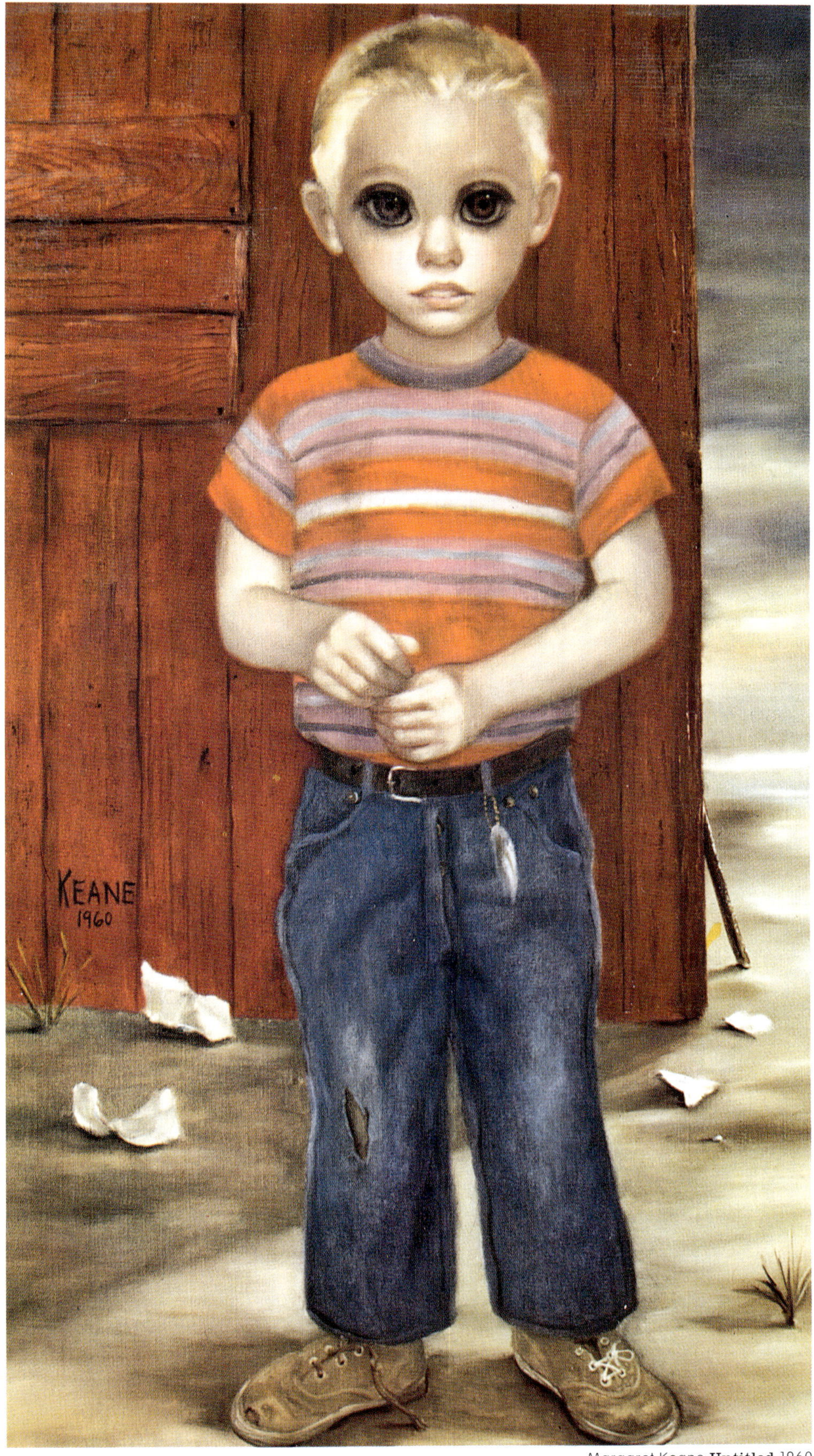

Margaret Keane **Untitled** 1960

Margaret Keane **Peace on Earth** 1961

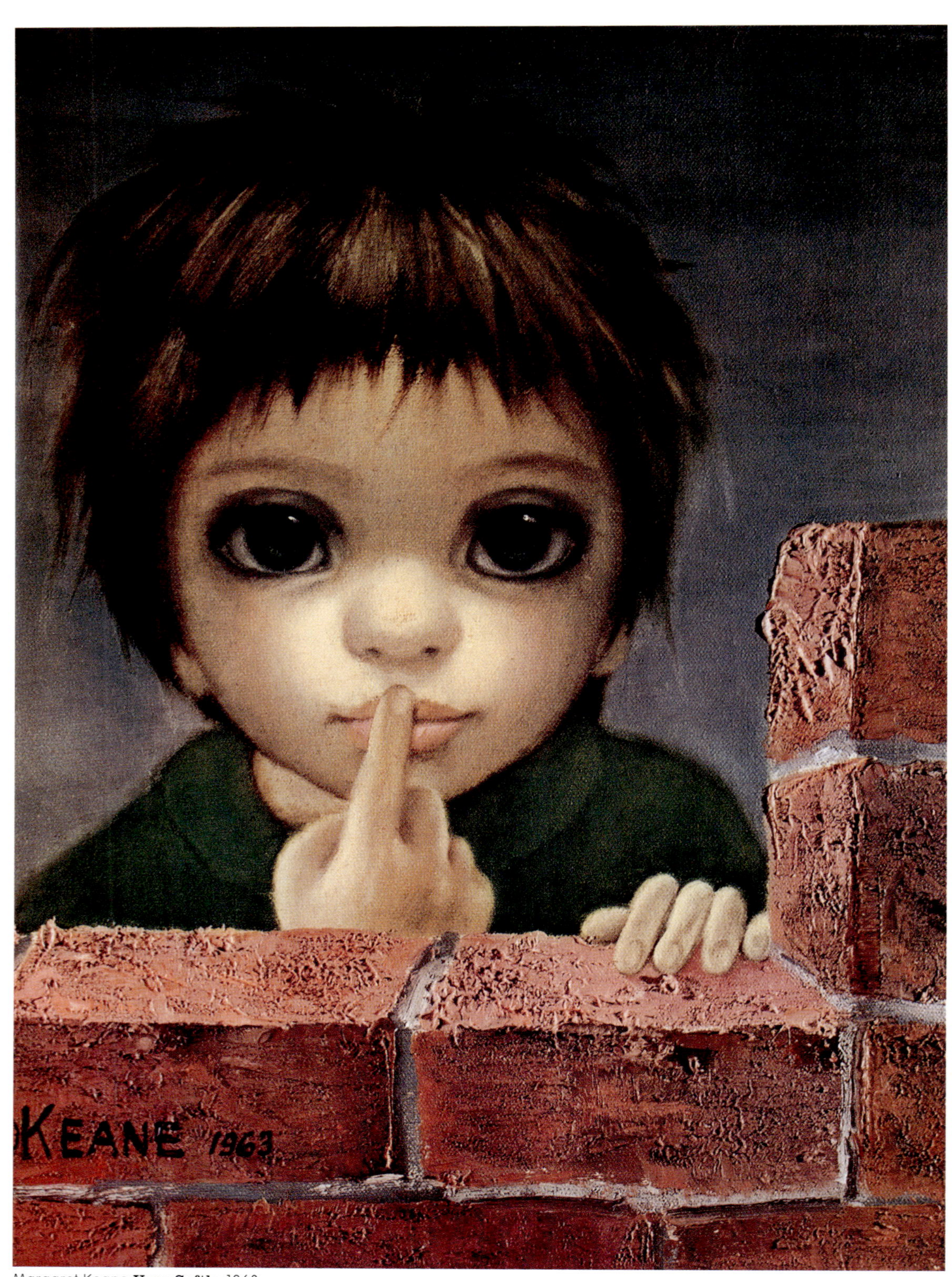

Margaret Keane **Very Softly** 1963

Margaret Keane **The Little Thinker** 1963

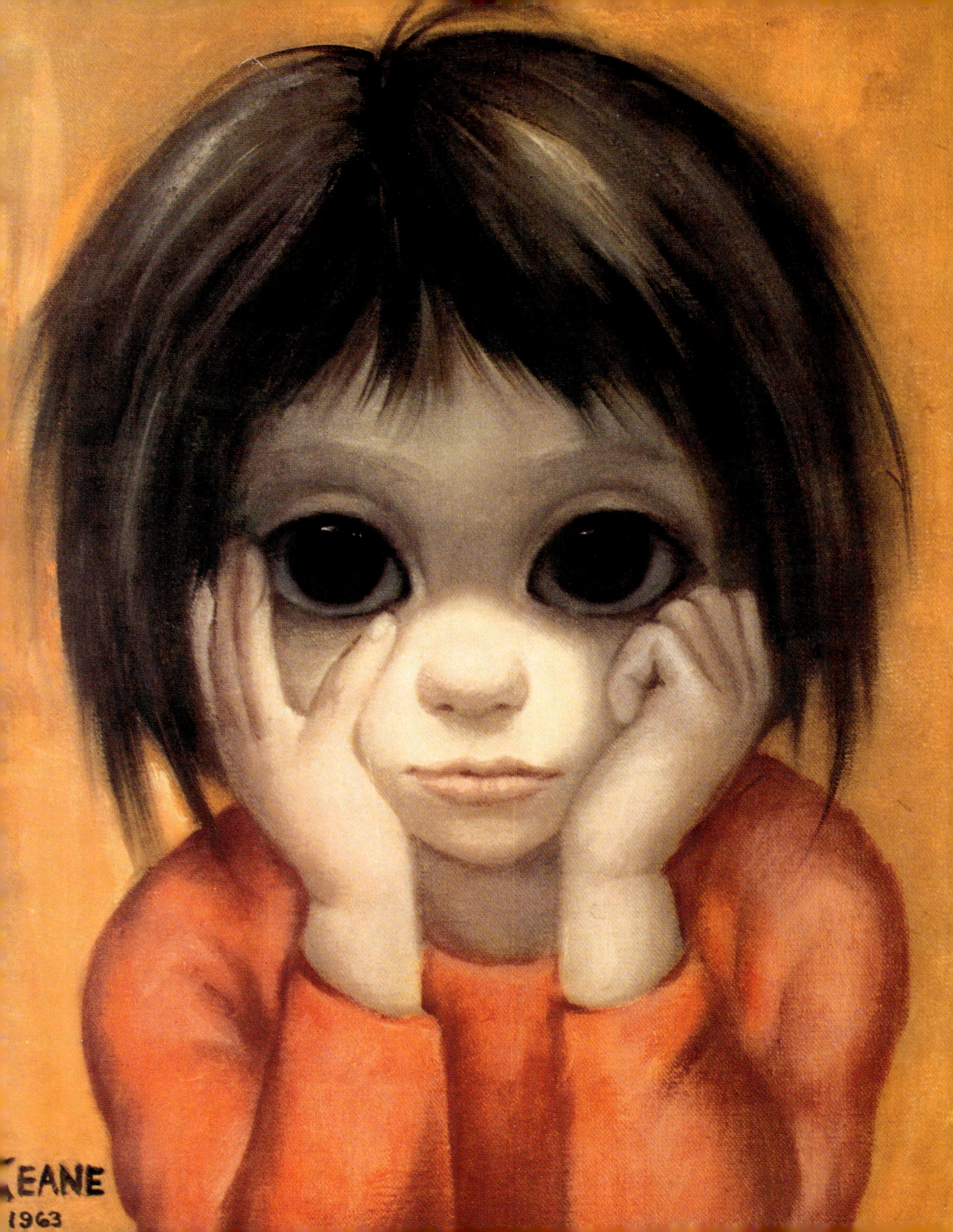

EANE
1963

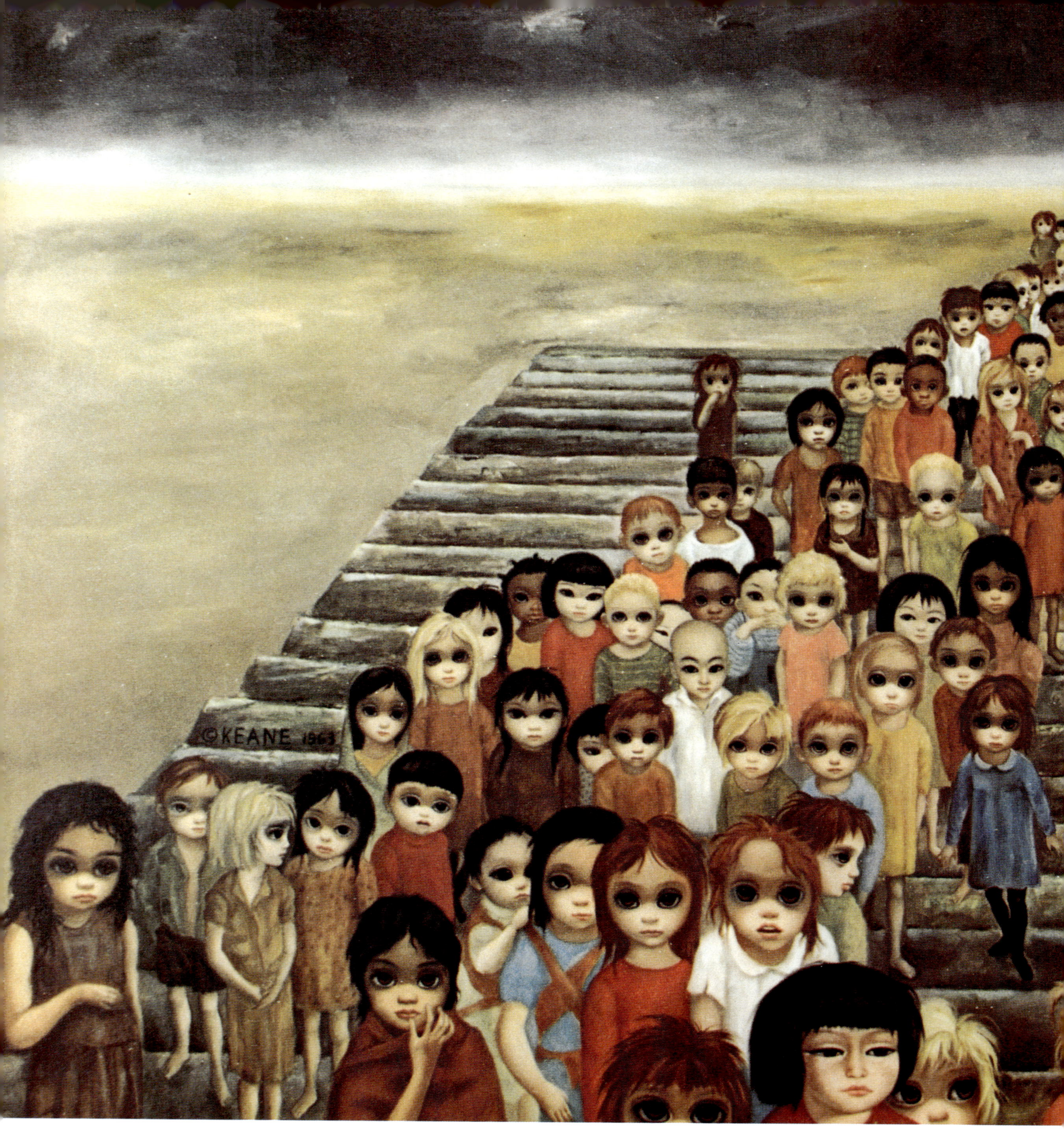

Margaret Keane **Tomorrow Forever** 1964

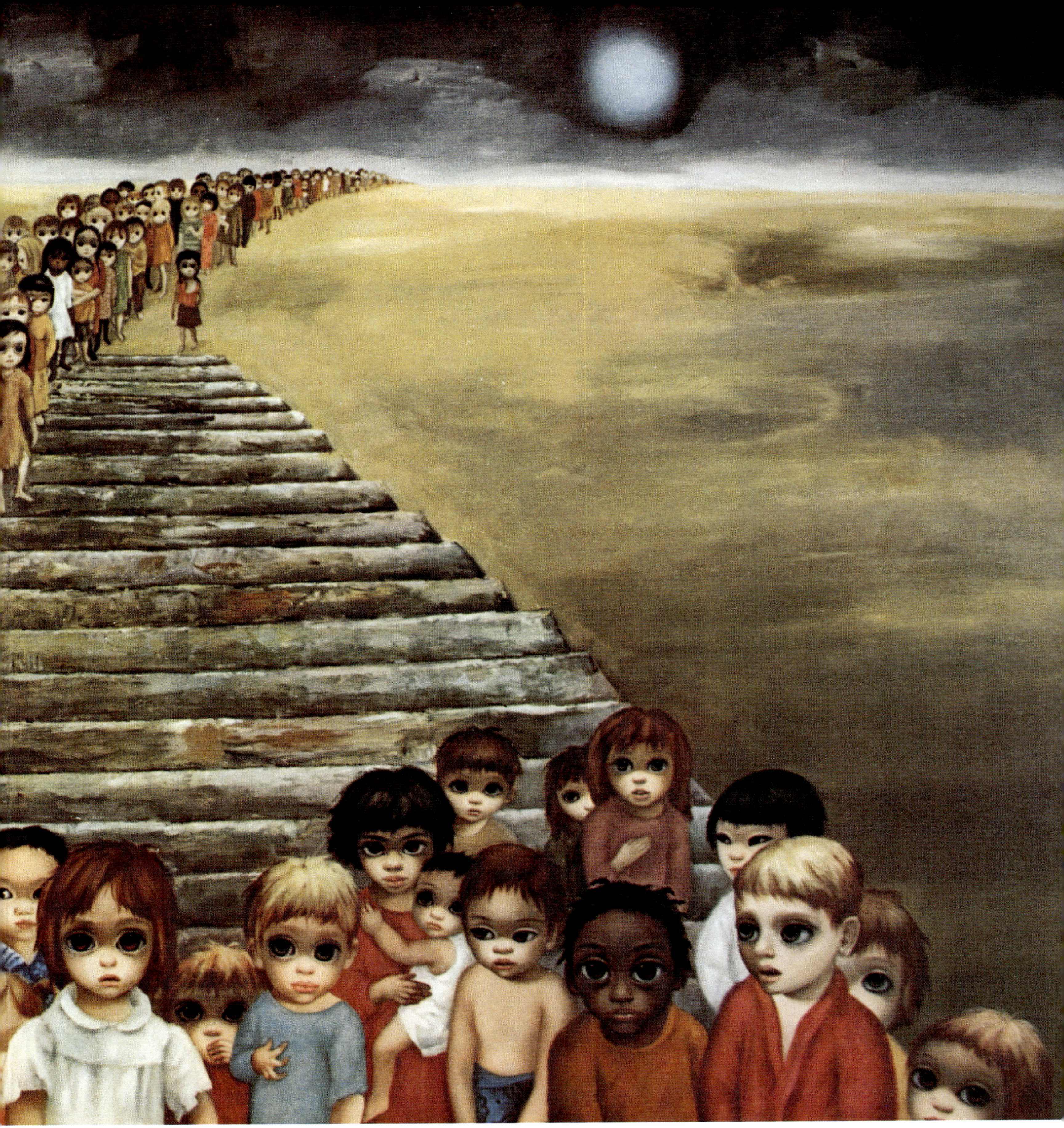

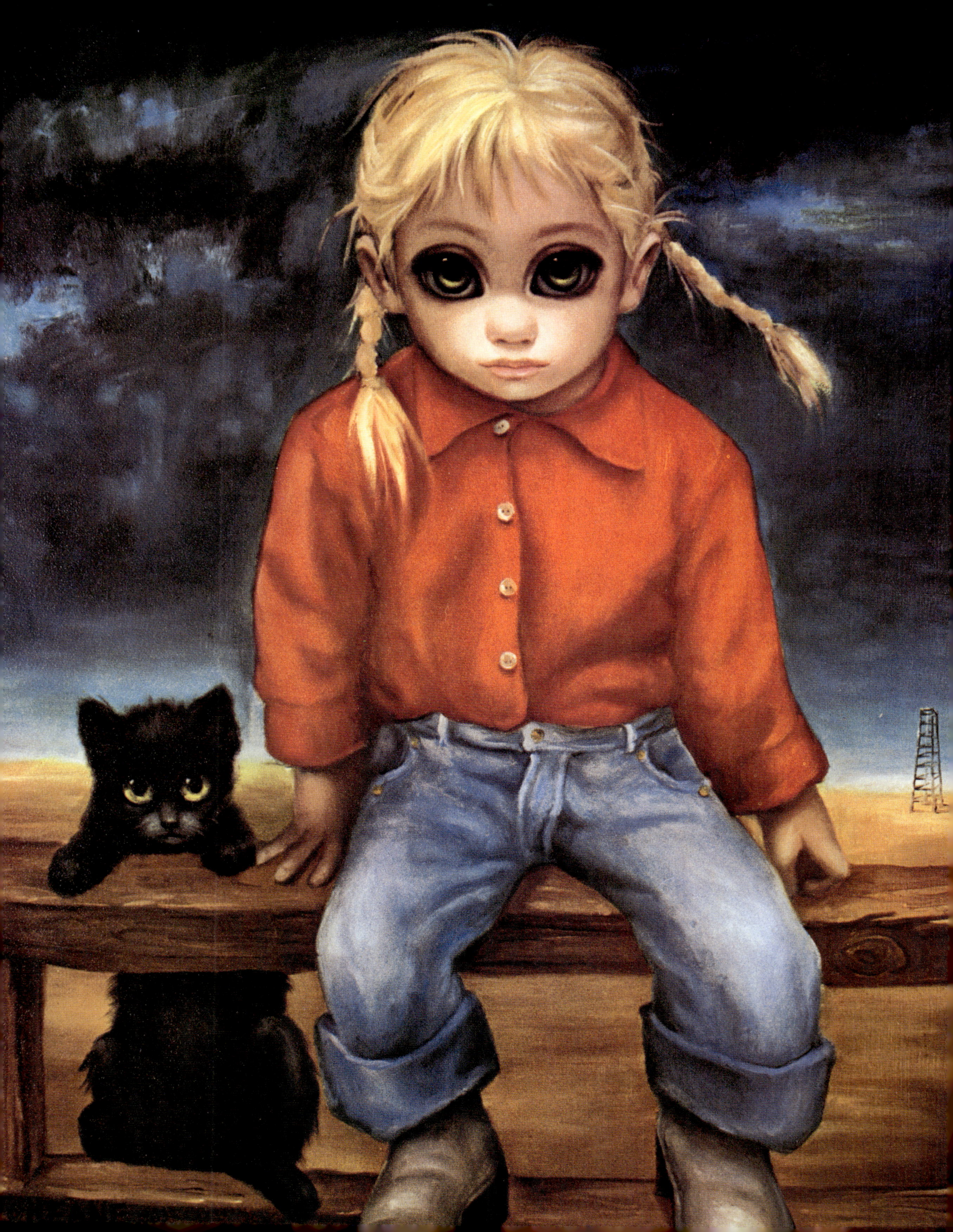

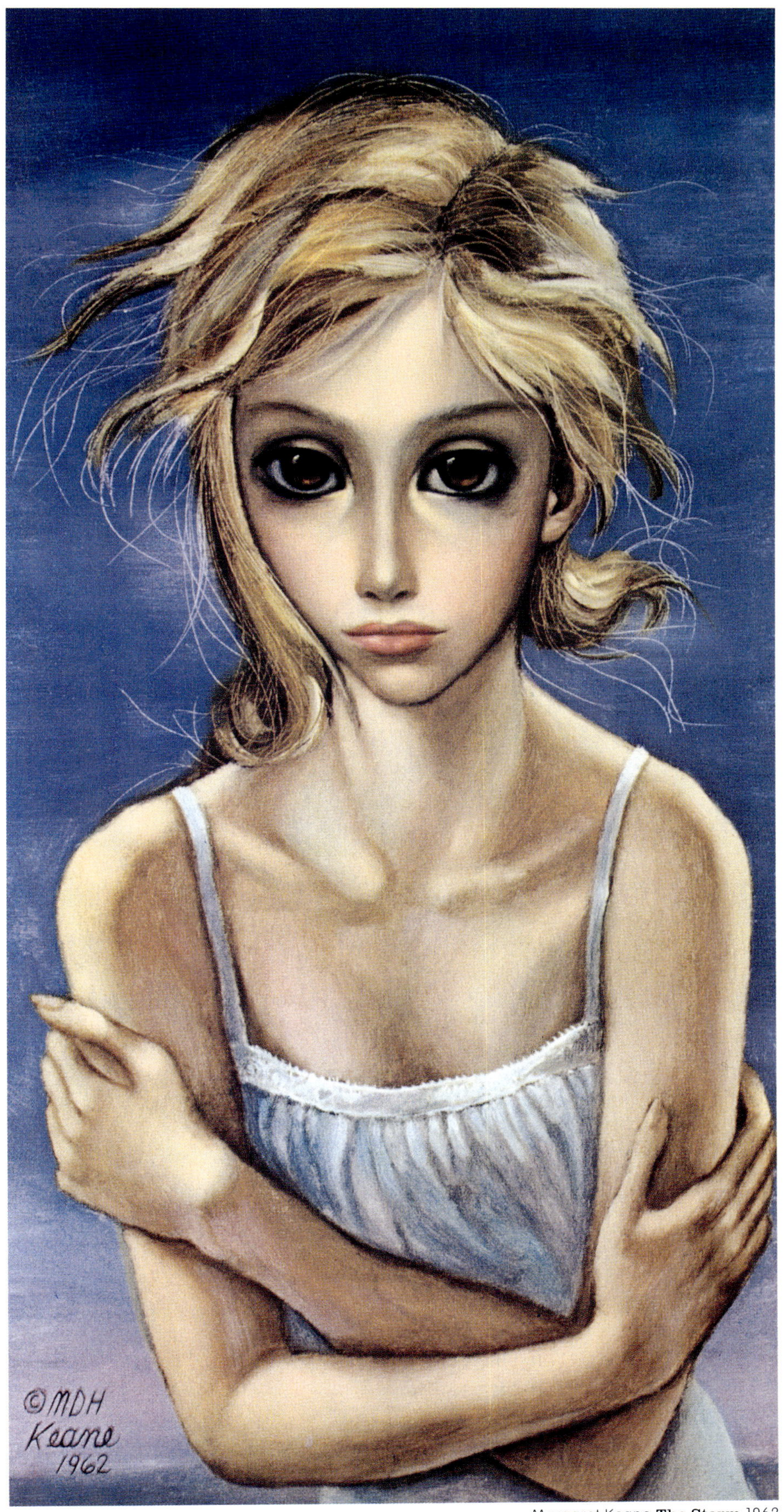

Margaret Keane **The Storm** 1962

Margaret Keane **The Wild Cat** 1963

Margaret Keane **The Flight** 1963

Margaret Keane **The Lively Puppet** 1963

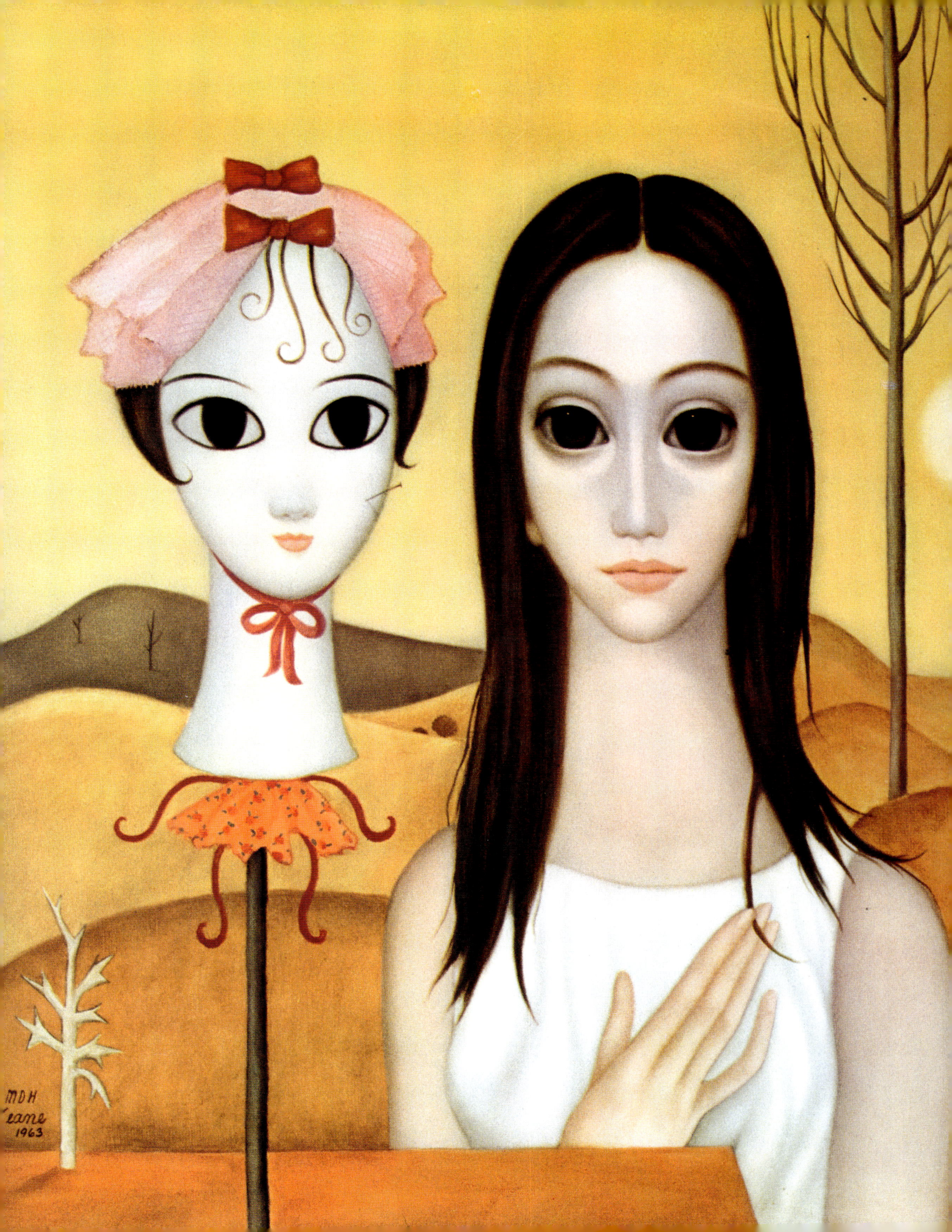
MDH
1963

Why do I spend hours of my valuable time trawling car boot sales or swap meets in the search for paintings of moon-eyed moggies, doleful dogs or ragamuffin kids with saucer eyes?

I've agonized over the value of Big Eye art and am still agonizing. I've been through my kitsch-obsessed twenties and my post-ironic early thirties. I now appreciate the value of minimalism and if I had too much money I would buy Saatchi's collection. Yet when I see the haunting expression of a scrawny cat, sitting in an alleyway next to a dustbin, I have to buy. Have those mesmerizing eyes transported me to a world far removed from what we are told is cool? Unlikely, and anyway, that's art critics' speak. More straightforwardly, in a sophisticated age, there is a beauty and a value in naivety, innocence and simplicity. Expressing the human emotions of happiness and sadness may be as far as this art form goes, but aren't these the most powerful of human emotions?

Old Big Eyes Is Back

If you accept this, then you can begin to think about the lasting success of Big Eye art in terms that make sense, even if they do not appear in the language of art critics. You can analyse it till the cows come home, but the fact that Big Eye art is alive forty years after its conception gives this art form a place in art history which it has hitherto been denied.

I first came into contact with Big Eye art in 1968, when I was seven years old. A print of a kid with bright, wide eyes and his streetwise mongrel, both peering round the corner of a Mediterranean village street, had captivated my grandmother Ida, who had spotted it for sale in a seafront gift-shop in Morecambe. Even though I was always dressed immaculately, this urchin reminded her of me. Isn't it natural for mothers to imagine bringing happiness to deprived children? This strangely haunting painting captured a gamut of expressions of childhood: innocence, sorrow and hope.

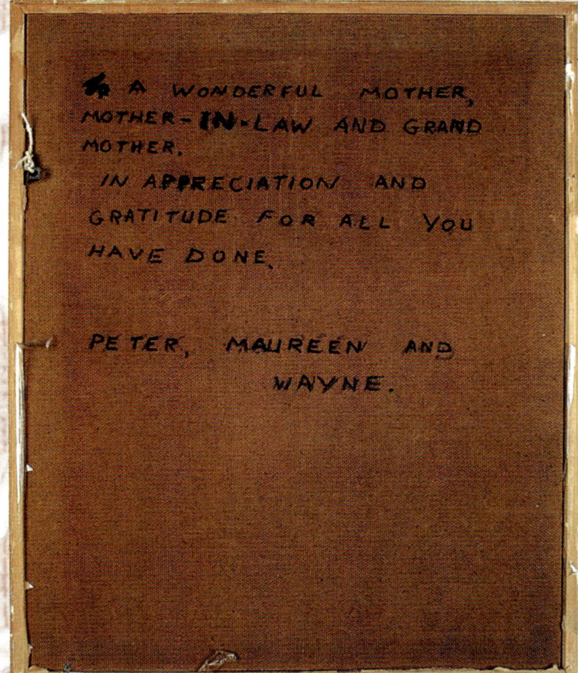

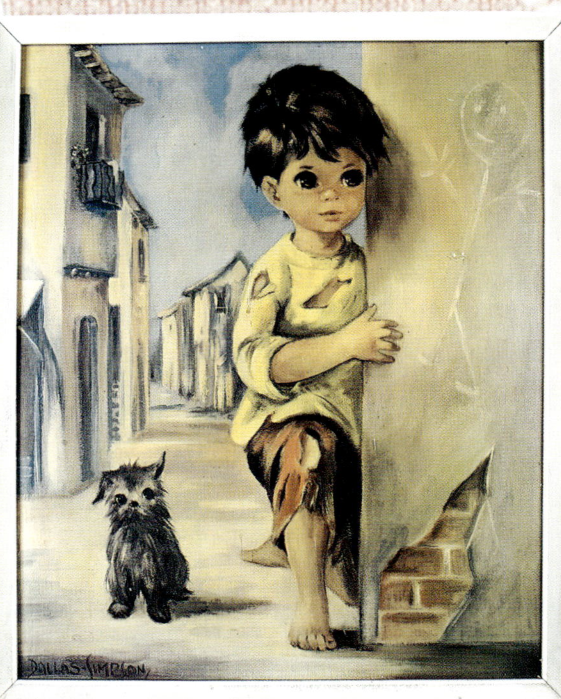

Dallas Simpson **Little Wayne and Bedraggled Dog** 1967

Dallas Simpson, the artist behind the first big-eyed painting I ever saw and many others in my collection, was just one of a multitude of artists who followed in the footsteps of **Margaret Keane**. It was **Keane** who started the movement in the late 1950s in North Beach, San Francisco, where her then husband **Walter** began to mass-market the paintings and prints with unprecedented success.

It was after Diane Keaton squealed, **'It's Keane, it's pure Keane!'** when given a Big Eye painting in Woody Allen's **Sleeper** (1973) and after these paintings became visible in films such as **Whatever Happened to Baby Jane?** that imitations blossomed. In America the genre was taken up by such painters as **Igor** (collected by John Waters), **Ozz Franca** (bought by Frank Sinatra), **Gig**, **Eve**, **Lee Eden**, **Mikki**, **Maiv**, **Gunilla**, **Luke Gibney**, **Jean Calogero**, **Sherle**, **Barbara**, **Pepi**, **Fellarda Leighton-Jones**; and in Europe by **Dallas Simpson**, **Idylle**, **Raphael**, **Cominoff** and **Genet**.

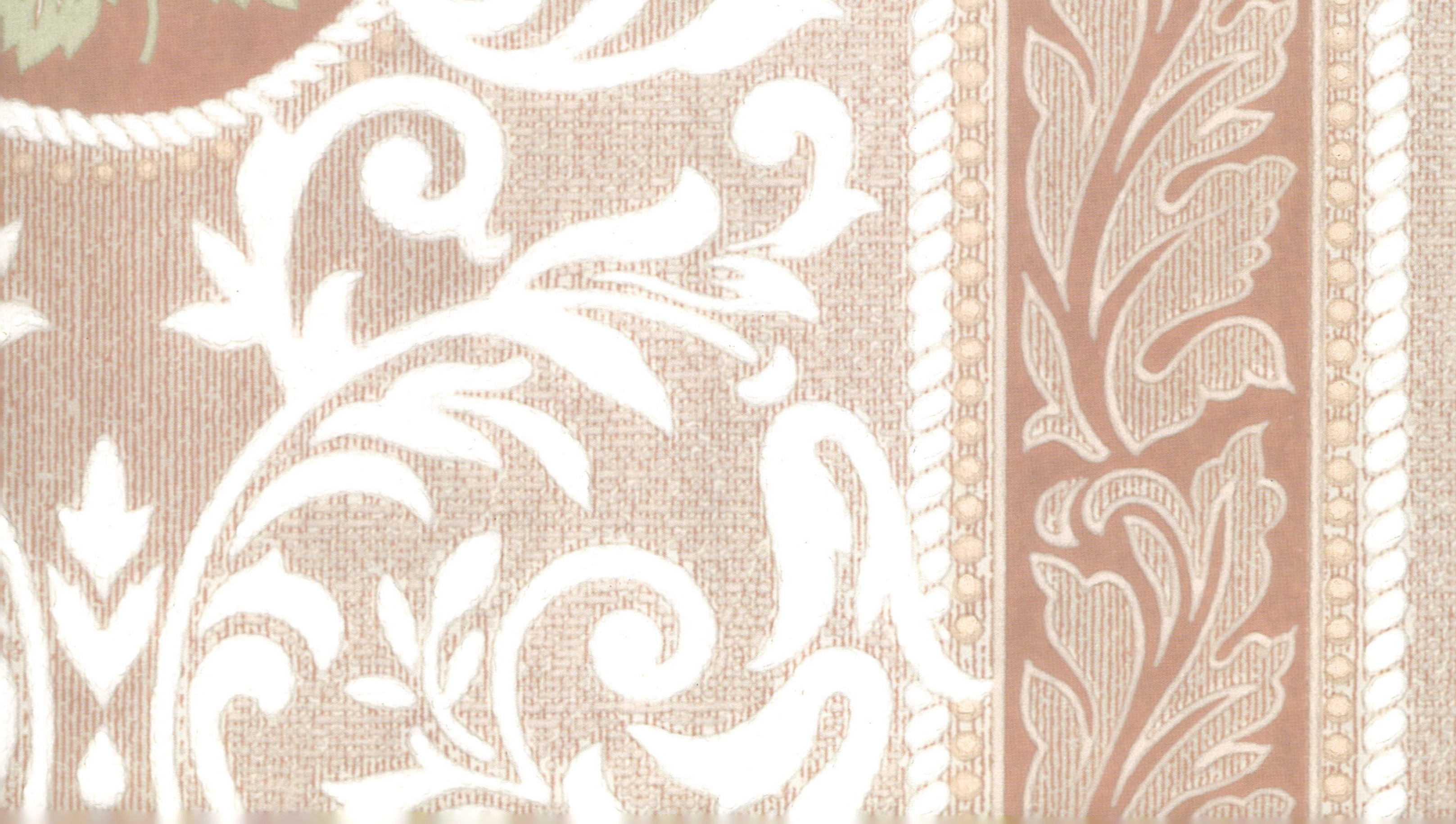

Today Big Eye art is returning as an affordable naïve art form for a new generation. It can increasingly be found on the walls of urban dwellers in the UK, USA and Tokyo, where stores like **Dept** and **Anna Sui** use Big Eye as decoration. I swap e-mails and digital images of new finds with fellow collectors in the States and there is a healthy transatlantic exchange of both prints and originals.

For the artists themselves, the placing of their work alongside the art of the **Sensation** generation jars. As British Big Eye artist **Betty Raphael** puts it, **'cut up cows and hung up horses – it's the emperor's new clothes. People are told they've got to like something with no skill in it.'** I can live with the two extremes in my life; I swing between the soft emotions of fatherhood, the beauty of children and the desire to explore and extend boundaries. Big Eye art plays a part in my life as it has with millions of people.

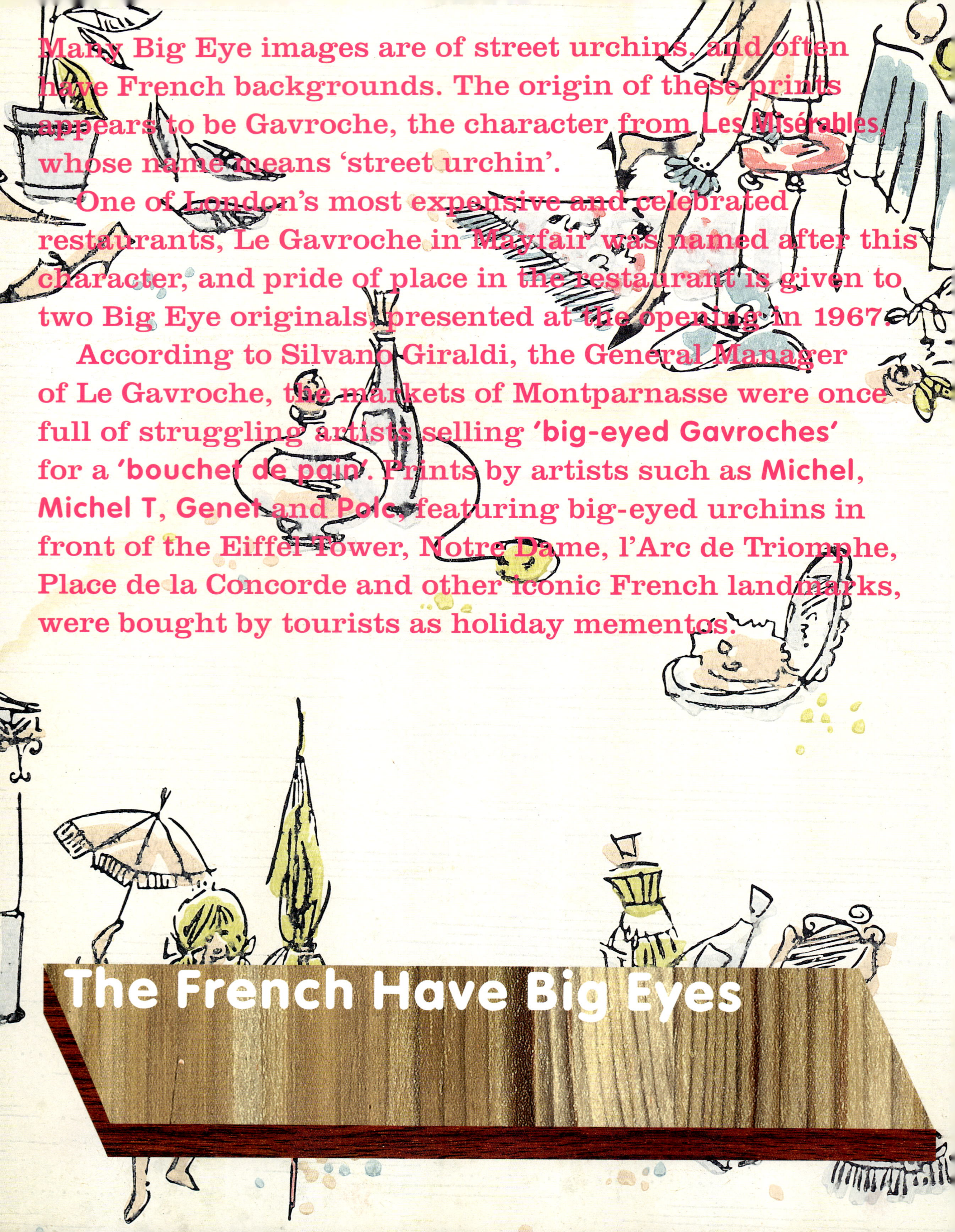

Many Big Eye images are of street urchins, and often have French backgrounds. The origin of these prints appears to be Gavroche, the character from **Les Misérables**, whose name means 'street urchin'.

One of London's most expensive and celebrated restaurants, Le Gavroche in Mayfair was named after this character, and pride of place in the restaurant is given to two Big Eye originals, presented at the opening in 1967.

According to Silvano Giraldi, the General Manager of Le Gavroche, the markets of Montparnasse were once full of struggling artists selling **'big-eyed Gavroches'** for a **'bouchet de pain'**. Prints by artists such as **Michel**, **Michel T**, **Genet** and **Polo**, featuring big-eyed urchins in front of the Eiffel Tower, Notre Dame, l'Arc de Triomphe, Place de la Concorde and other iconic French landmarks, were bought by tourists as holiday mementos.

The French Have Big Eyes

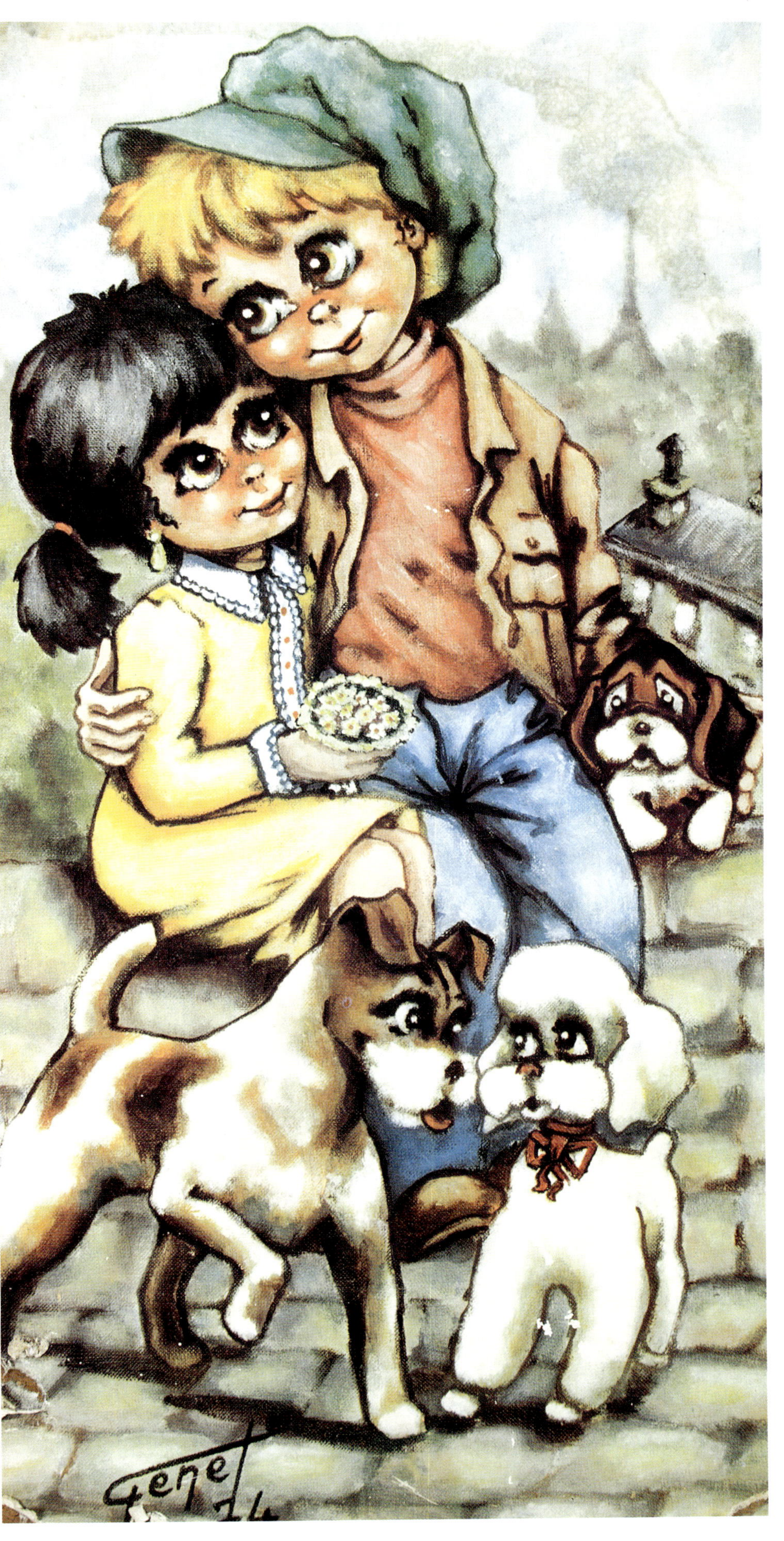

Genet Cute 70s Boy and His Big-Eyed Mongrel Meet Big-Eyed Rich Girl and Her Big-Eyed Pristine Poodle

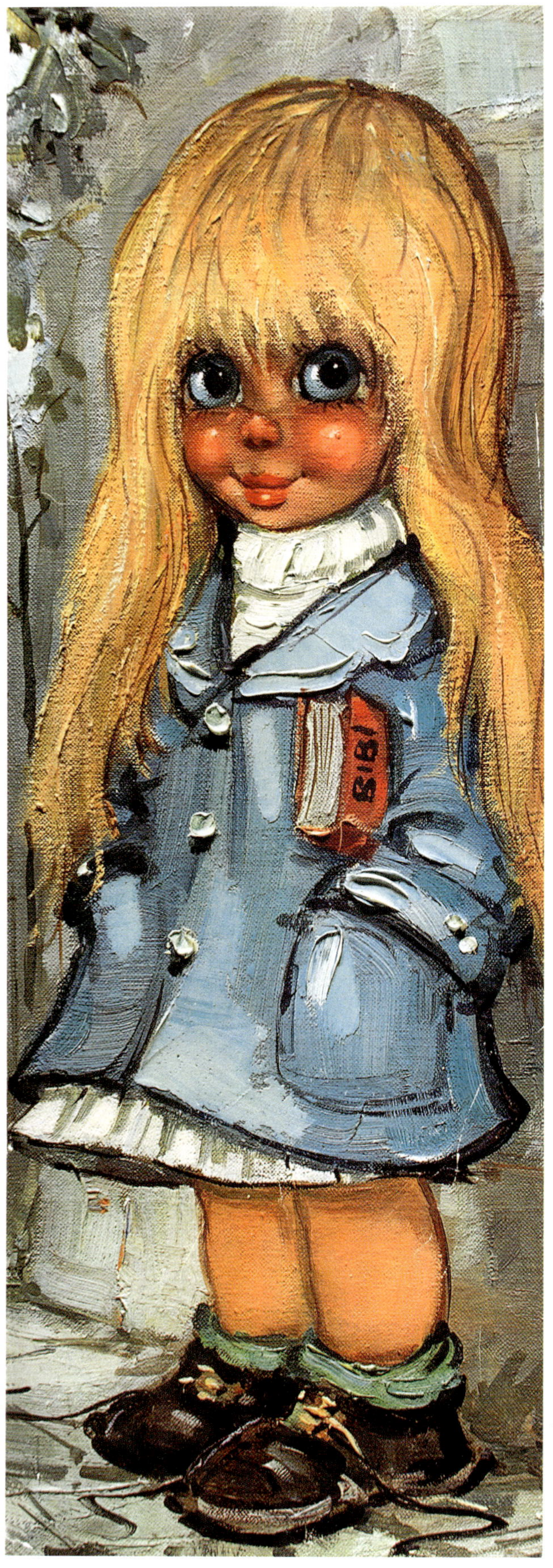

Michel T **Donatella V**

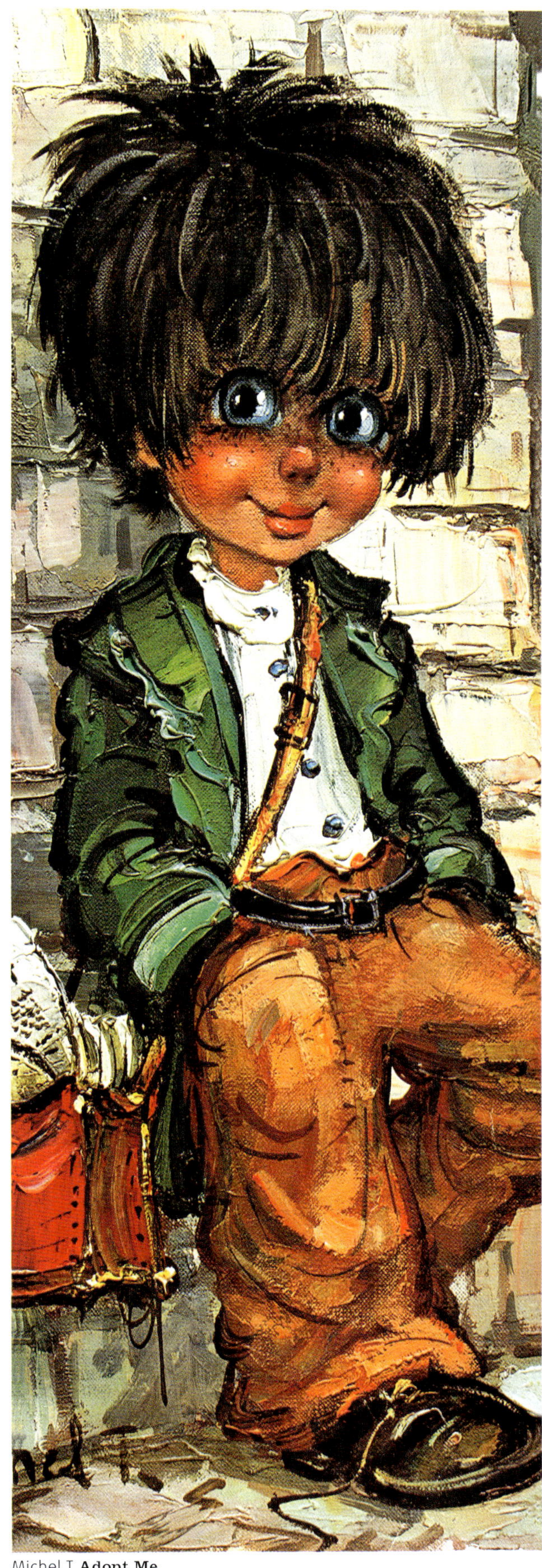

Michel T **Adopt Me**

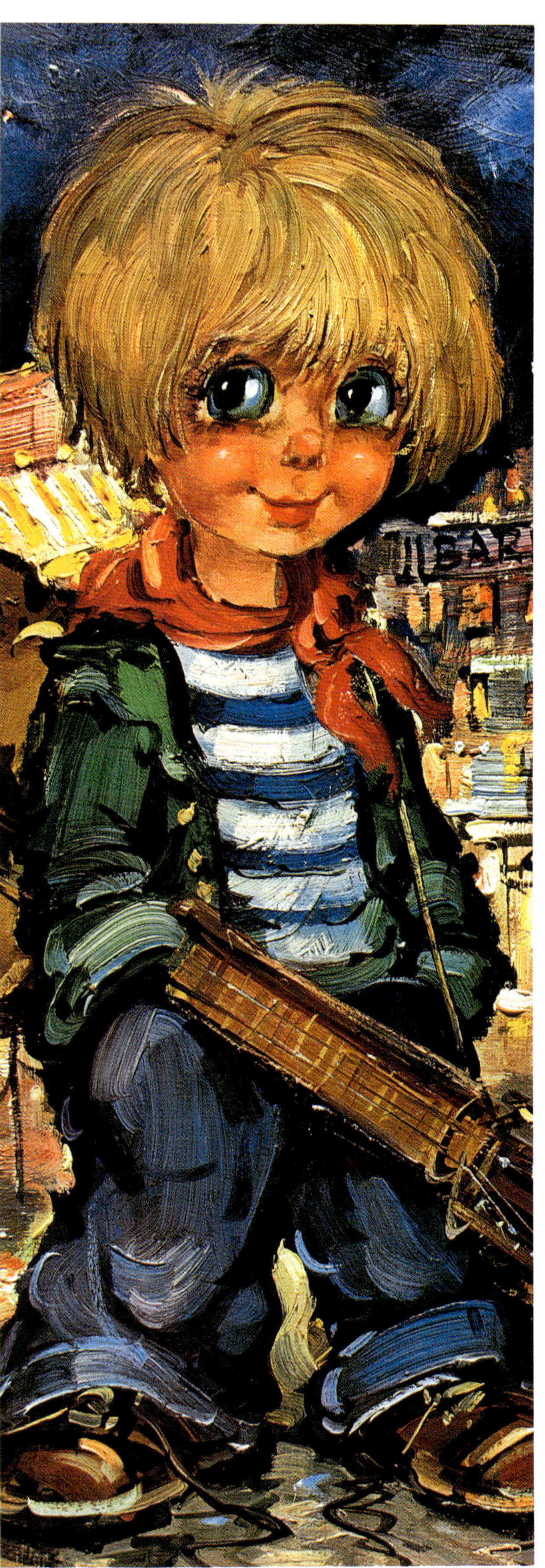

Michel T **Breton Bum Note**

following pages: Michel T **Ce Soir**; Michel T **Get Down Shep**

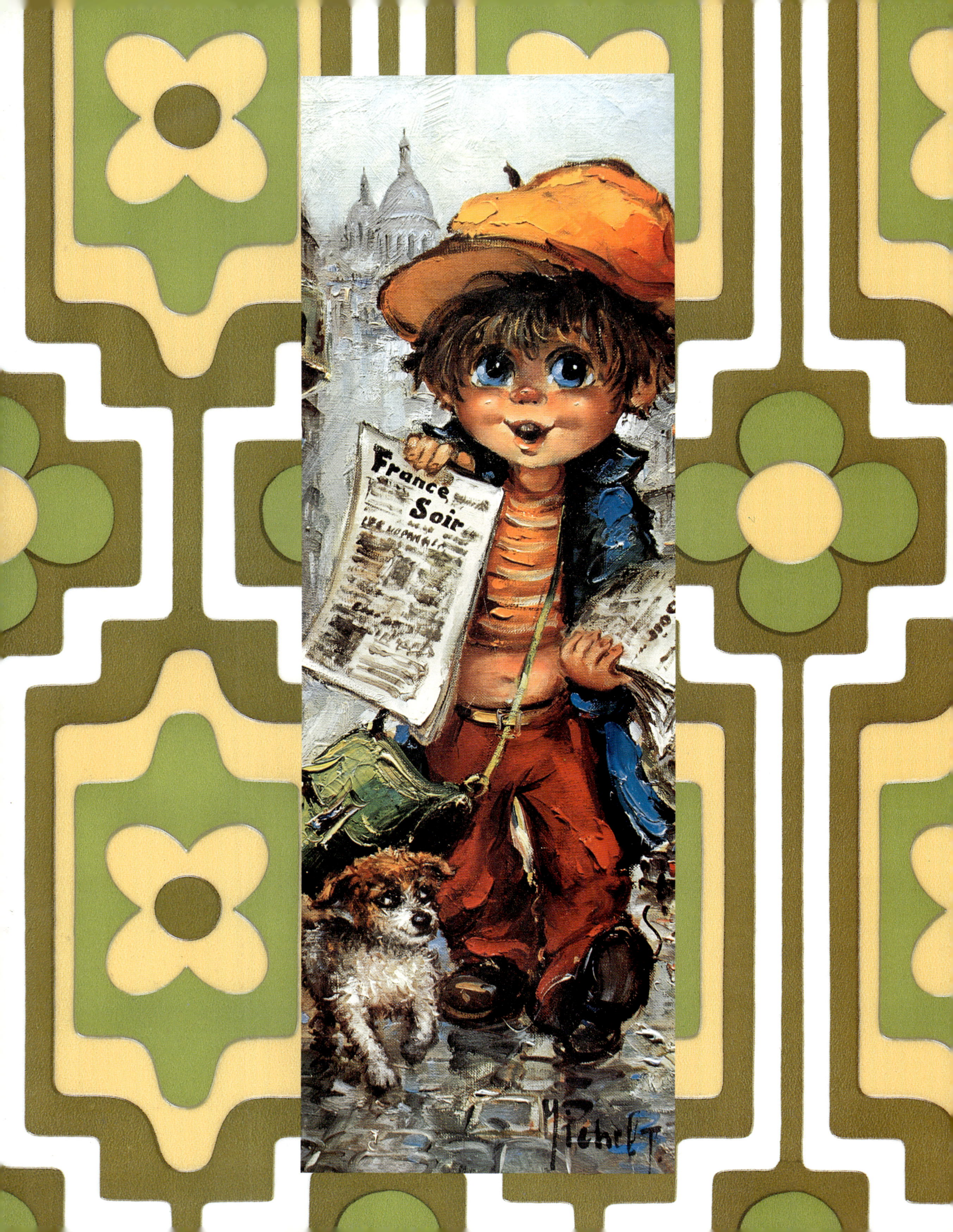
France Soir

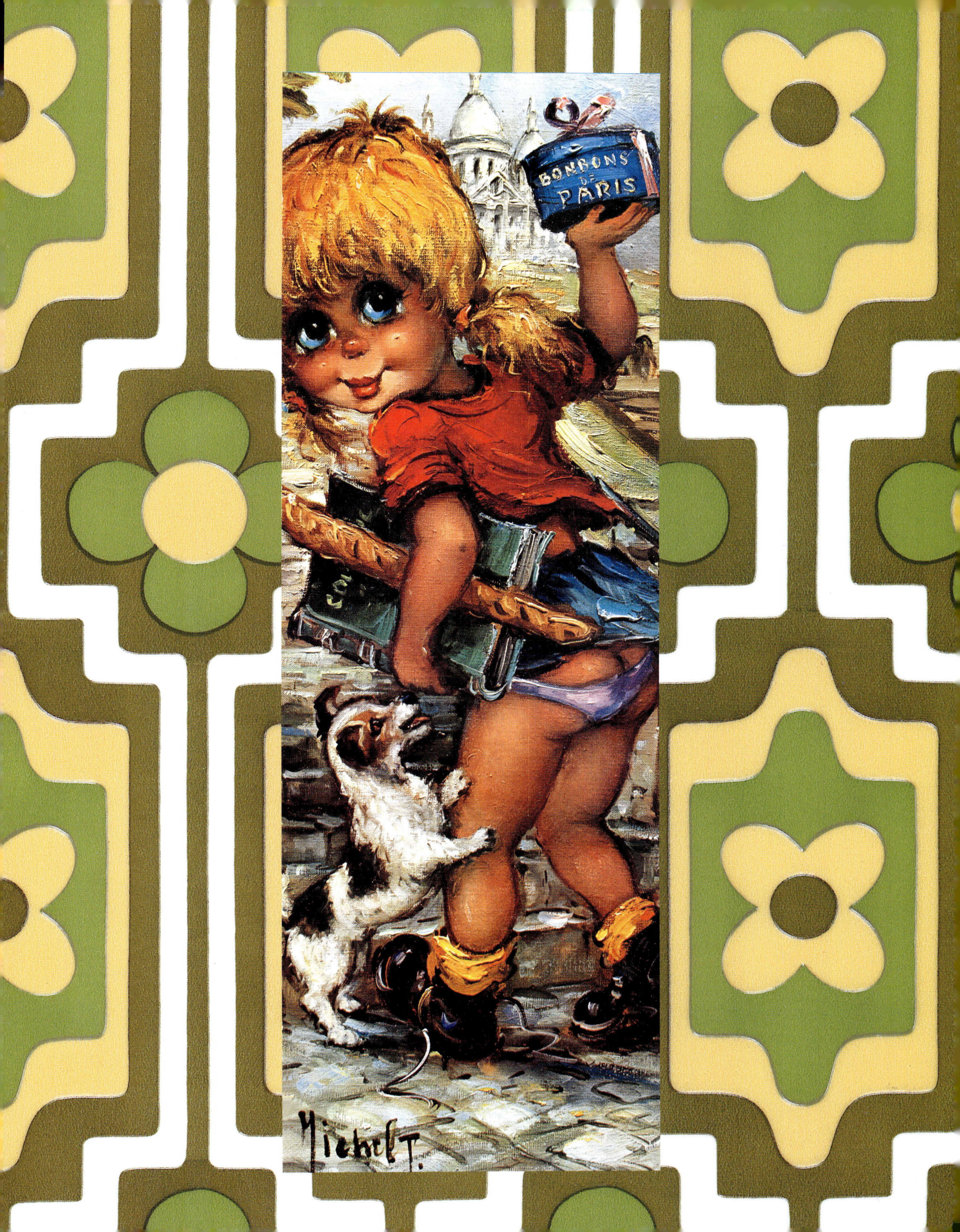
BONBONS
PARIS
Michel T.

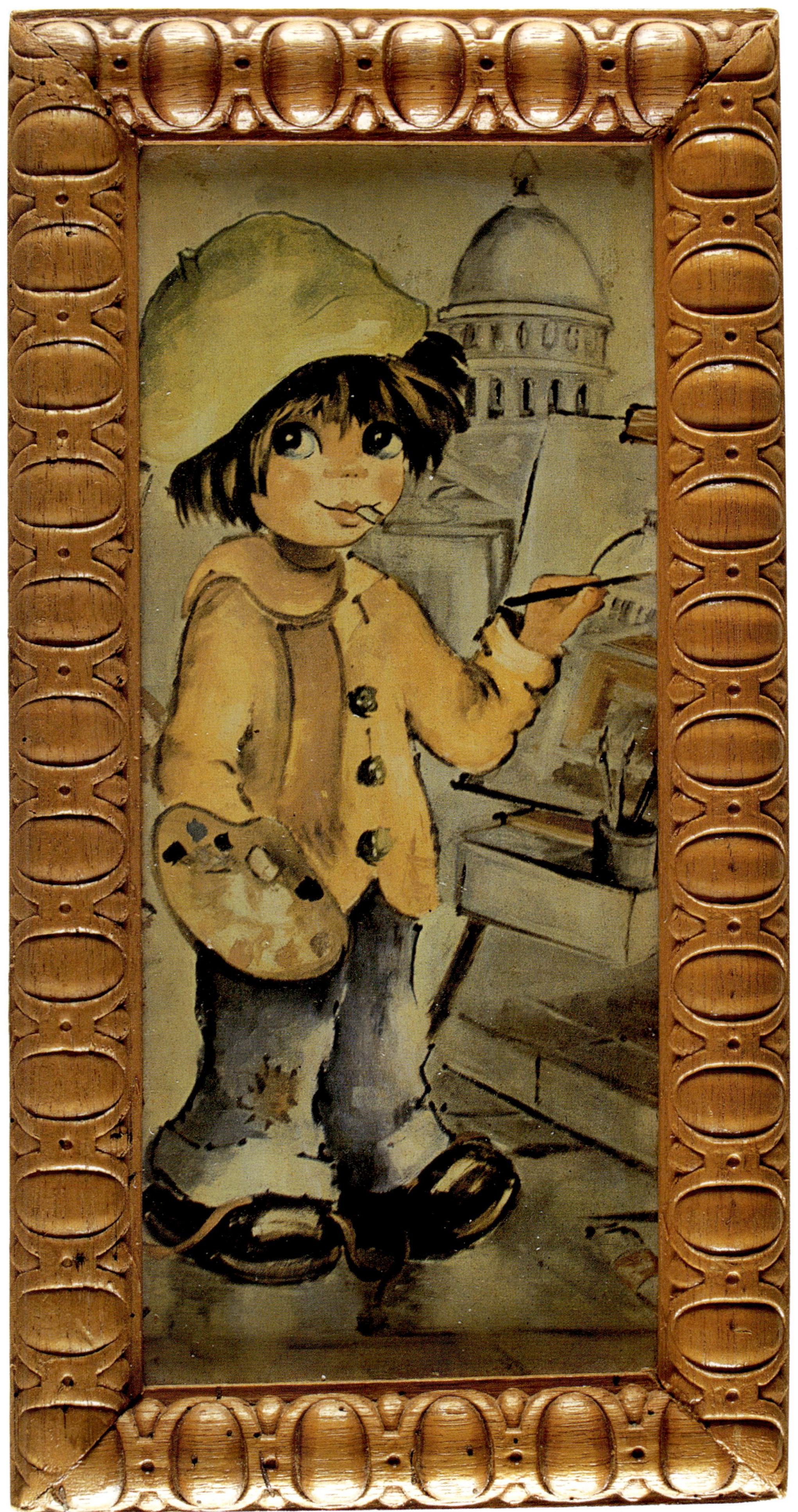

Unknown Artist **Montmartre**

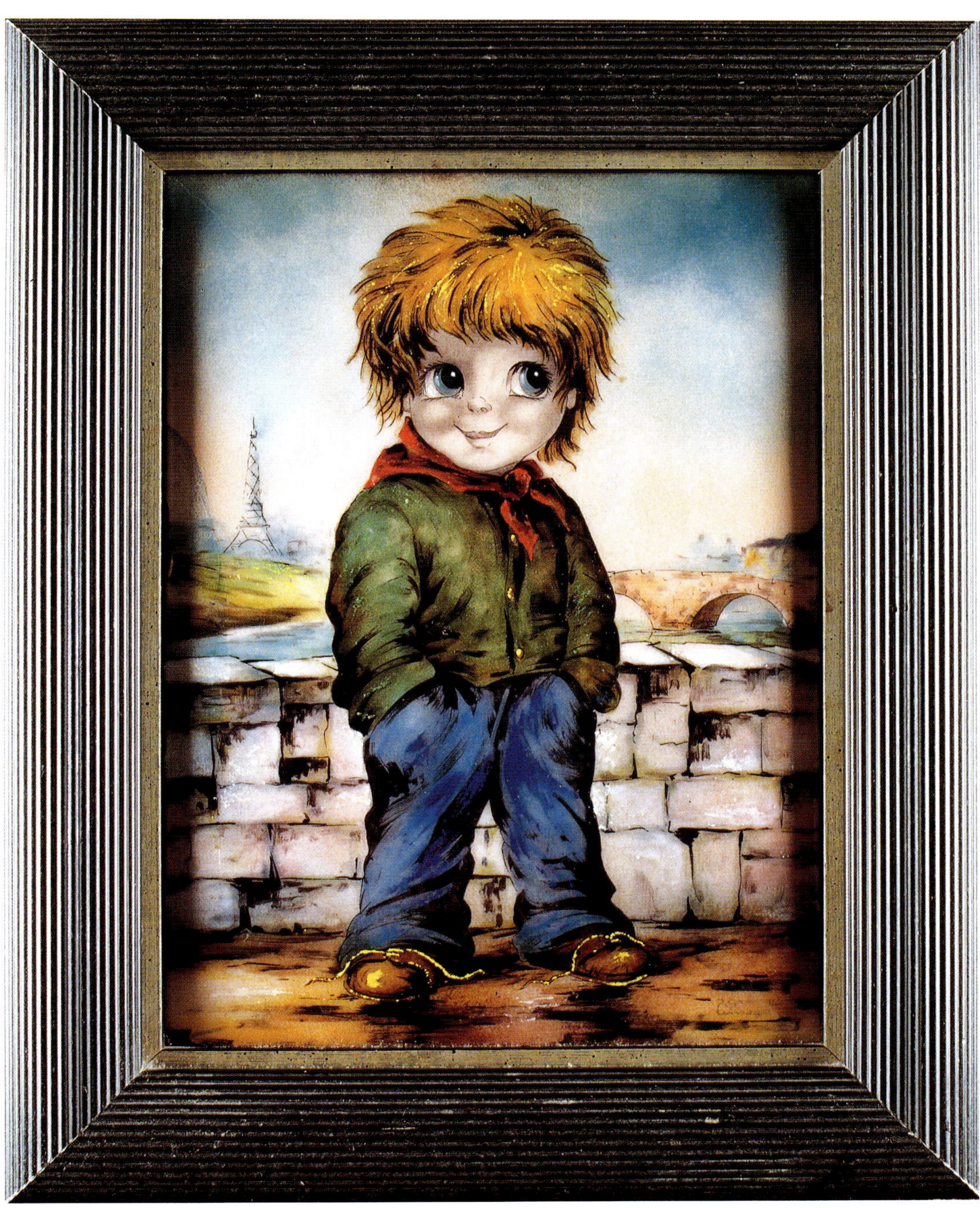

Granger **Young Parisian** 1981

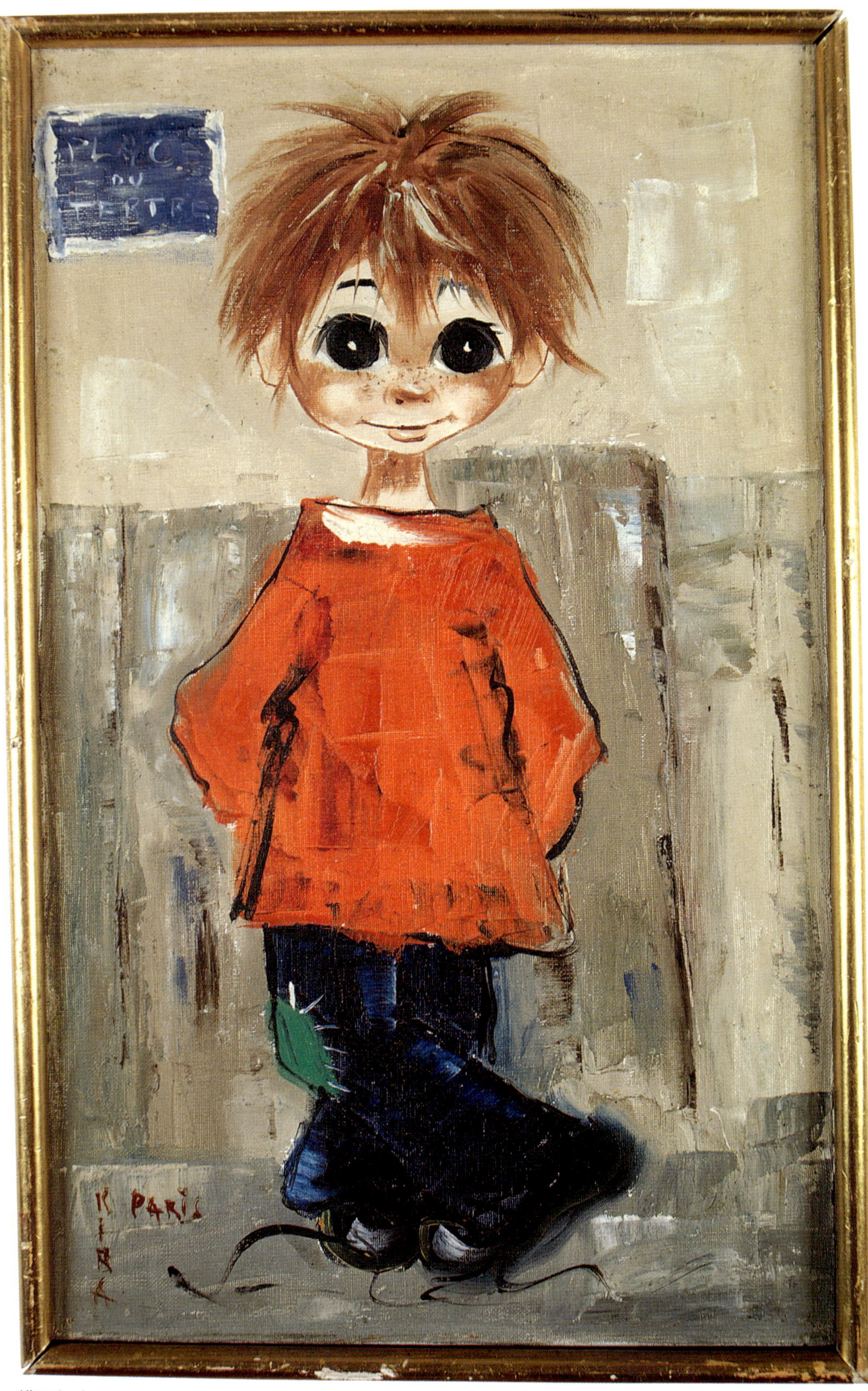

Kira **Androgyny**

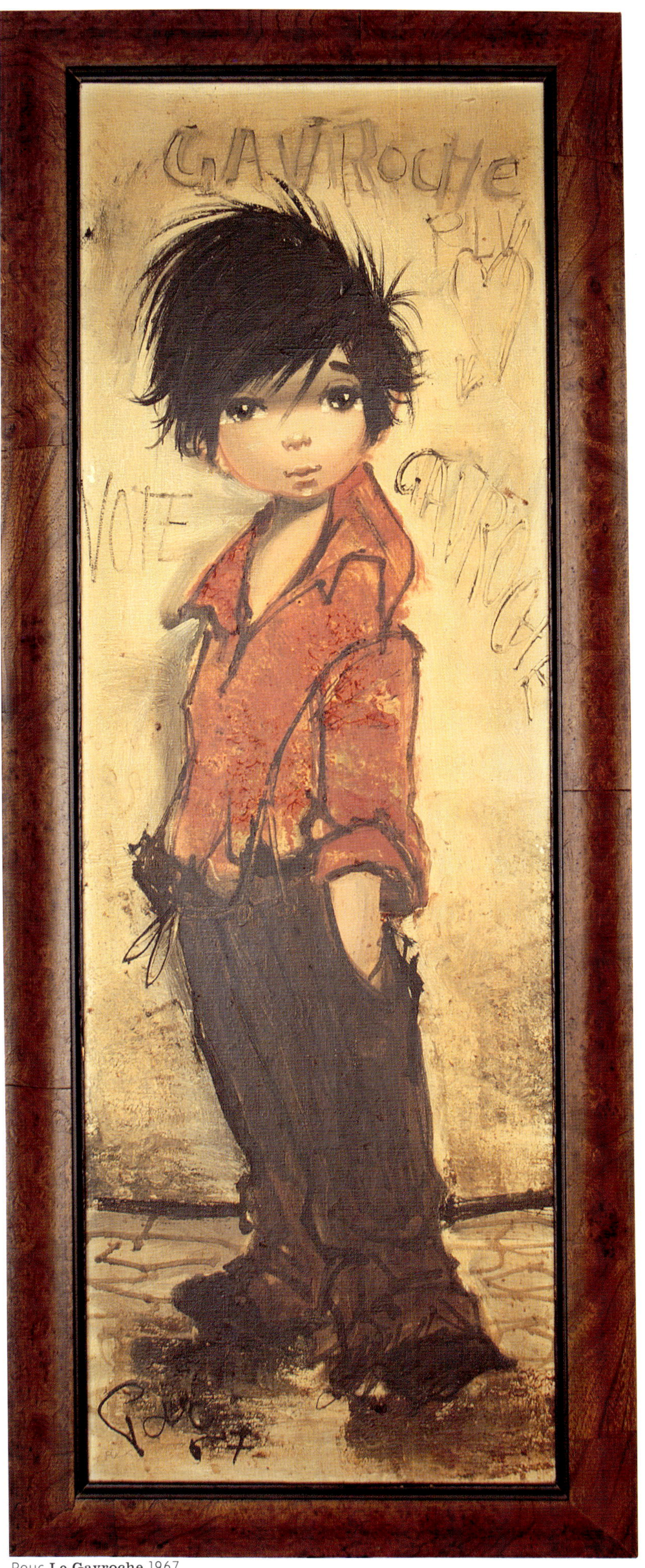

Pouc **Le Gavroche** 1967

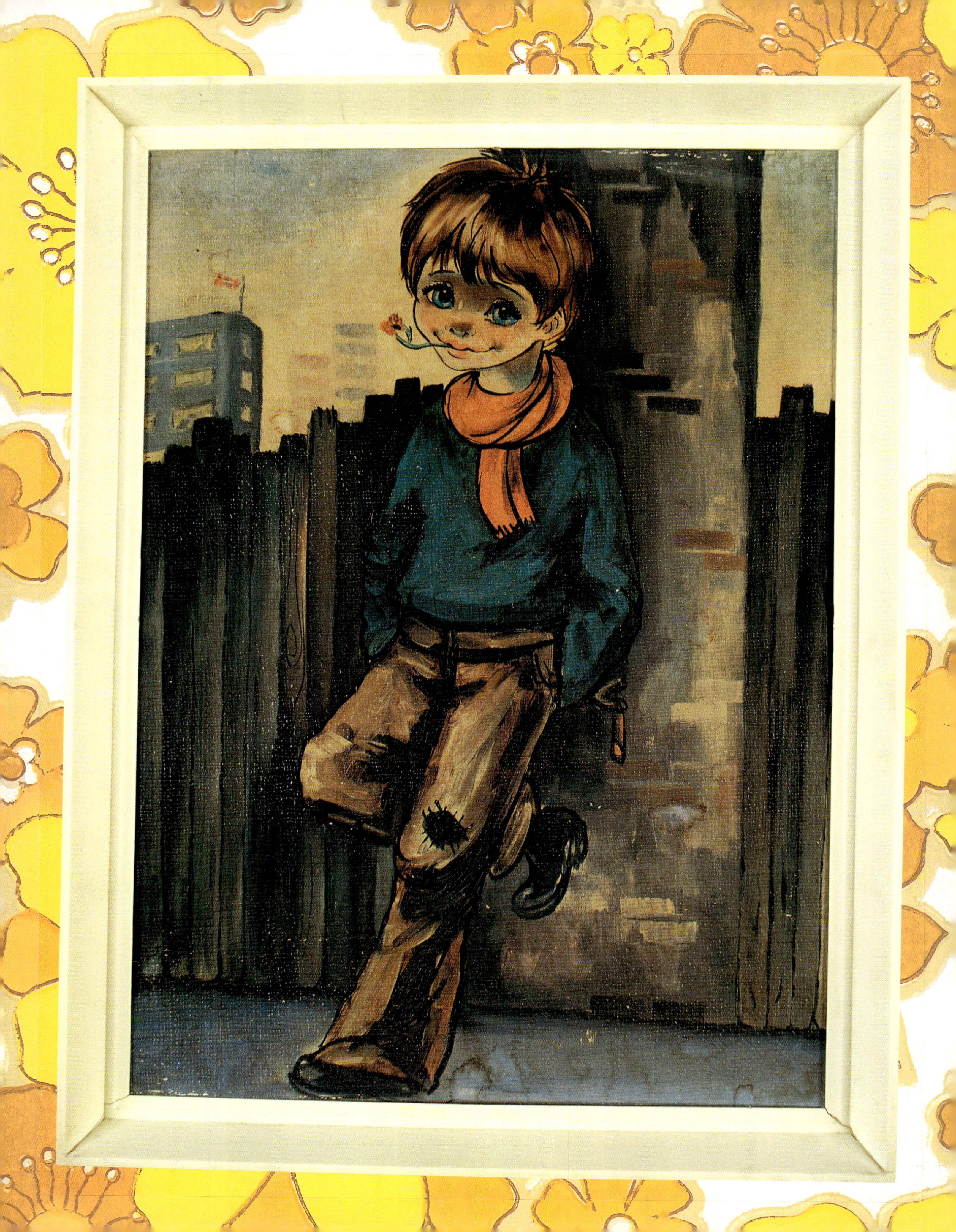

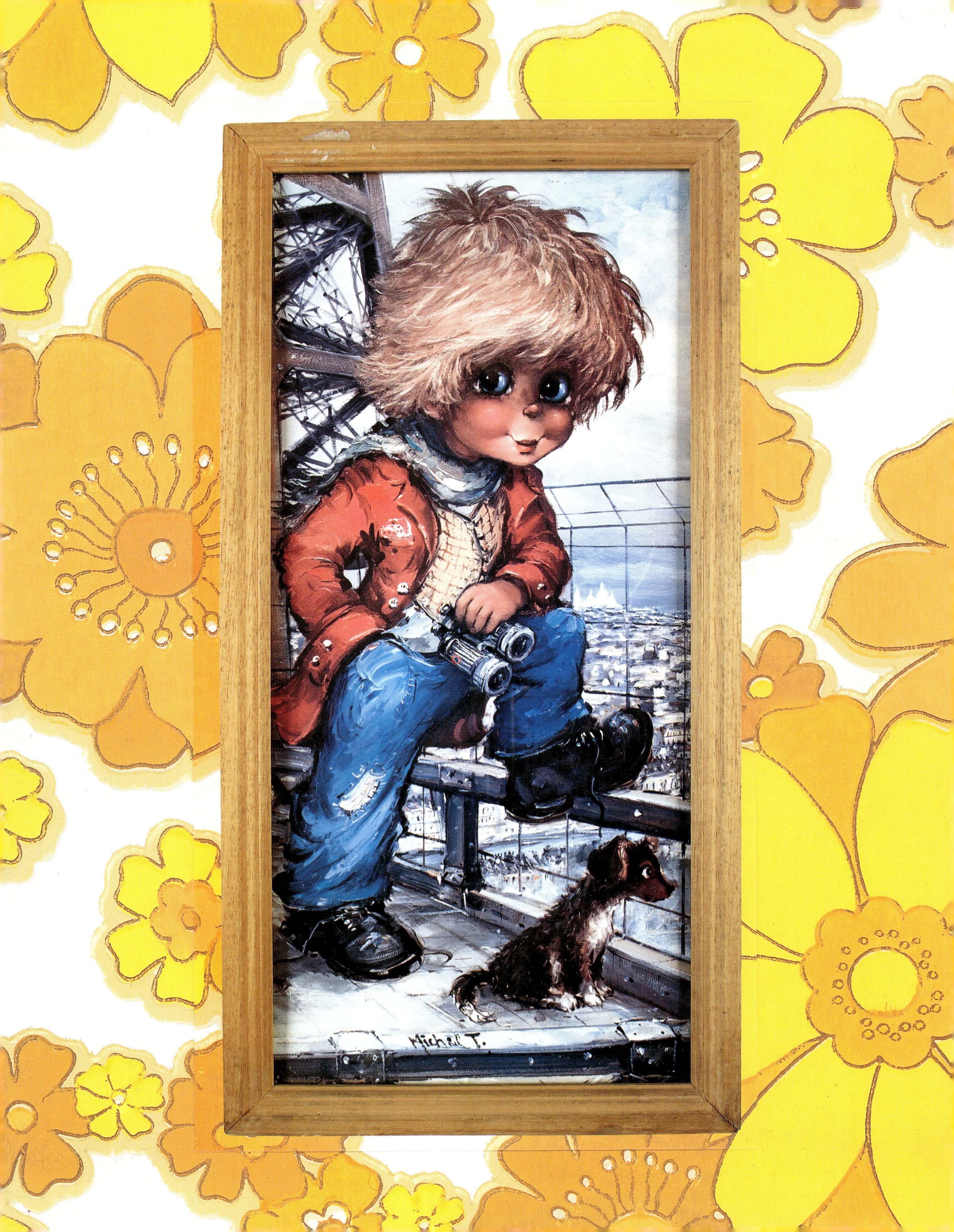
Michel T.

preceding pages: Unknown Artist **Pipe Boy;** Michel T **On Tour**

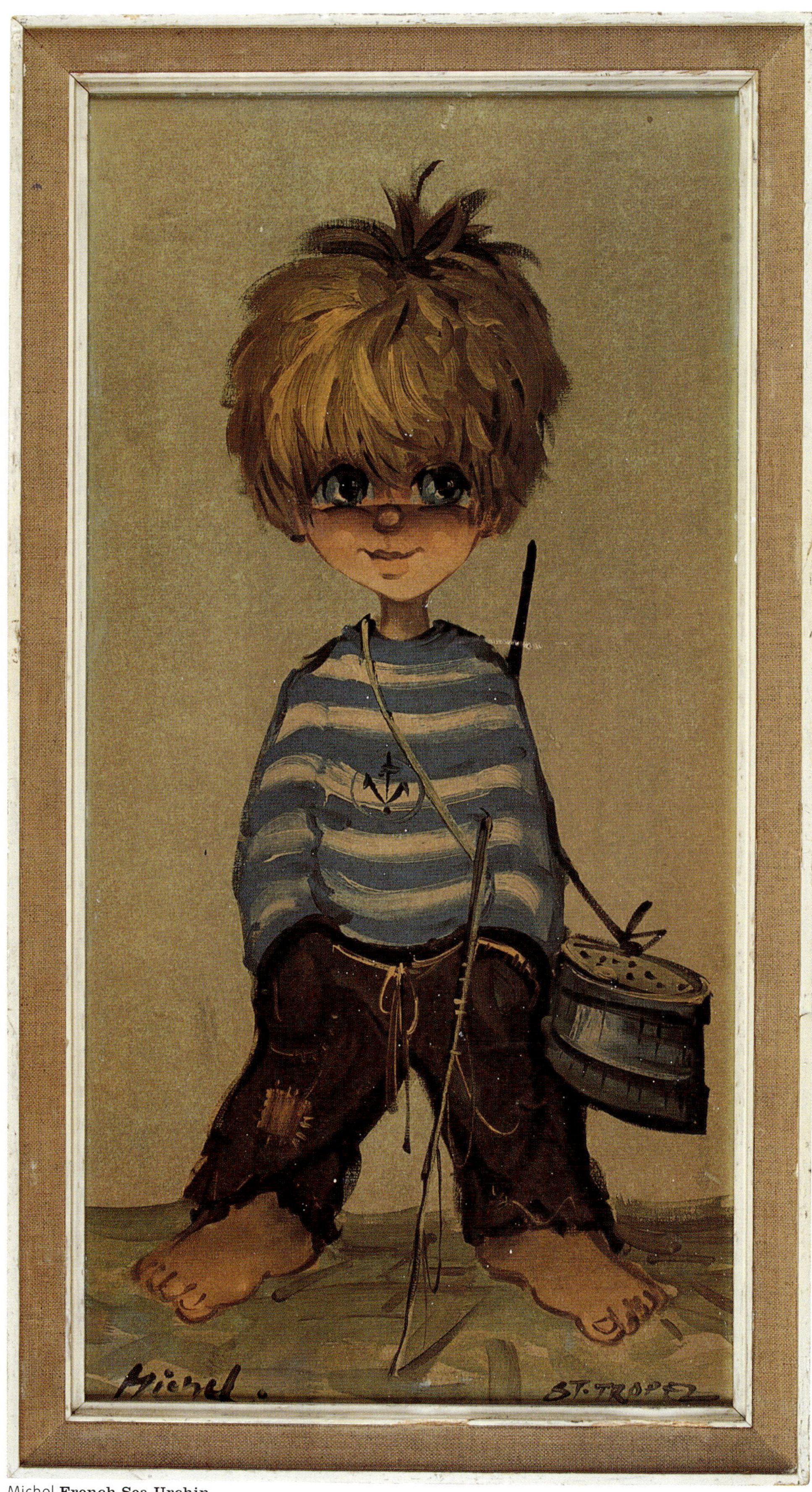

Michel **French Sea Urchin**

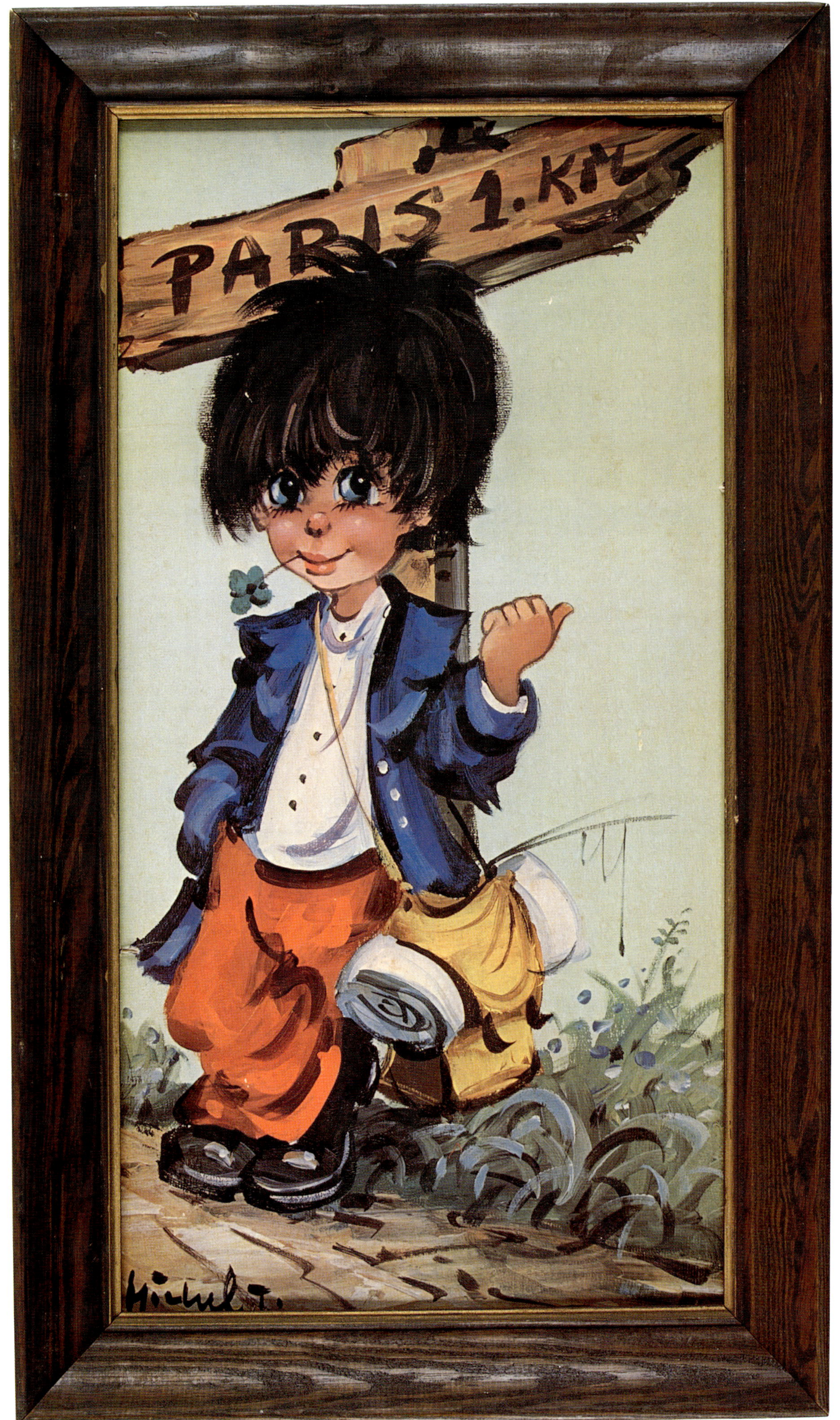

Michel T **Hitchin' a Ride**

British Big Eye artists were heavy on childhood sentimentality. A recurrent 'before and after' theme ran through the works of **Dallas Simpson**, **Idylle** and **Golding**. 'Adopt me' doe-eyed urchins were miraculously transformed into healthy bright-eyed rich kids, their soiled, ripped shirts giving way to pristine, whiter-than-white cotton, their cut-off 'beach bum' shorts replaced by Little Lord Fauntleroy tailored breeches, and their home-made toys replaced by violins.

In the late 60s, as holidays to the Costa del Sol took off, the Big Eye kids took on a Mediterranean pallor and background scenes became a little more exotic. What more could you ask for? Cute kids in need of help in exotic Benidorm.

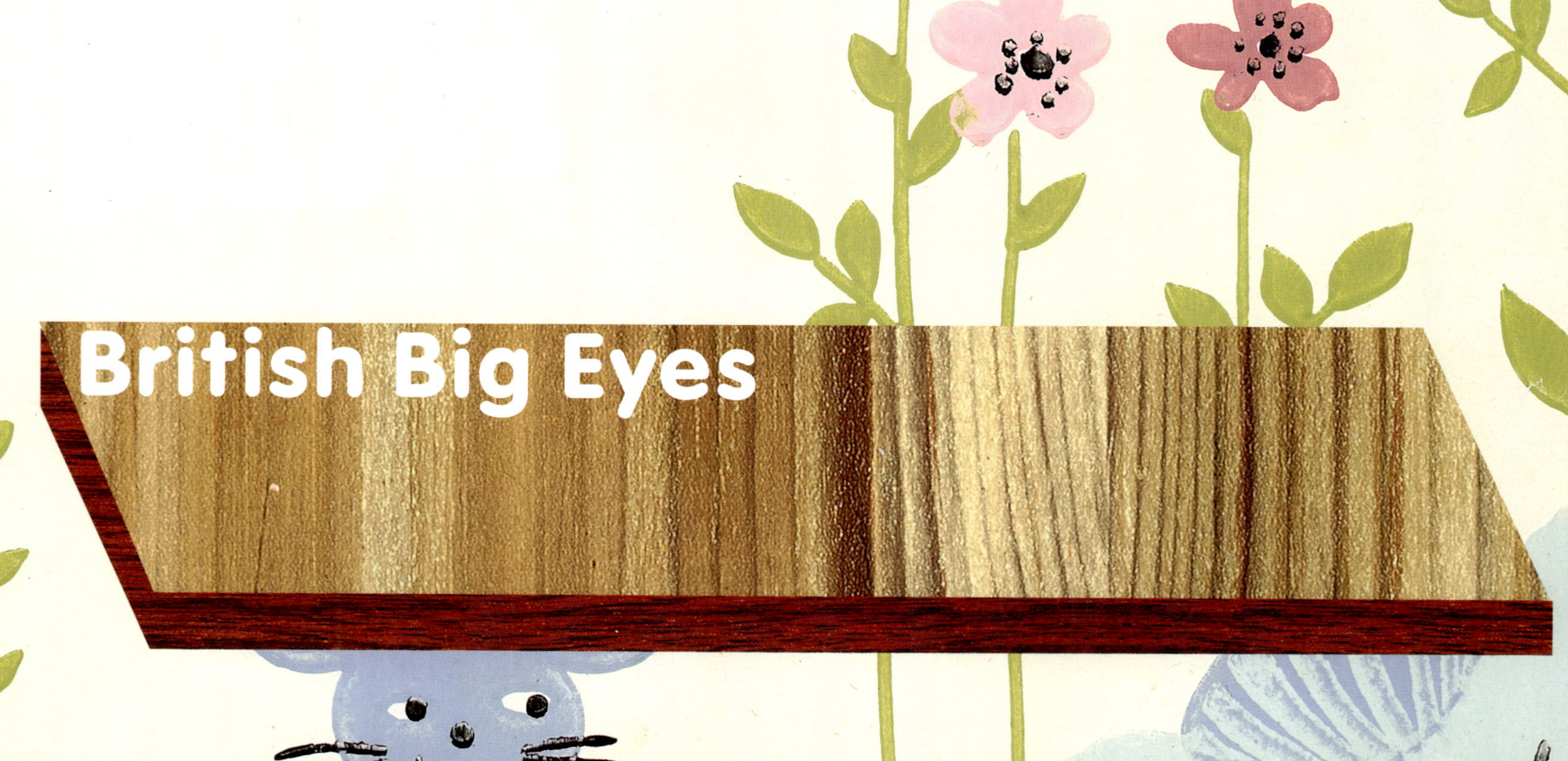

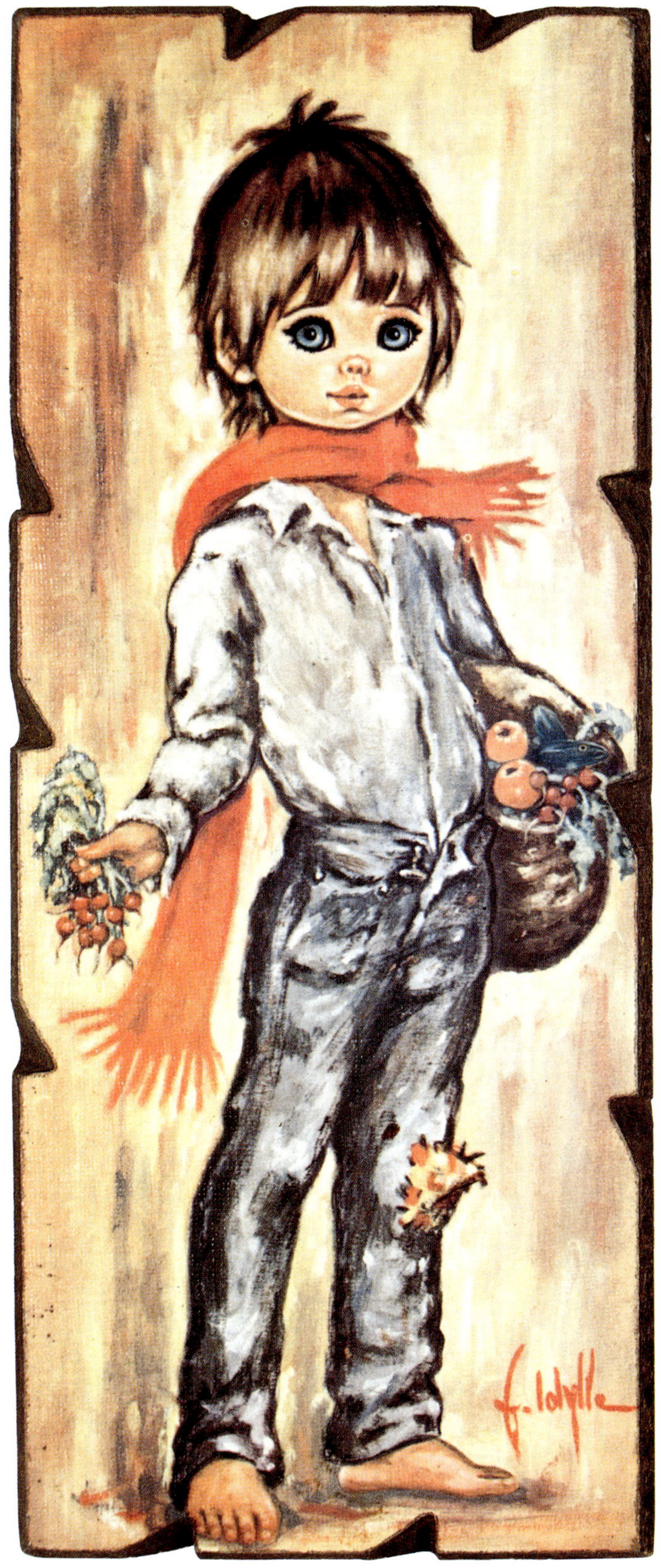

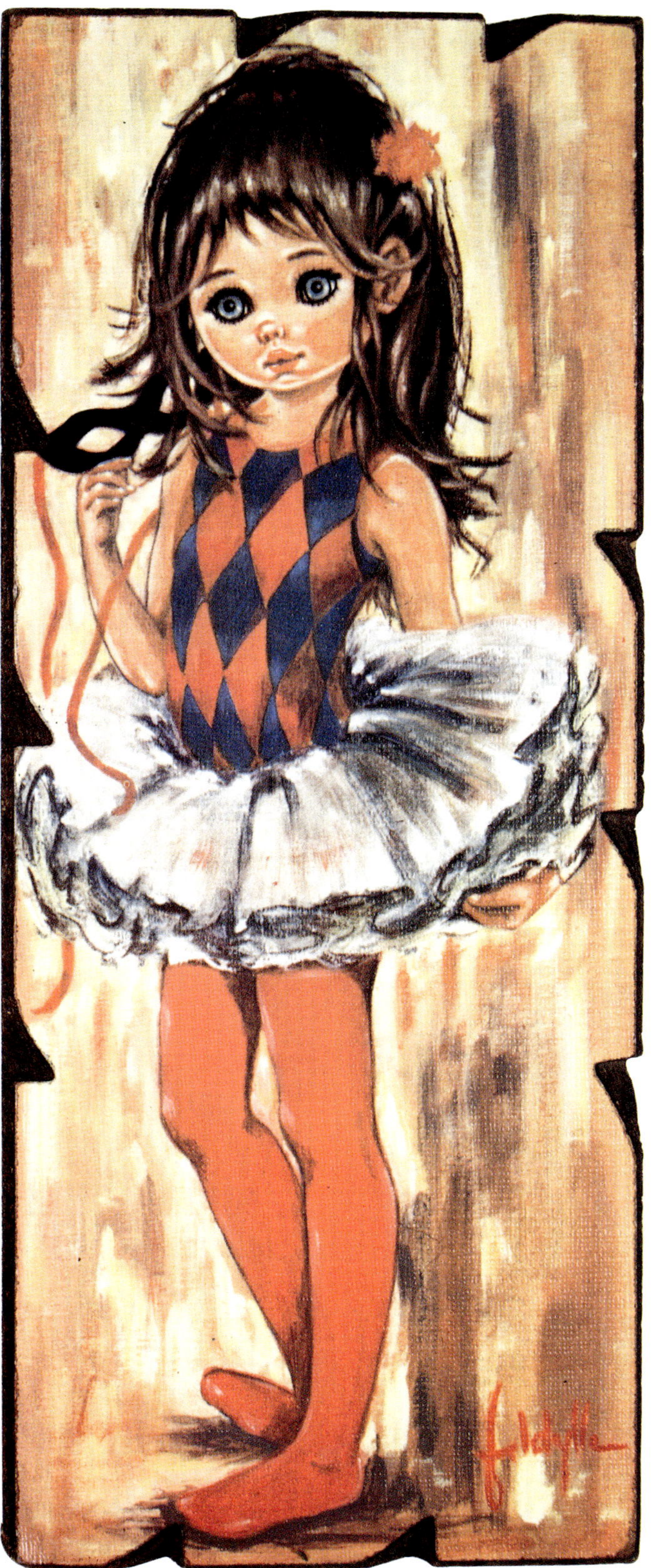

F Idylle **A Right Pair**

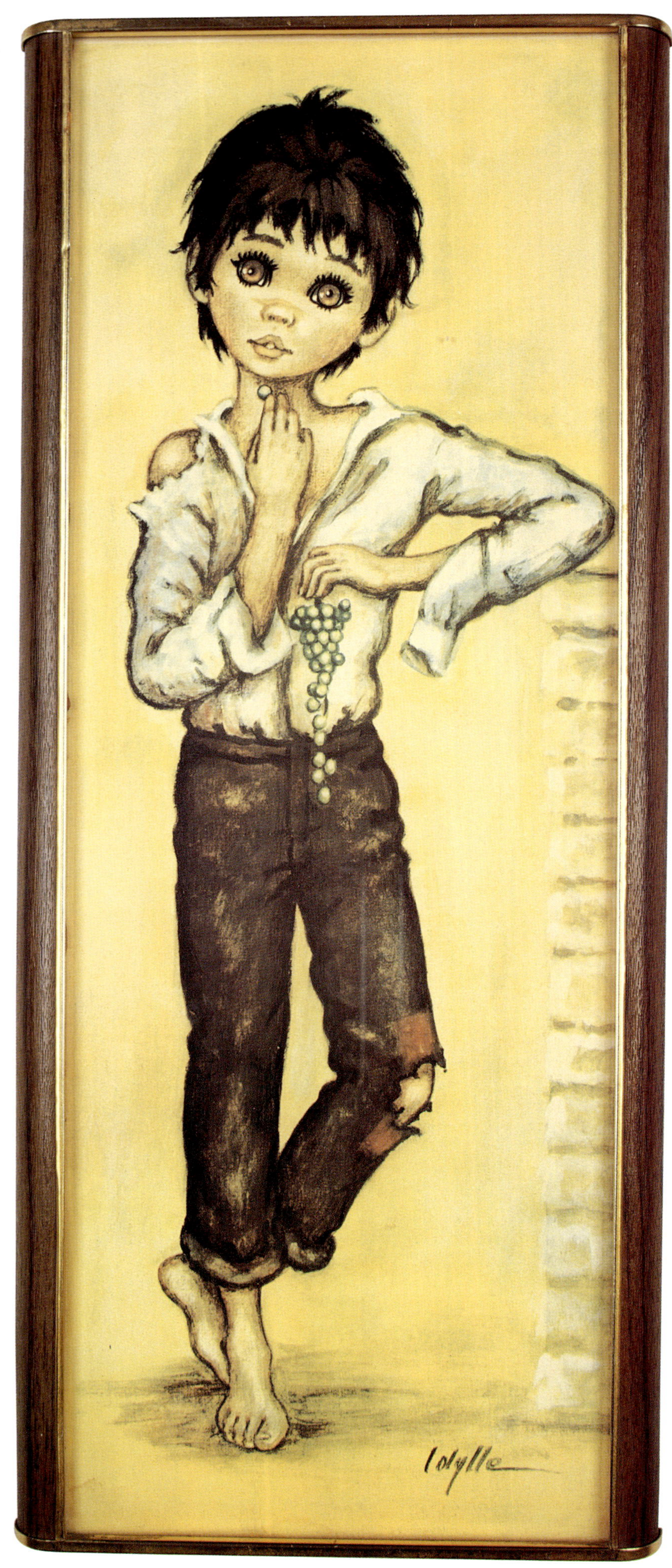

F Idylle **Before and After**

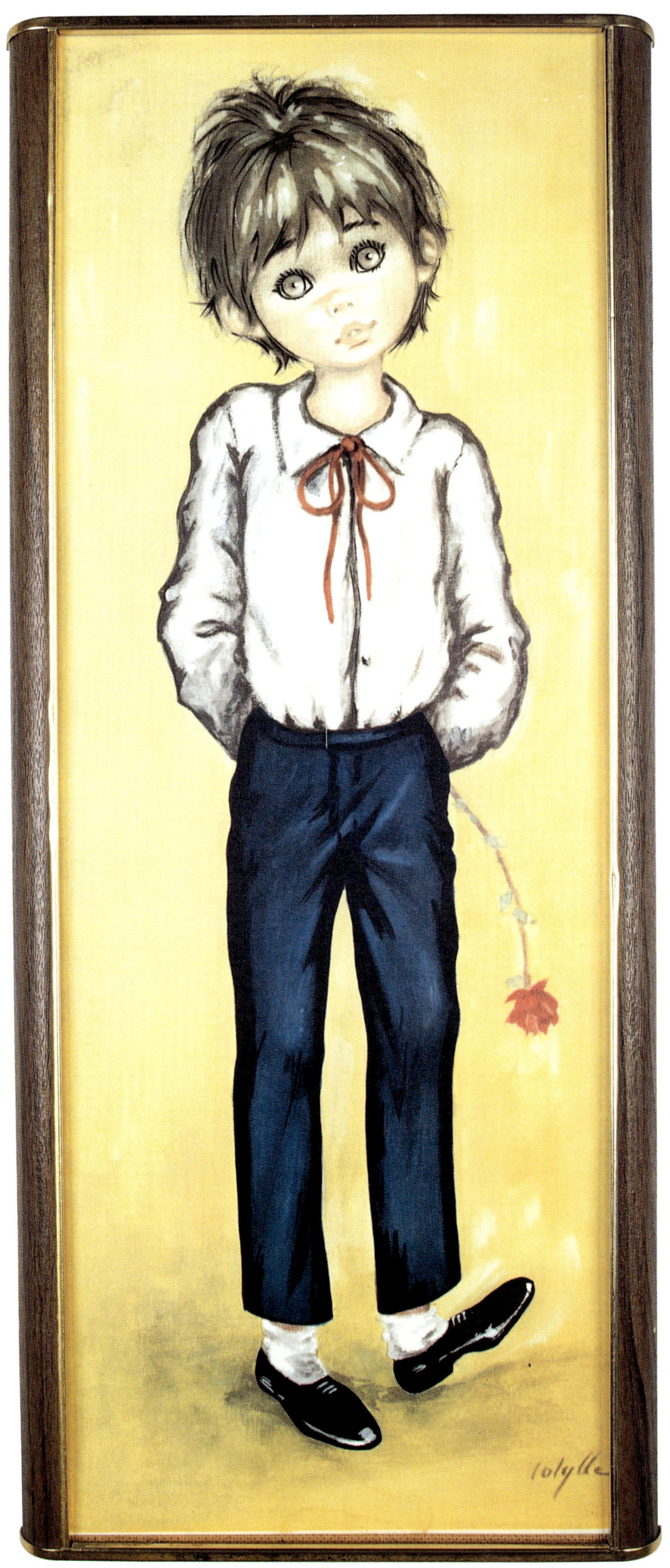

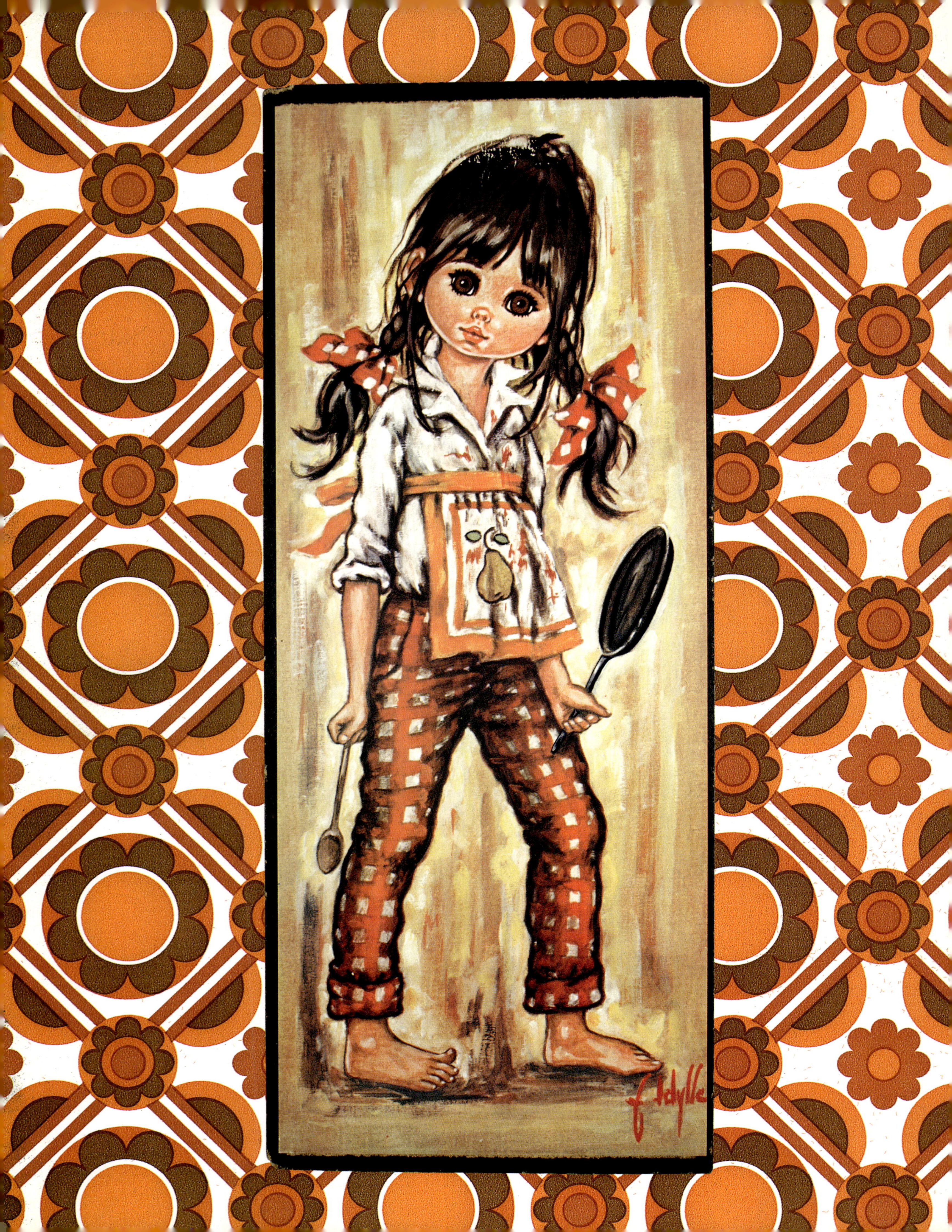
f. Idylle

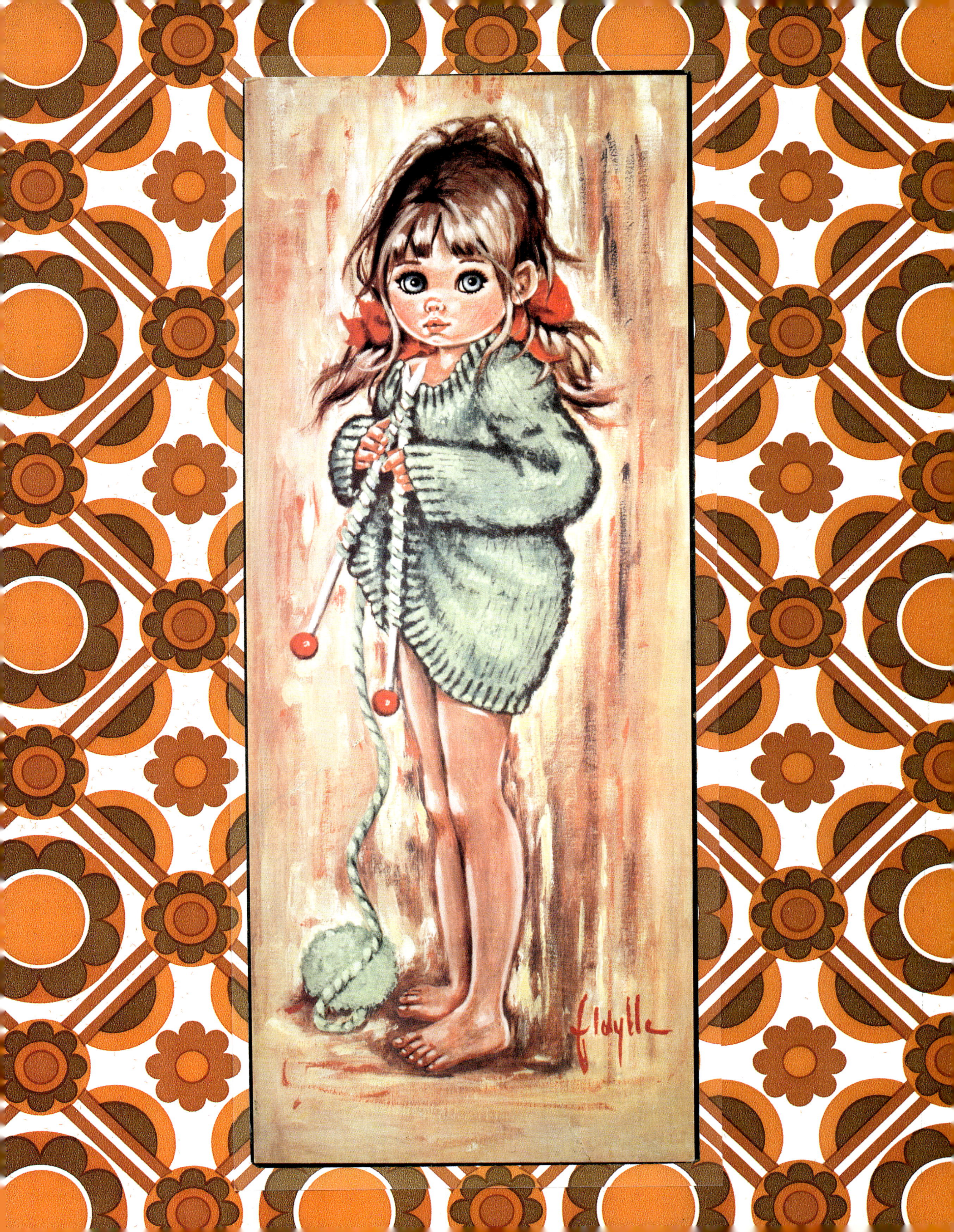

preceding pages: F Idylle **We Have To Cook For Ourselves and Knit Our Own Clothes**

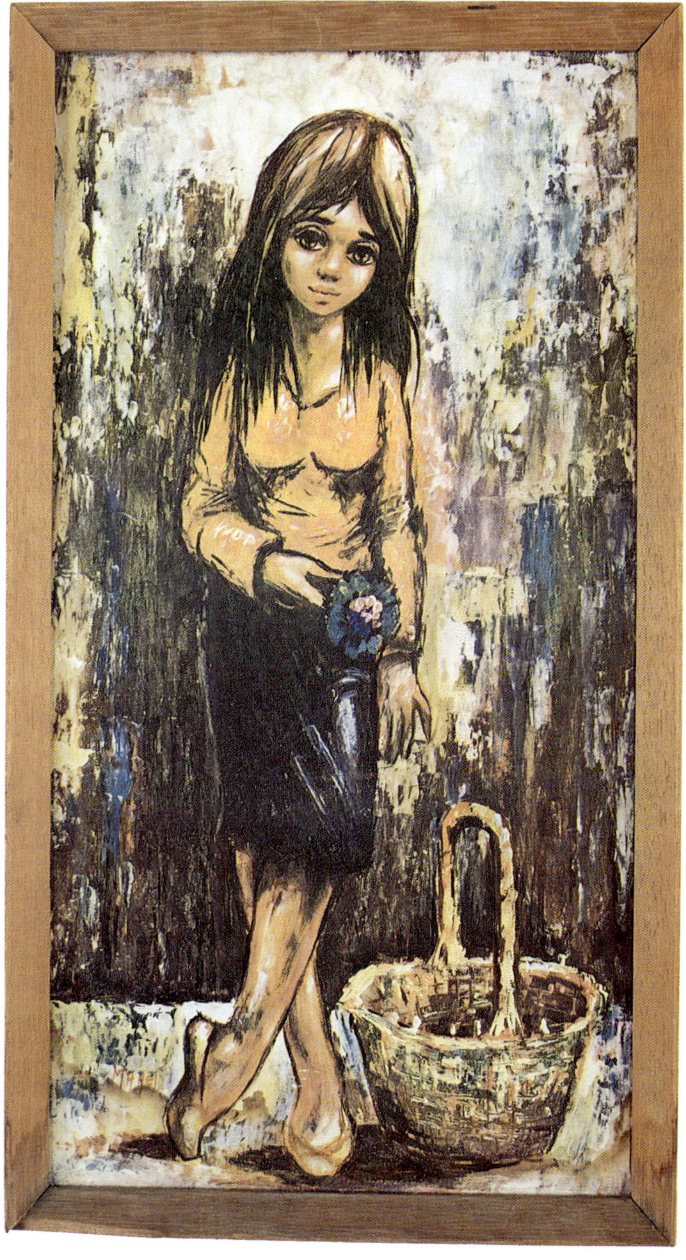

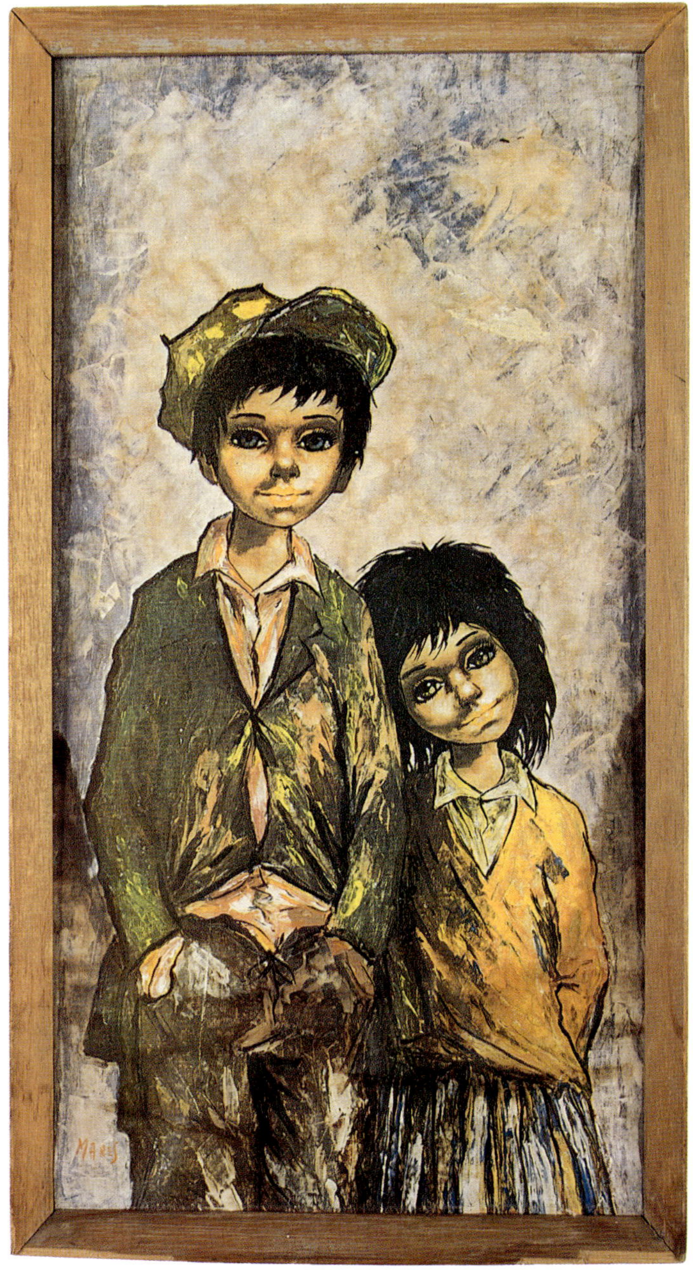

Manes **Shabby Chic**

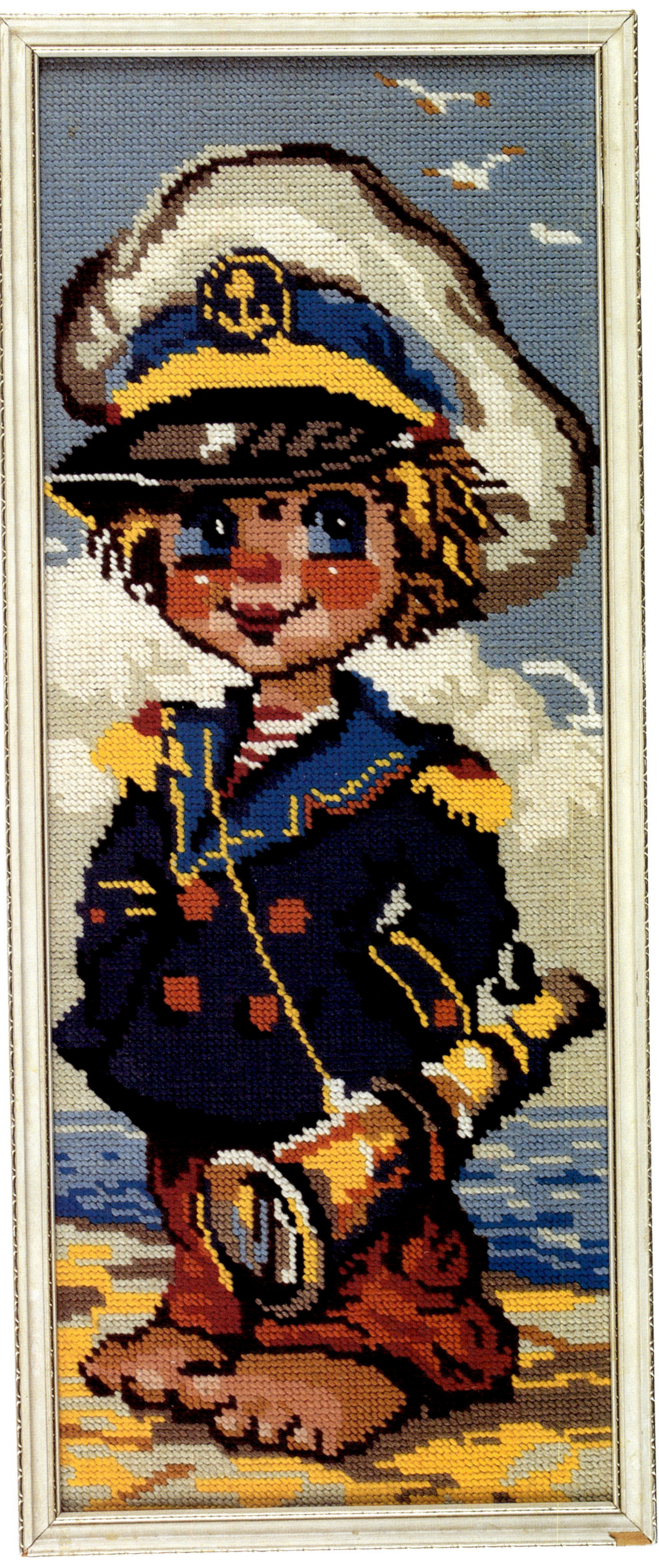

Unknown Artist **Needlecraft Sailor**

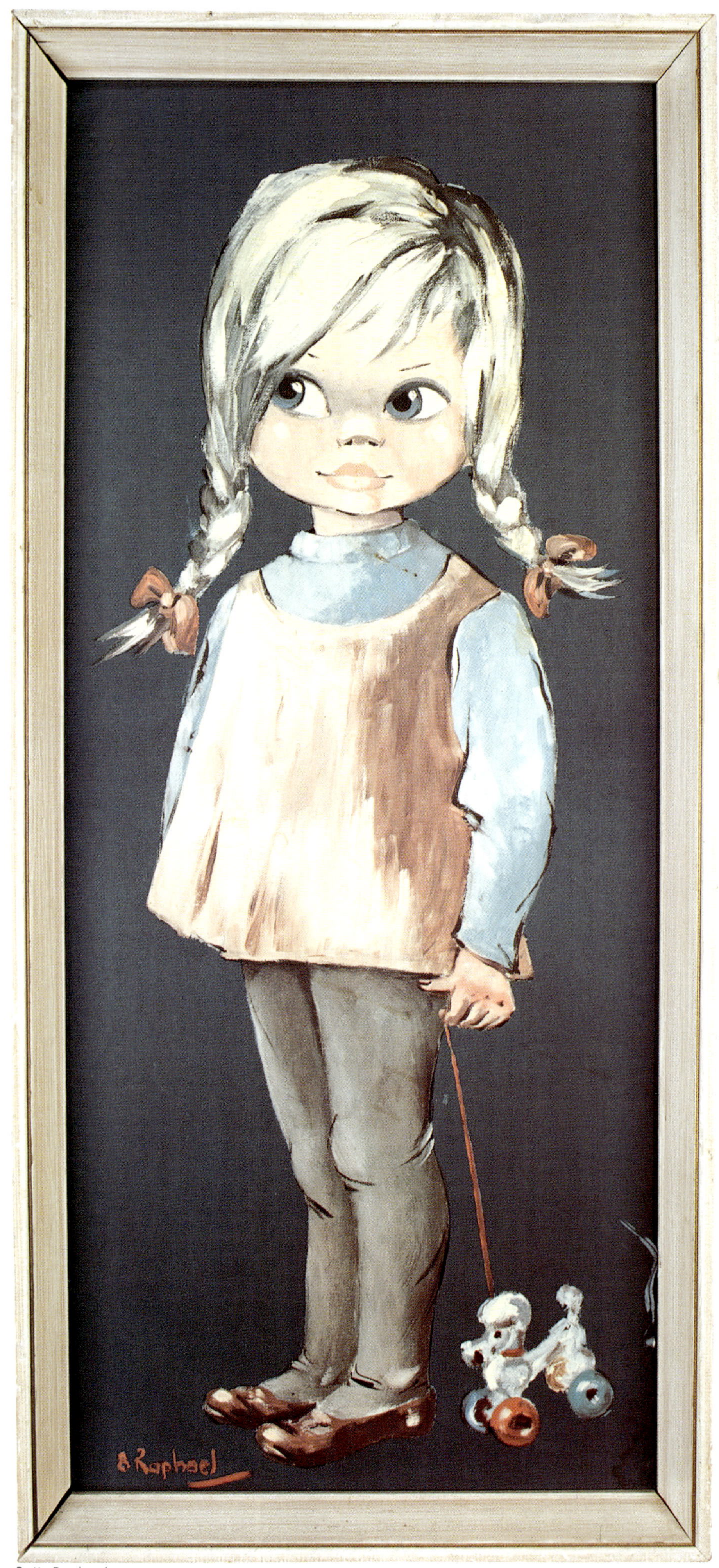

Betty Raphael **Big Eyes, Cute Hair No 1**

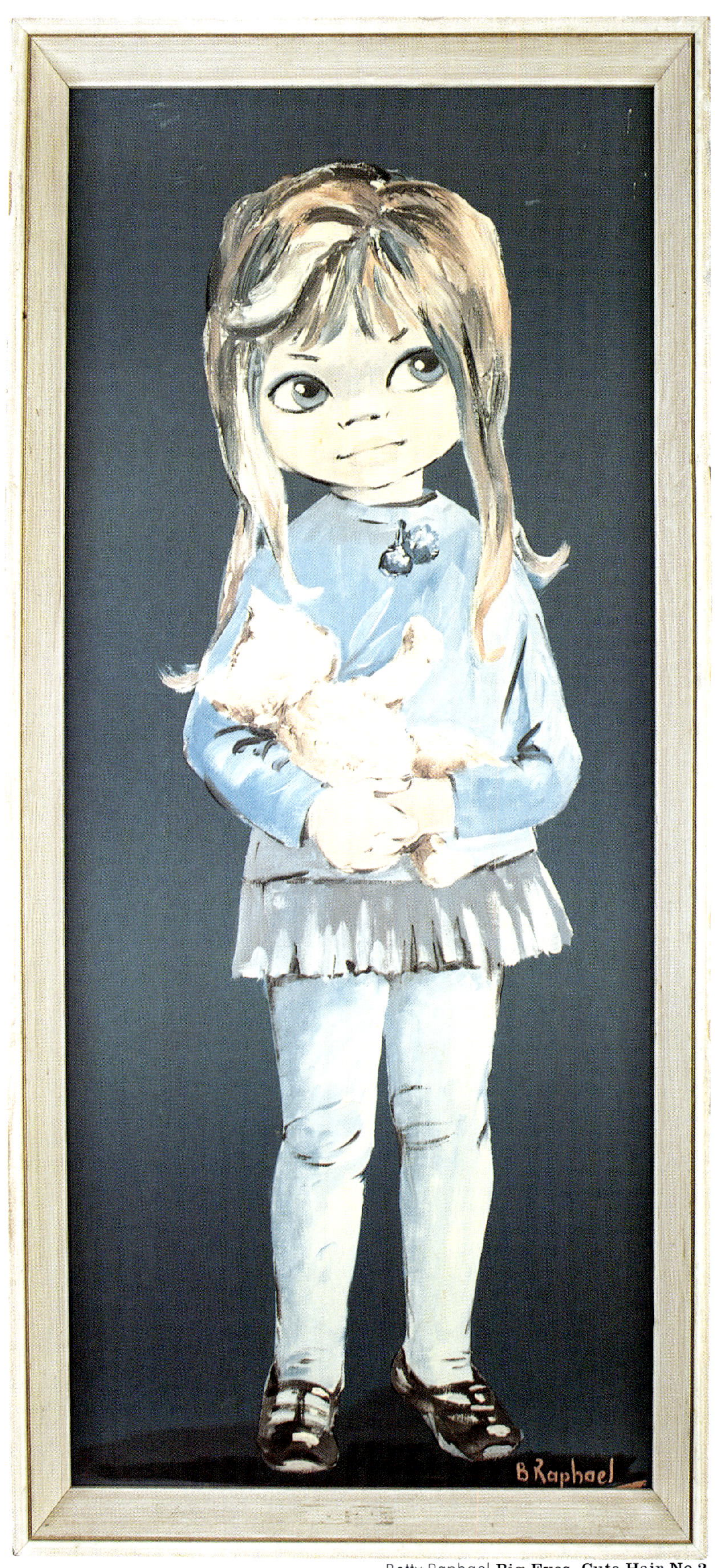

Betty Raphael **Big Eyes, Cute Hair No 2**

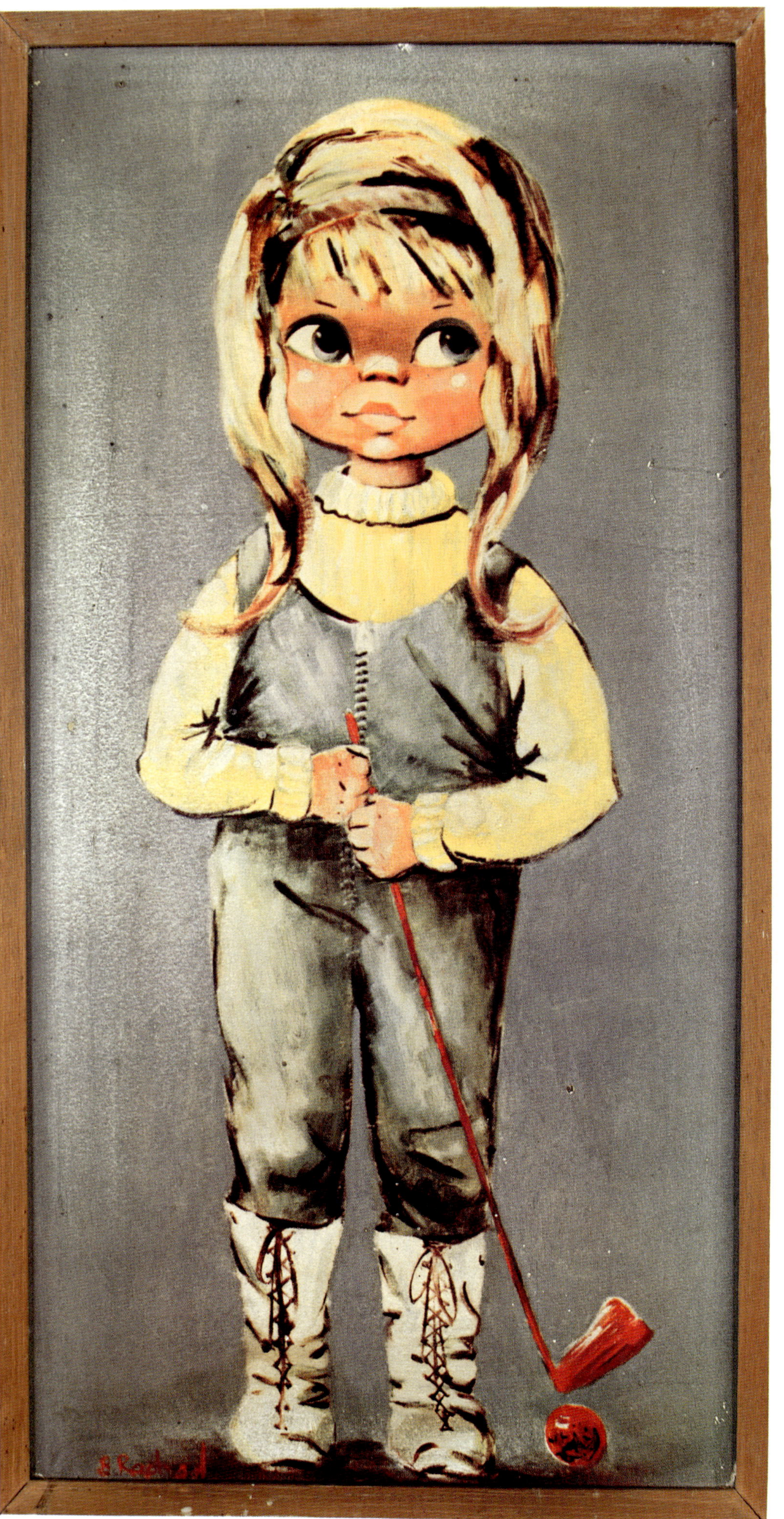

Betty Raphael **Anyone For Golf**

Betty Raphael **Red Tights**

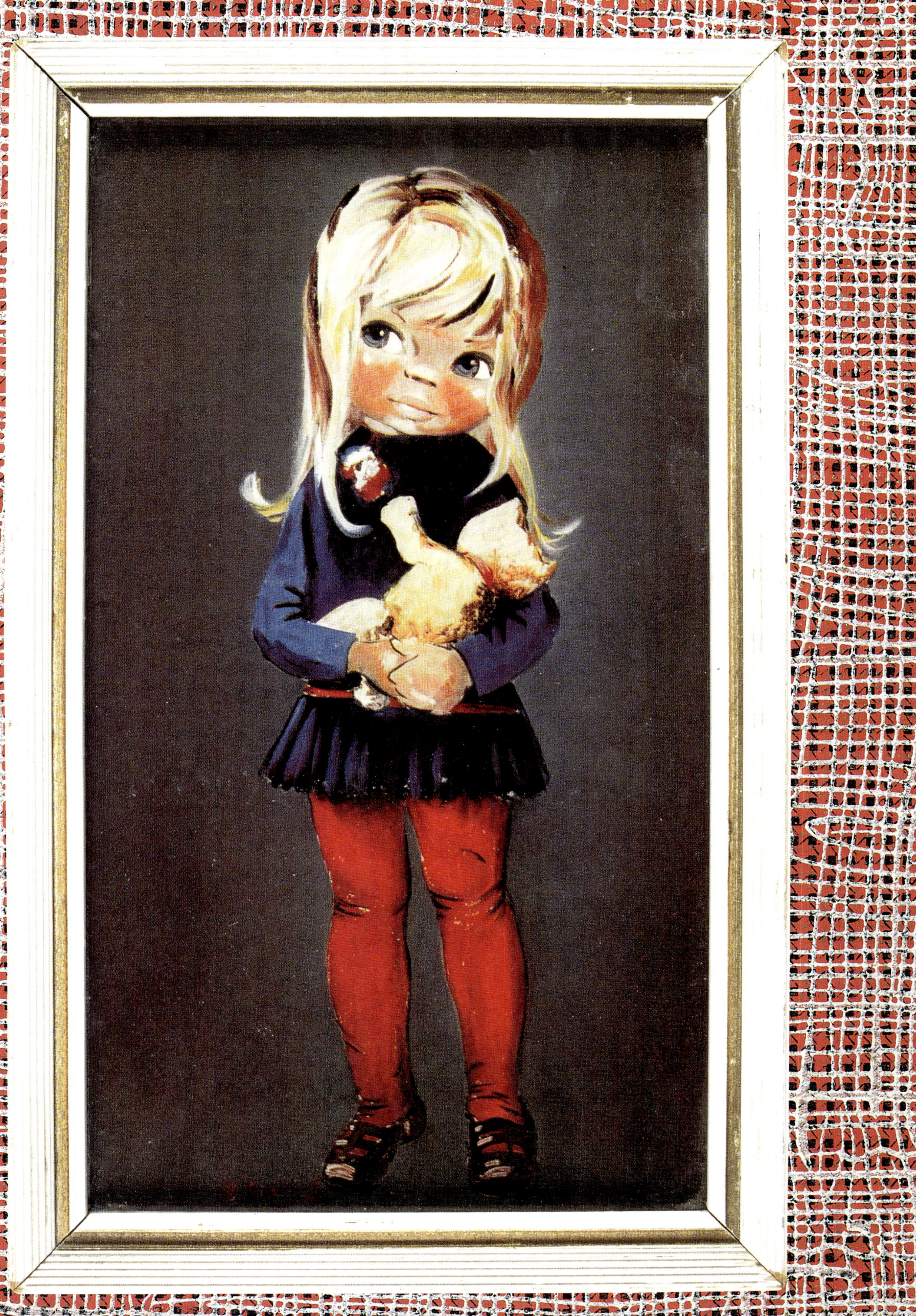

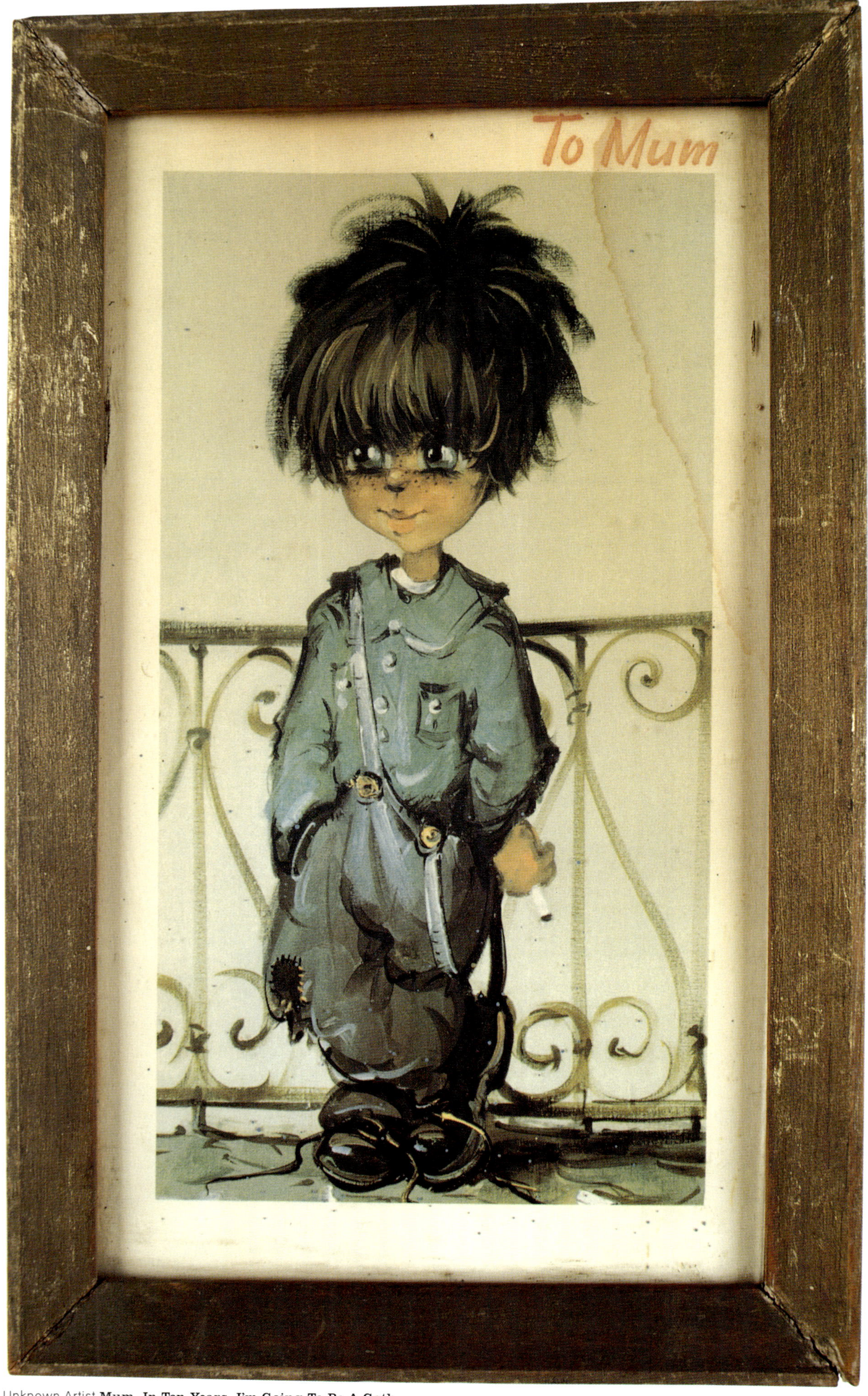

Unknown Artist **Mum, In Ten Years, I'm Going To Be A Goth**

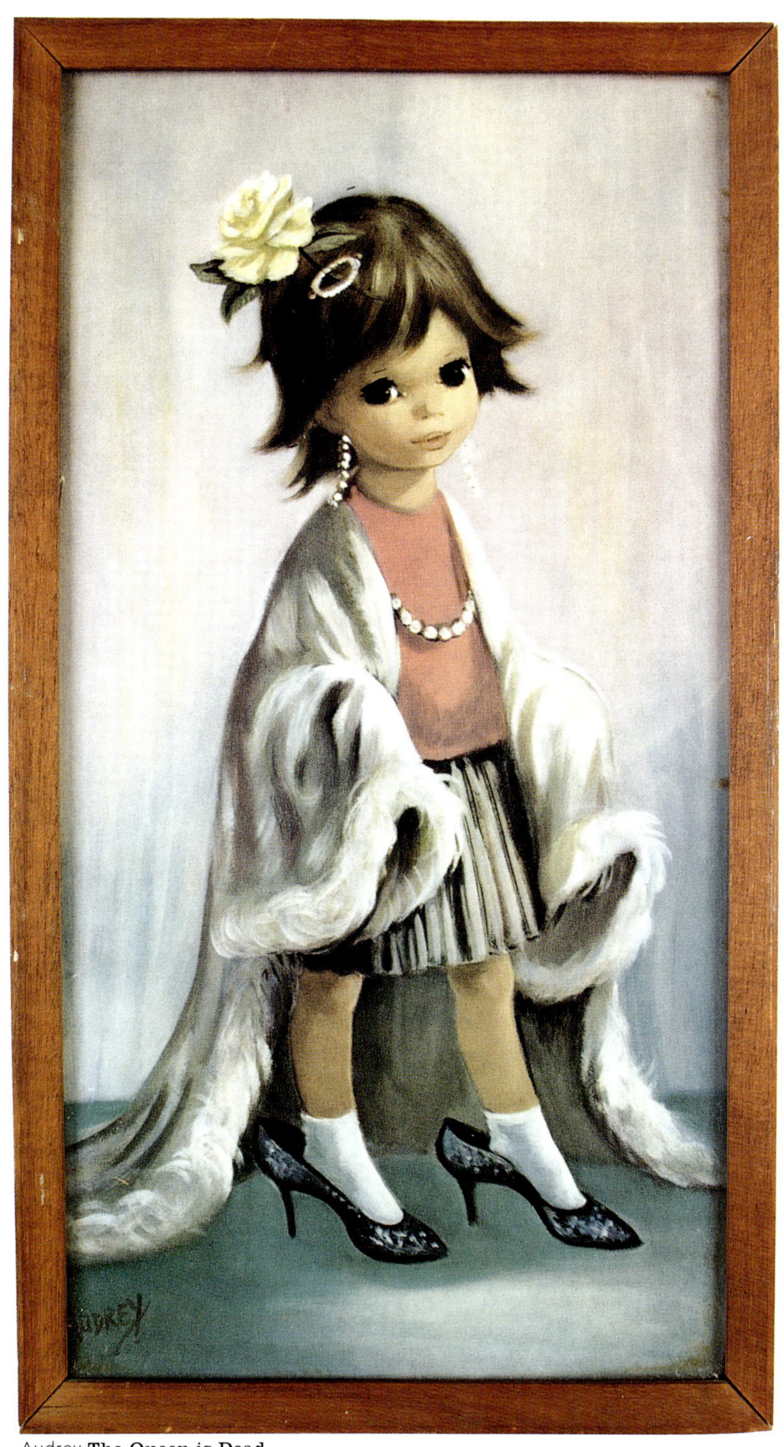

Audrey **The Queen is Dead**

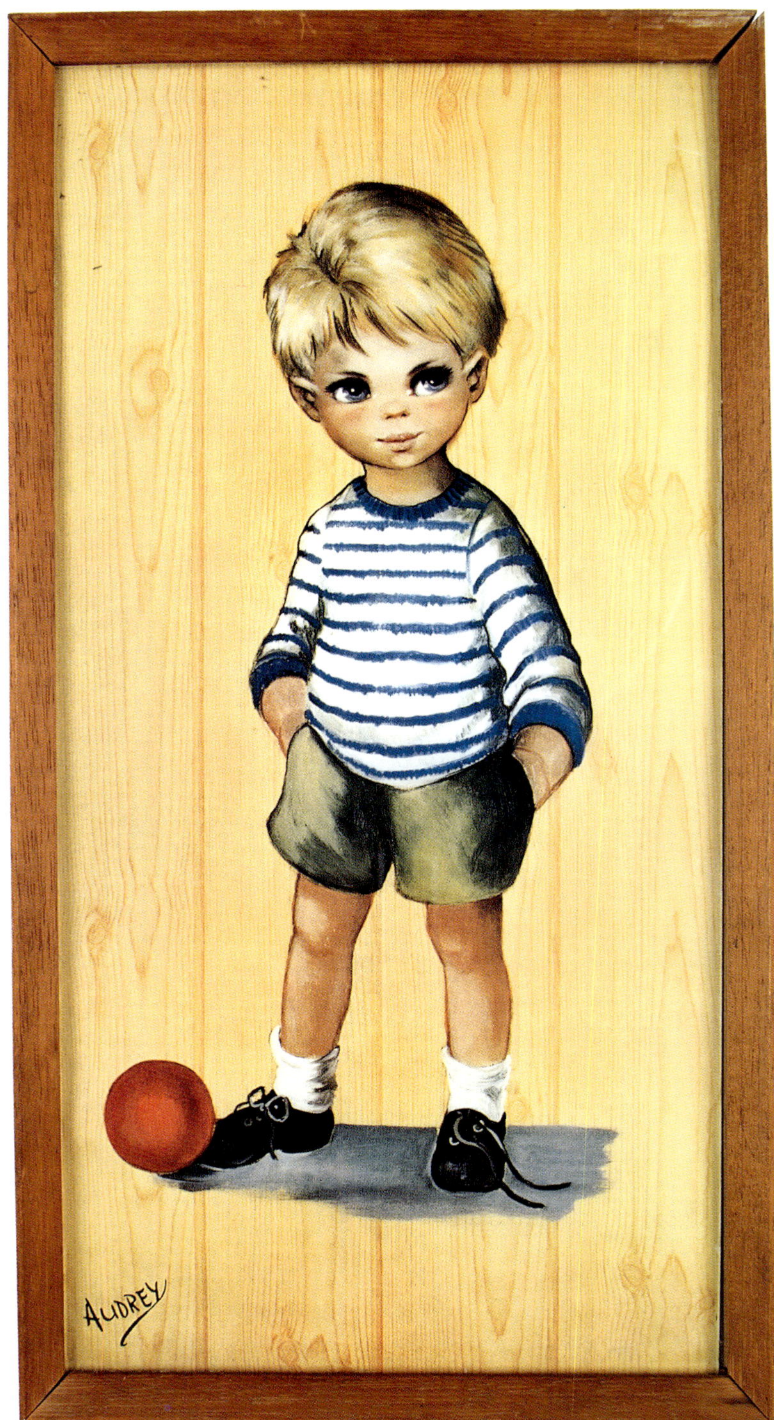

Audrey **I Want To Be Adored**

D Golding **Big Eyes and Big Hair No 2**; D Golding **Tiddler**

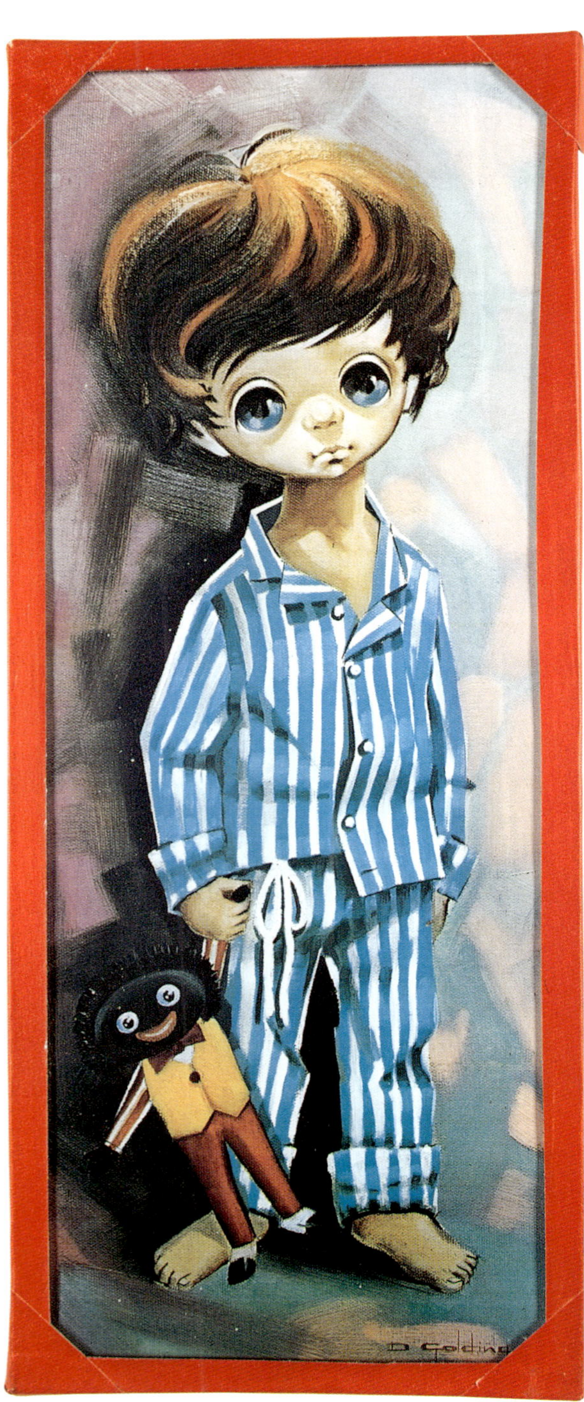

D Golding **Gollywogs Also Love Big Eyes**

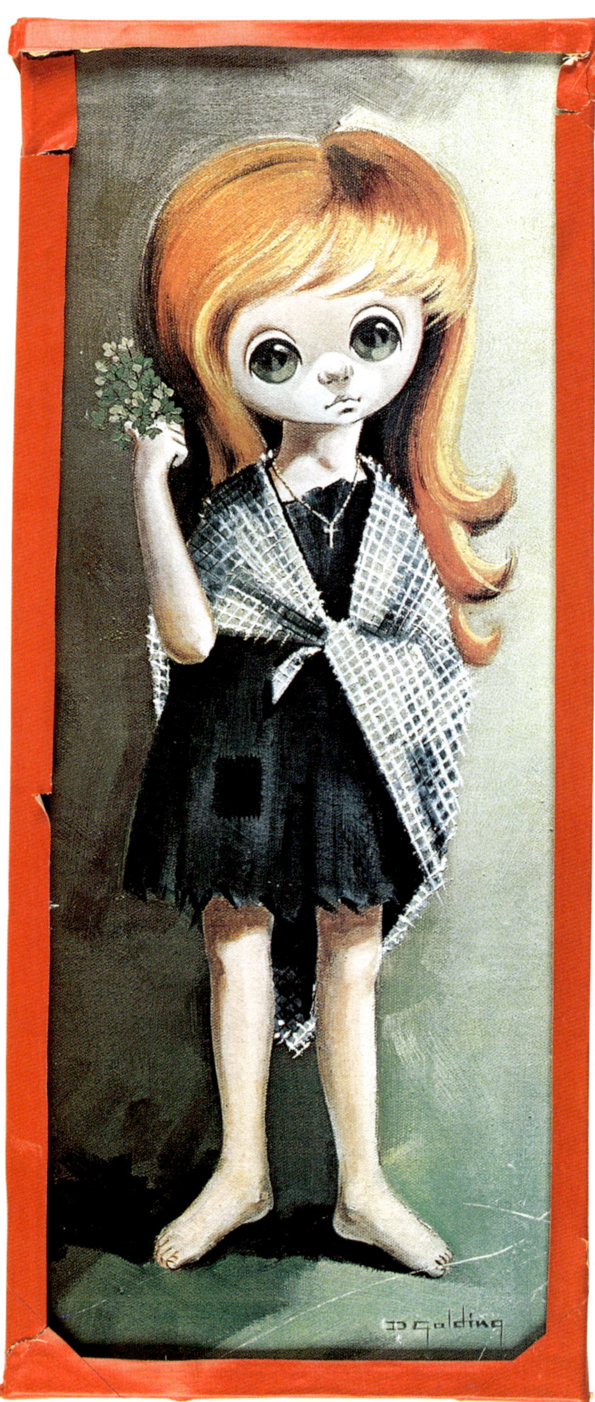

D Golding **Big Eyes and Big Hair No 1**

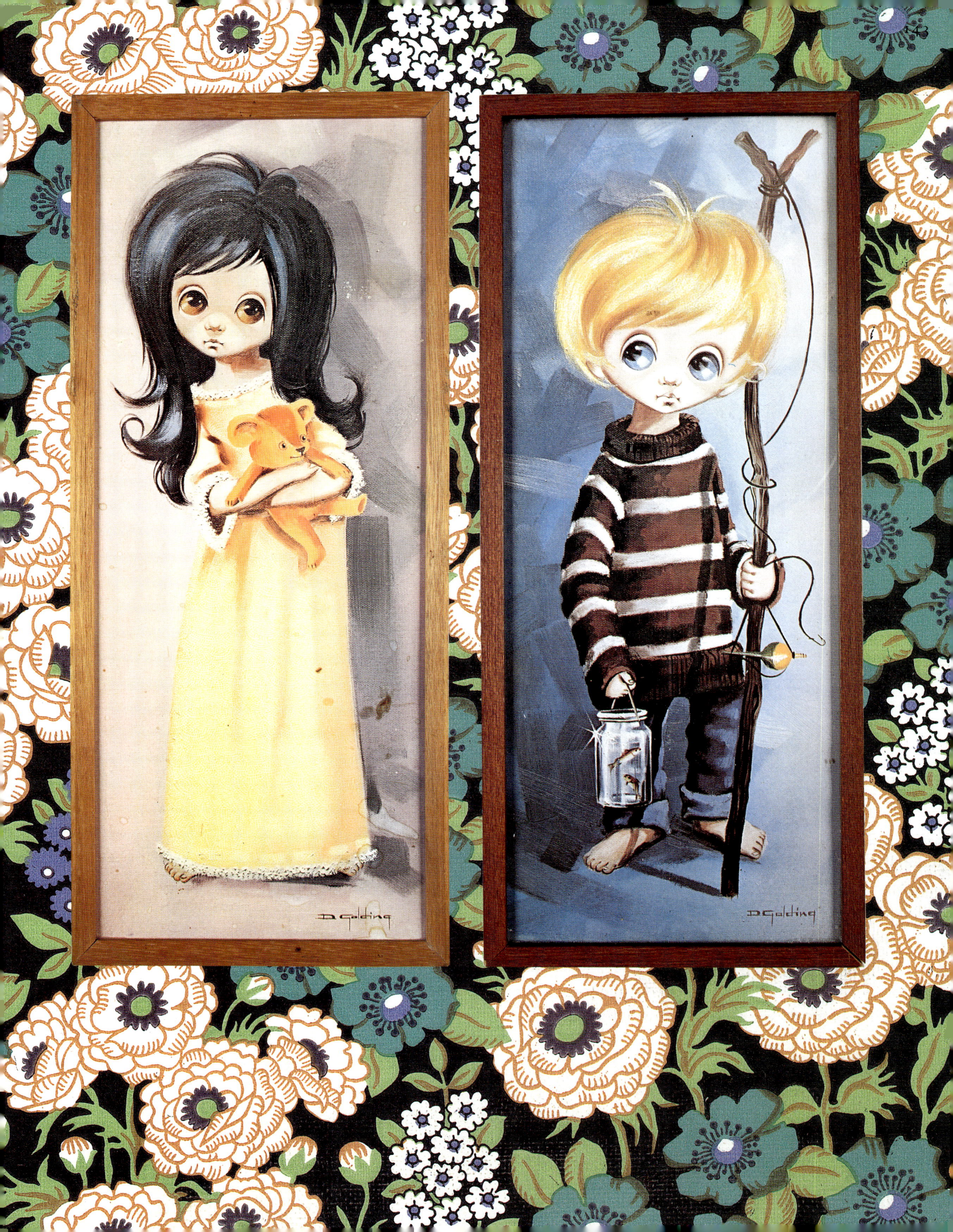
D.Golding
D.Golding

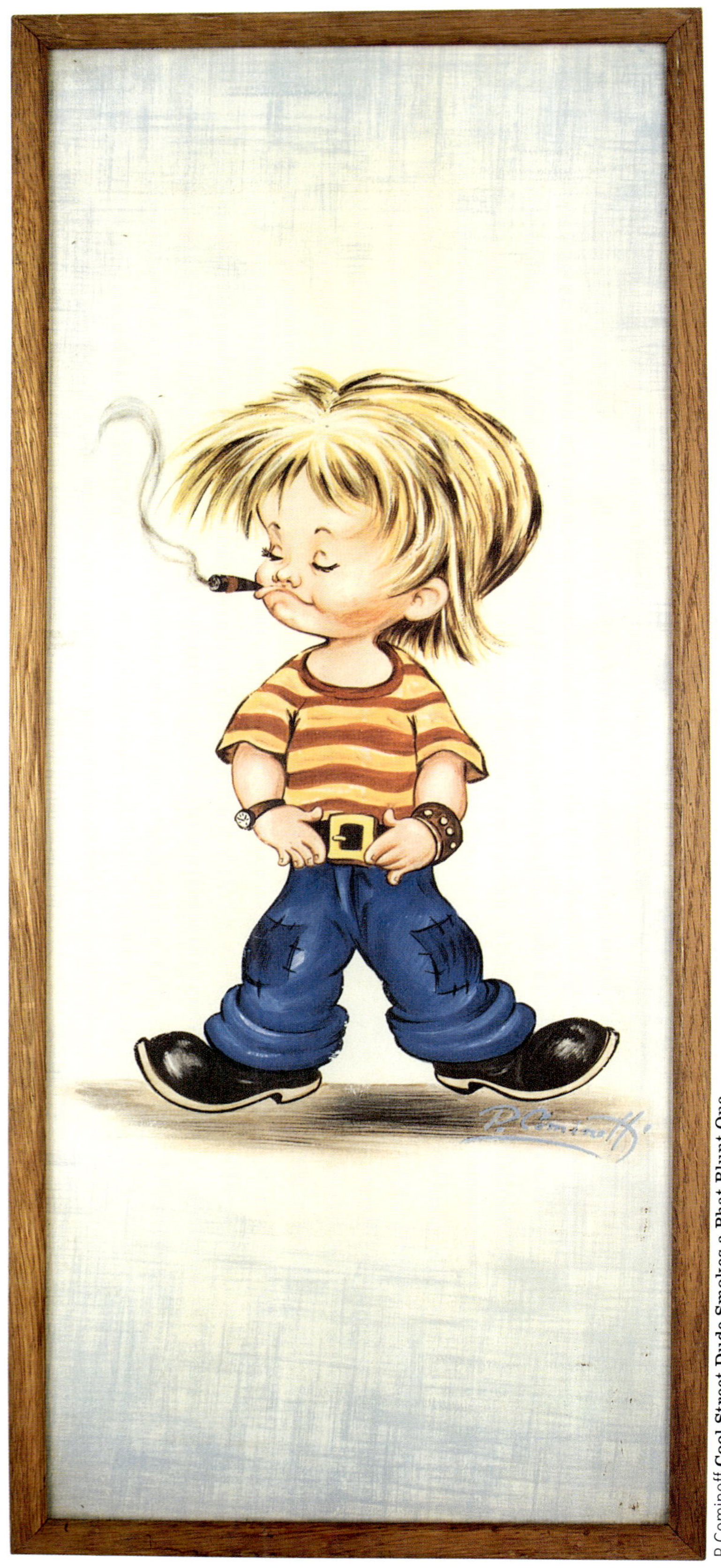

P Cominoff **Cool Street Dude Smokes a Phat Blunt One**

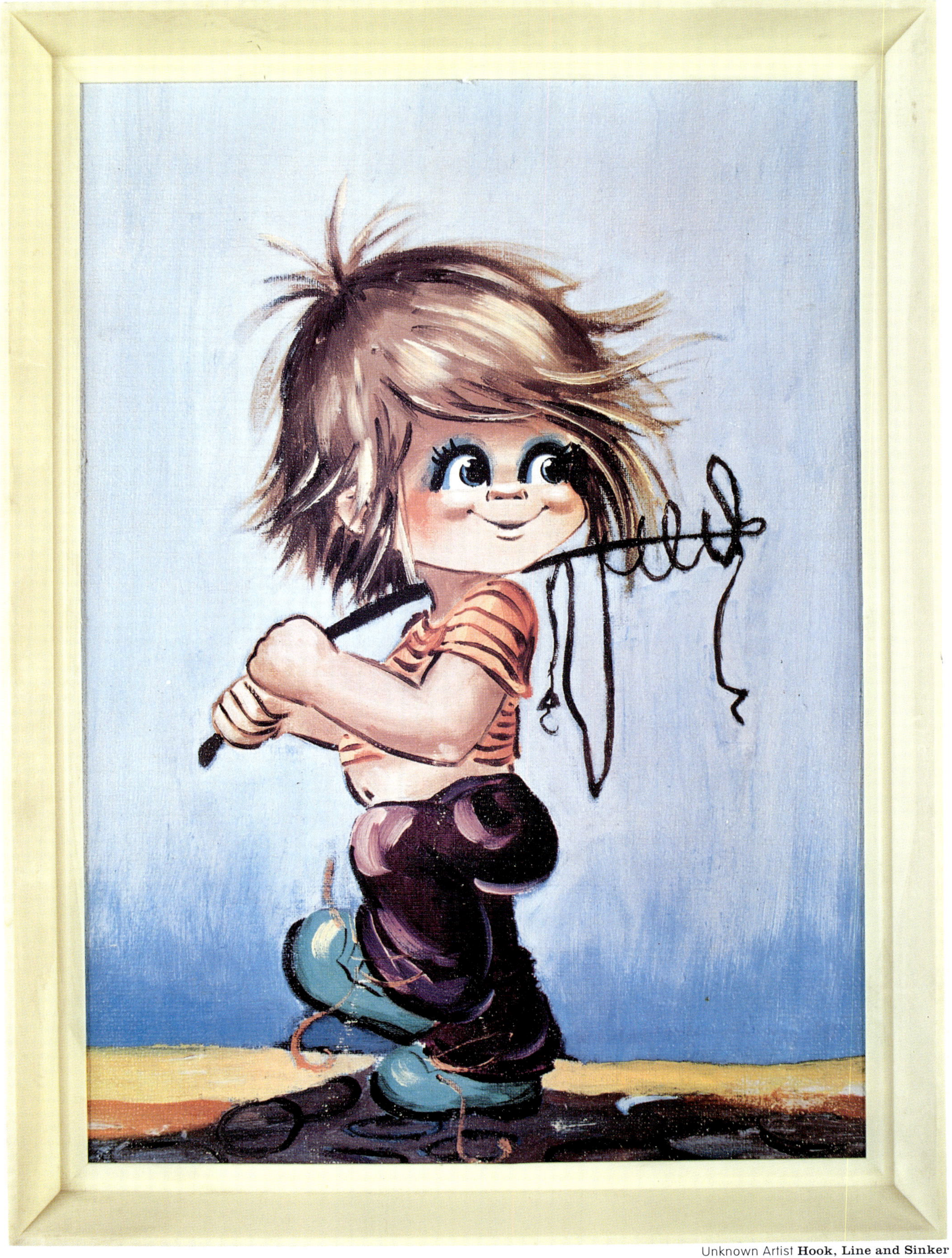

Unknown Artist **Hook, Line and Sinker**

Between October 1965 and June 1970, **Dallas Simpson** painted seventy big-eyed urchins from her caravan near Worthing, West Sussex. She had no children of her own. She received between £30 and £50 from an art publisher for the originals and the worldwide reproduction rights. Over five million of her prints were sold. She also painted under the pseudonym **Emma Louise** (pages 164-67), with a subtle change of style in painting, but with the same subject matter.

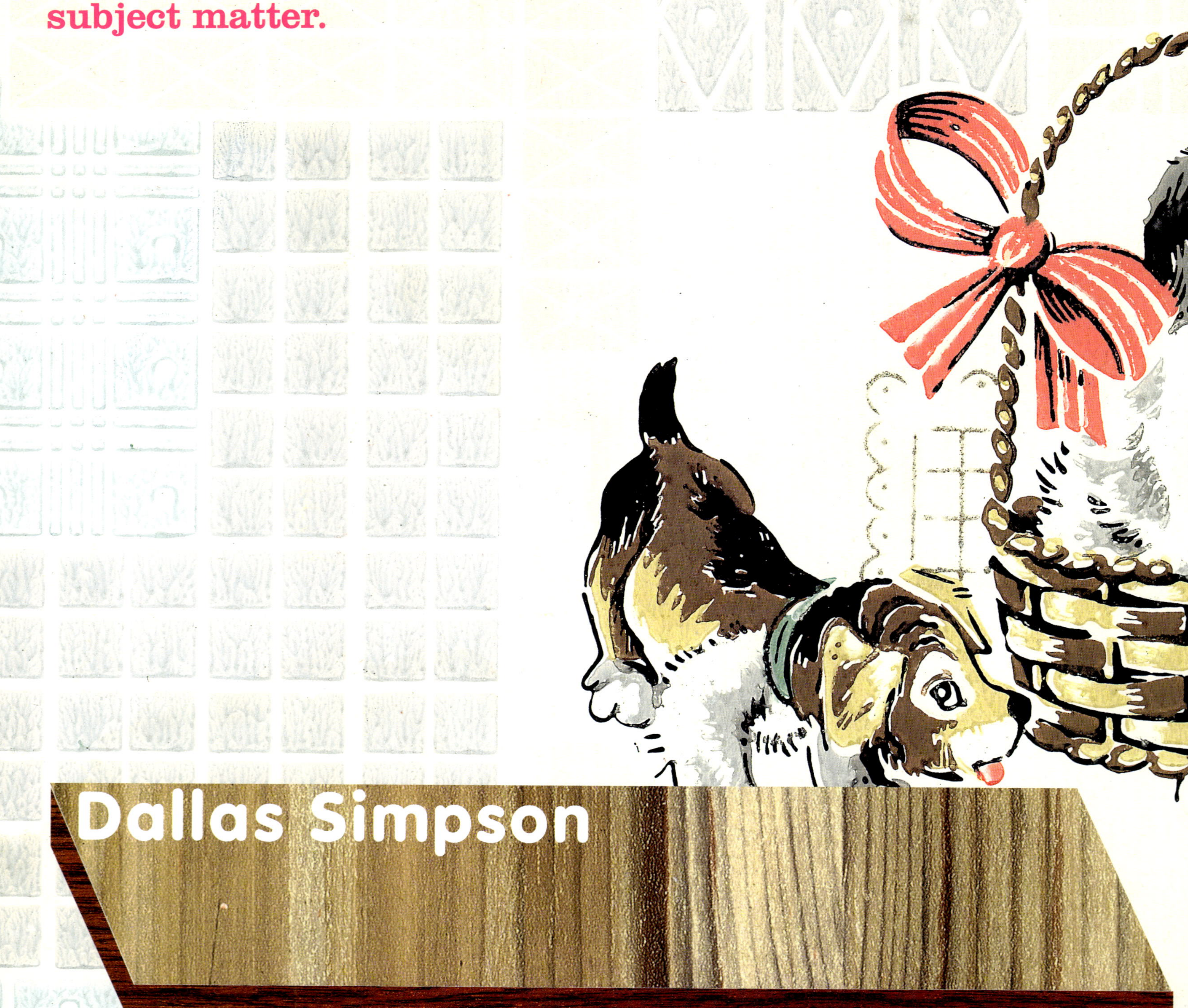

Dallas Simpson

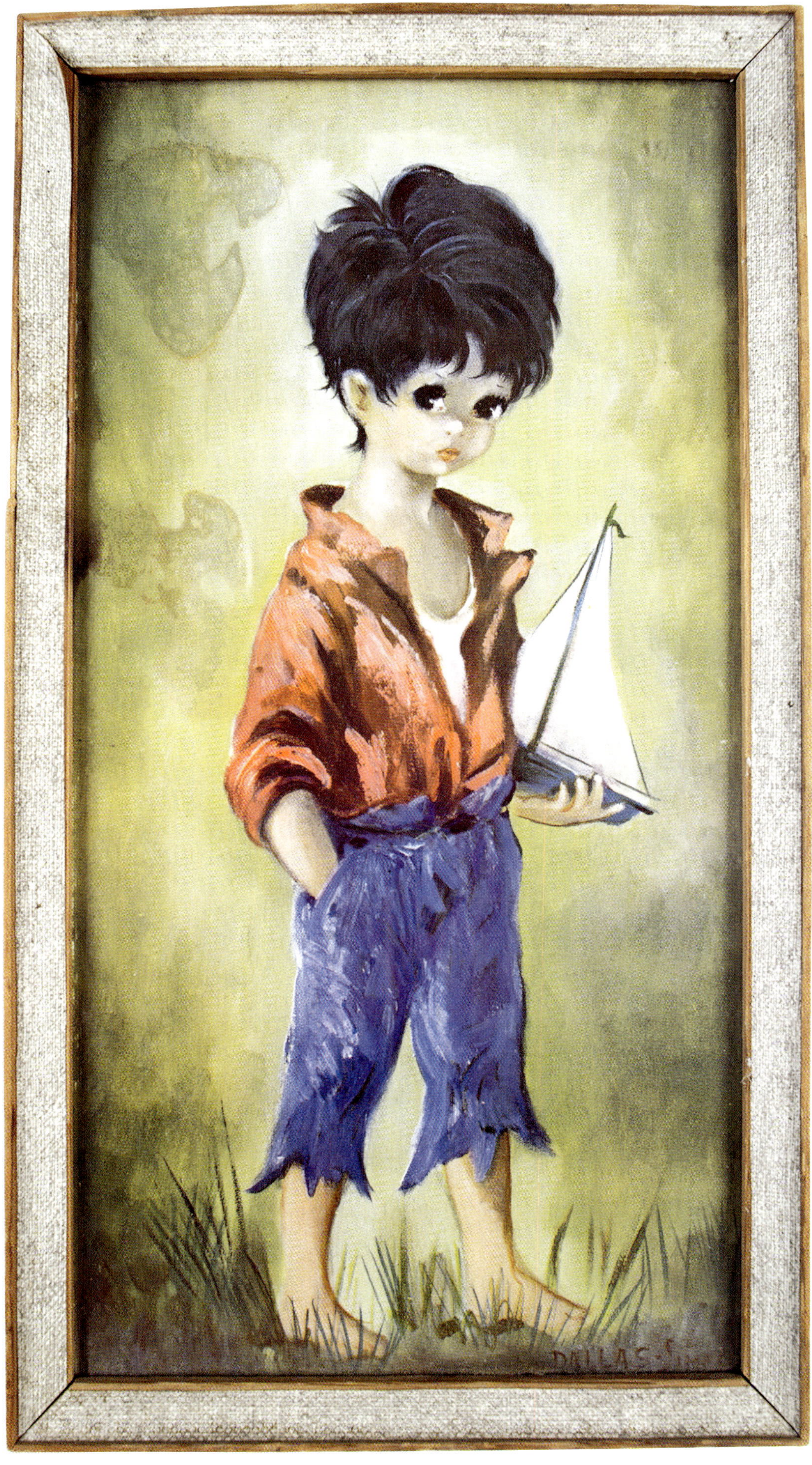

Dallas Simpson **Boy With Boat**

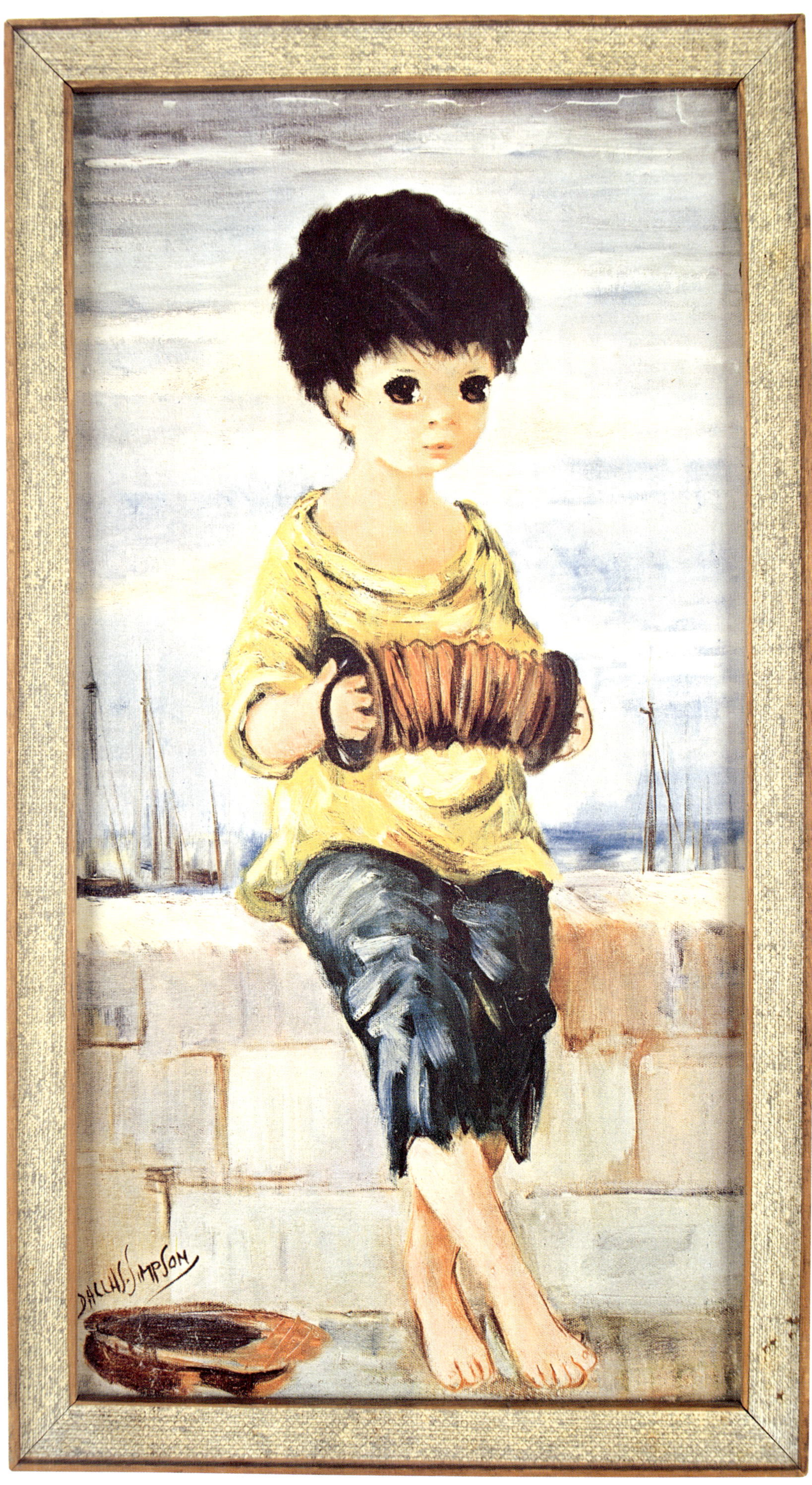

Dallas Simpson **Poor Musical Youth**

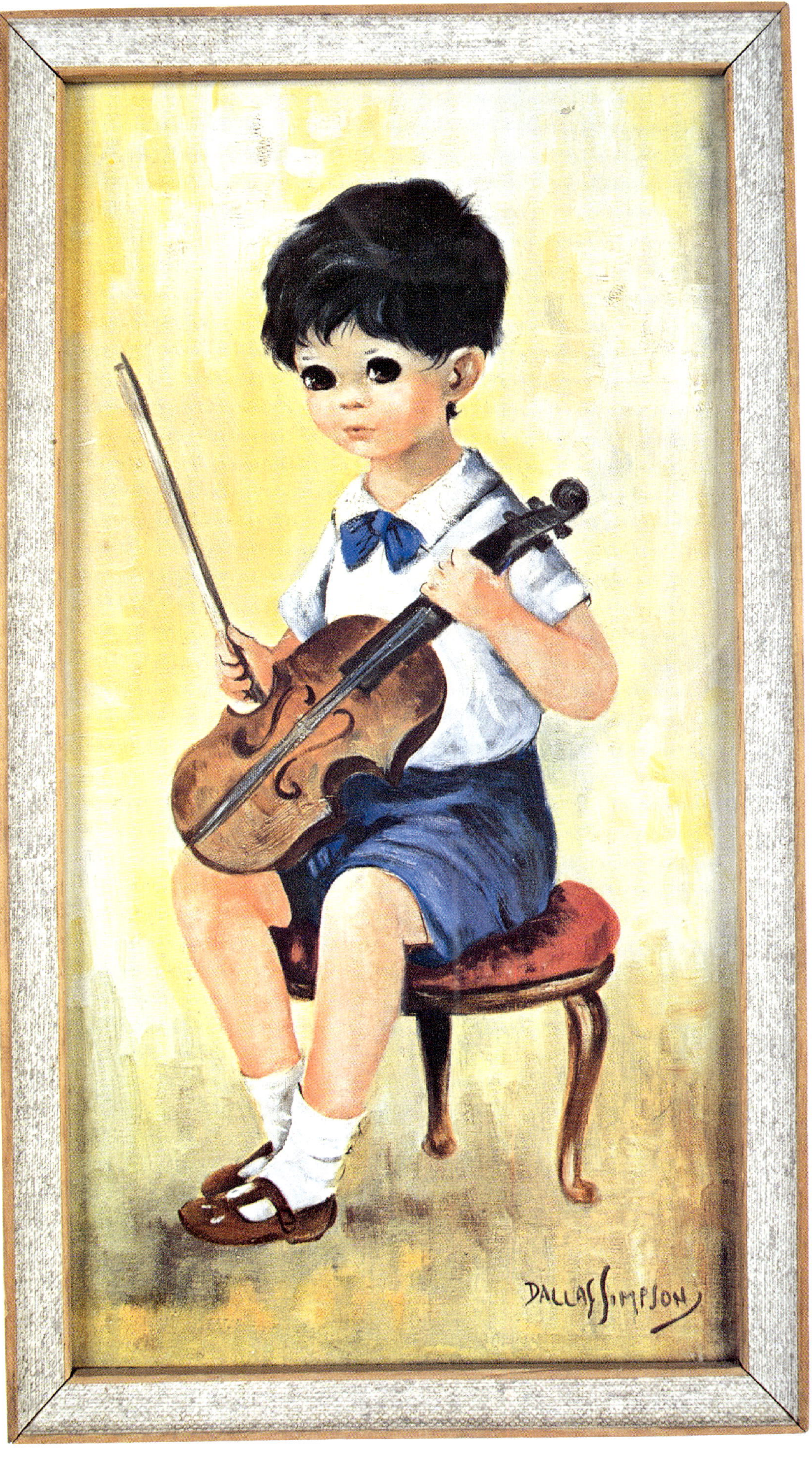

Dallas Simpson **Rich Musical Youth**

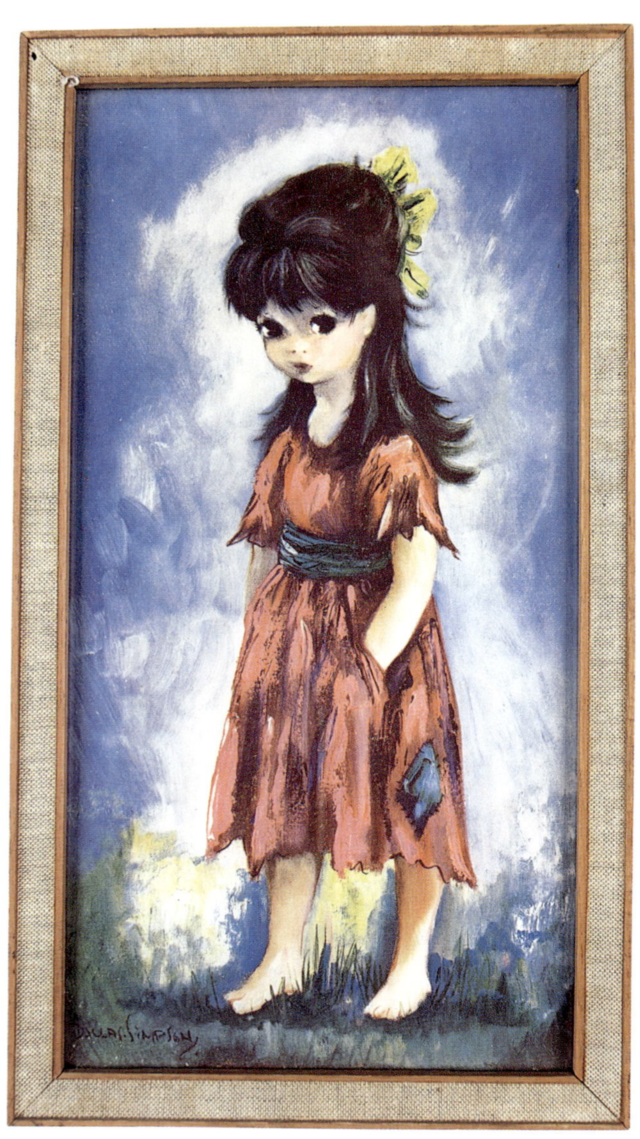

Dallas Simpson **Ripped Dress Lass**

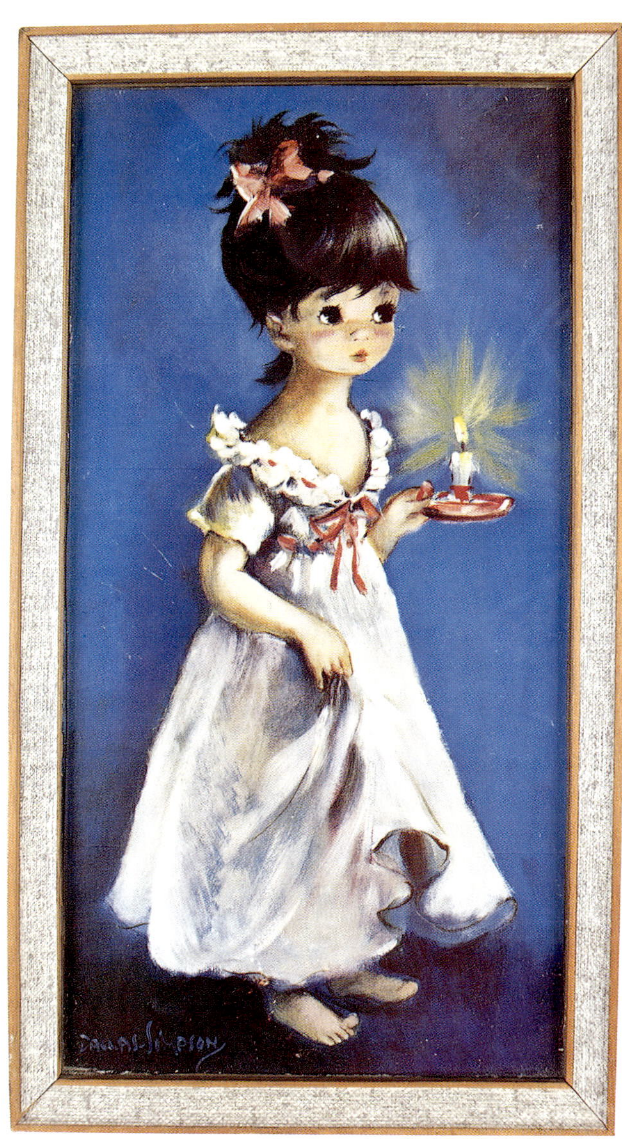

Dallas Simpson **Posh Little Candle Lass**

Dallas Simpson **Dressing-Gown Daniel**

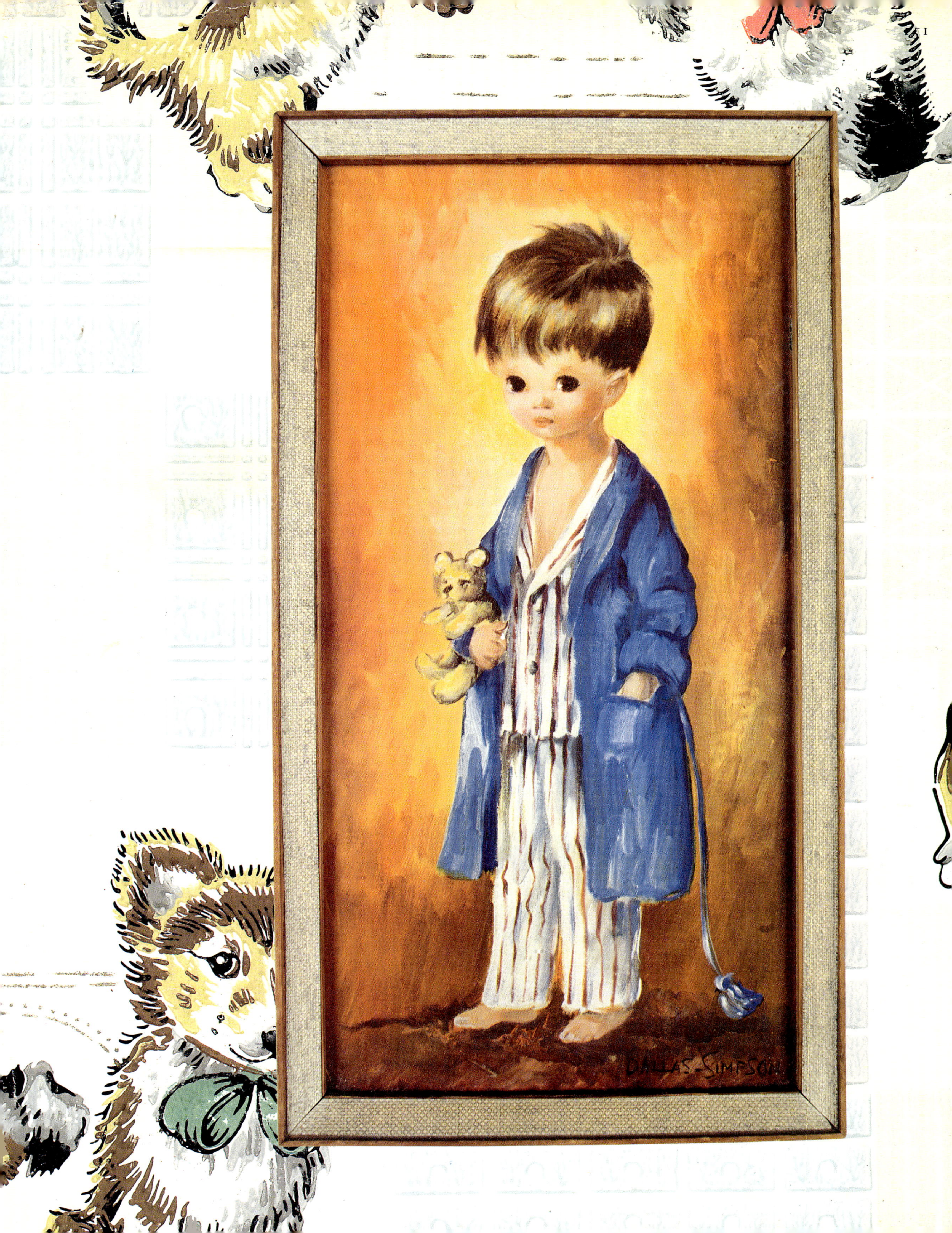
DALLAS-SIMPSON

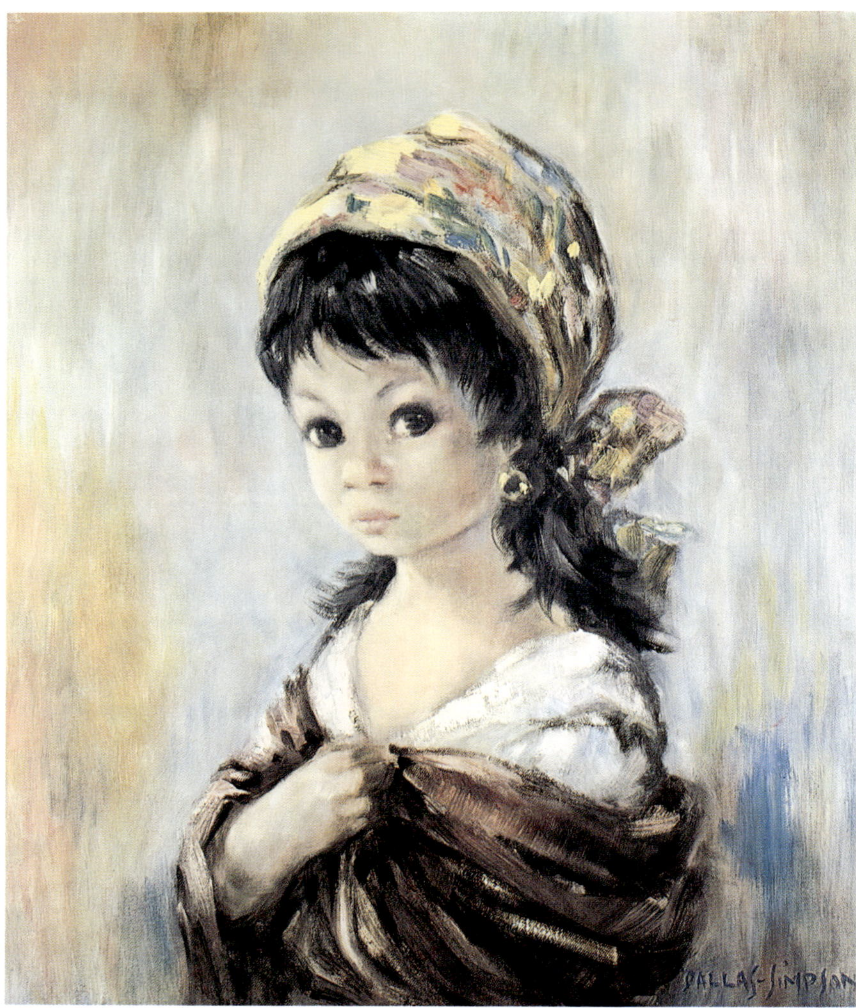

Dallas Simpson **Waif** 1965

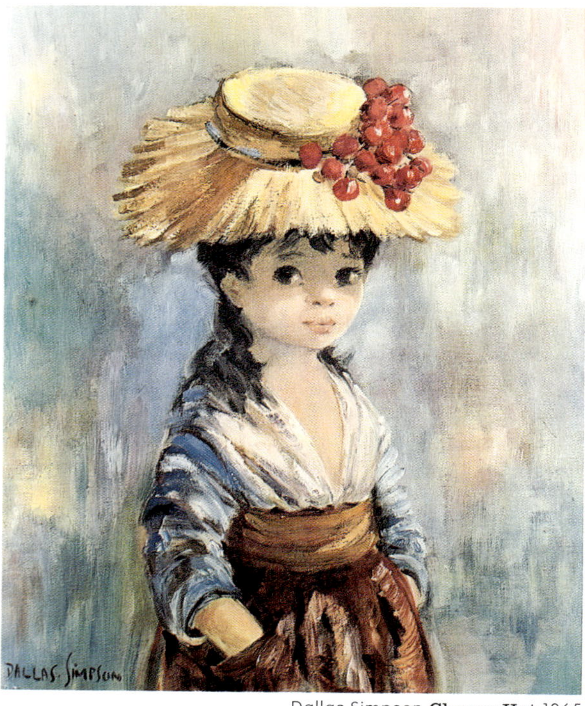

Dallas Simpson **Cherry Hat** 1965

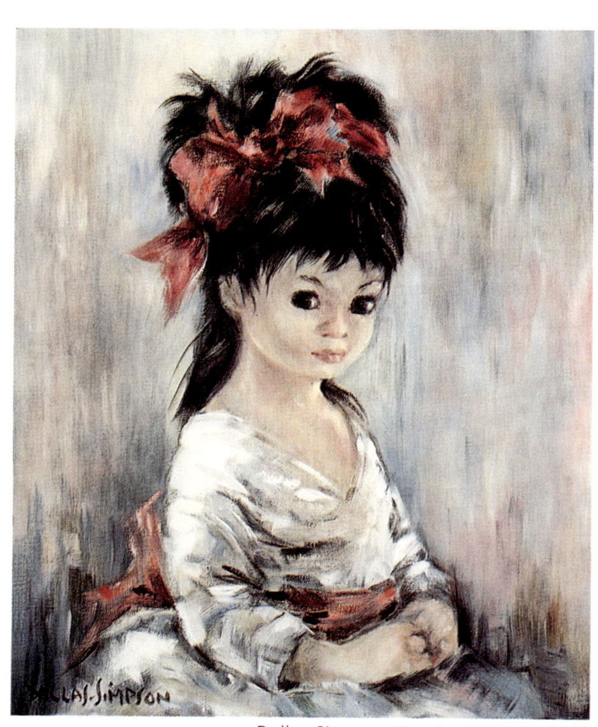

Dallas Simpson **Scarlet Ribbons** 1965

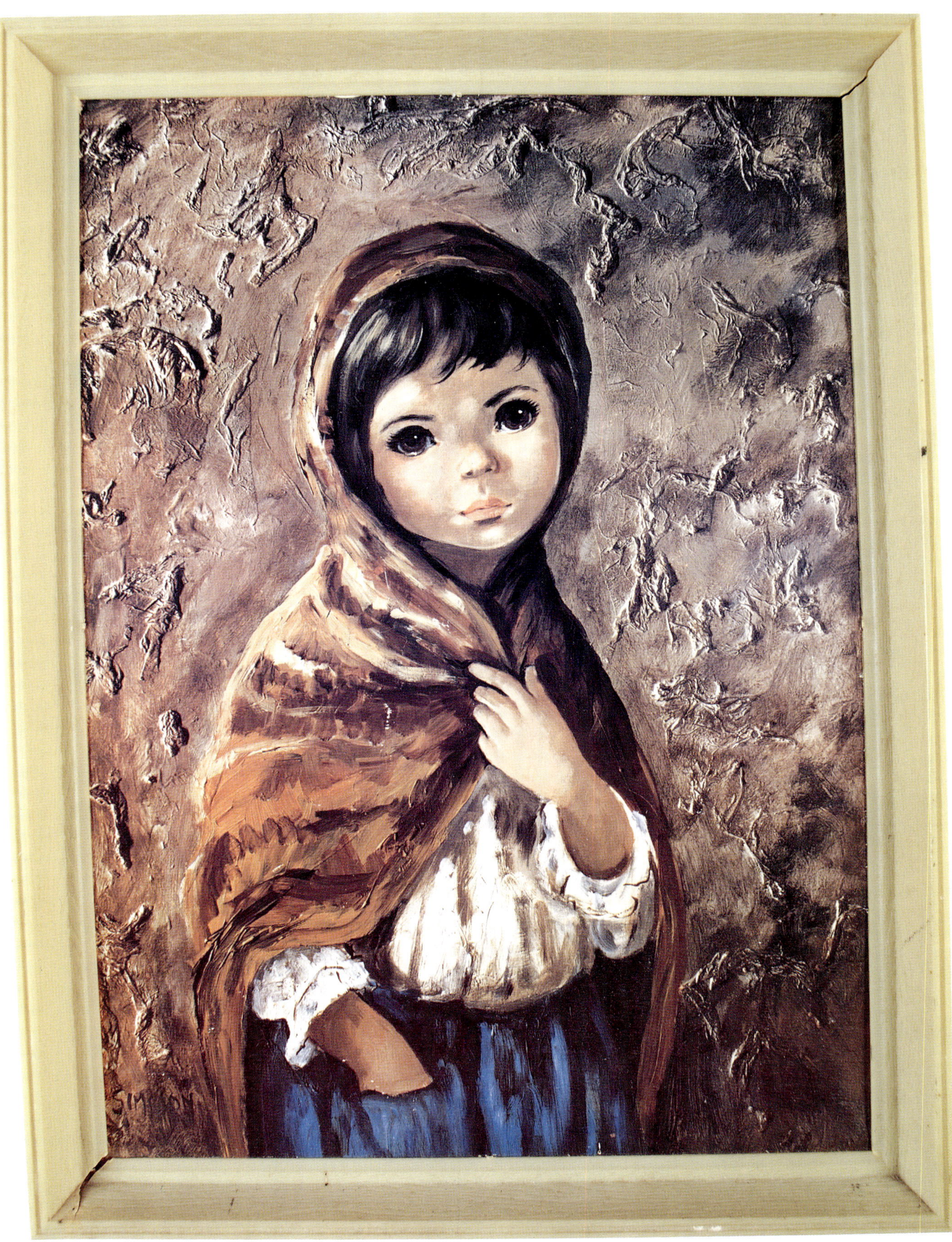

Dallas Simpson **Girl With Shawl**

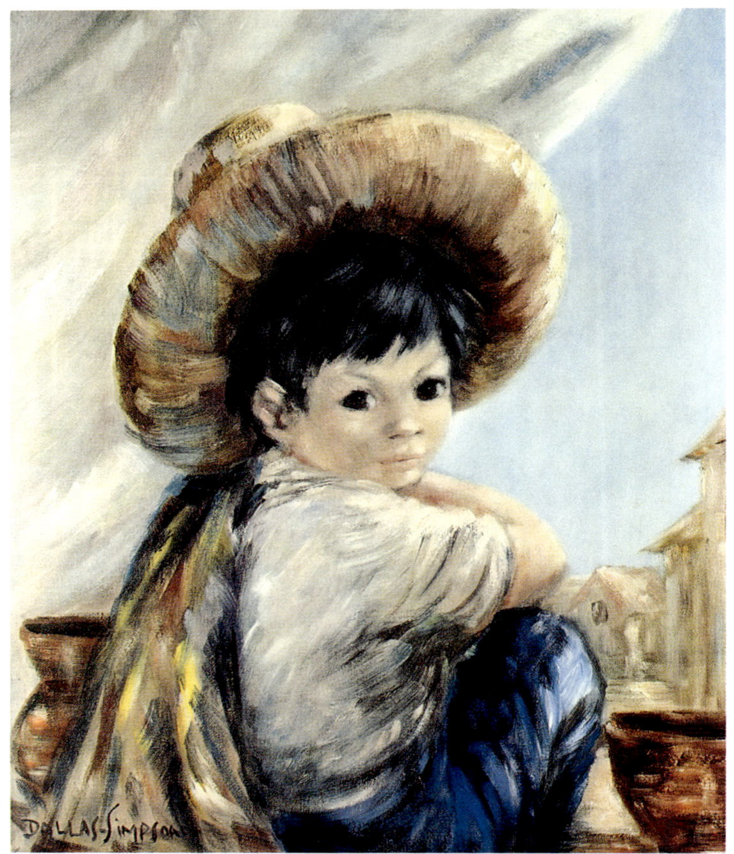

Dallas Simpson **Potter's Son** 1965

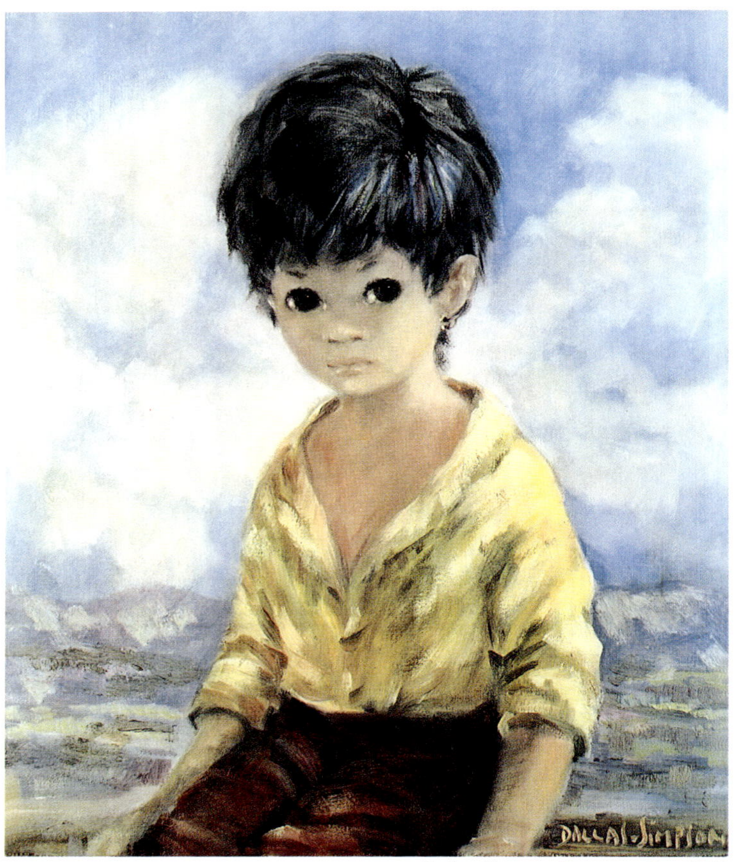

Dallas Simpson **Romany Boy** 1965

Dallas Simpson **Sea Urchin** 1965

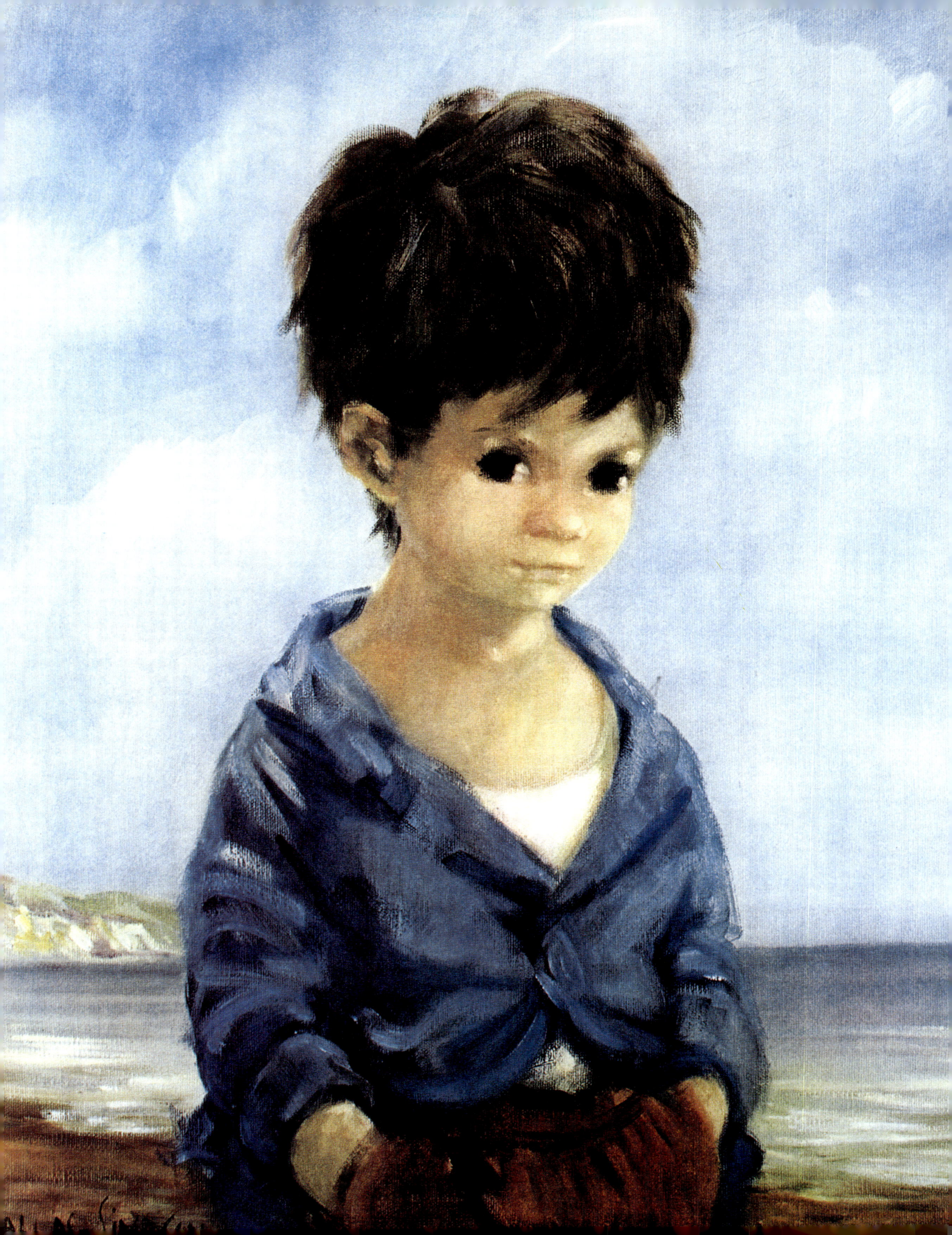

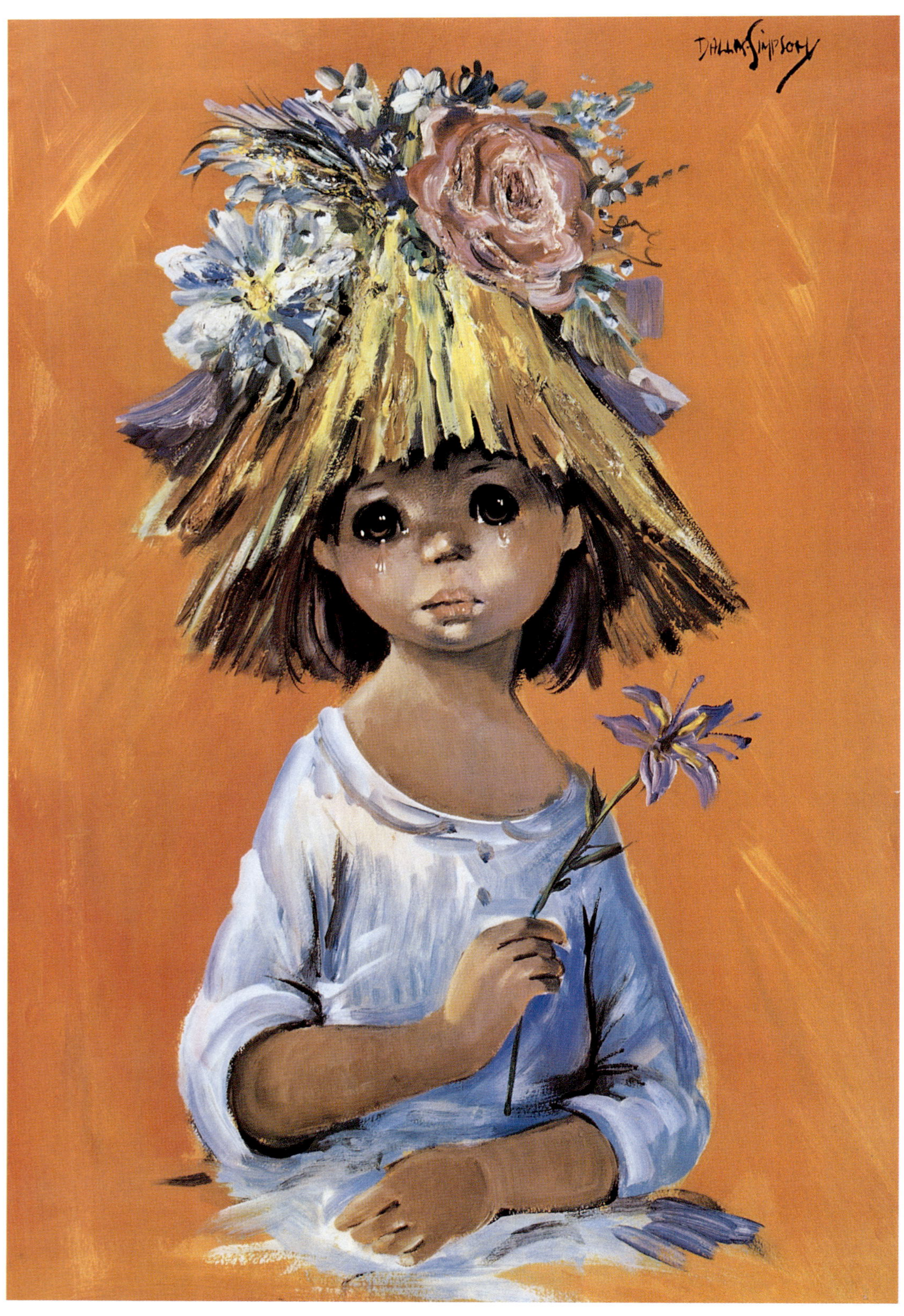

Dallas Simpson **Lucinda** 1972

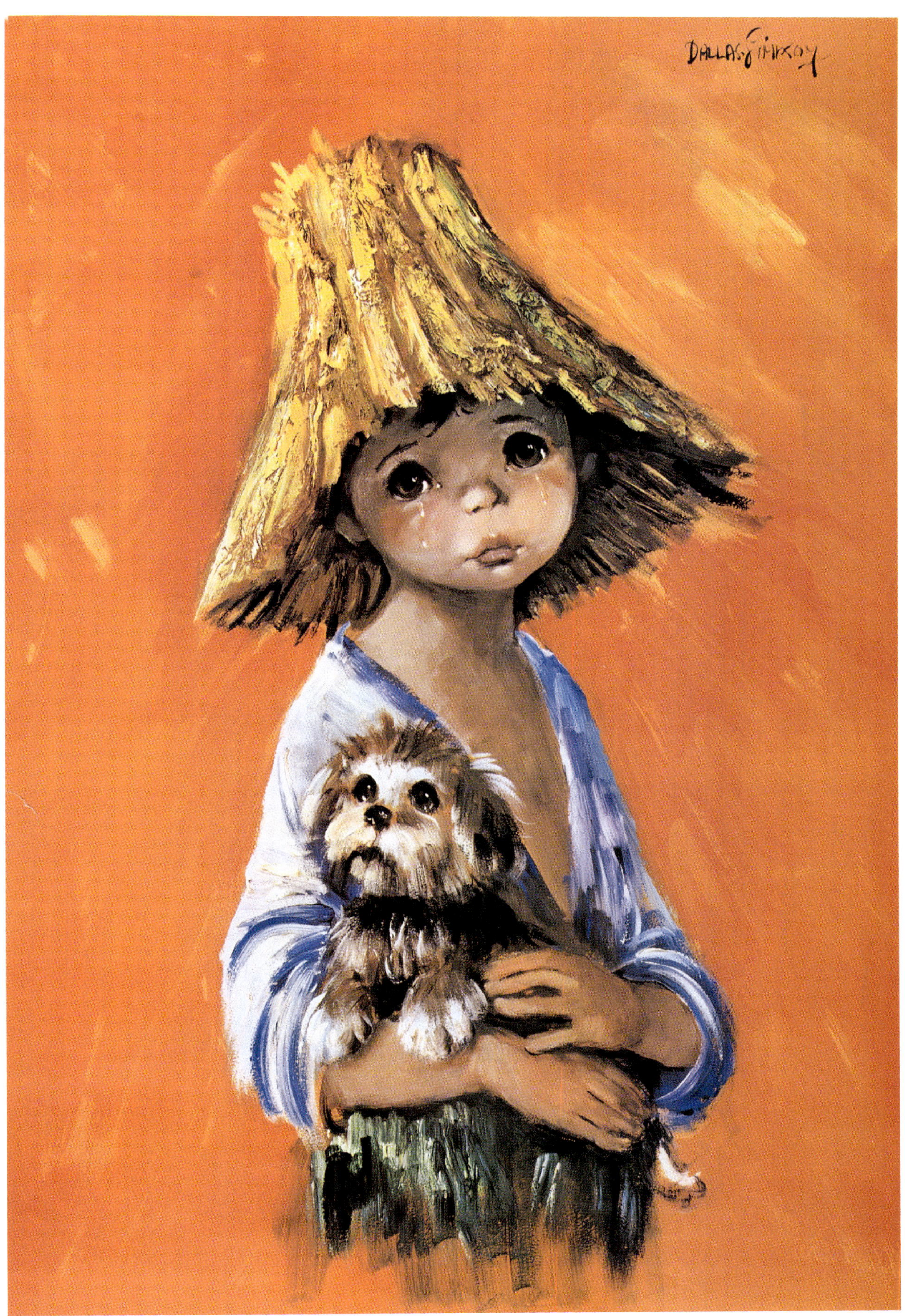

Dallas Simpson **Ramon** 1972

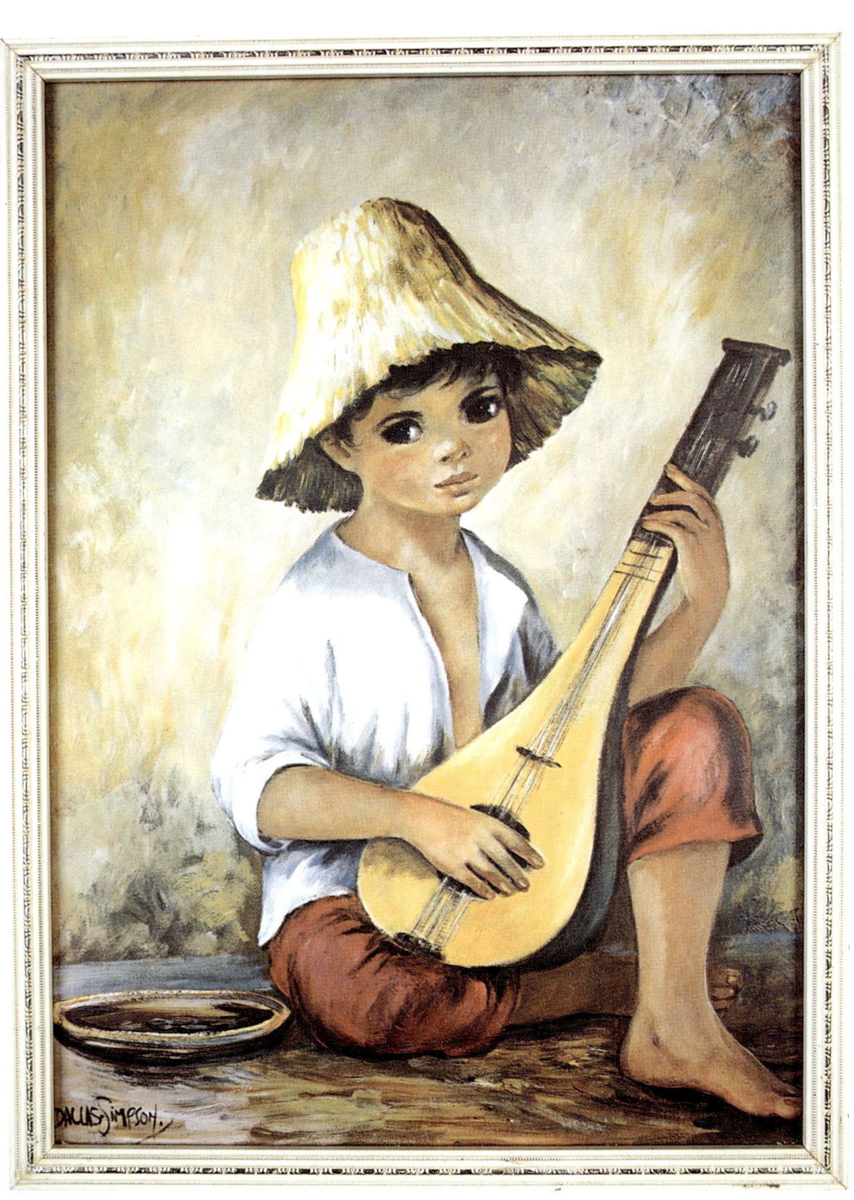

Dallas Simpson **Melancholy Maudlin Mandolin Boy**

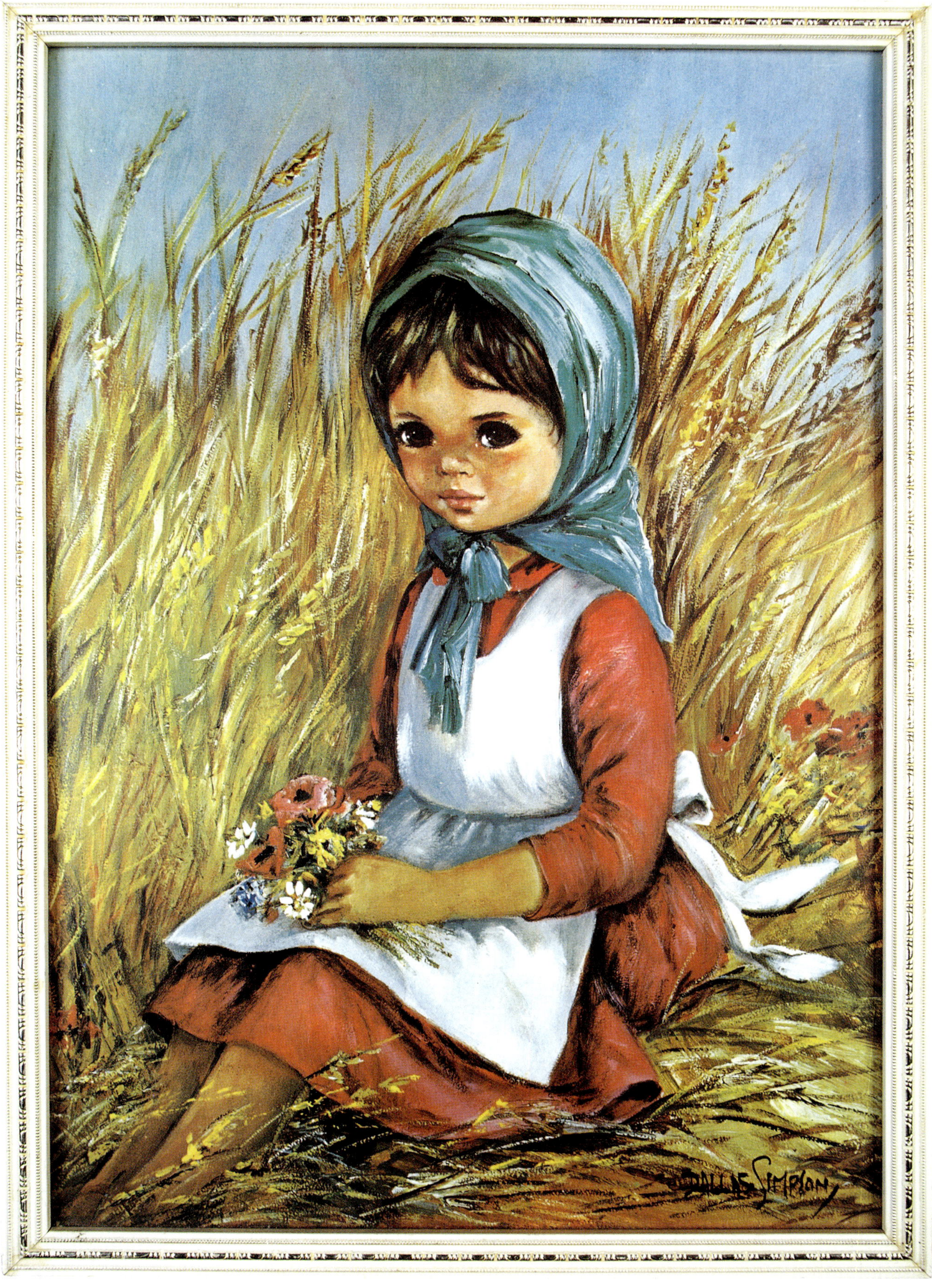

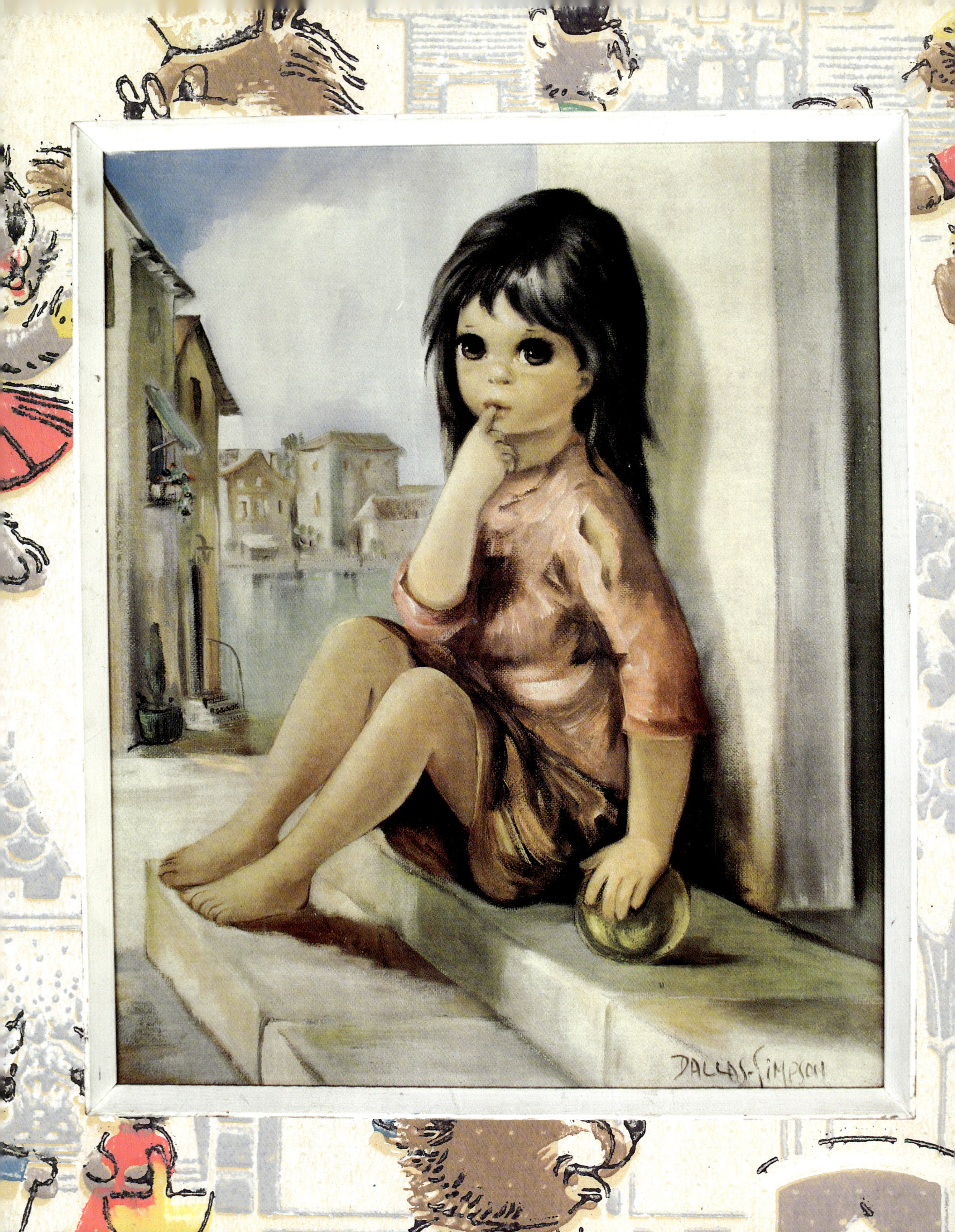
DALLAS-SIMPSON

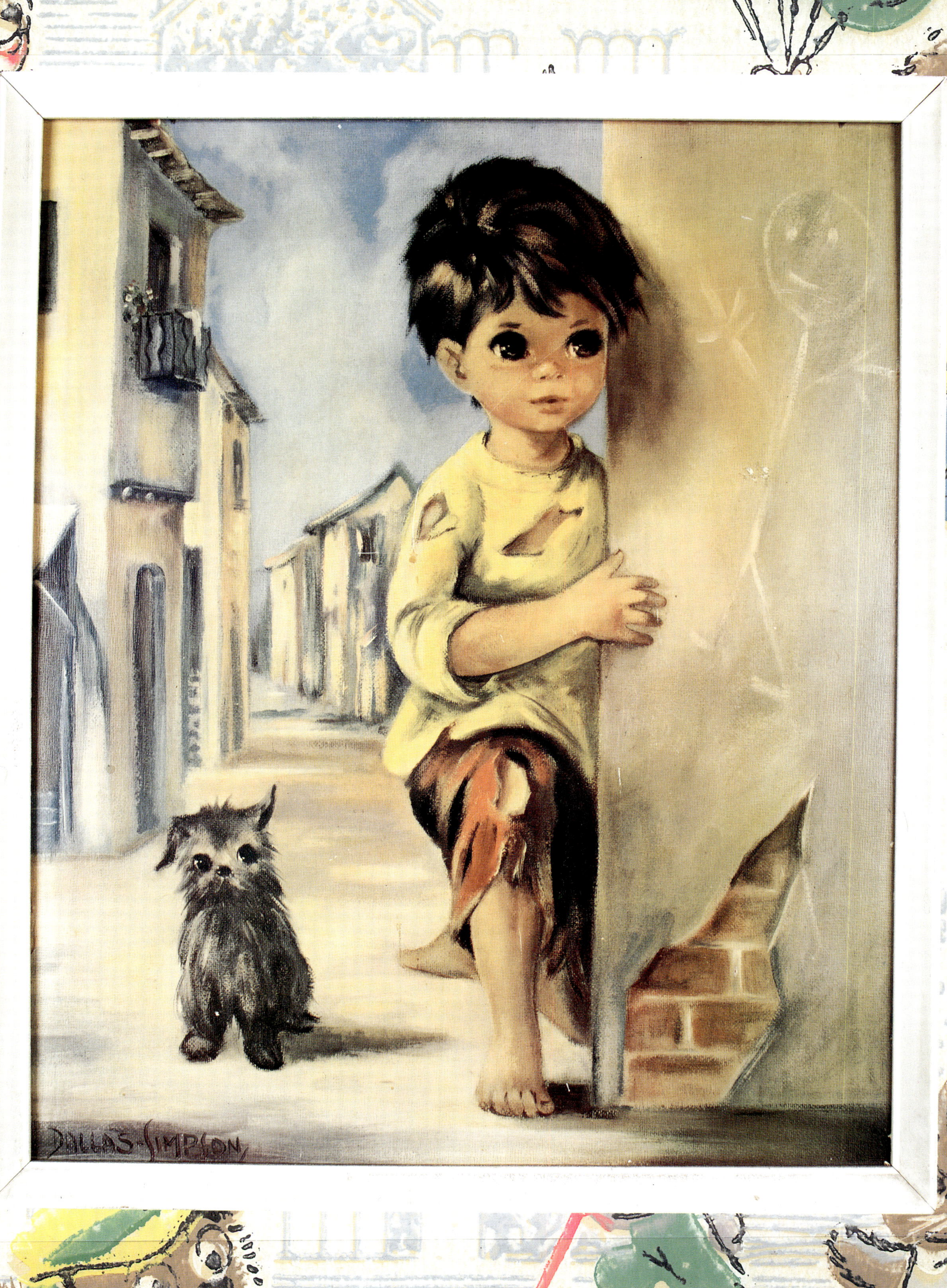
DALLAS-SIMPSON

preceding pages: Dallas Simpson **Pensive Urchin Girl** 1967
Dallas Simpson **Little Wayne and Bedraggled Dog** 1967

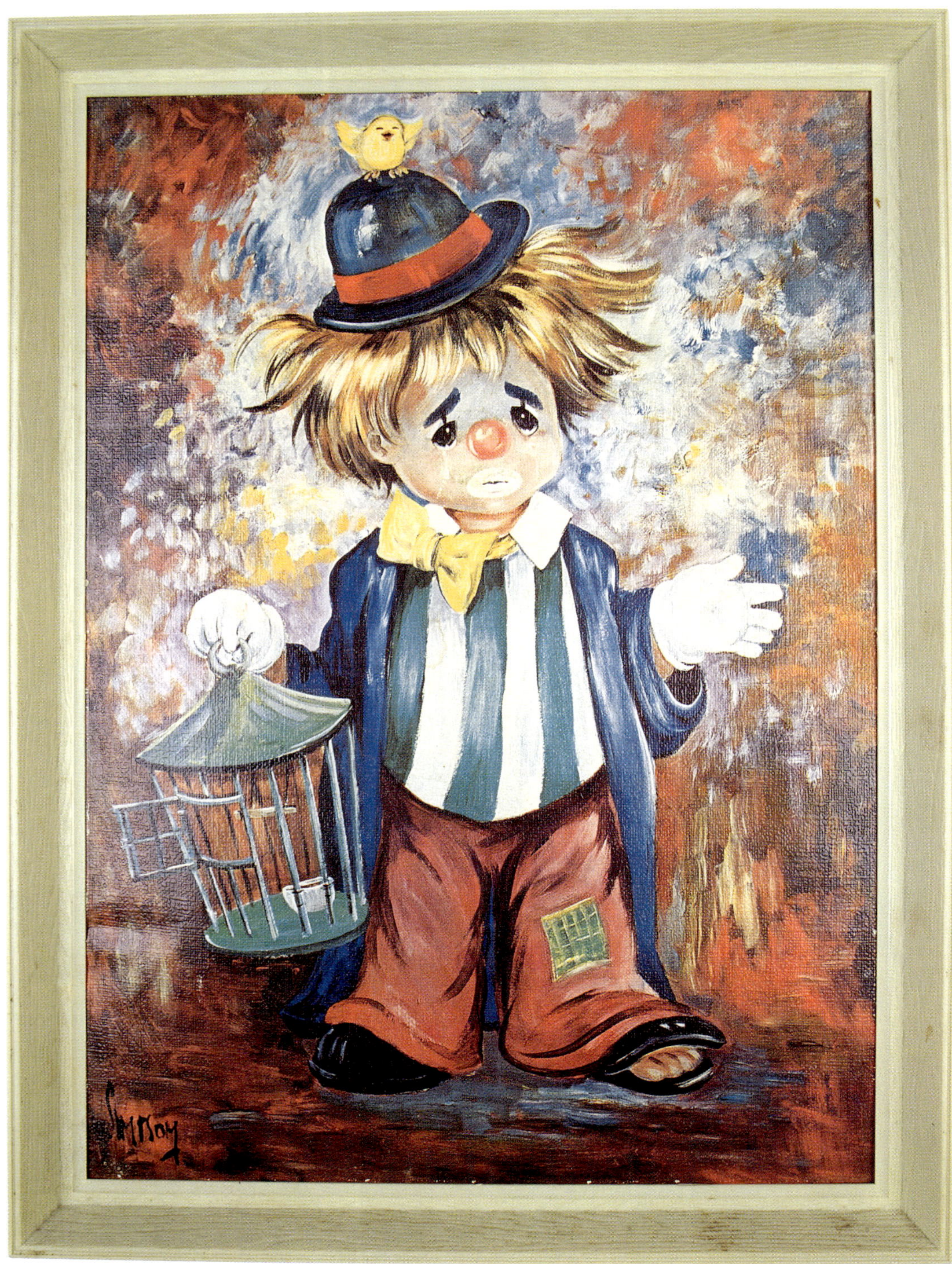

Dallas Simpson **Child Clown**

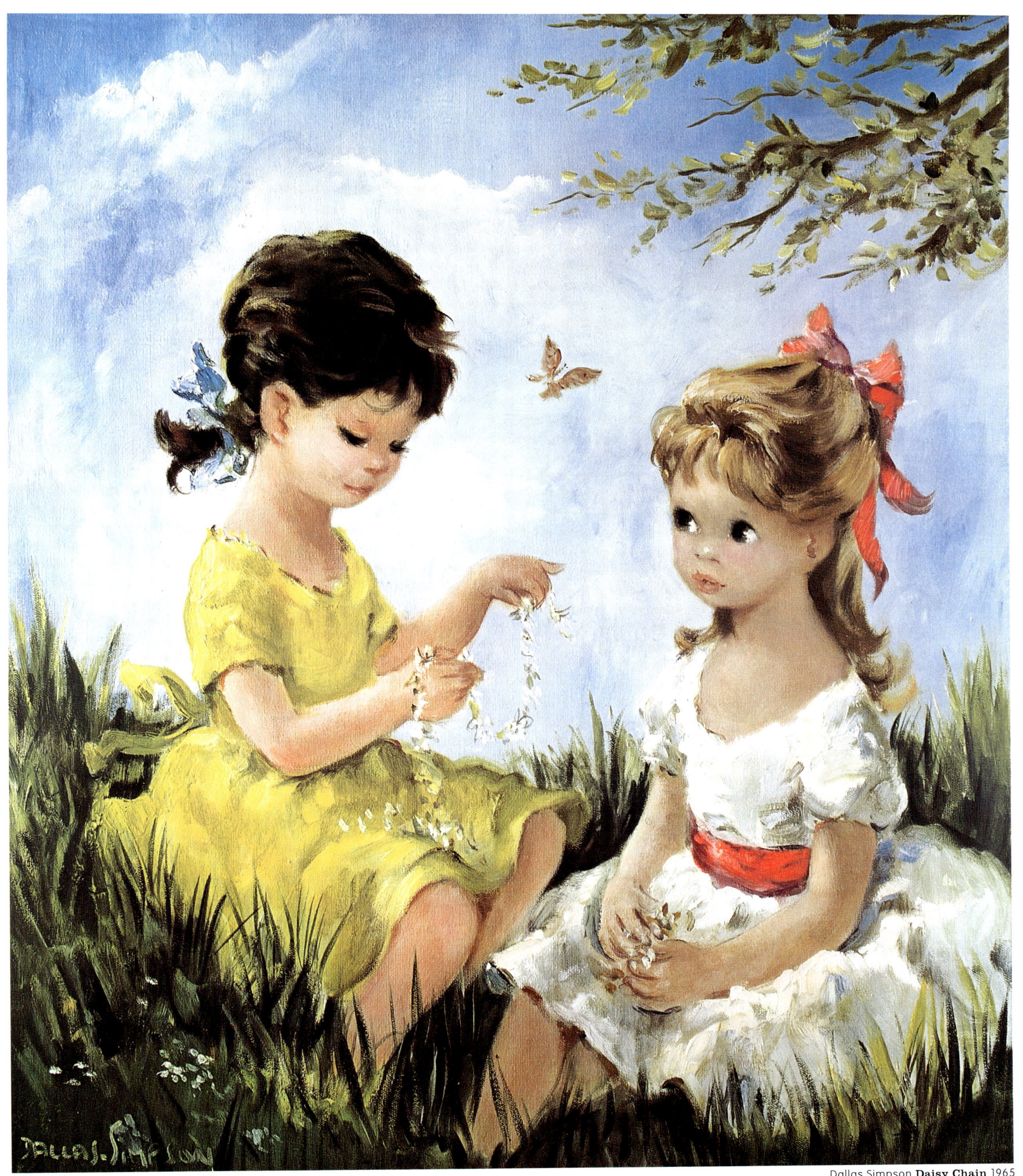

Dallas Simpson **Daisy Chain** 1965

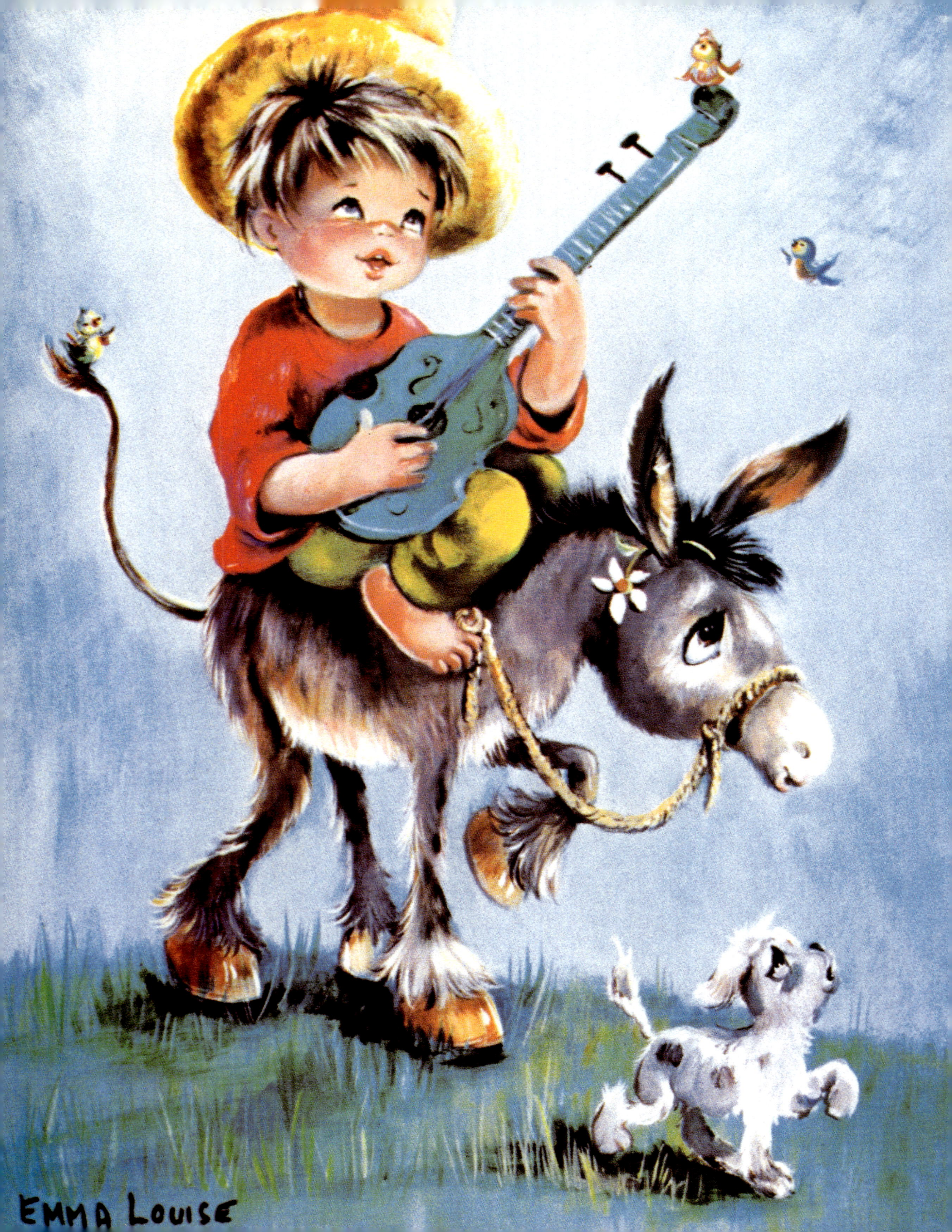
EMMA LOUISE

Dallas Simpson **Donkey Serenade**

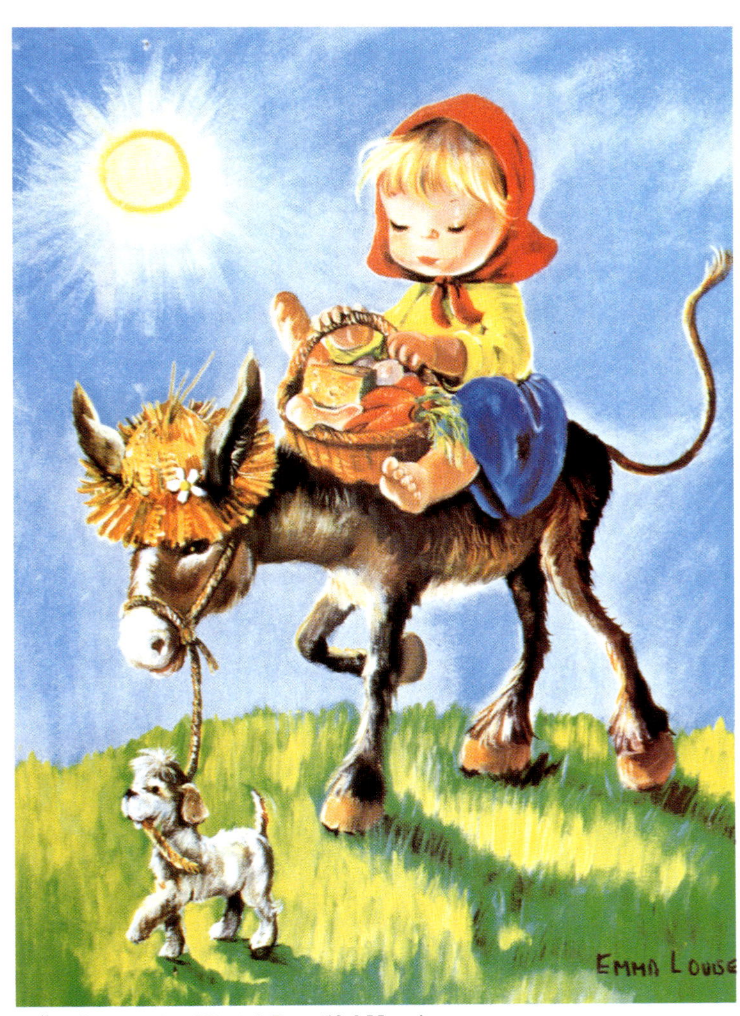

Dallas Simpson **Oh, What A Beautiful Morning**

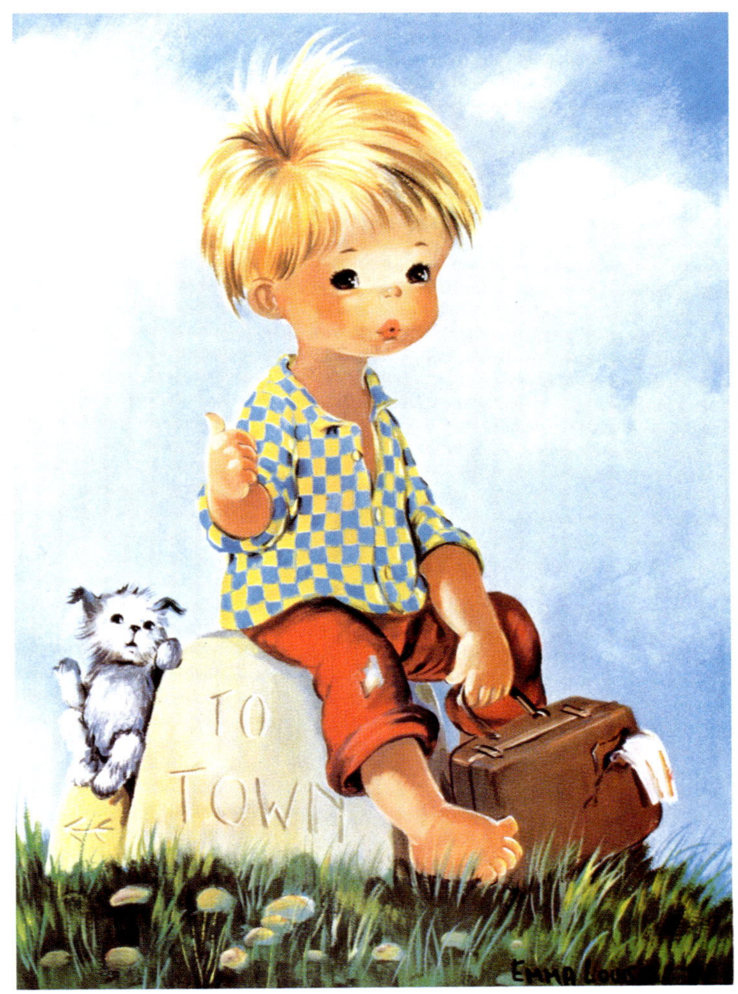

Dallas Simpson **Going My Way?**

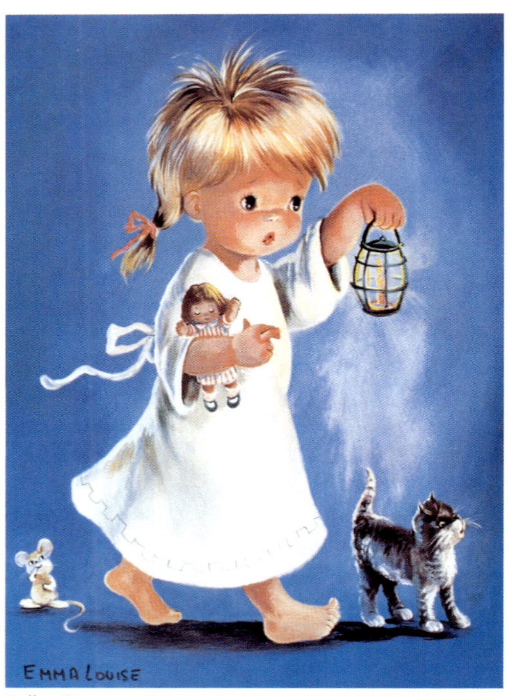

Dallas Simpson **Who's That Knocking At My Door**

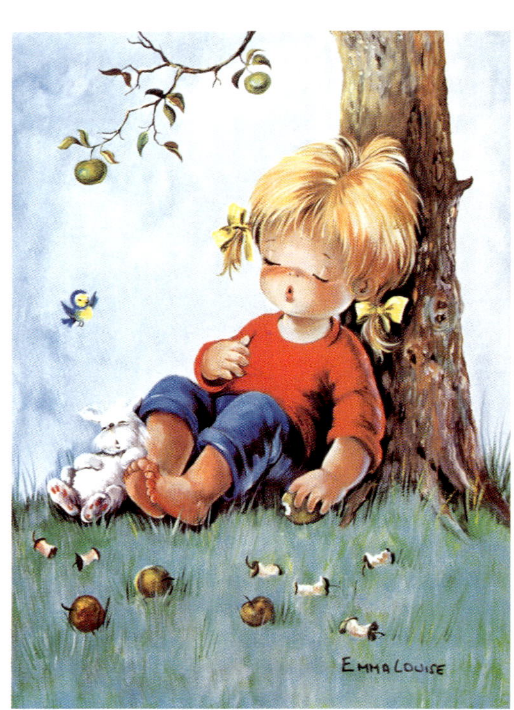

Dallas Simpson **Little Green Apples**

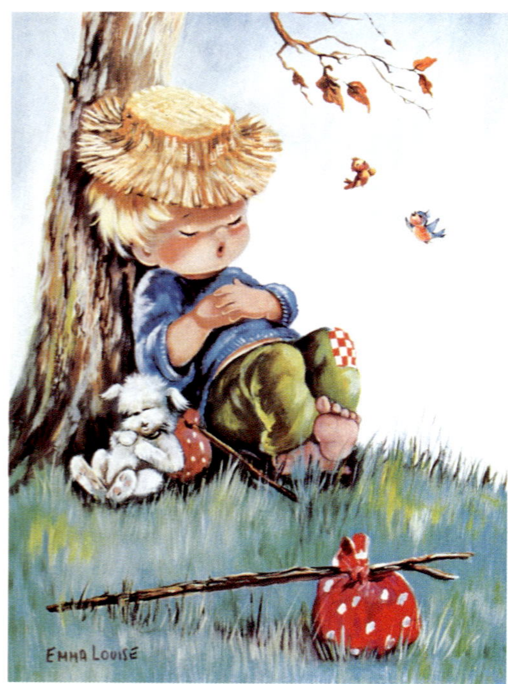

Dallas Simpson **King of the Road**

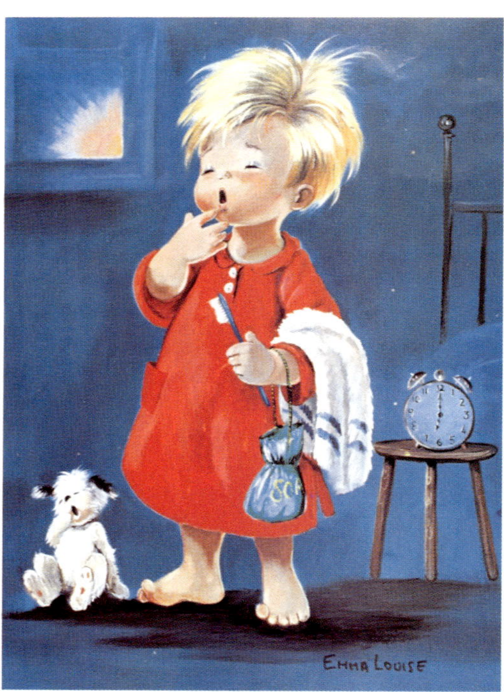

Dallas Simpson **So Early in the Morning**

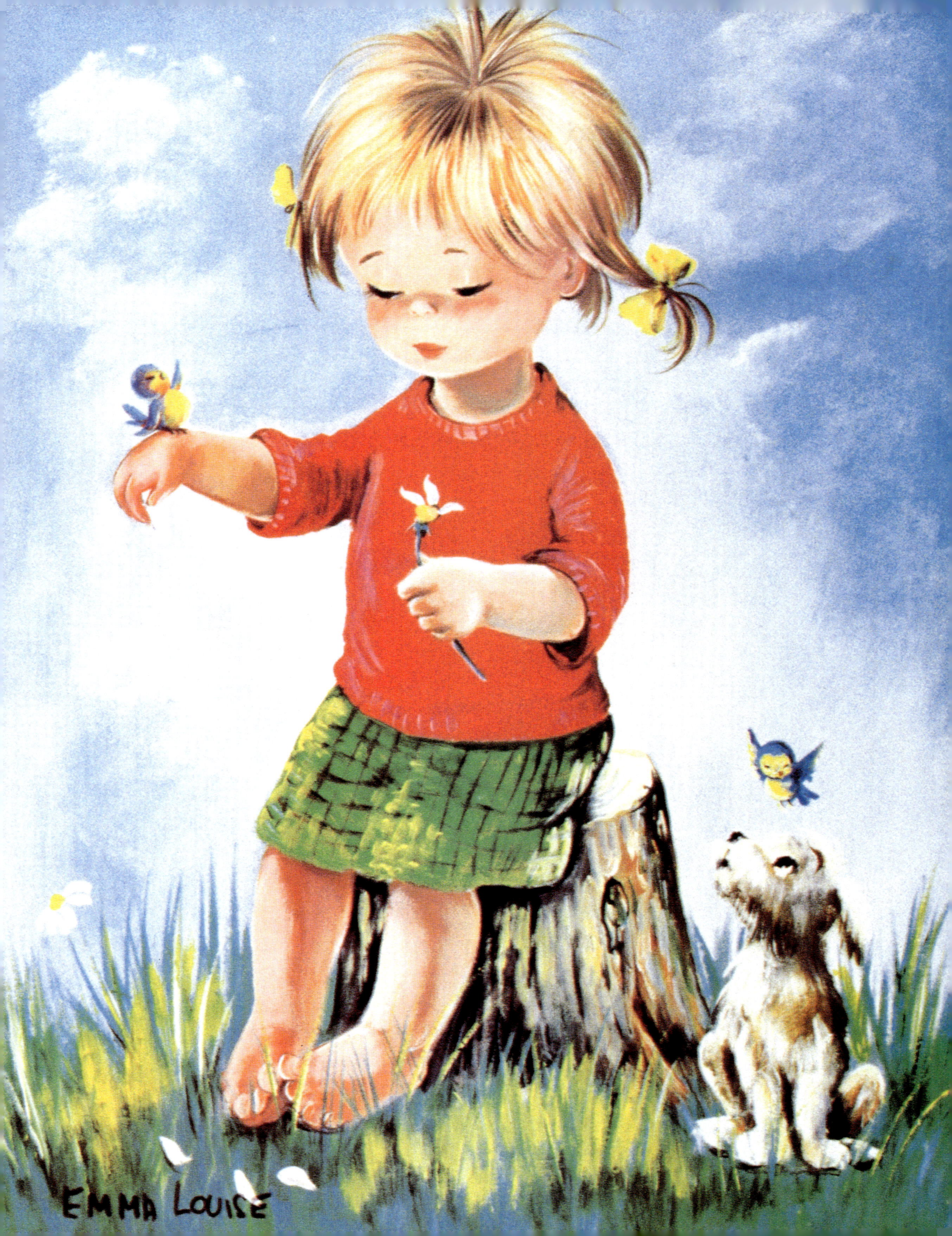
EMMA LOUISE

The US take on Big Eye was more varied than in Britain, permeating every aspect of life including big-eyed US marines in Korea. **Lee Eden** produced paintings in a similar 'adopt me' vein to British artists but along with **Eve** and **Kwatz** he also painted an enormous series of big-eyed 'mod' kids in various poses, glorifying the early 60s' teenage 'mod' phenomenon. Big-eyed, twisting, guitar-playing 'mod' kids, abandoning their schoolbooks and blazers to join the youth explosion.

Ugly big-eyed ballet dancers, harlequins and Robin Hood-style characters were specialities of **Goji** and **Eden**, to which **Ozz Franca** added a weird and sinister angle.

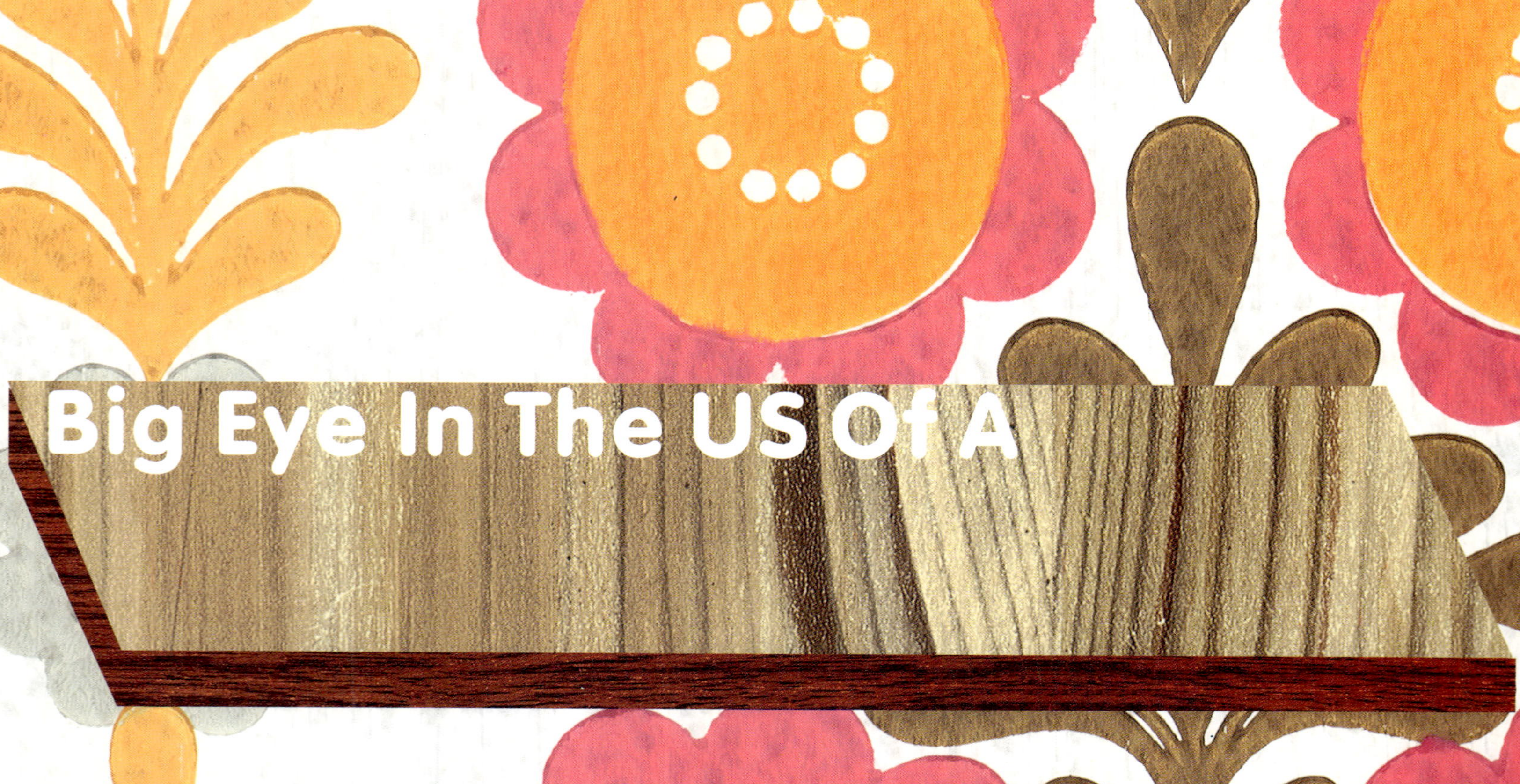

Big Eye In The US Of A

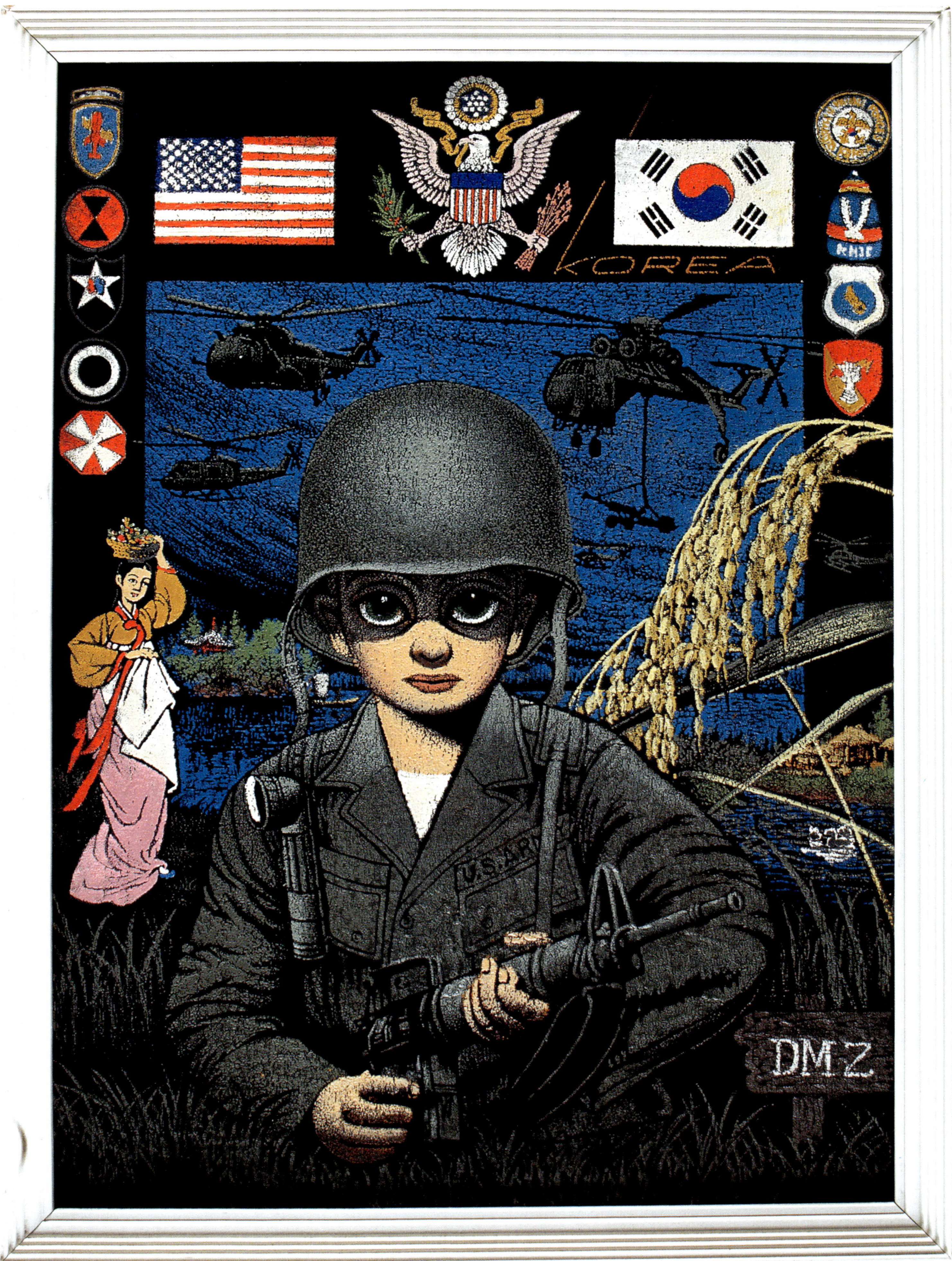

Unknown Artist **Big-Eyed Soldier Boy**

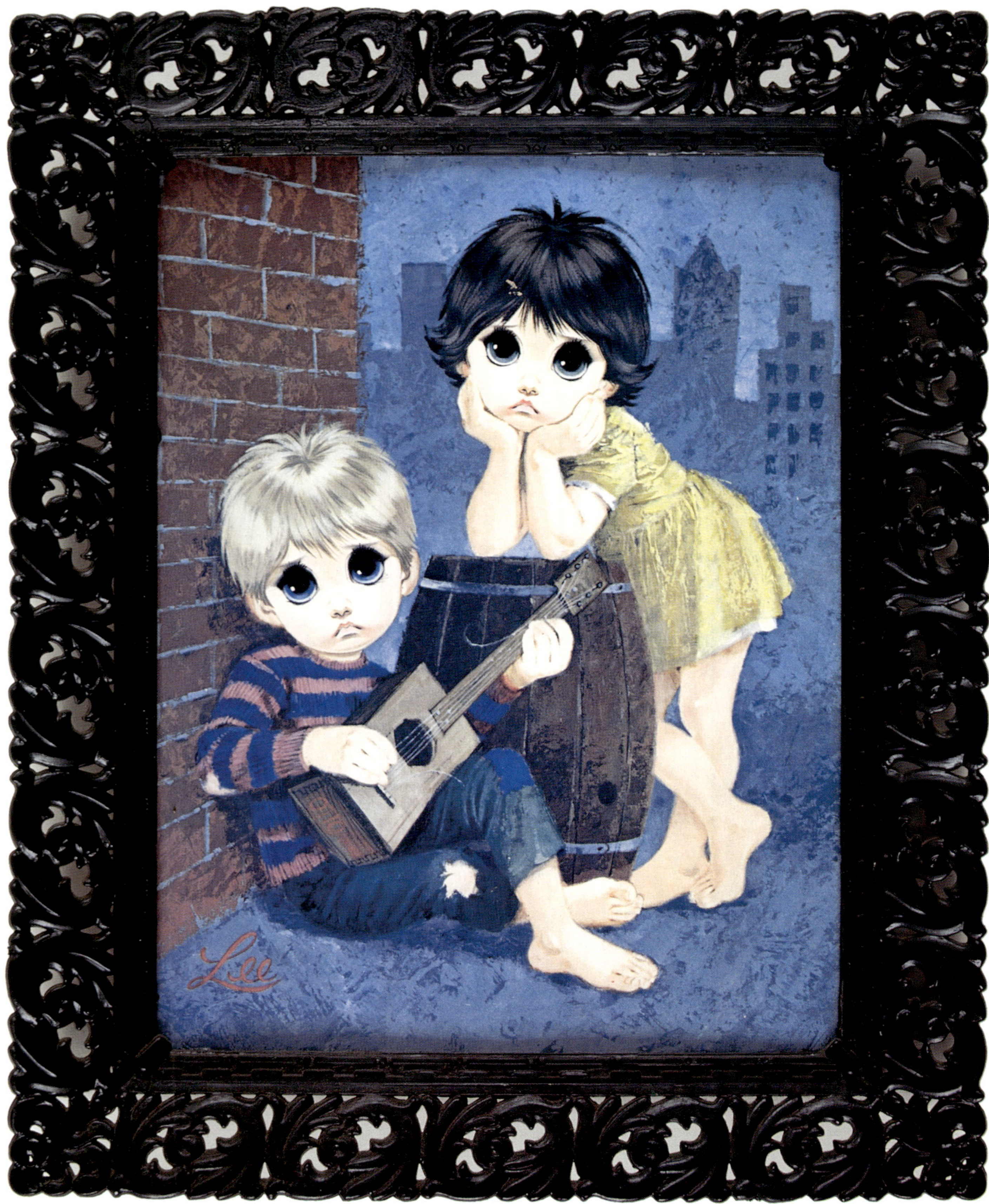

Lee **Sad Songs**

Lee **Feel My Warmth**

Lee **Flower Power**

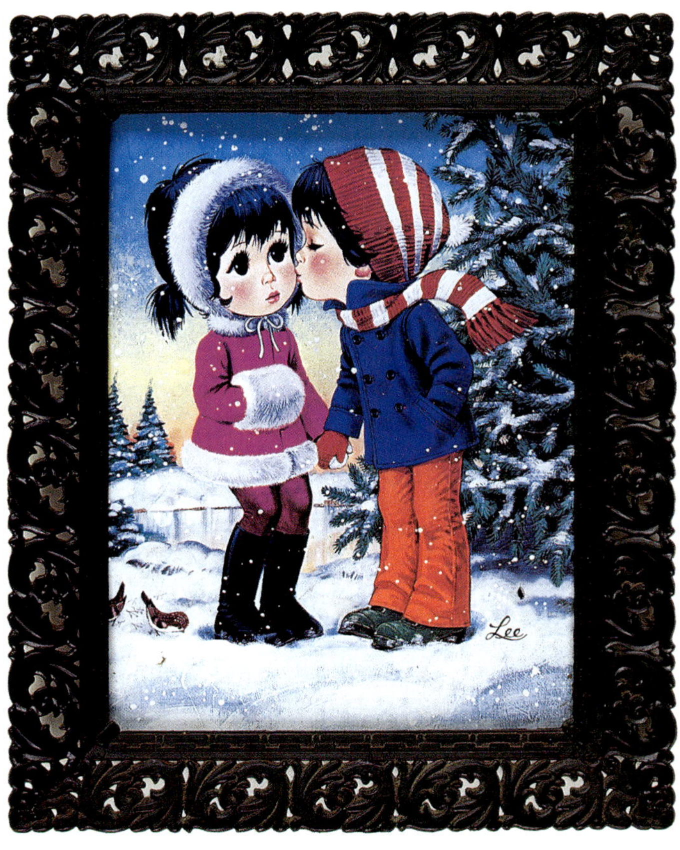

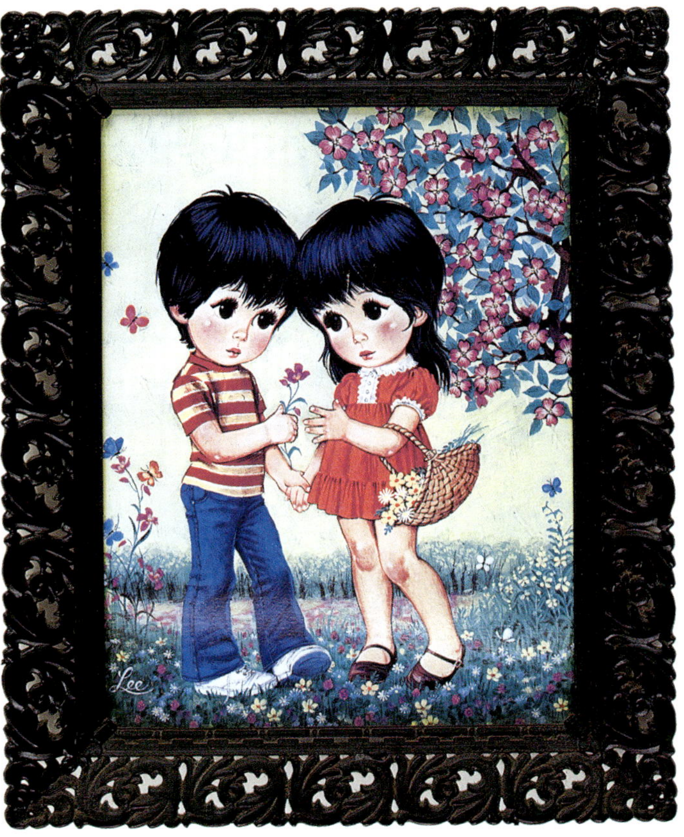

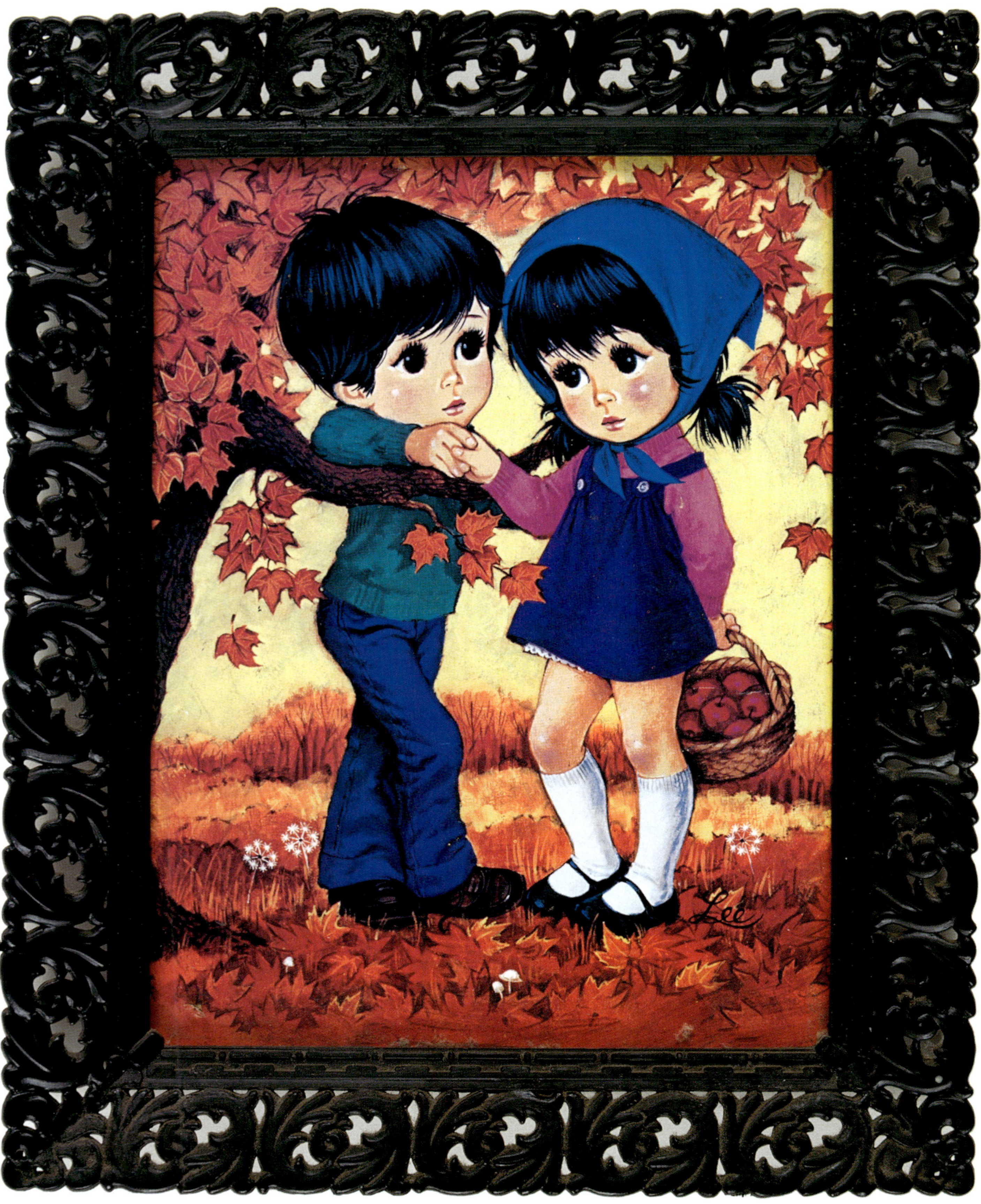

Lee **A Branch Between Us**

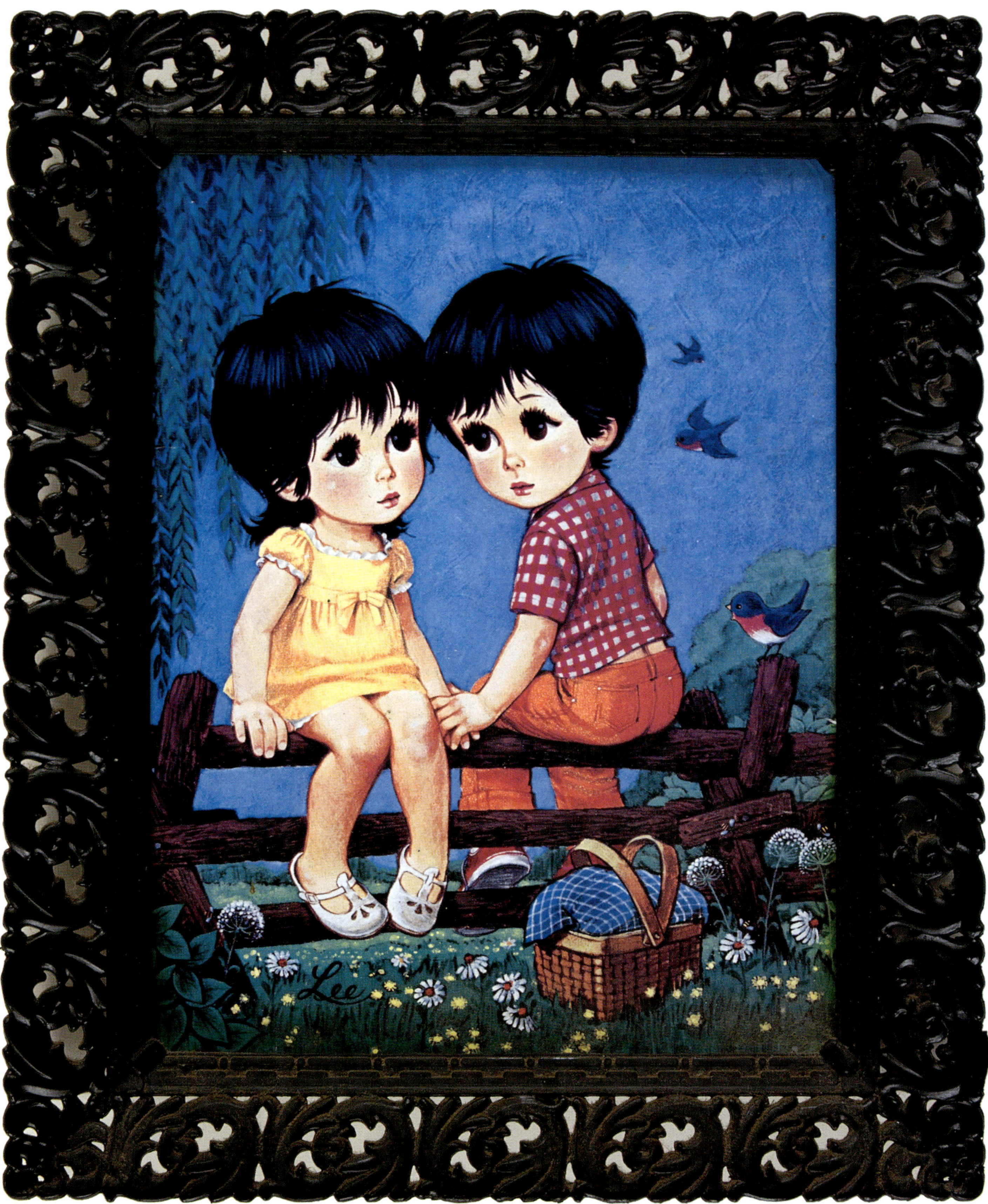

Lee **Fence Love**

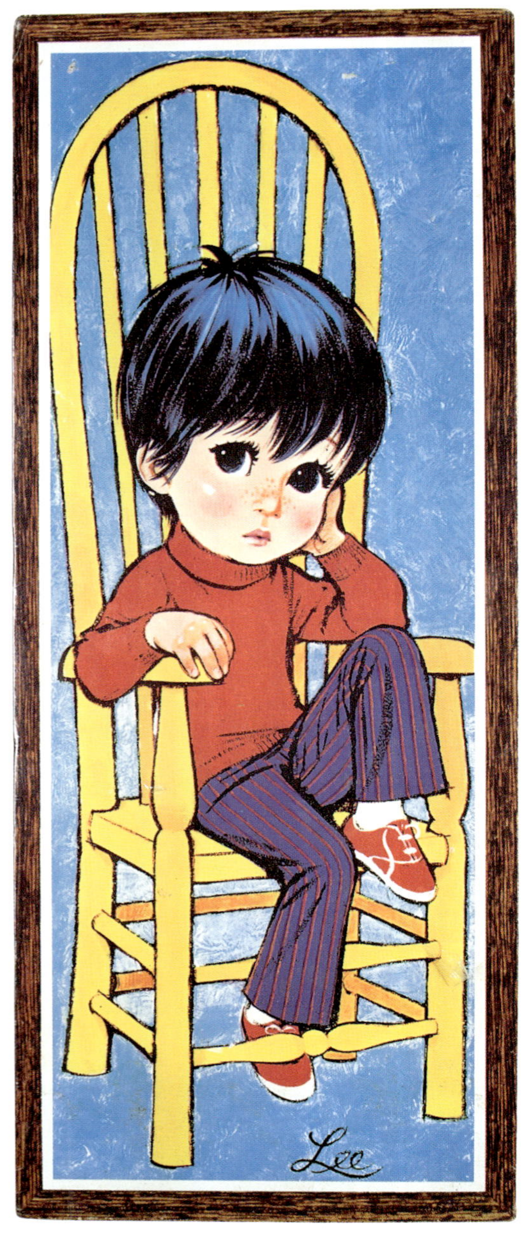

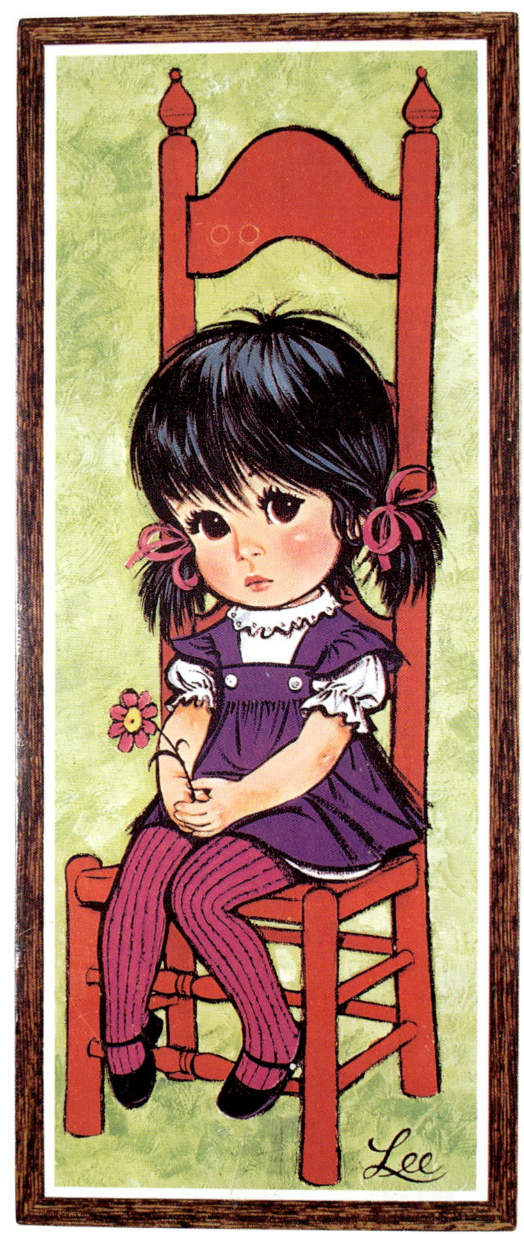

Lee **Big Eyes, Big Chairs, Little Kids**

Lee **Wet and Sad; Give Me Love; Sad Songs**

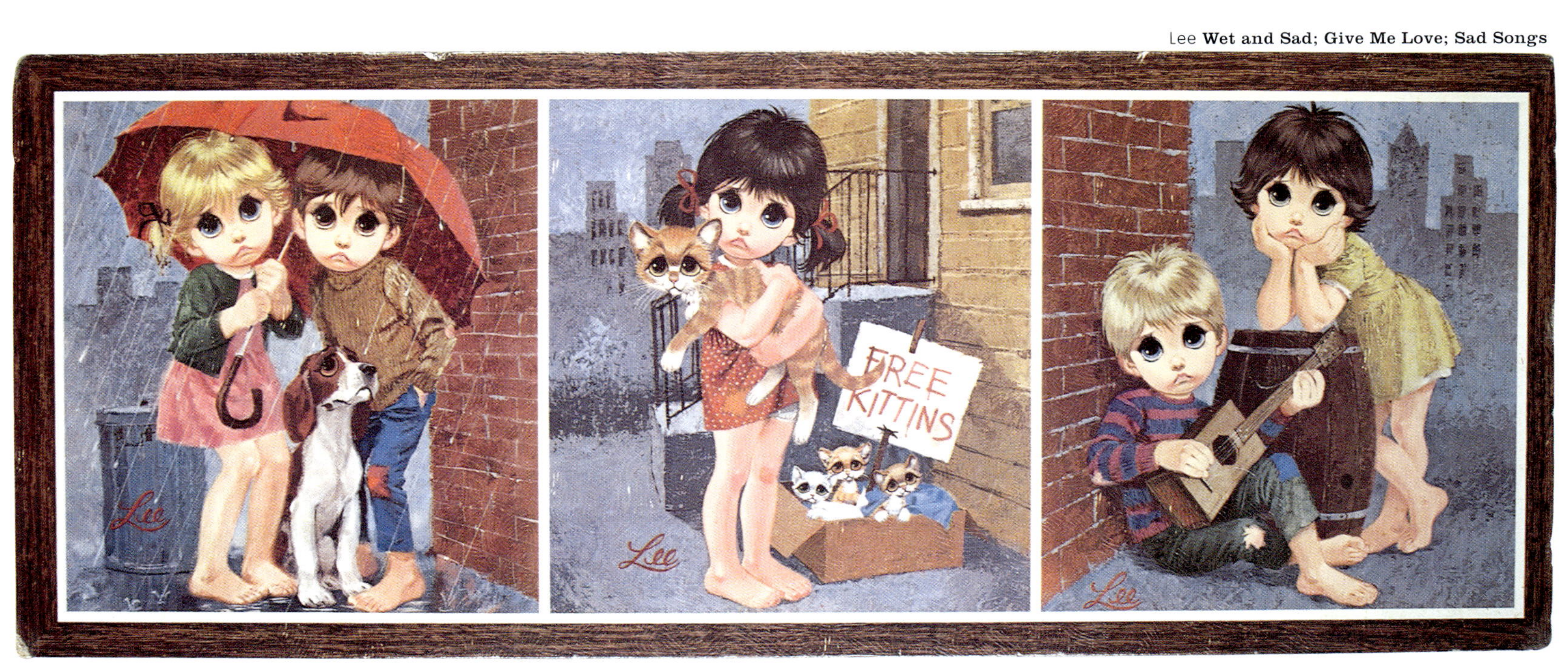

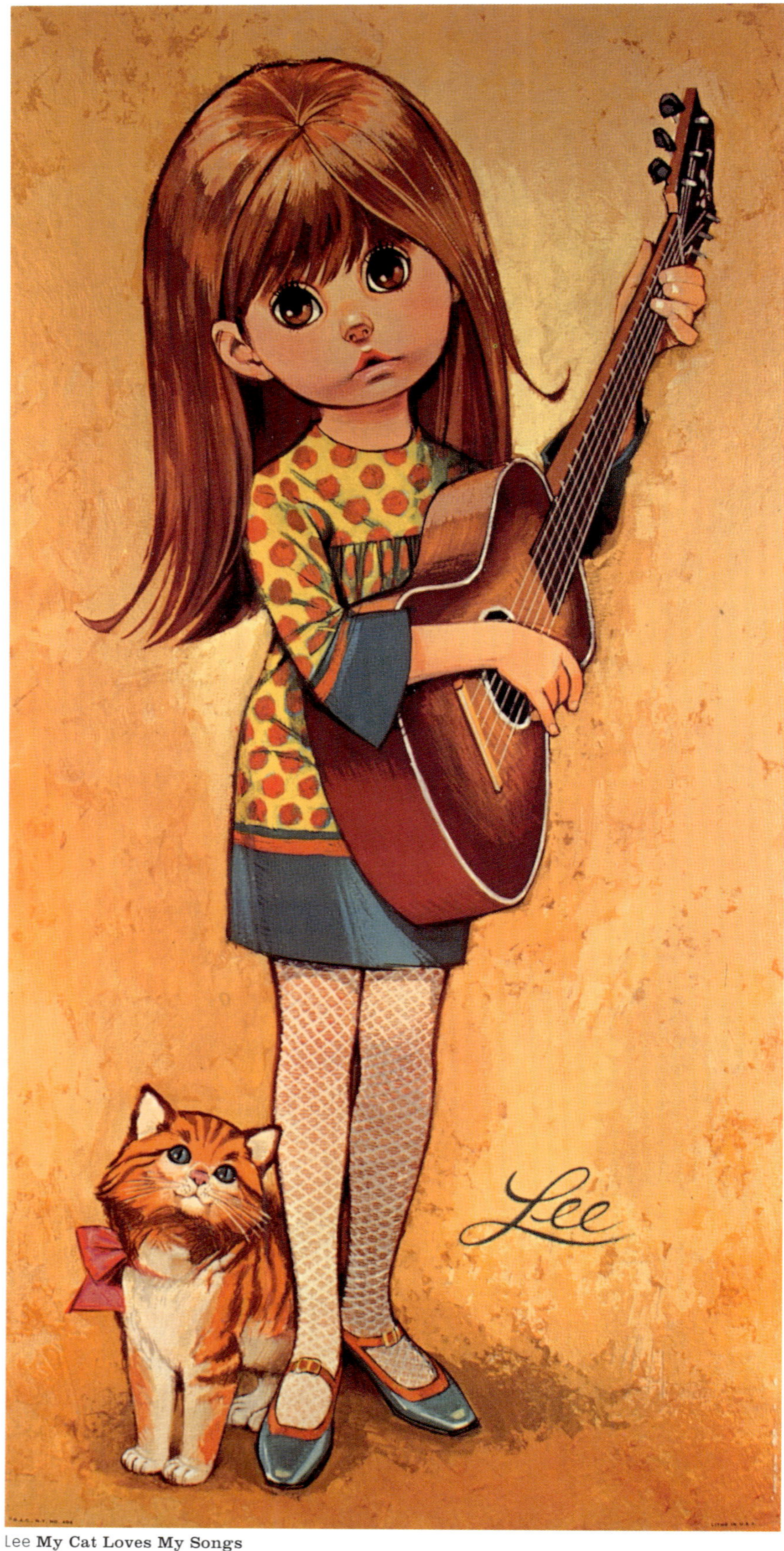

Lee **My Cat Loves My Songs**

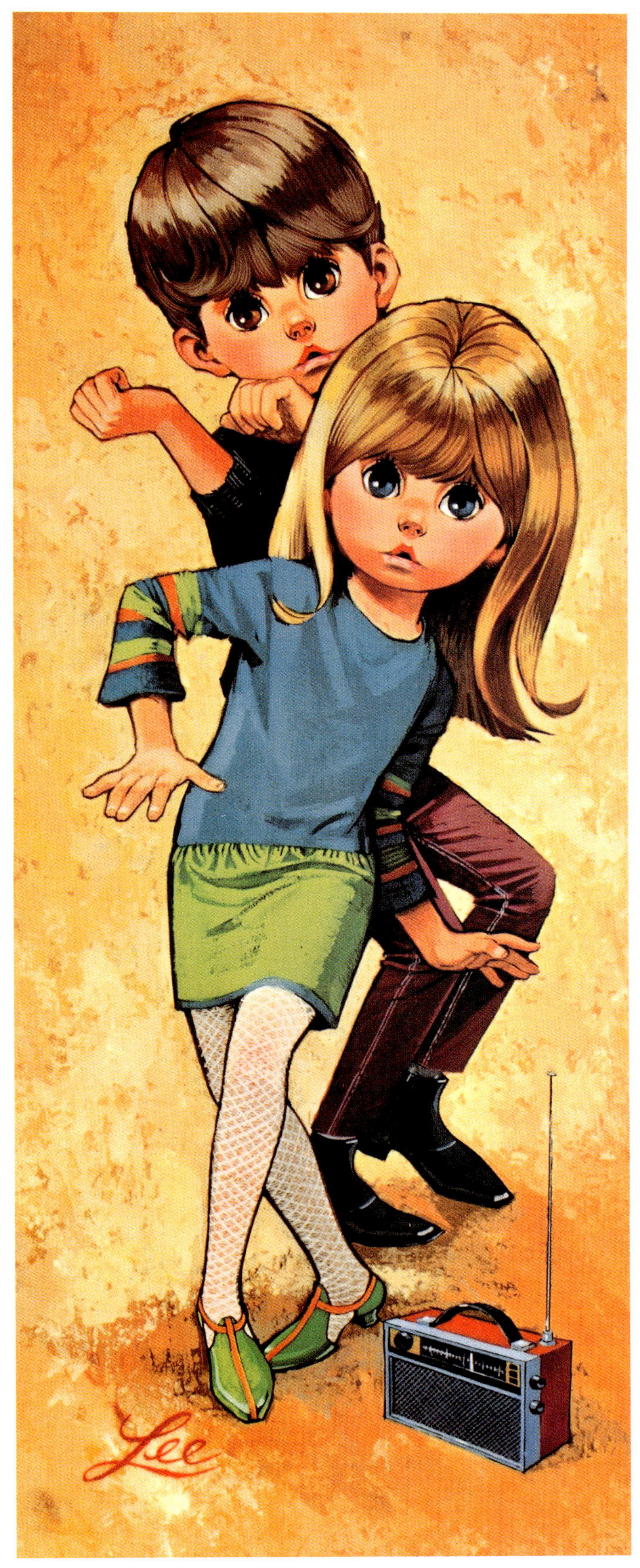

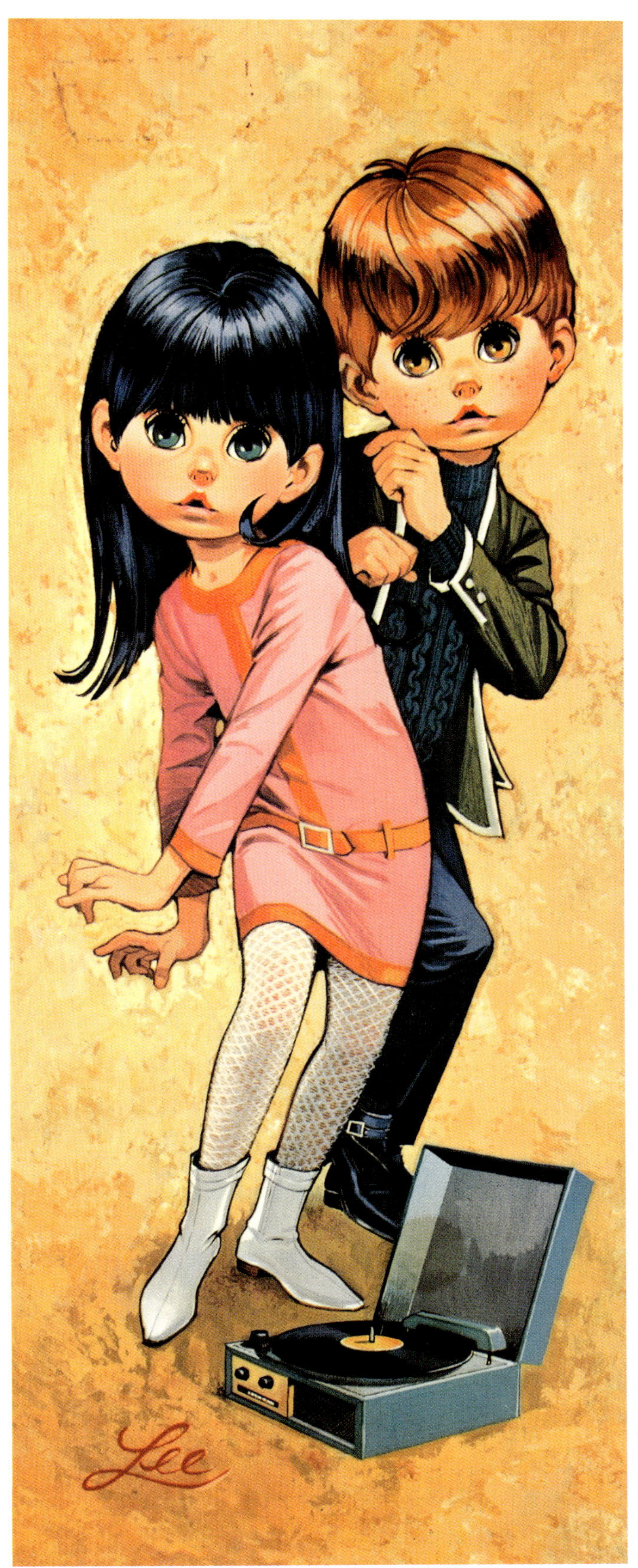

Lee **We Can Twist**

Eve **Dancing Makes Me Sad**

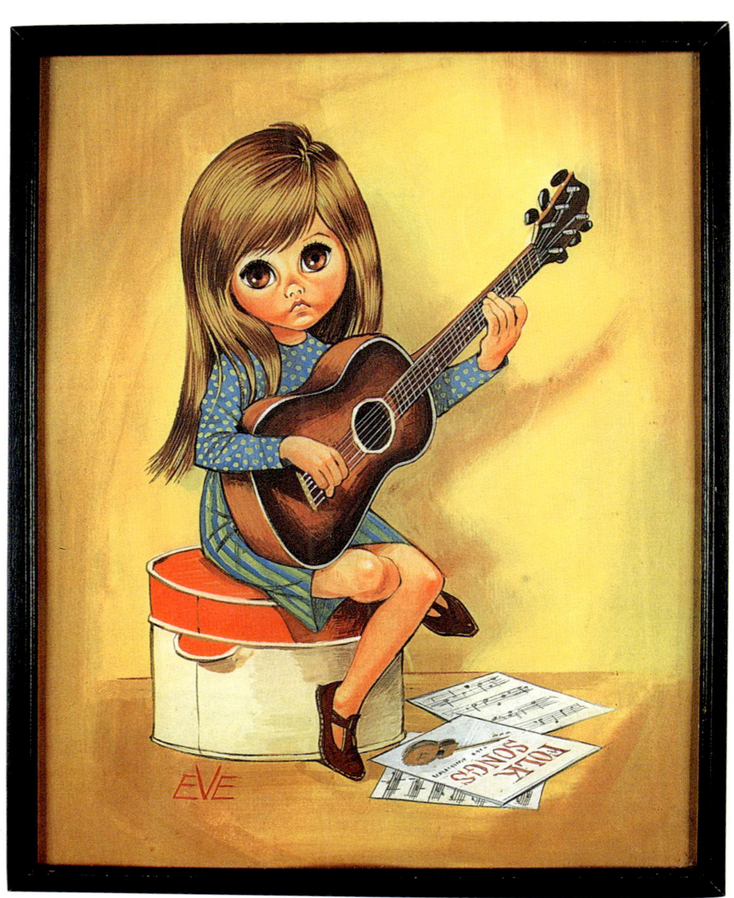

Eve **Singing Makes Me Sad**

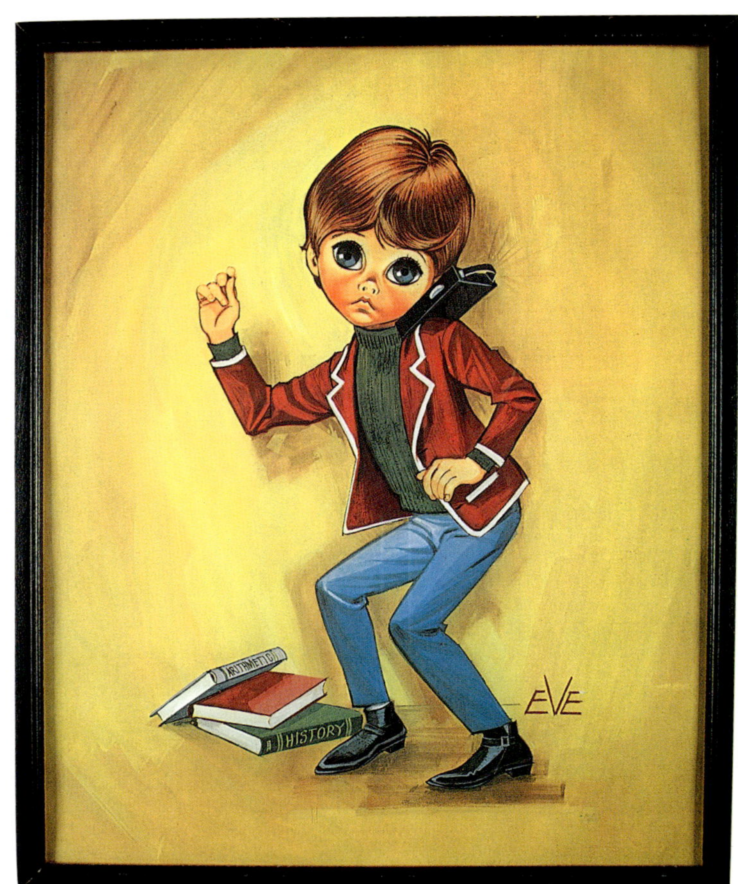

Eve **I've Dropped My Books**

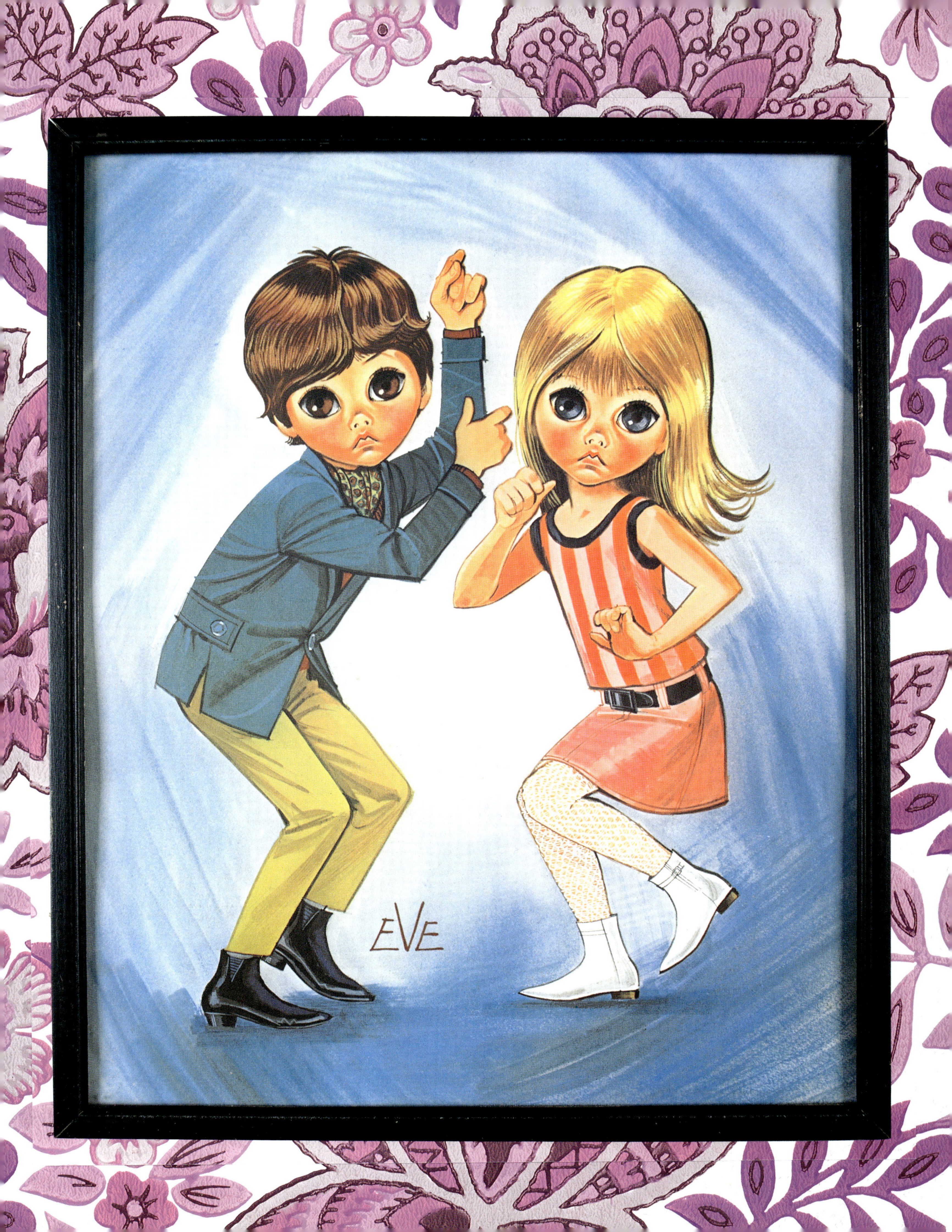
EVE

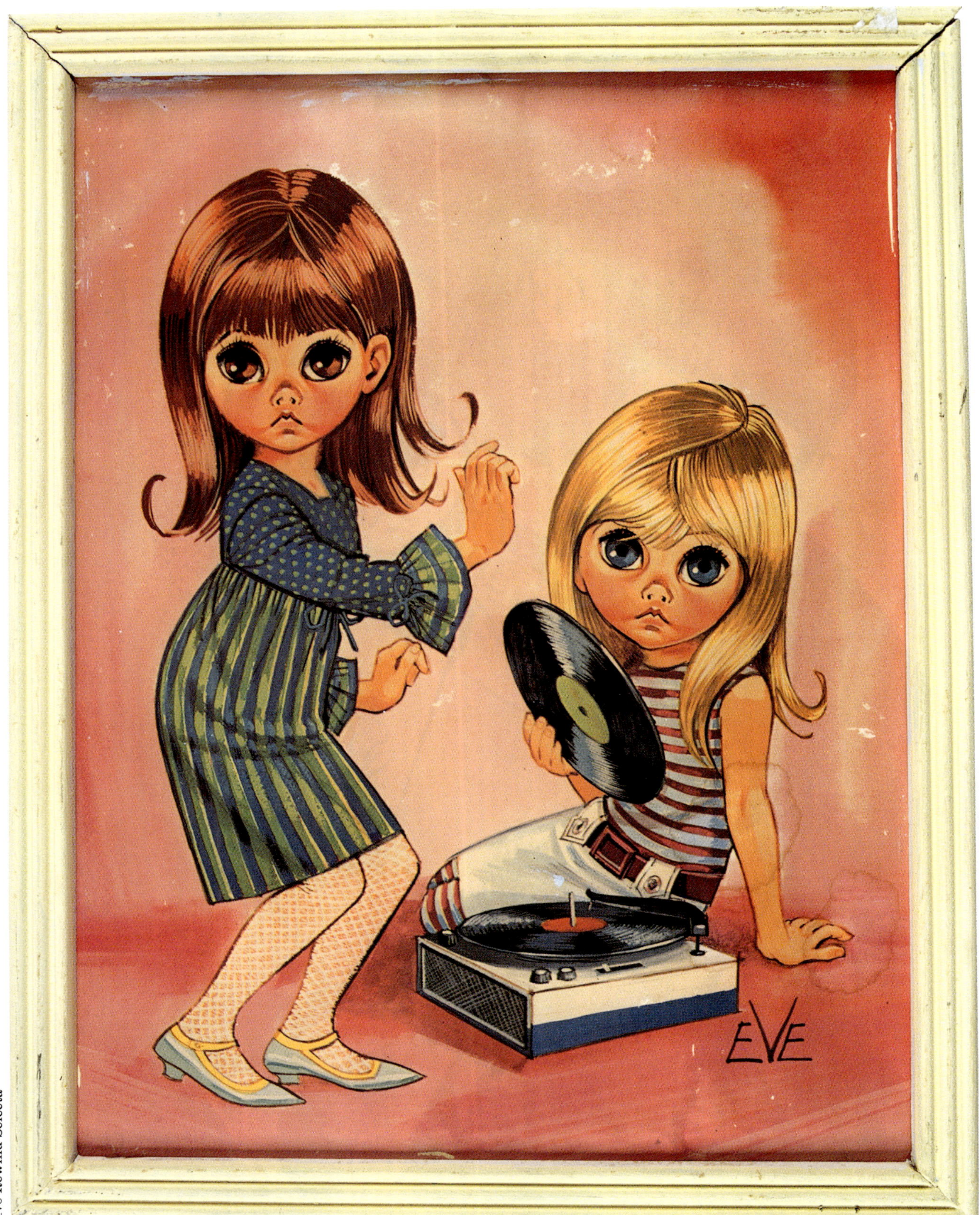

Eve **Rewind Selecta**

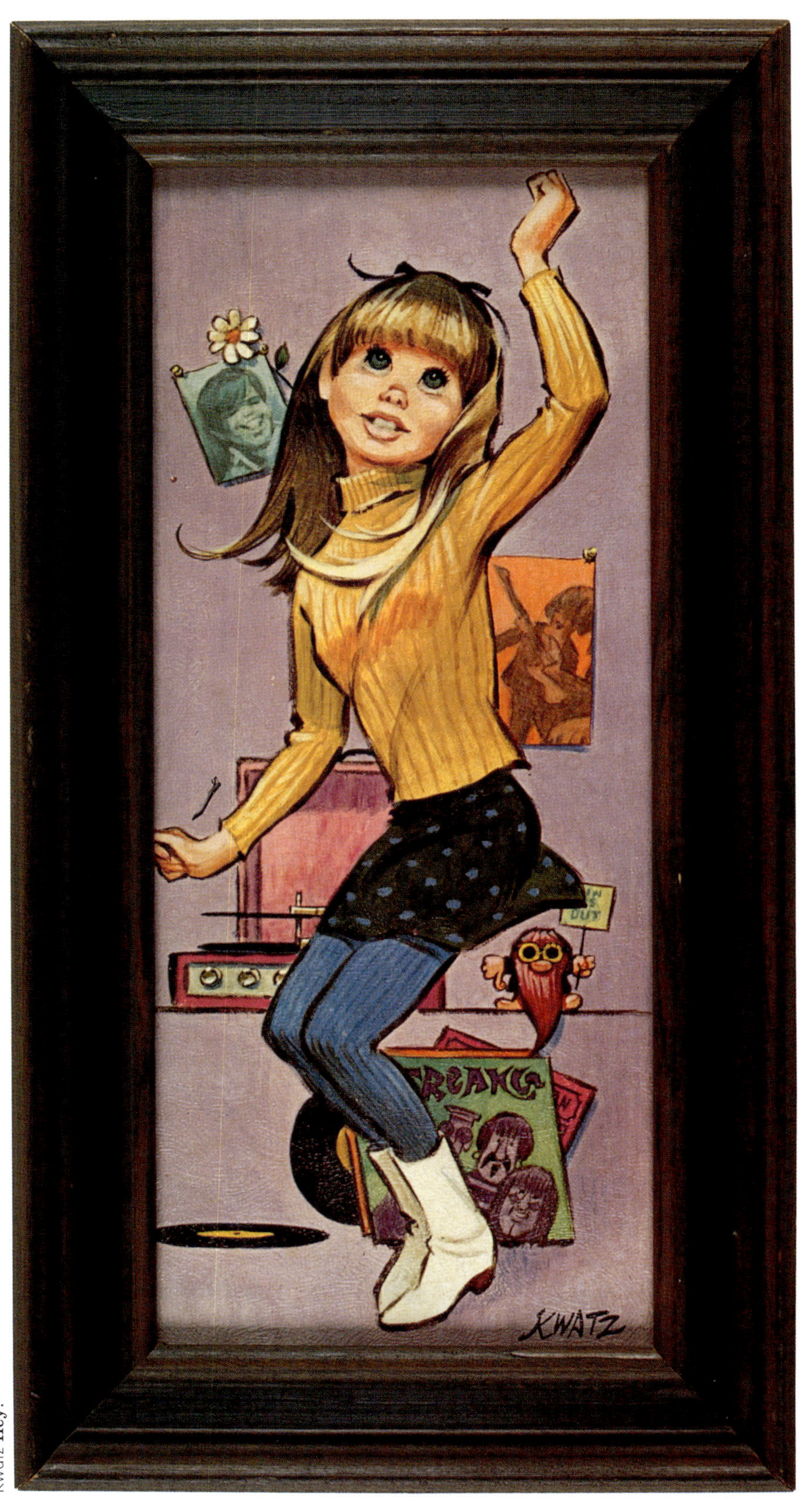

Kwatz **Hey!**

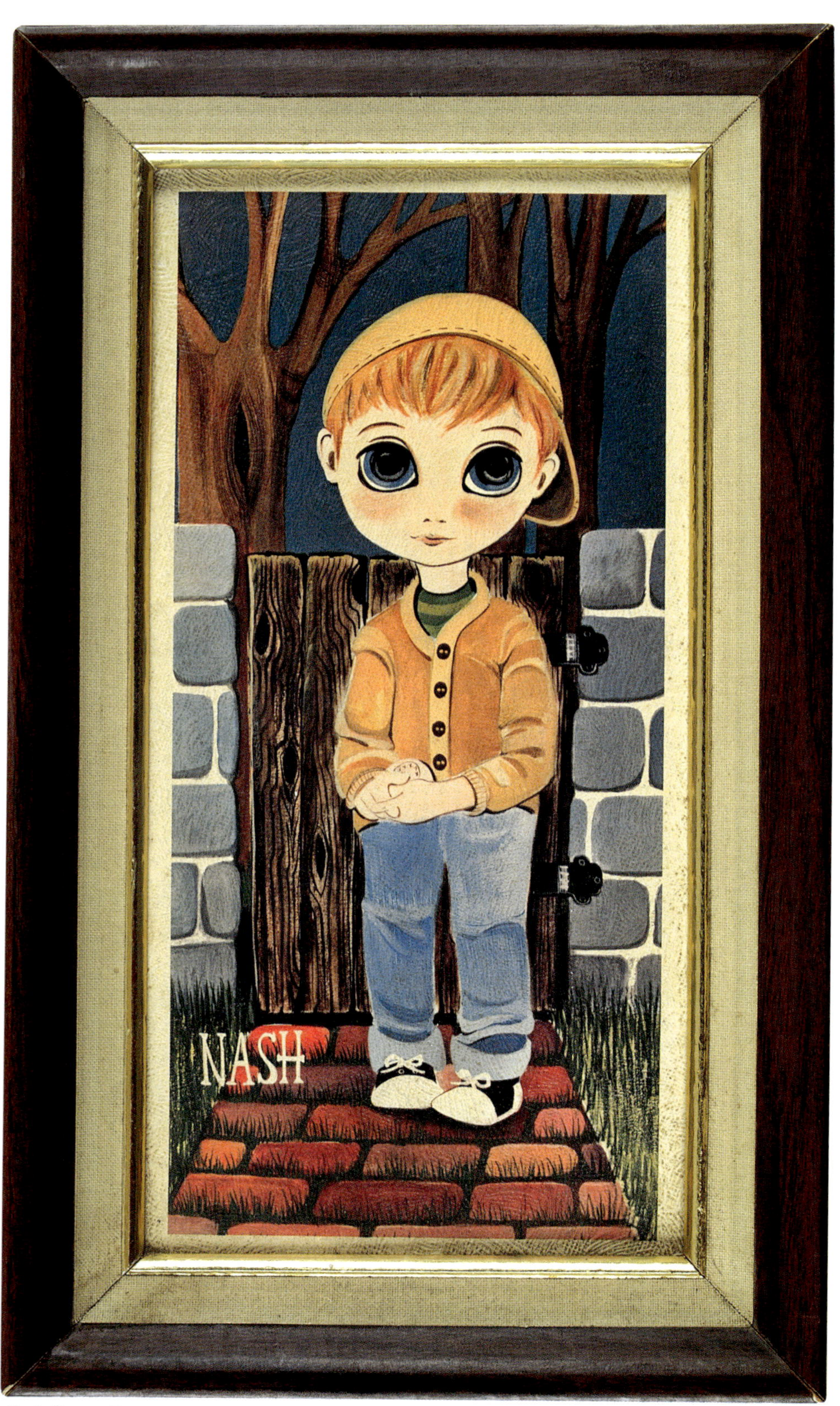

Nash **Saucer Boy**

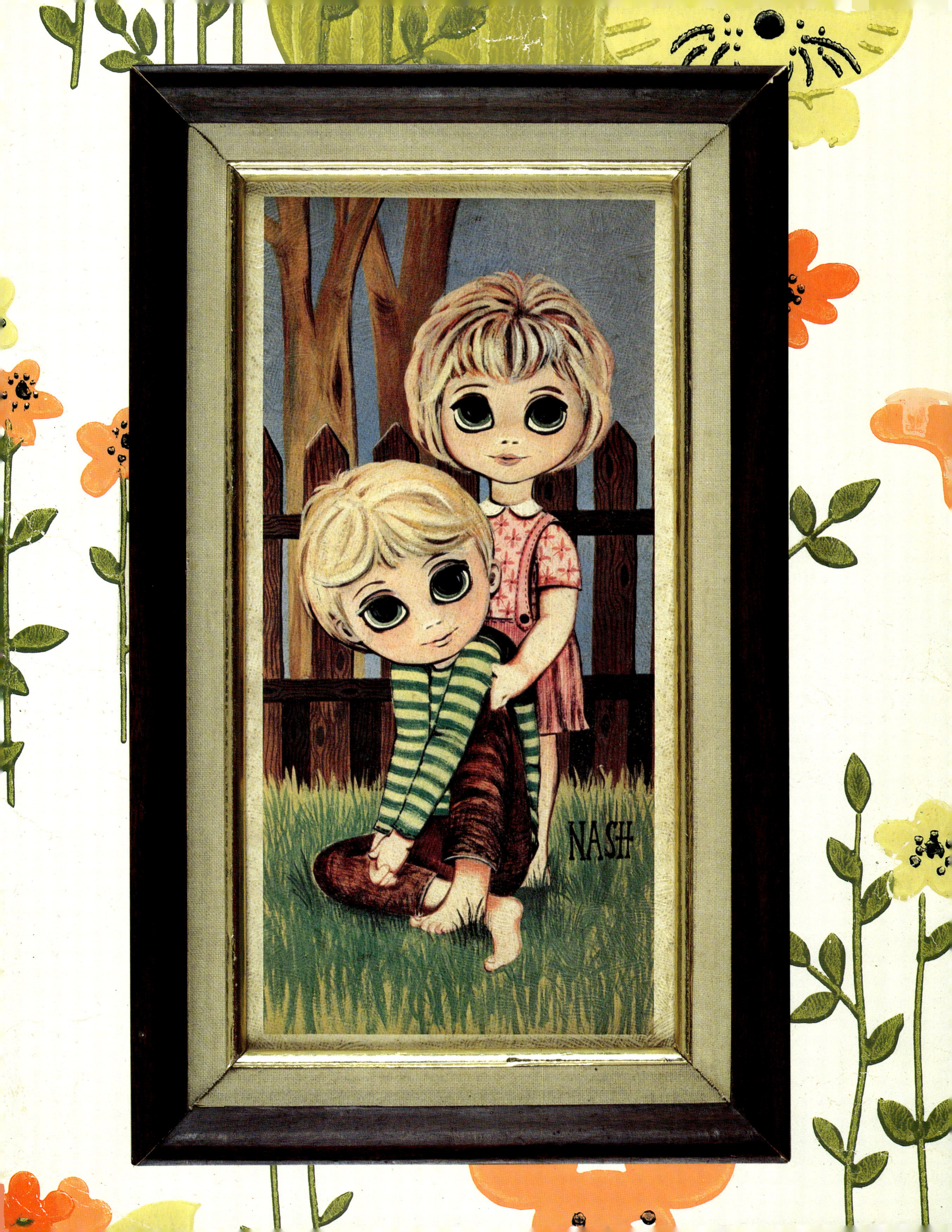
NASH

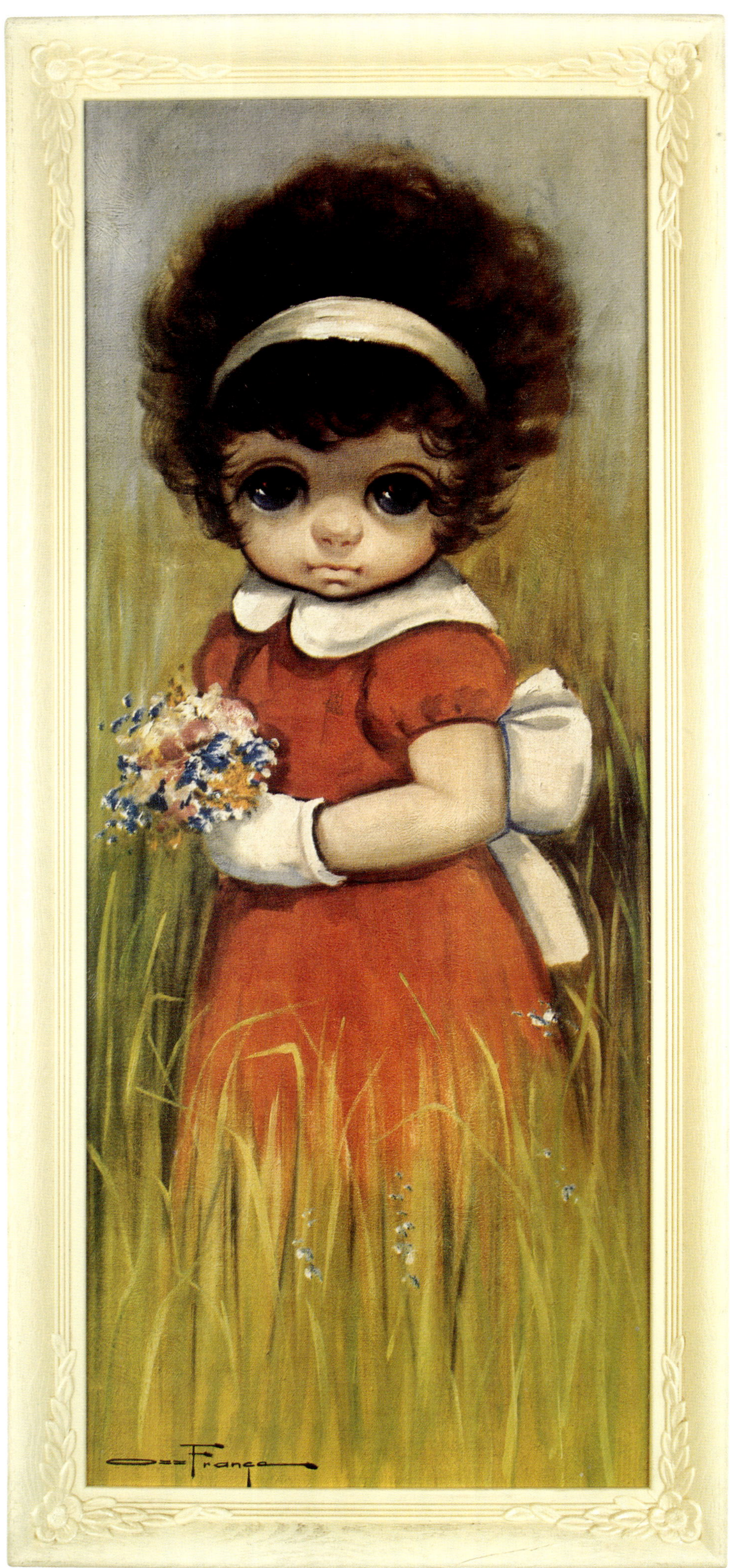

Ozz Franca **Pug Face**

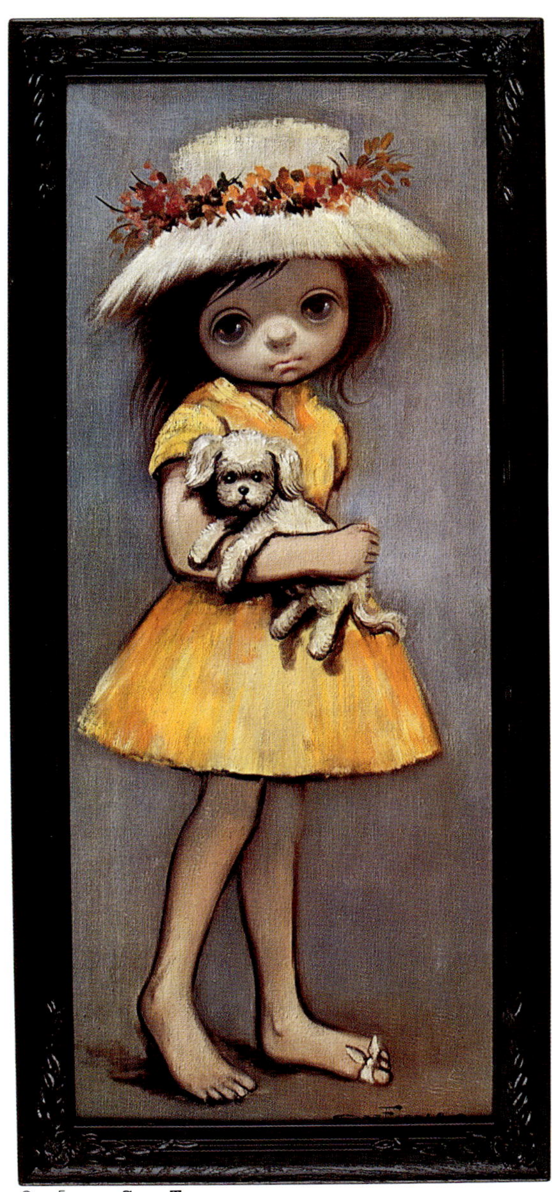

Ozz Franca **Sore Toe**

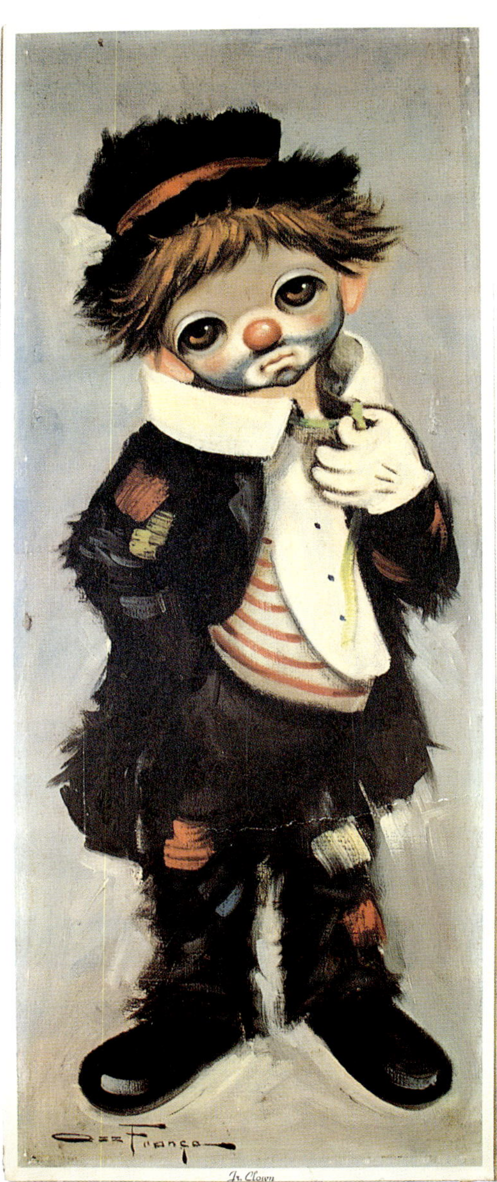

Ozz Franca **Big-Eyed Kid in Disguise**

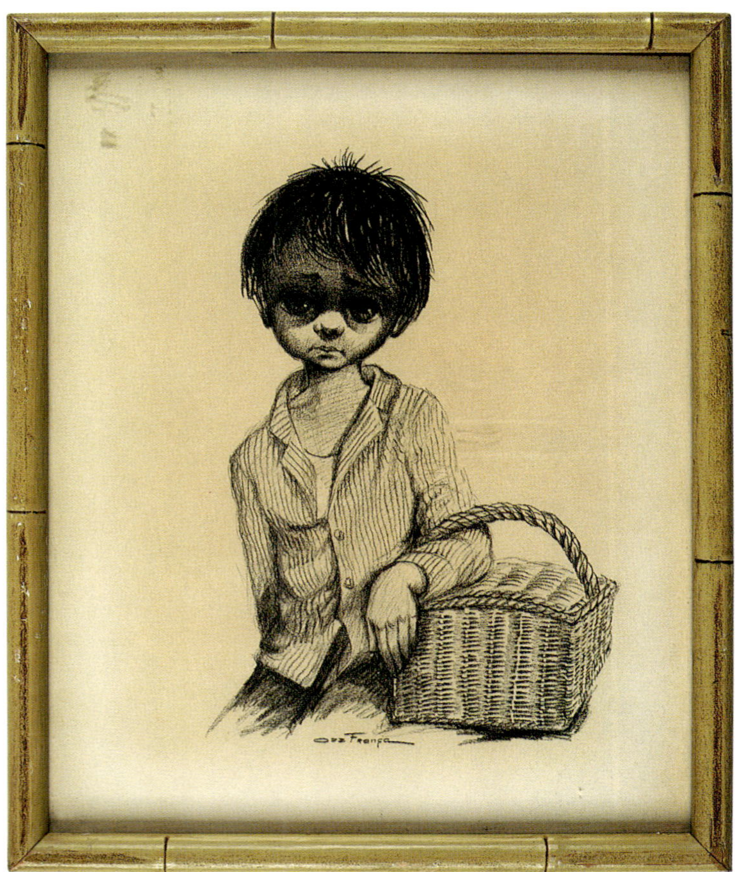

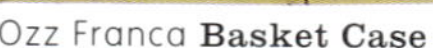

Ozz Franca **Basket Case**

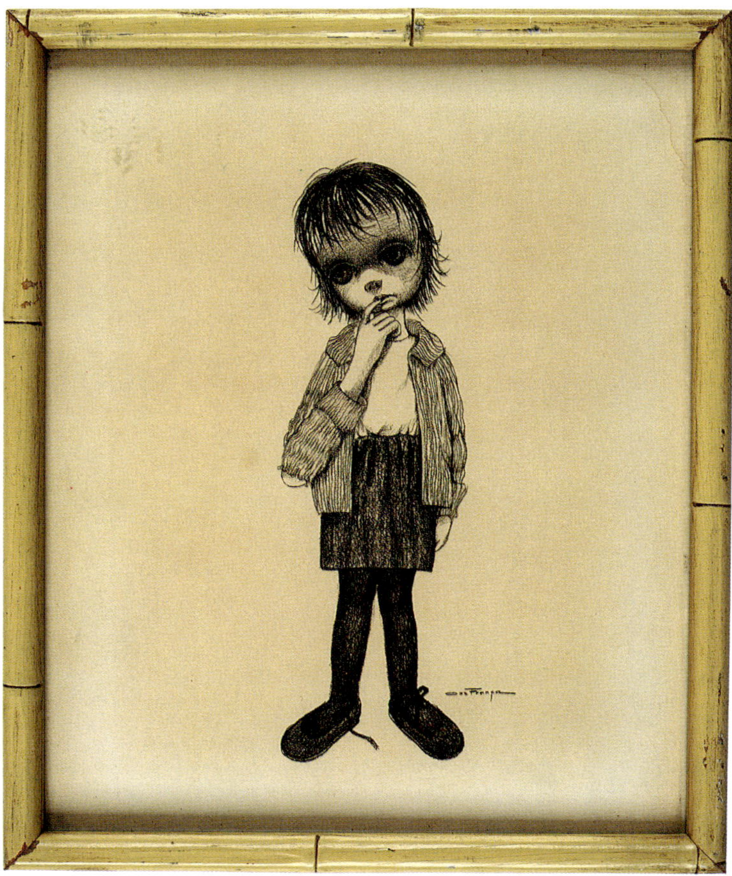

Ozz Franca **Pensive**

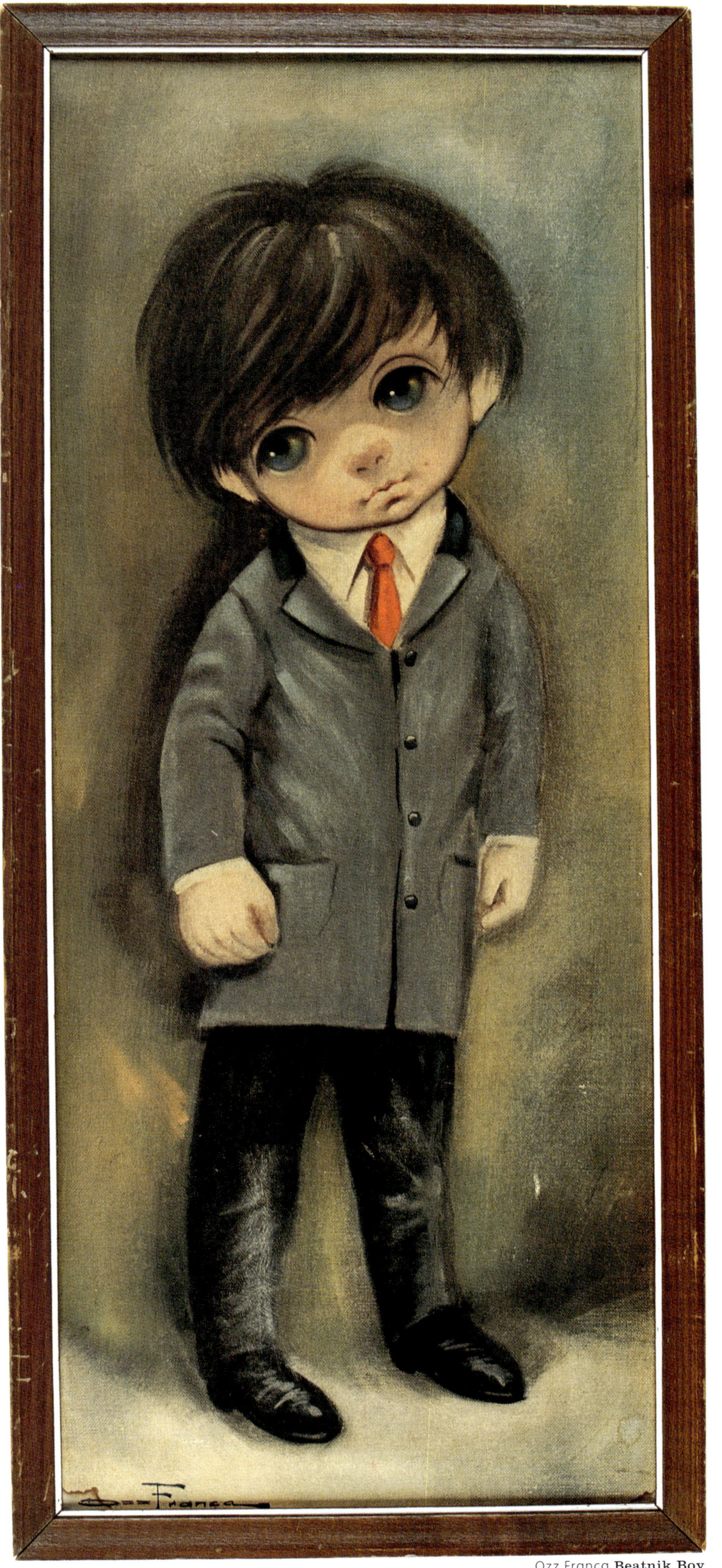

Ozz Franca **Beatnik Boy**

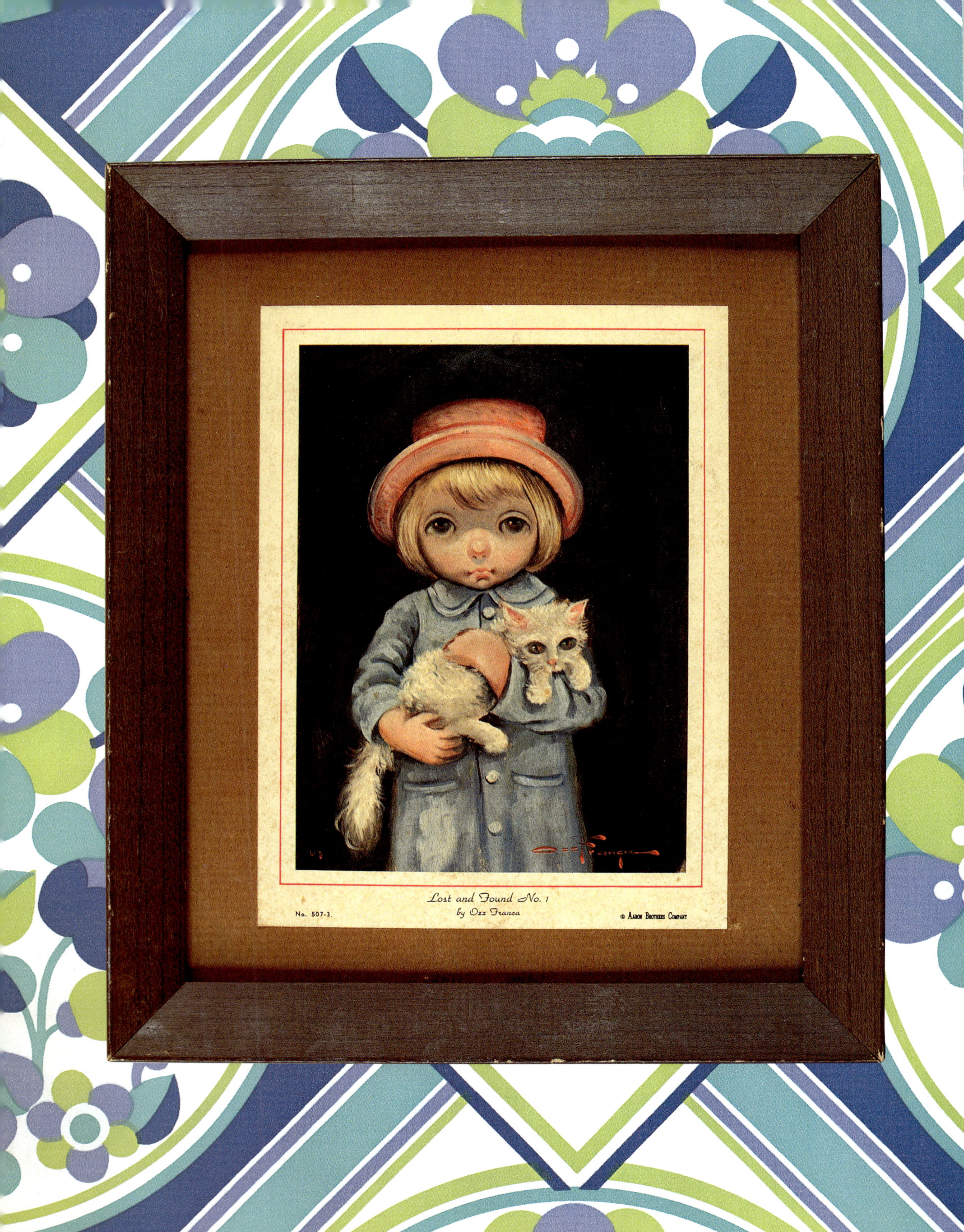
Lost and Found No. 1
by Ozz Franca
No. 507-3.
© Aaron Brothers Company

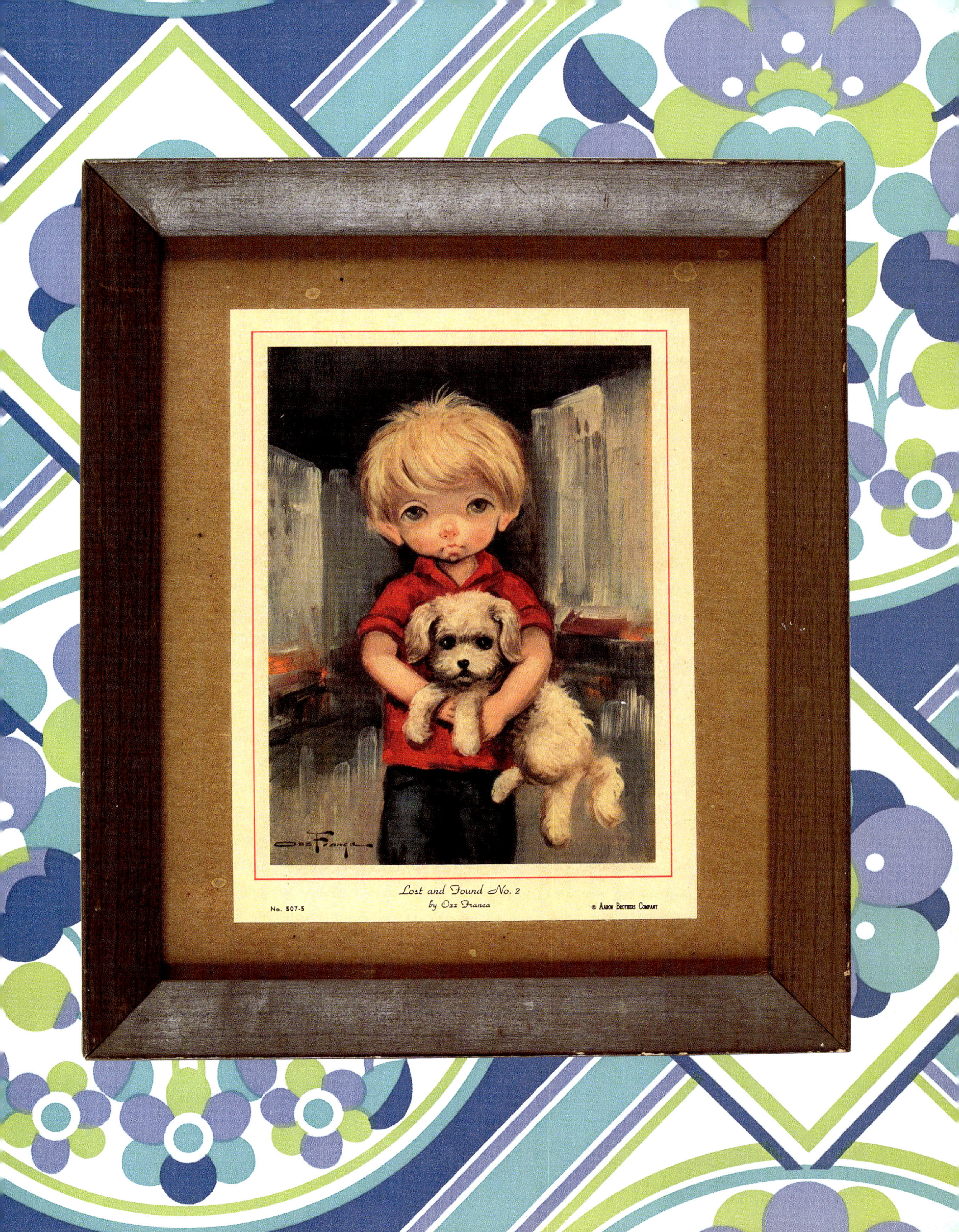
Ozz Franca
Lost and Found No. 2
by Ozz Franca
No. 507-5
© Aaron Brothers Company

preceding pages: Ozz Franca **Lost and Found No 1**; Ozz Franca **Lost and Found No 2**

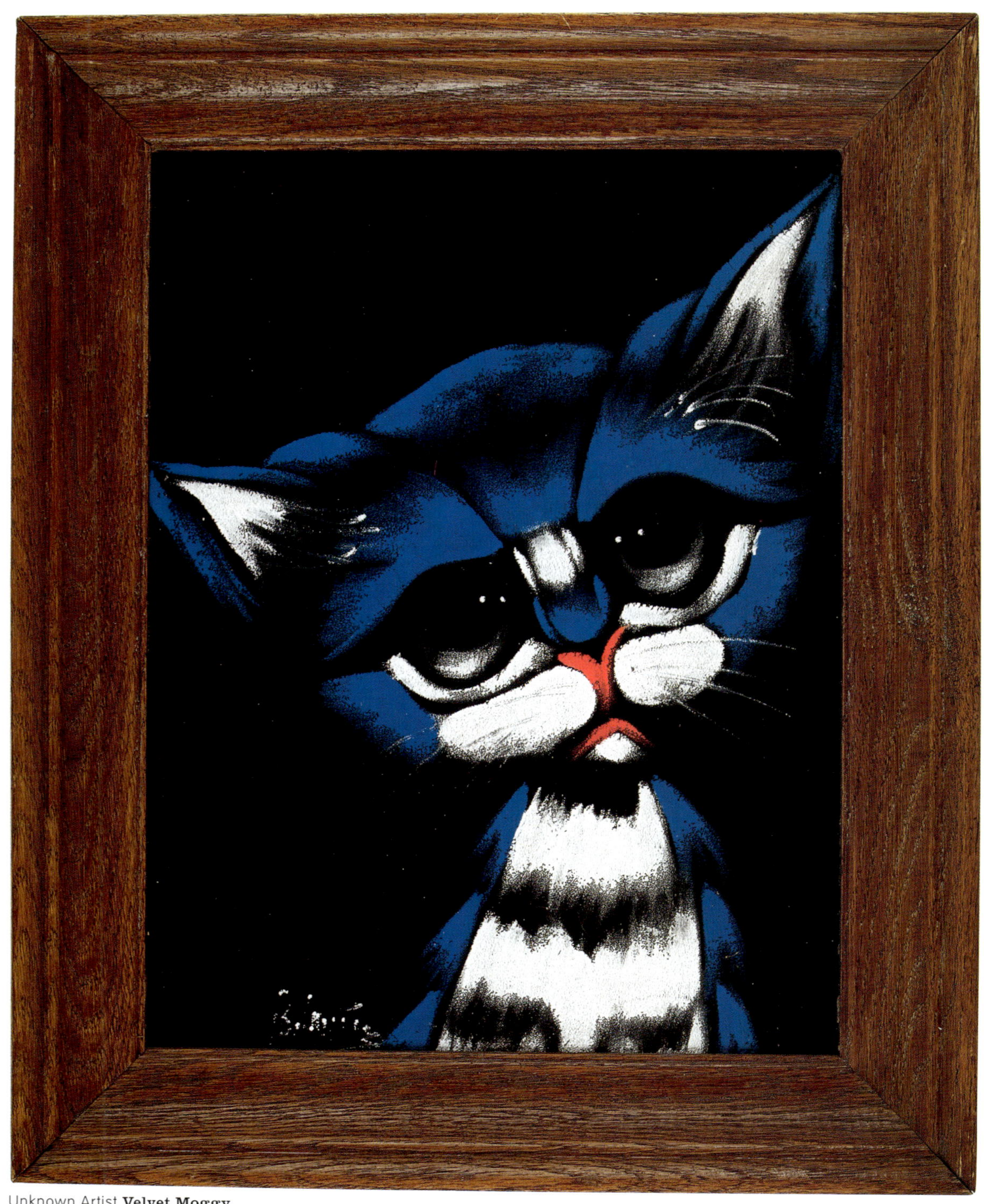

Unknown Artist **Velvet Moggy**

Unknown Artist **Velvet Girl and Poodle**

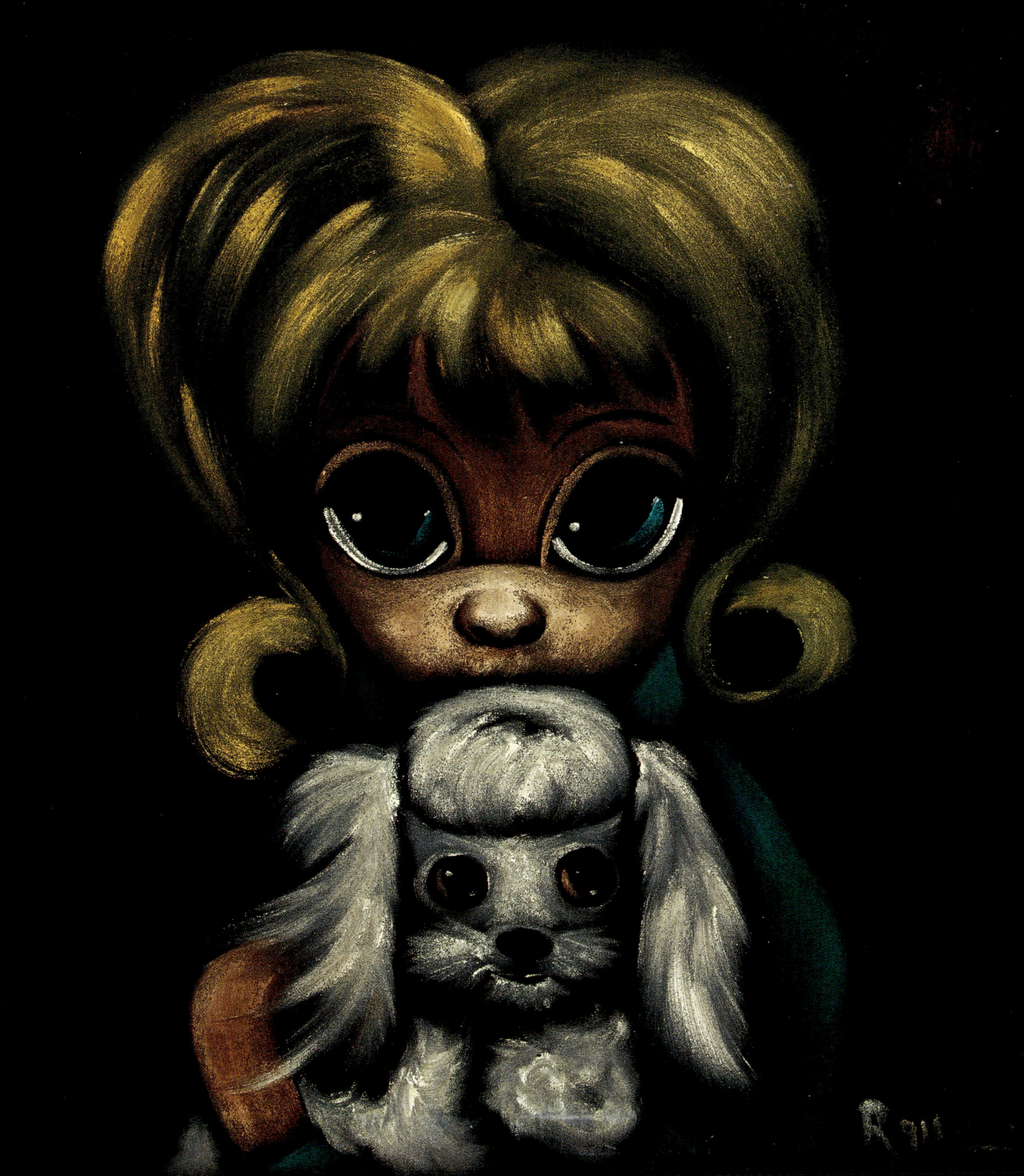

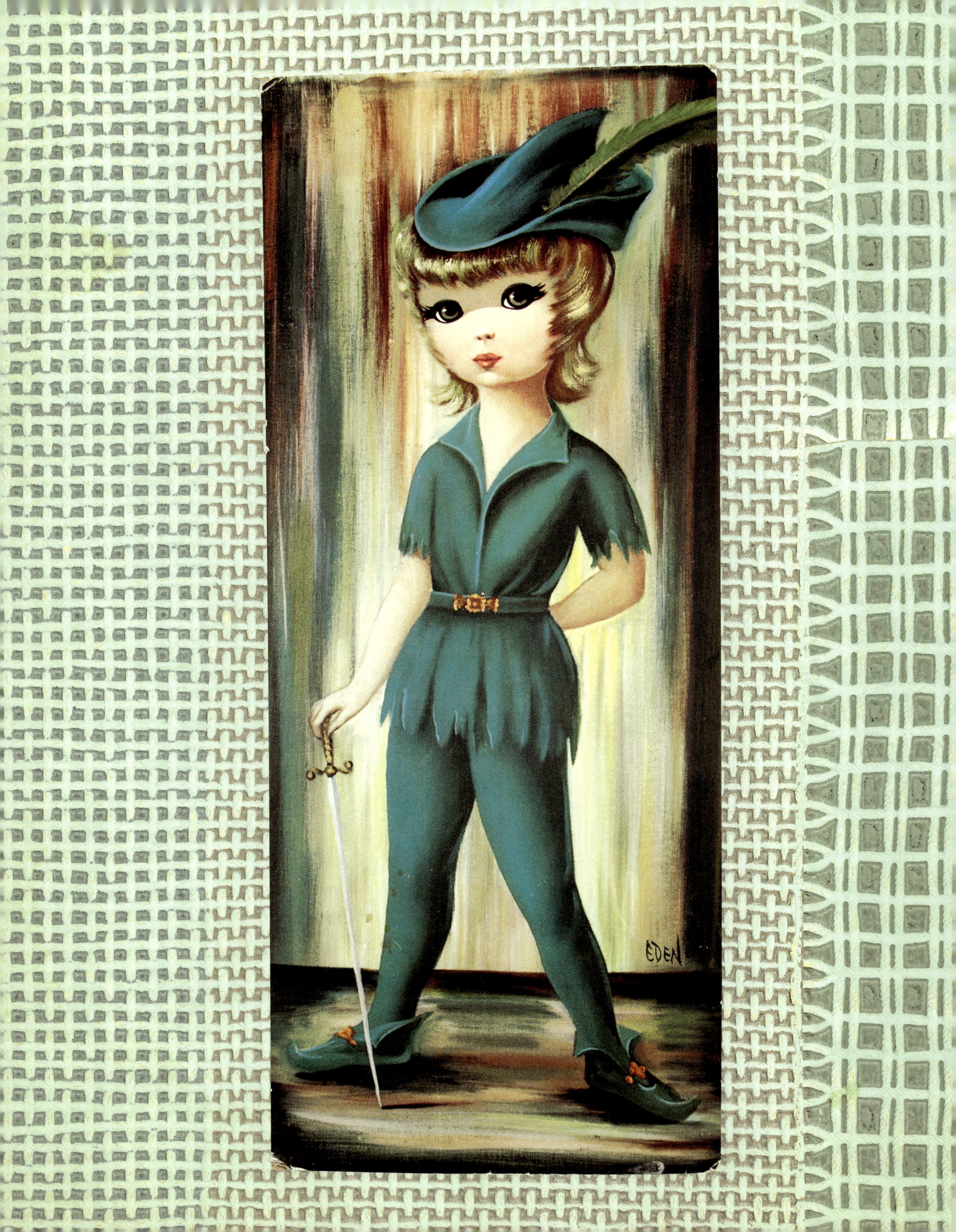
EDEN

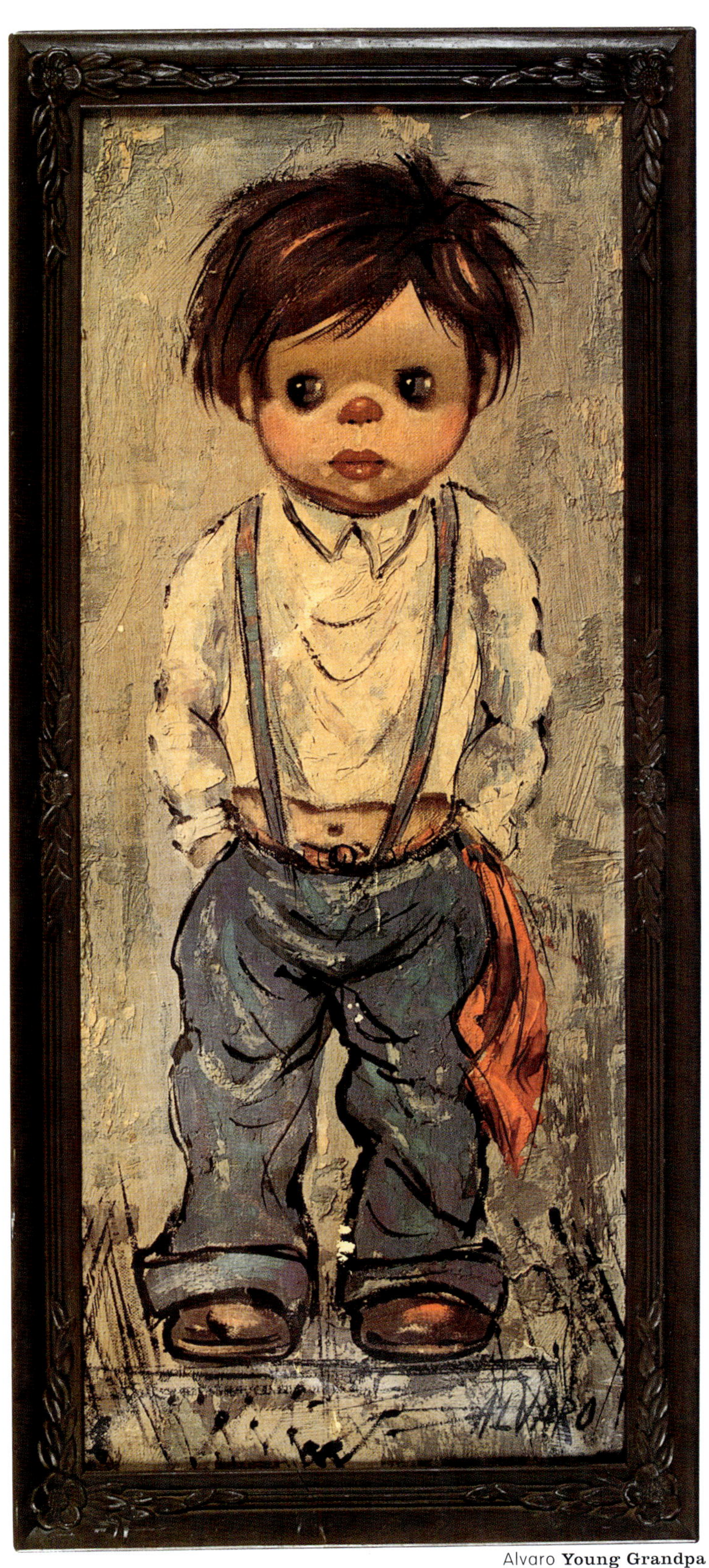

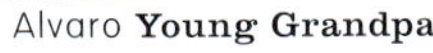
Alvaro **Young Grandpa**

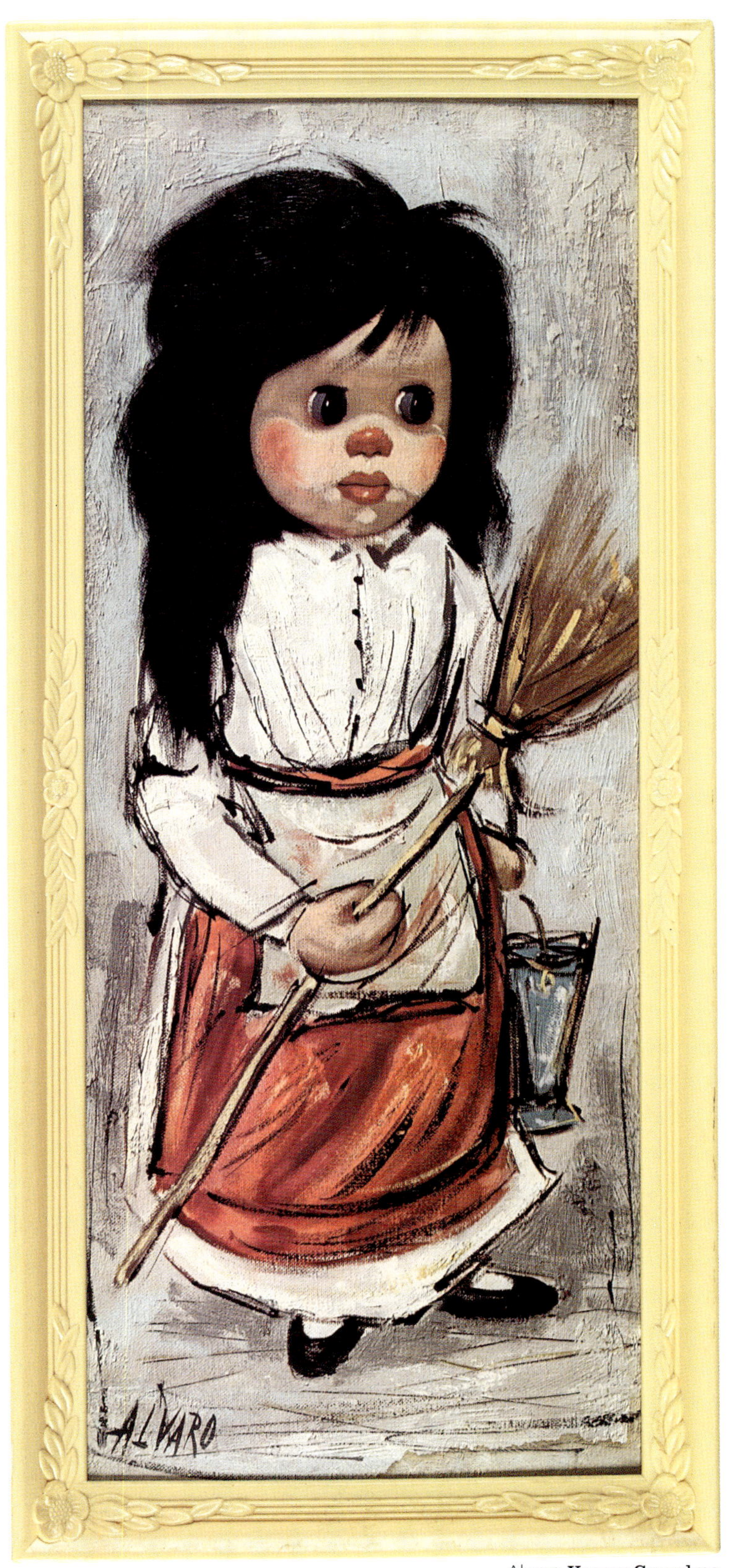

Alvaro **Young Grandma**

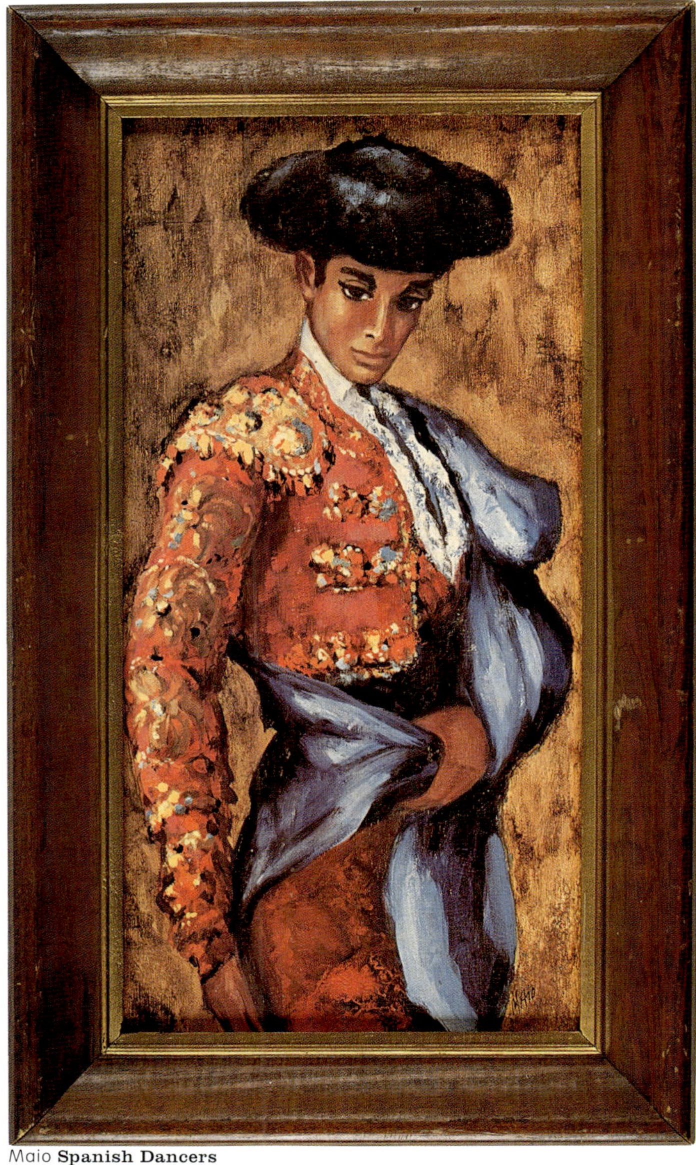

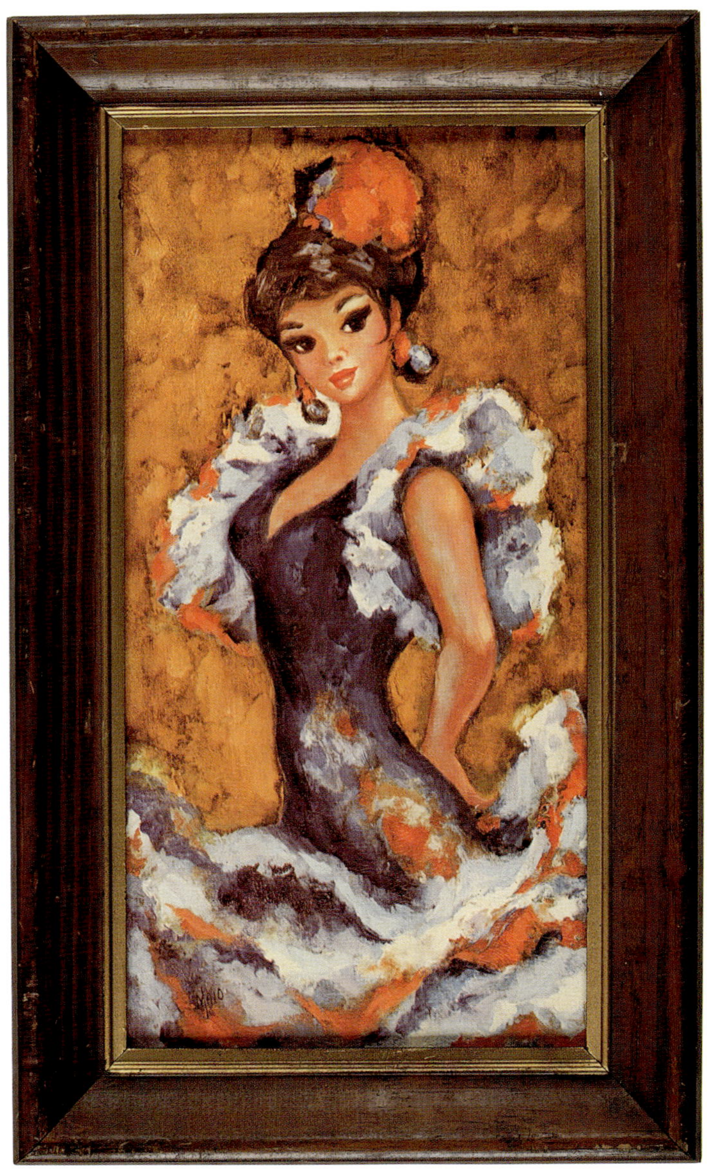

Maio **Spanish Dancers**

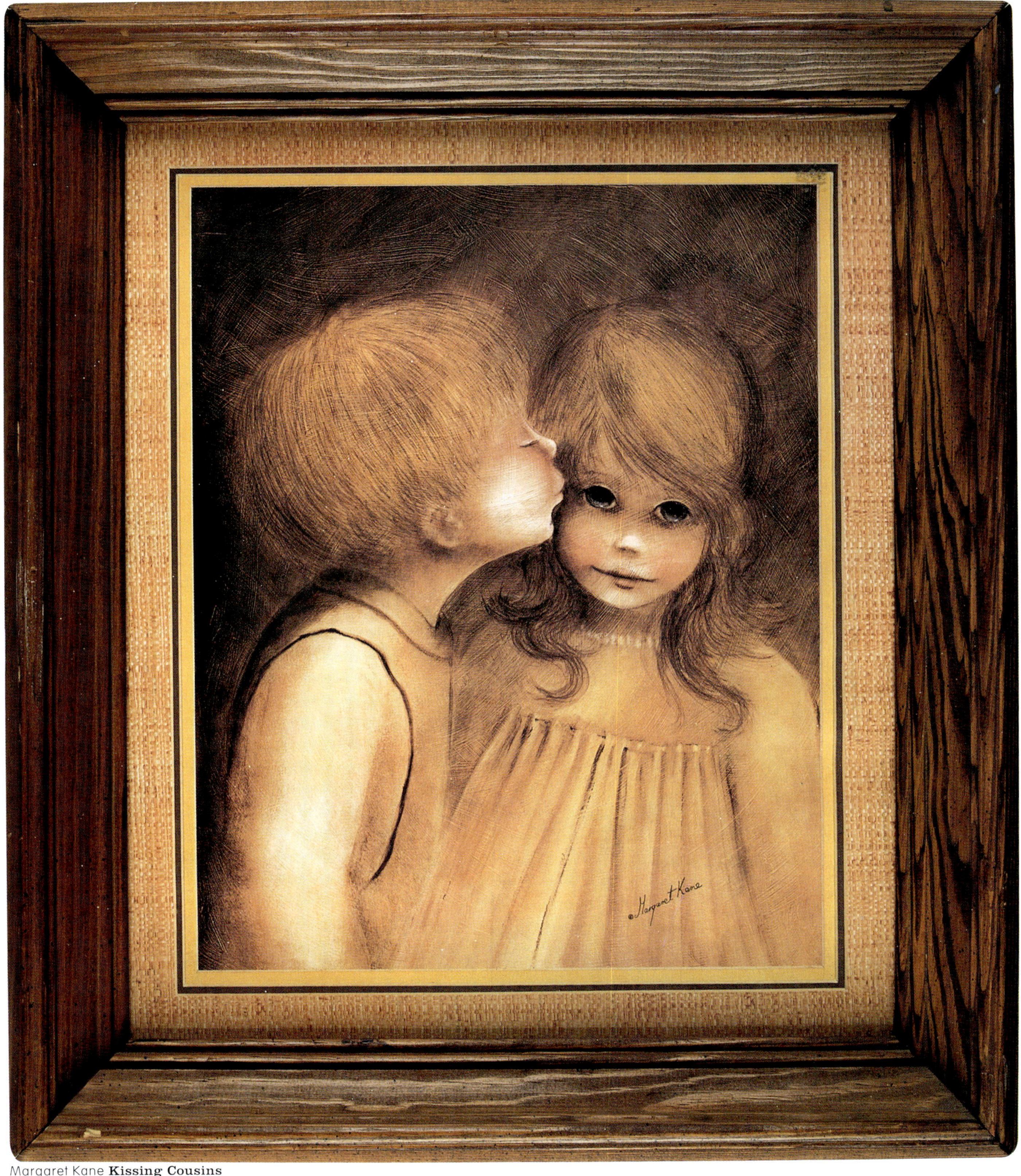

Margaret Kane **Kissing Cousins**

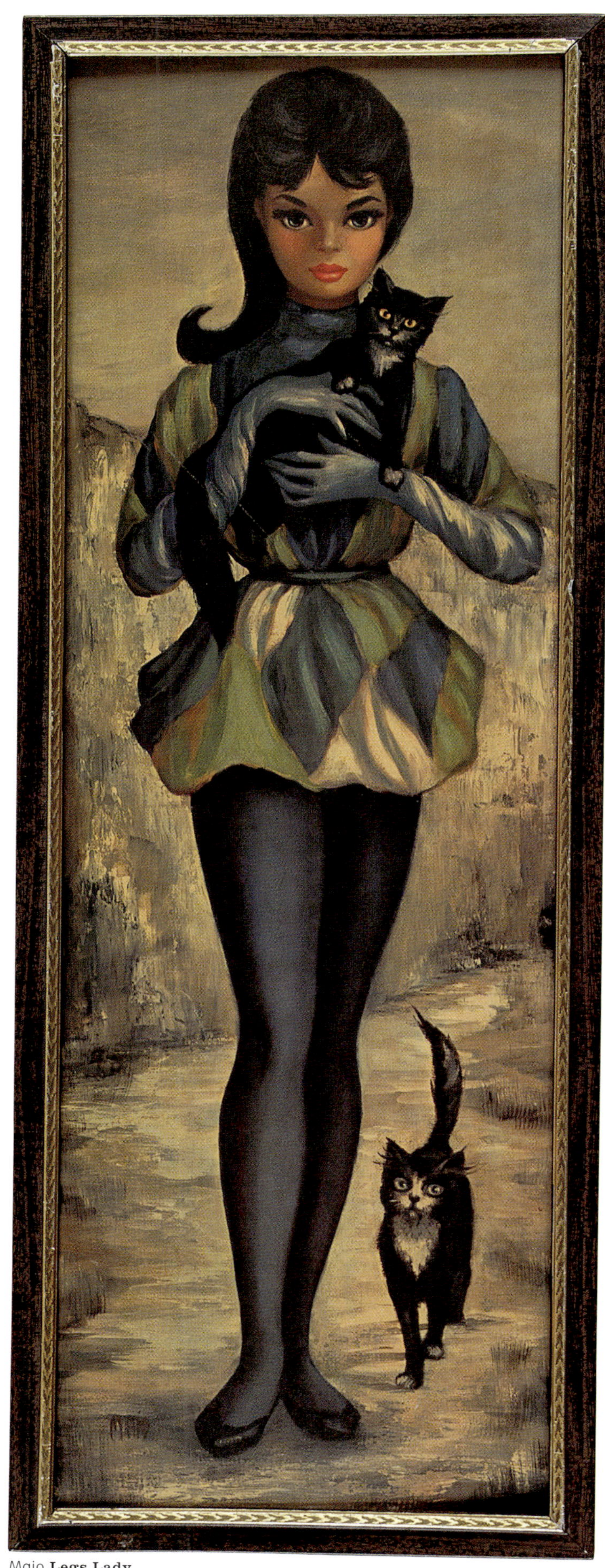

Maio **Legs Lady**

Maio **Mandolin Lass**; Maio **Parrot Girl**

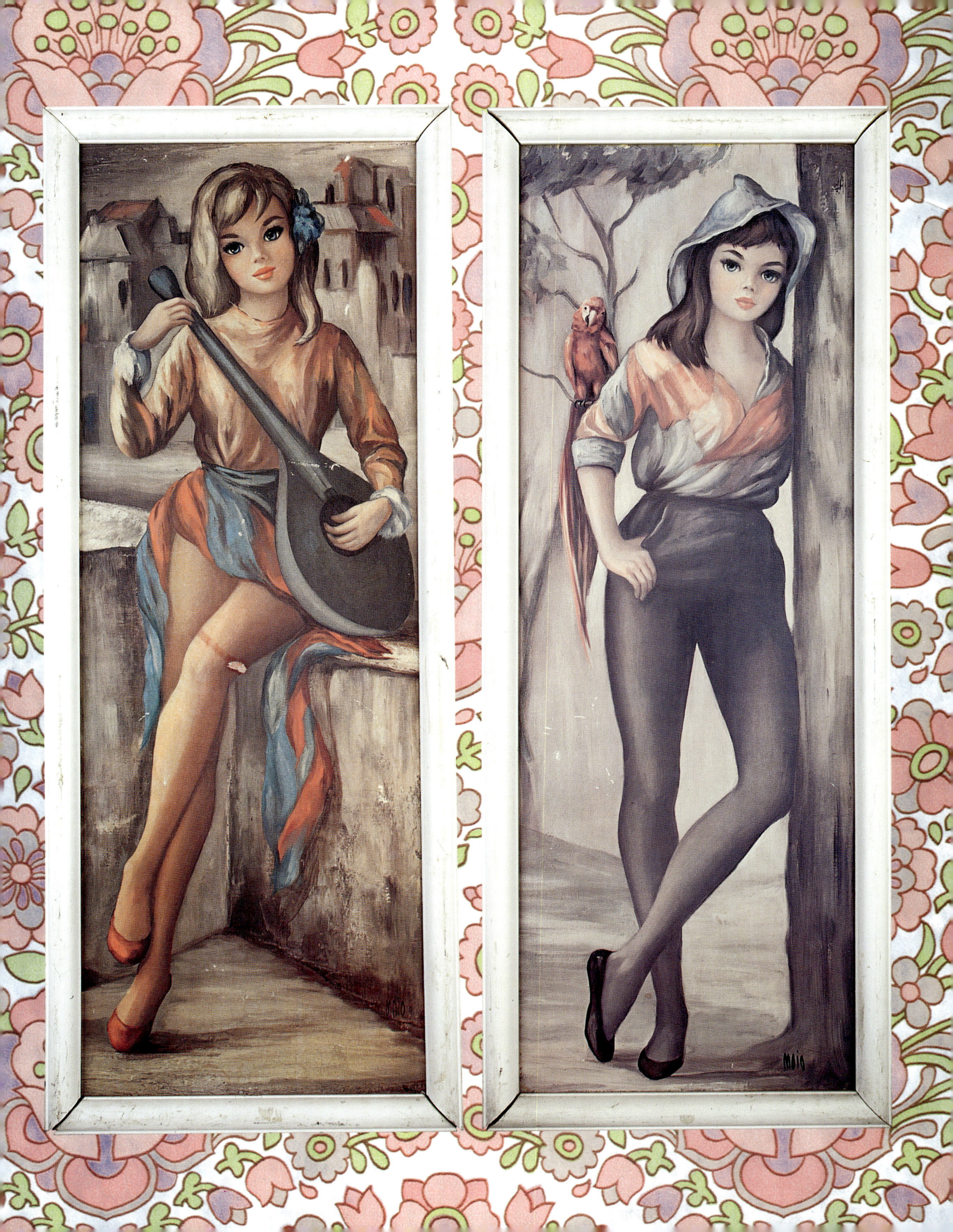

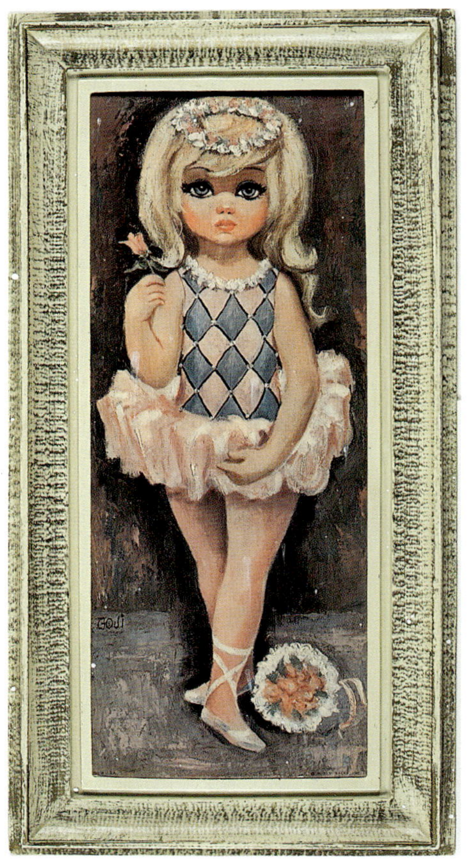

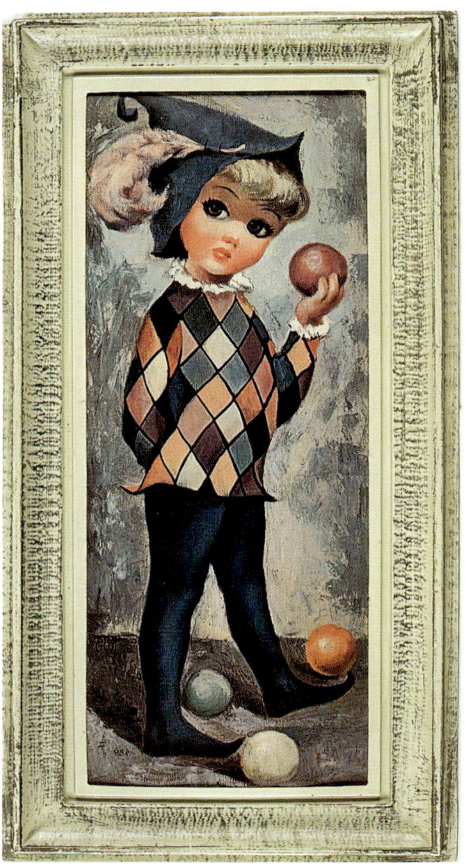

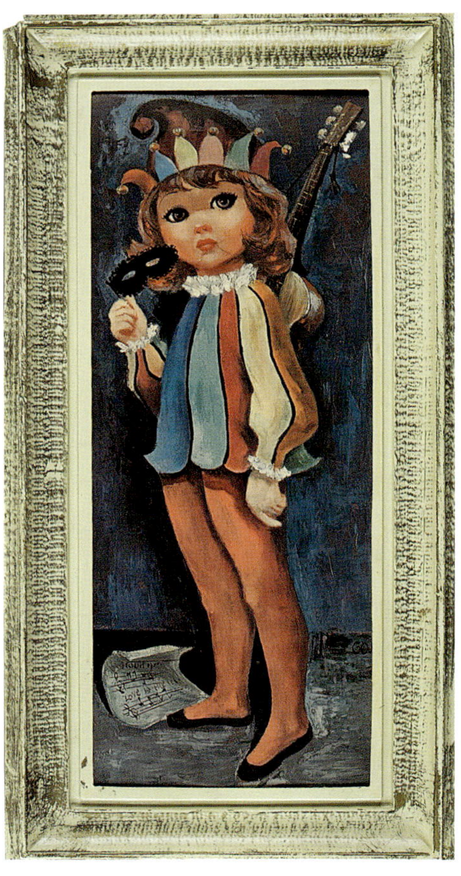

Unknown Artist **Four Fat Harlequins**

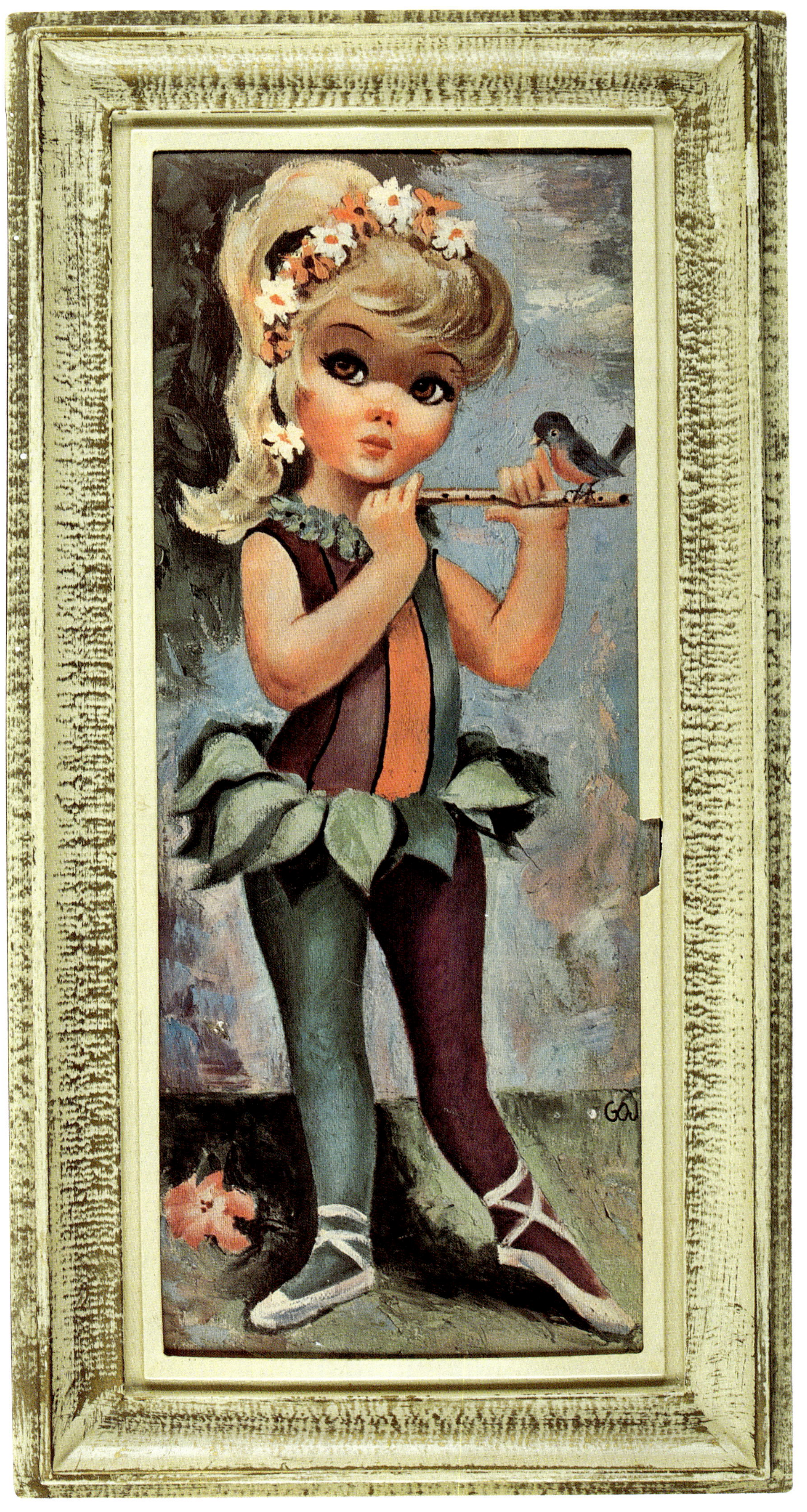
GØ

Sales of **Gig**'s Big Eye animal art must be in the millions but collectors have thus far failed to trace the American artist. **Gig** used every trick in the book to give the paintings 'cuteness'. Puppies in pet-shop windows, at bus stops and on railway lines. Stray dogs with one ear up, one ear down, with black patches on eyes, behind bars at the dogs' home, and abandoned, tethered to lampposts. Hungry cats in alleyways, foxes playing tennis and lonely lion cubs all had one thing in common – uncommonly doleful saucer eyes.

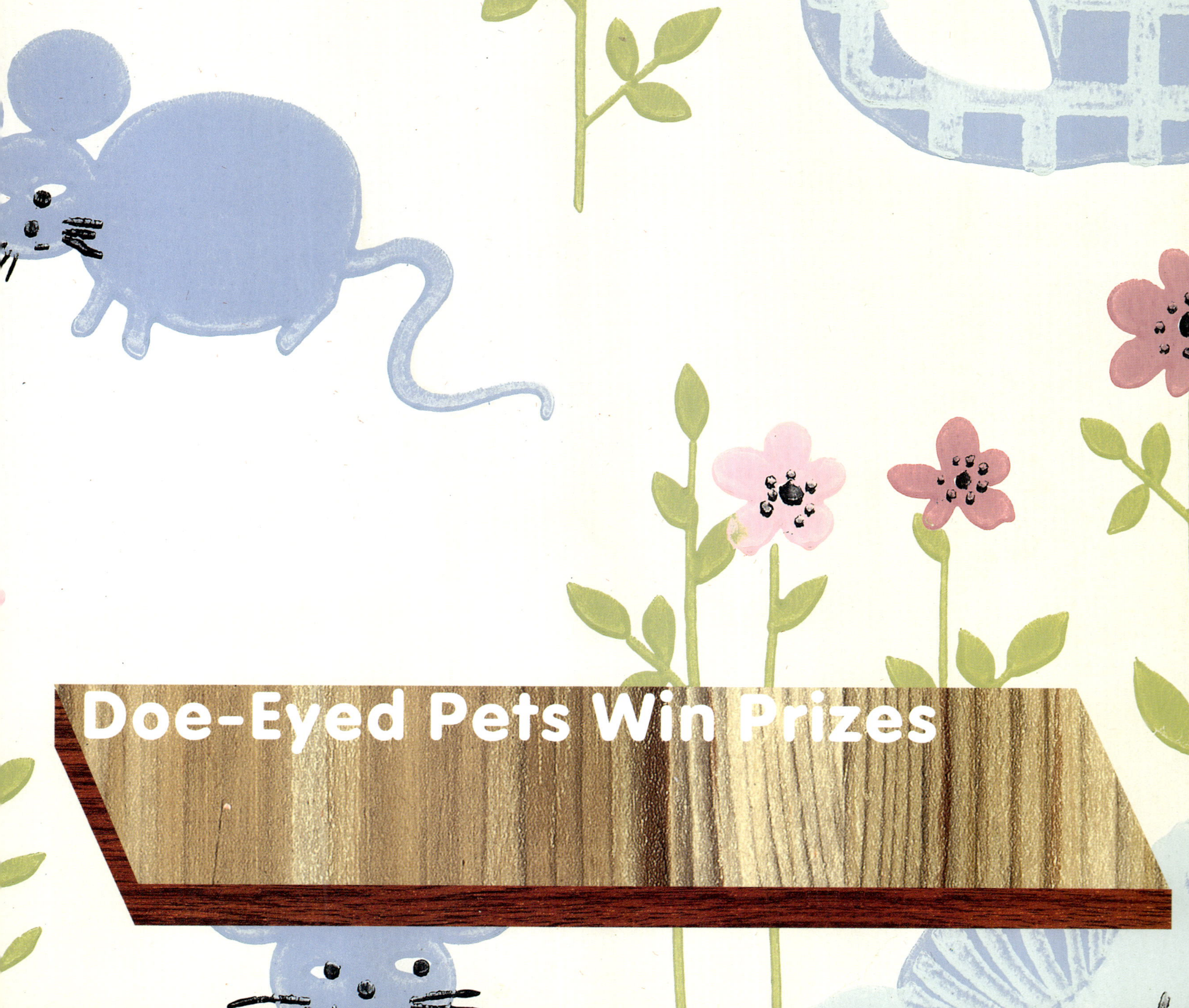

Doe-Eyed Pets Win Prizes

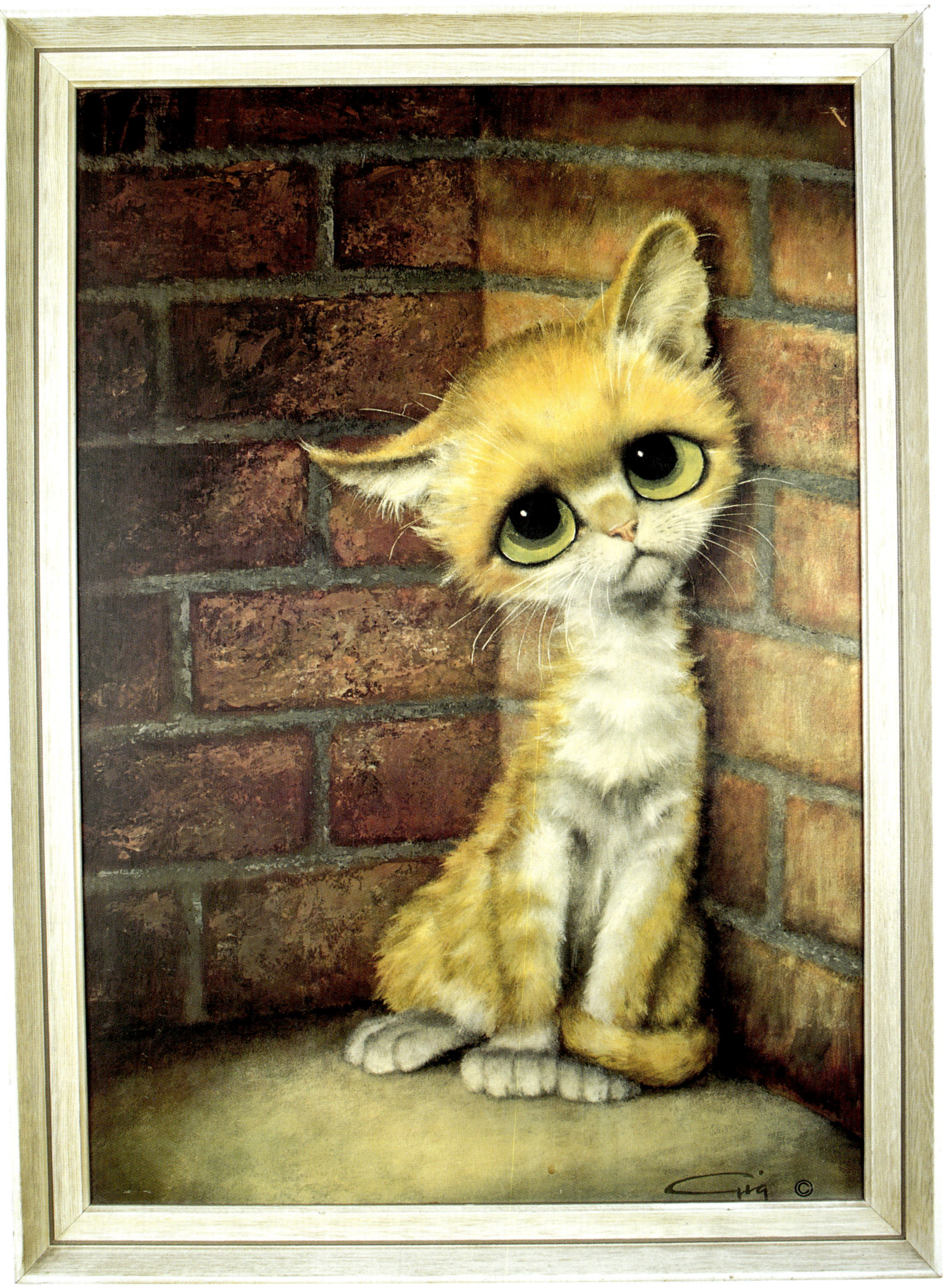

Gig **Posing**

Gig **Let Me Out**

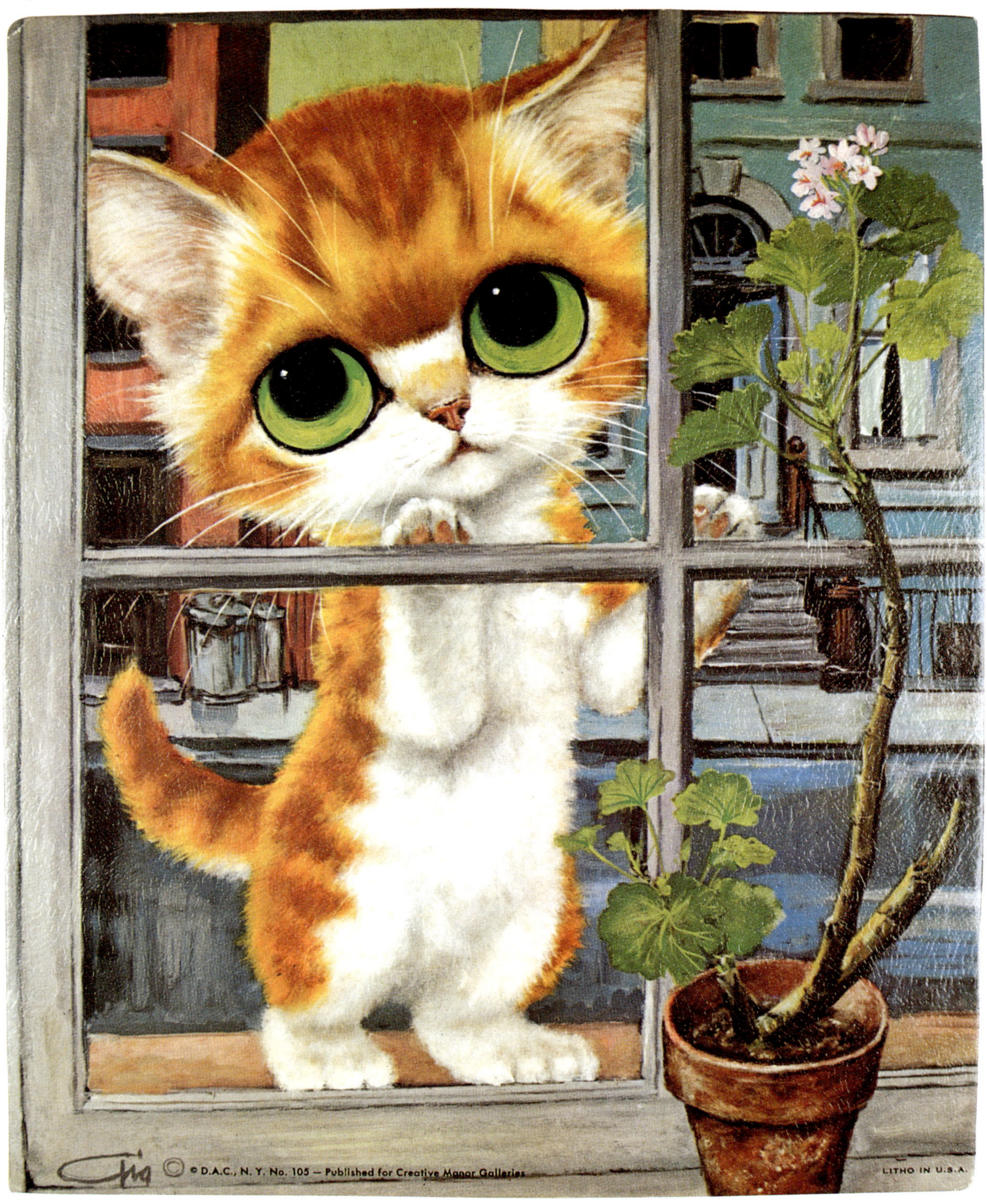

Gig **Escape**

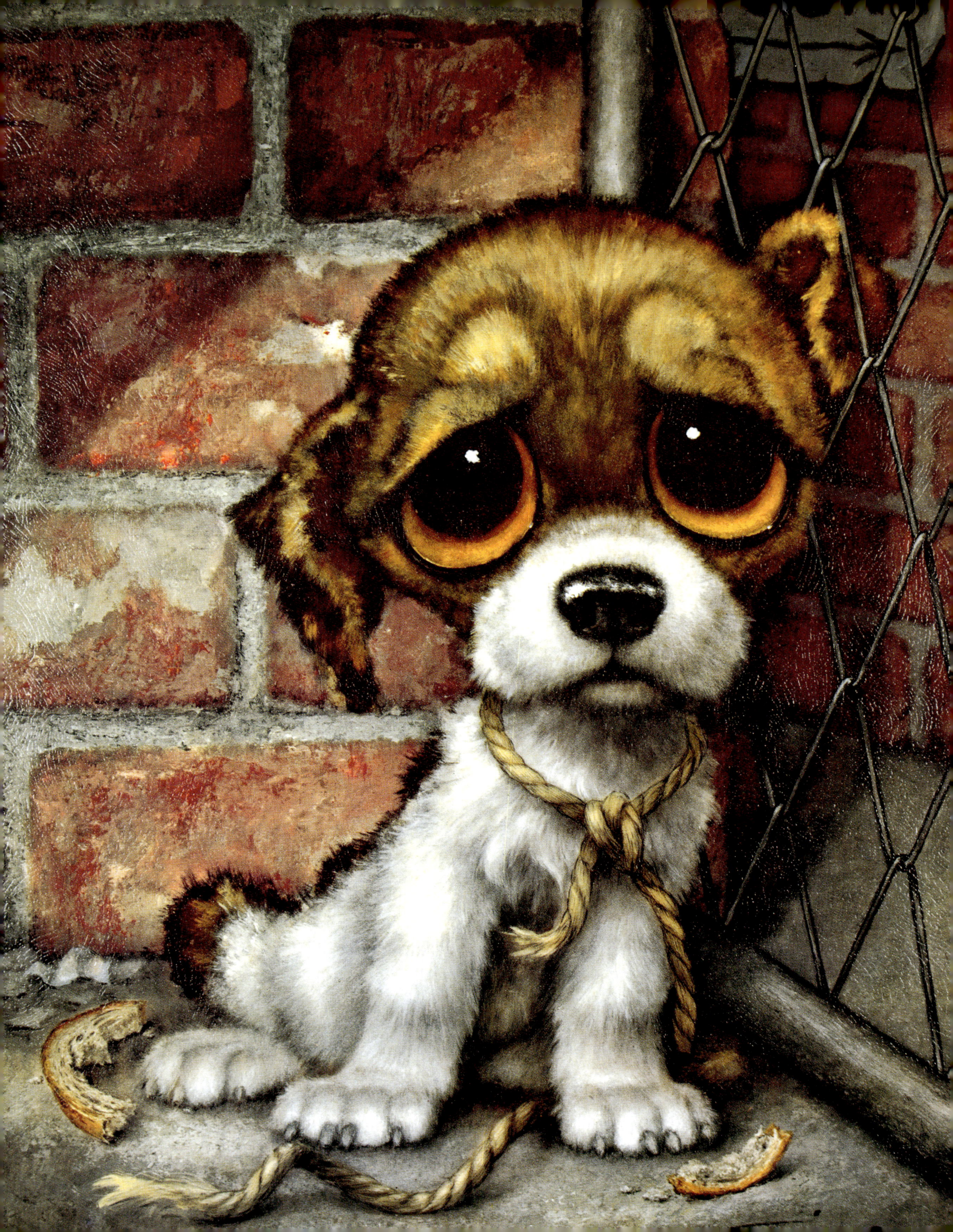

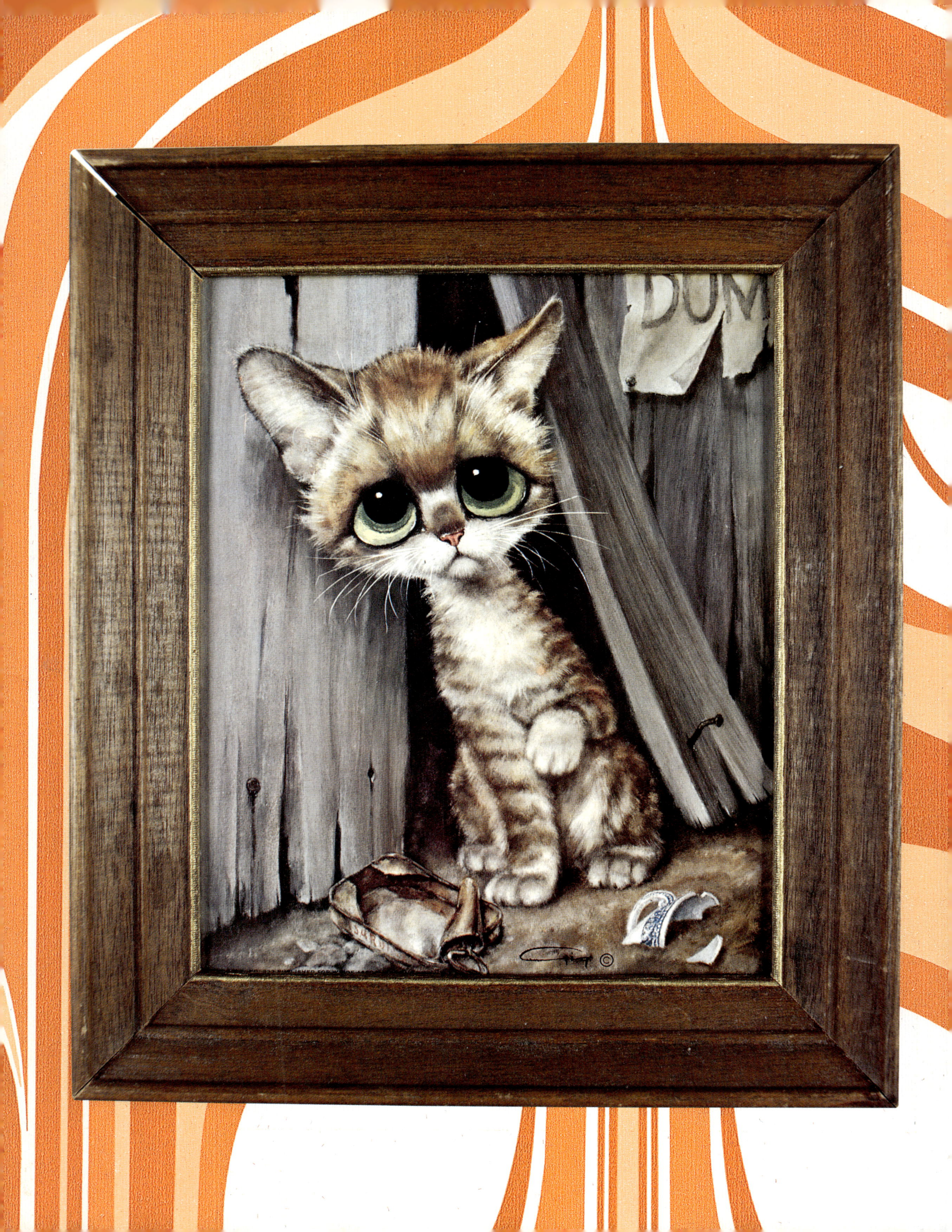
DUM

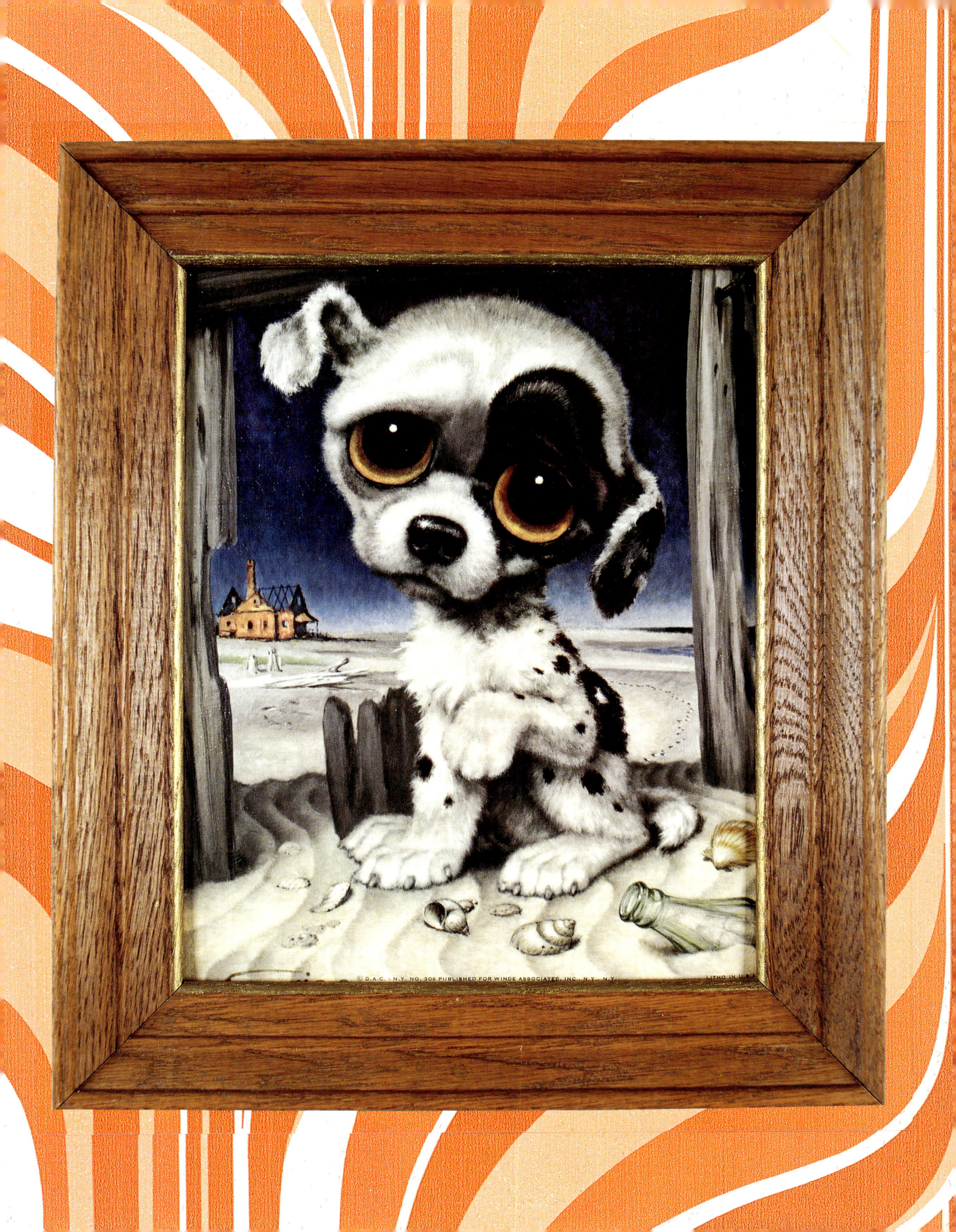
© D.A.C. - N.Y. NO. 306 PUBLISHED FOR WINDE ASSOCIATES, INC., N.Y., N.Y.
LITHO IN U.S.A.

preceding pages: Gig **Broken**; Gig **Help**

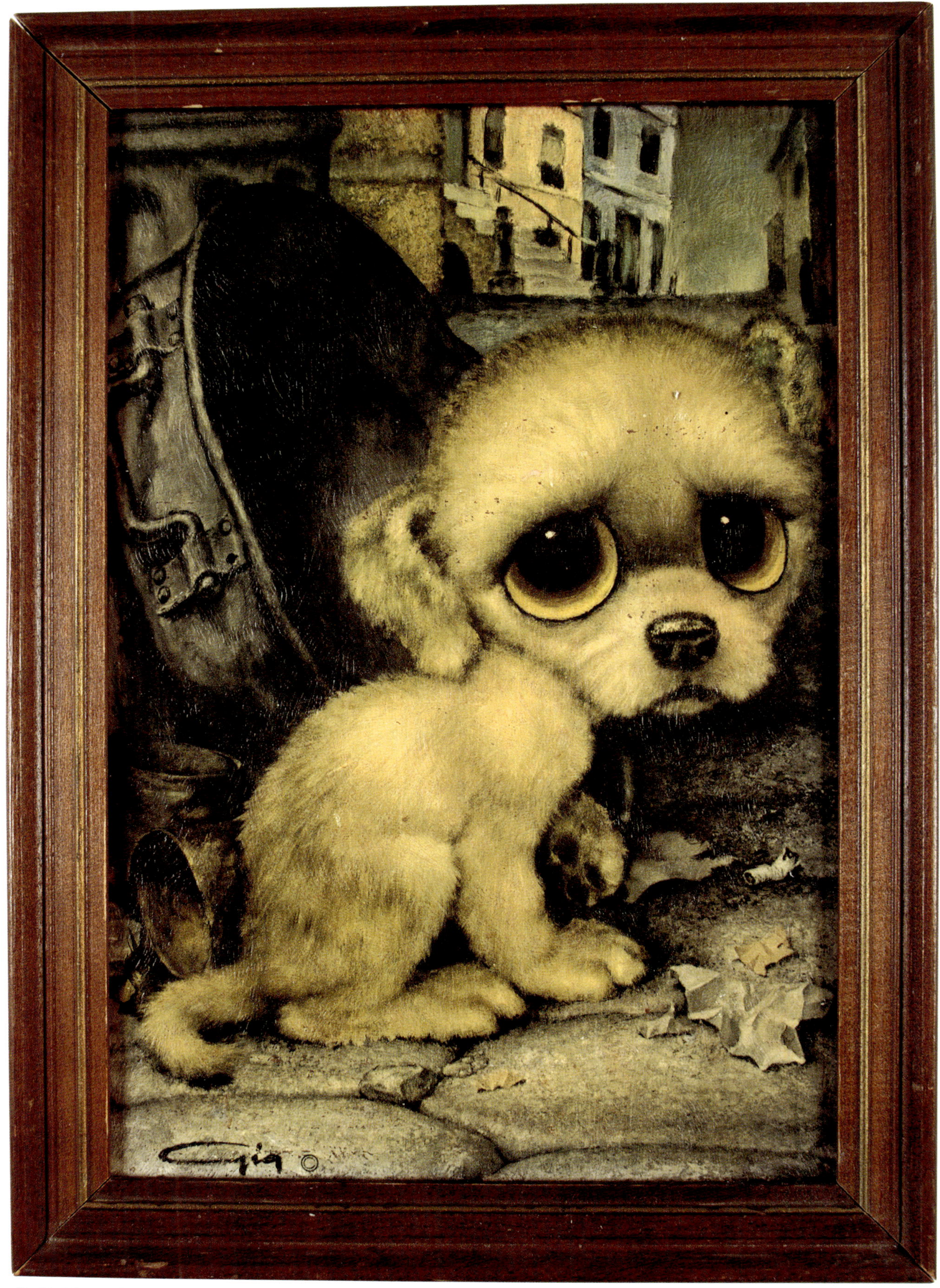

Gig **Nothing Left**

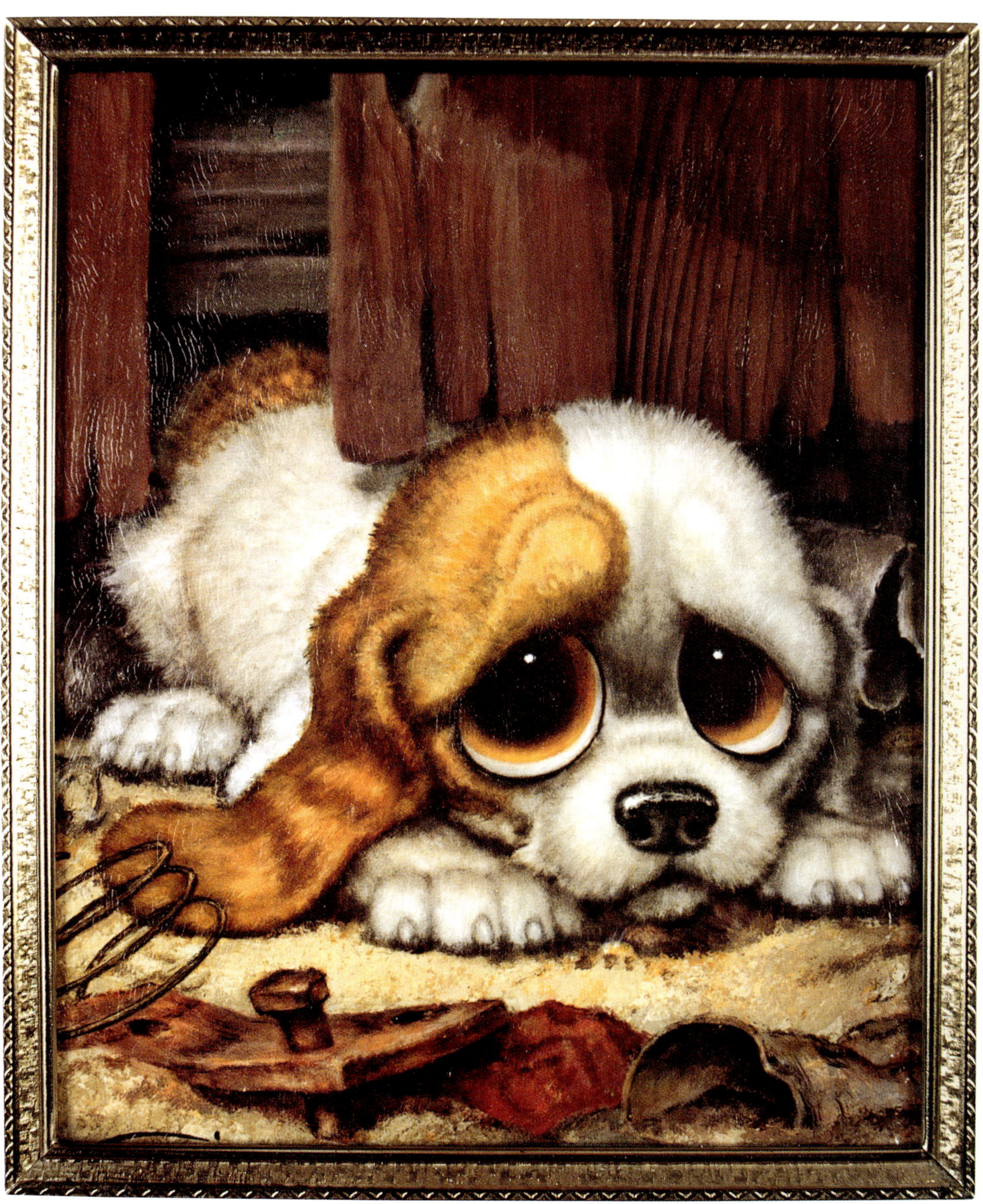

Gig **Guilty**

following pages: J R **Shabby Kittens;** Lee **Honeybear**

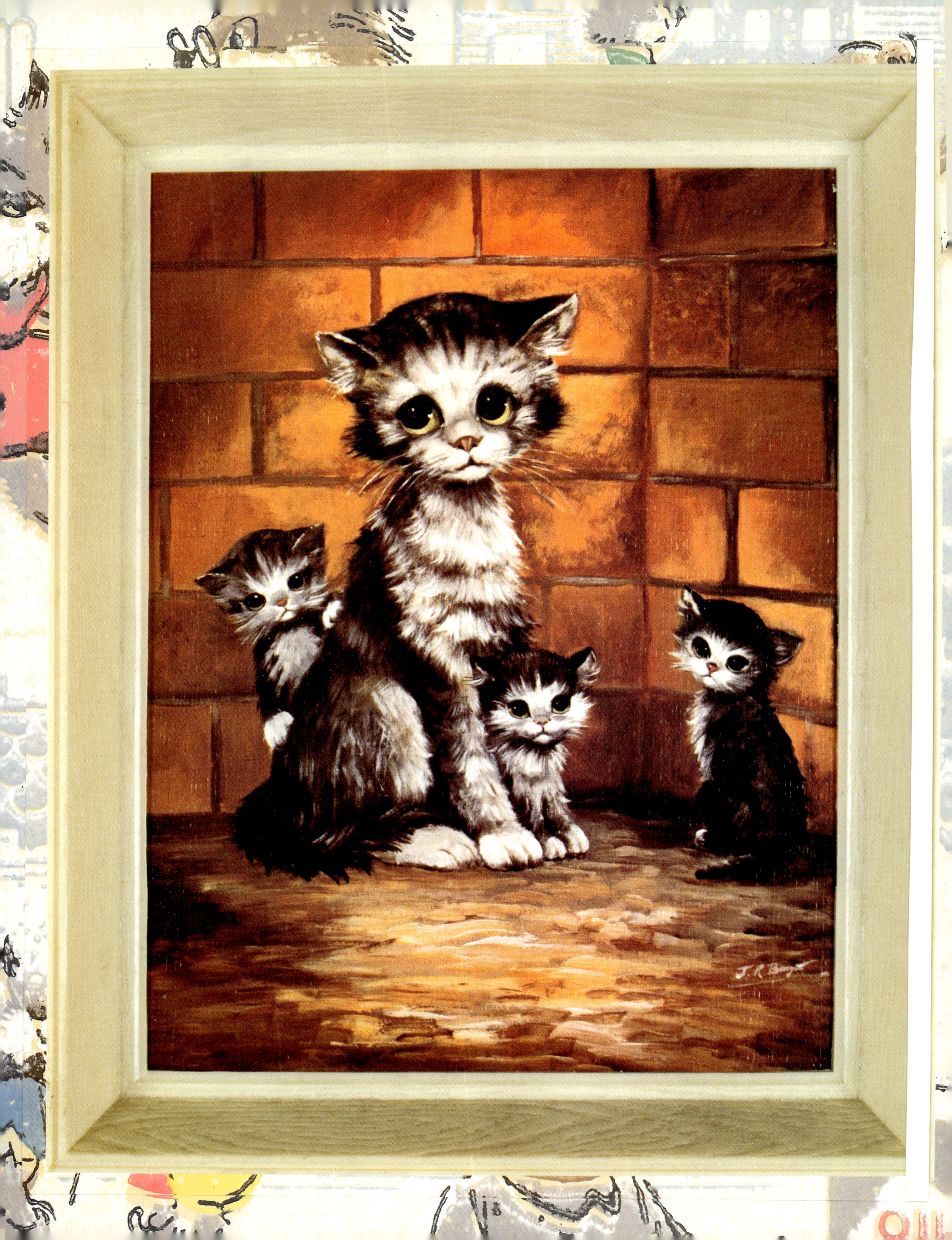

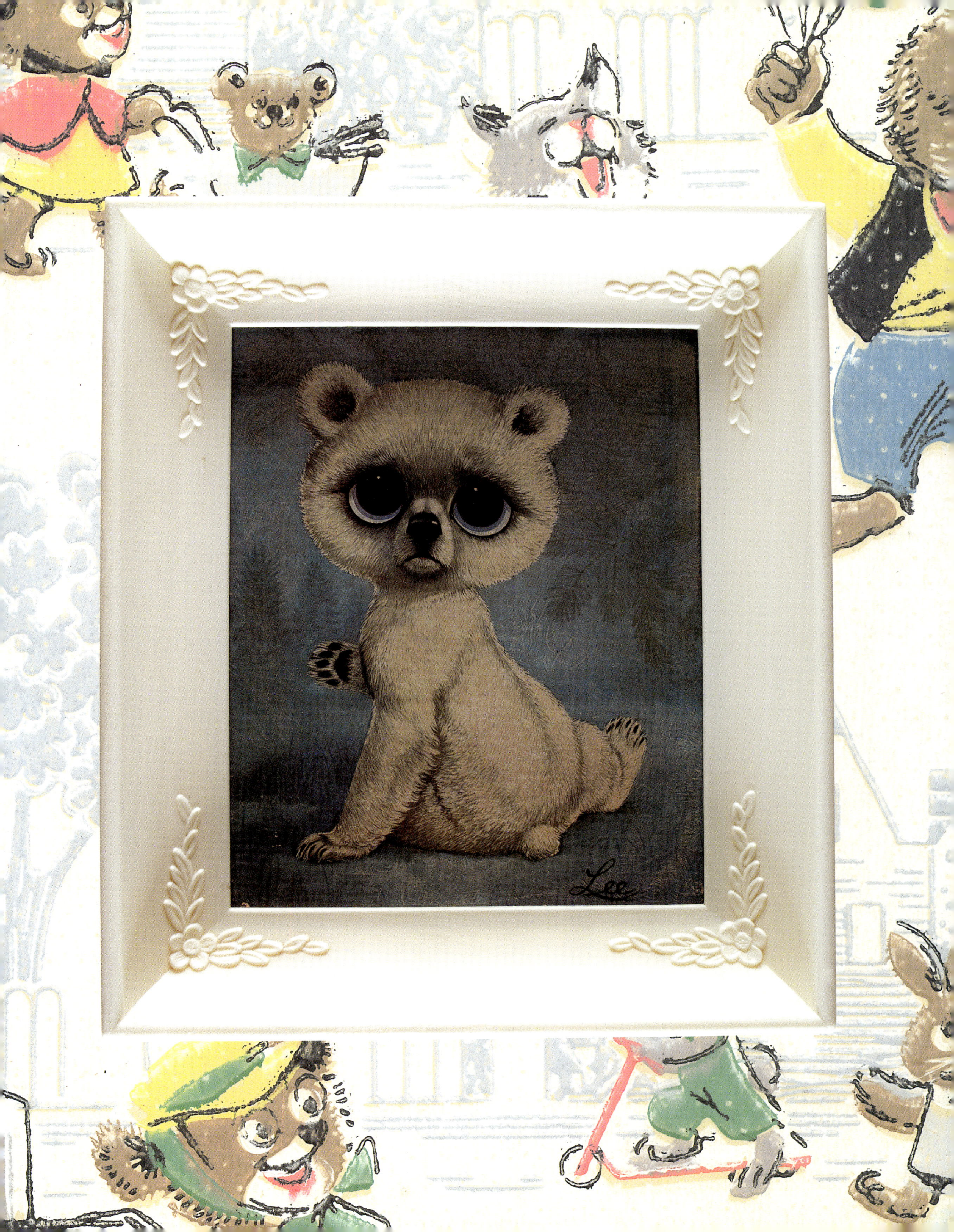
Lee

preceding pages: J R **Shabby Kittens;** Lee **Honeybear**

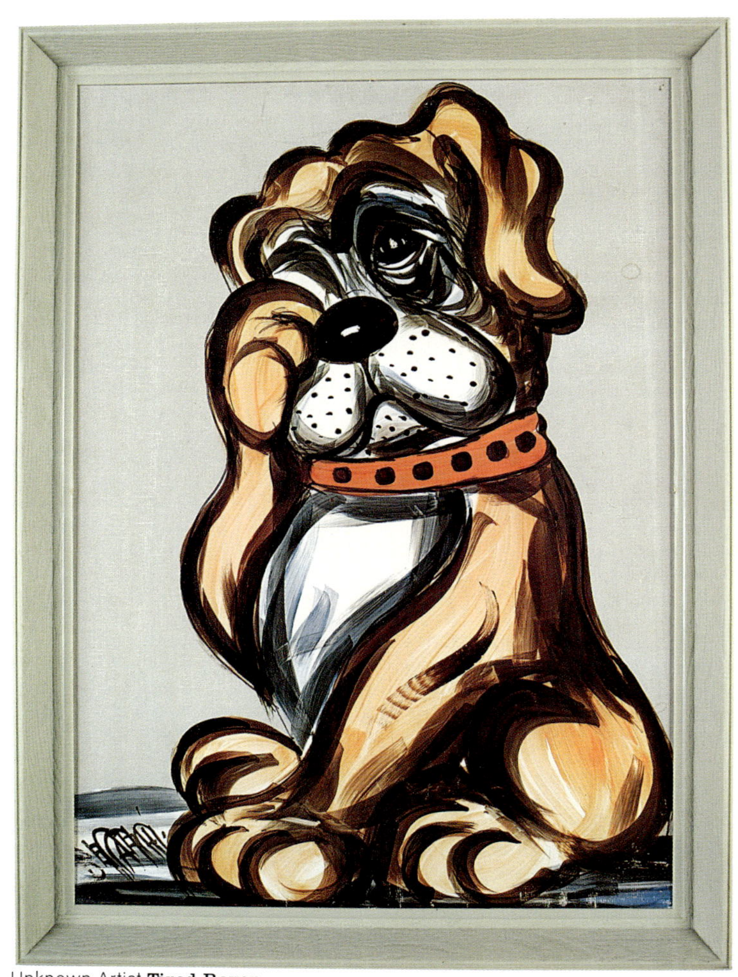

Unknown Artist **Tired Rover**

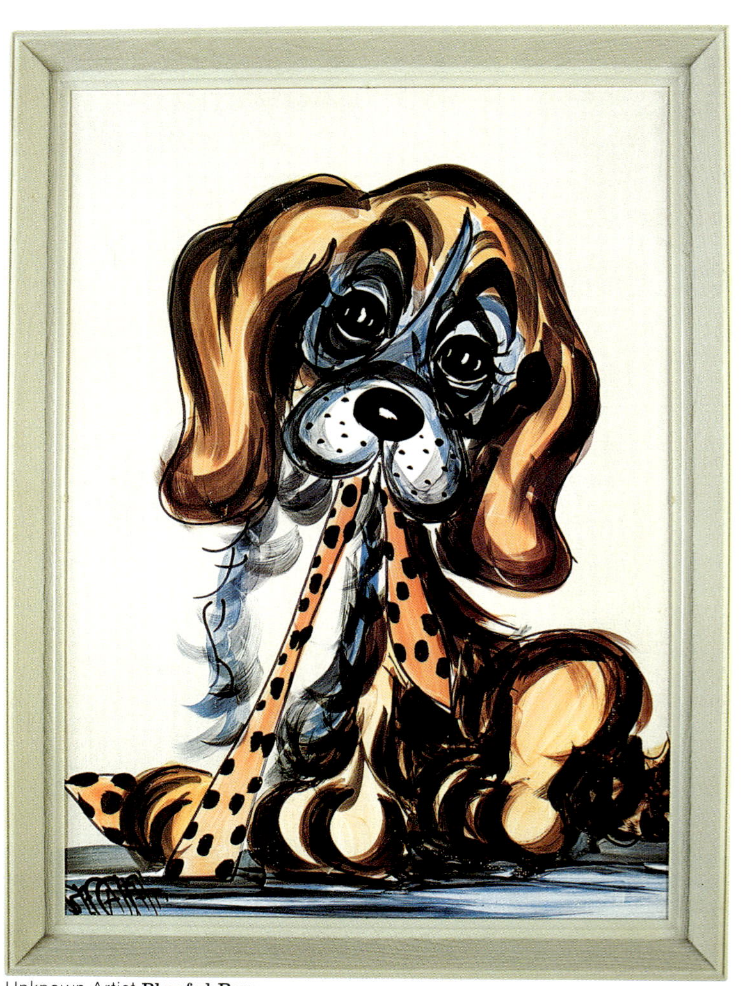

Unknown Artist **Playful Rex**

Unknown Artist **Surprised**

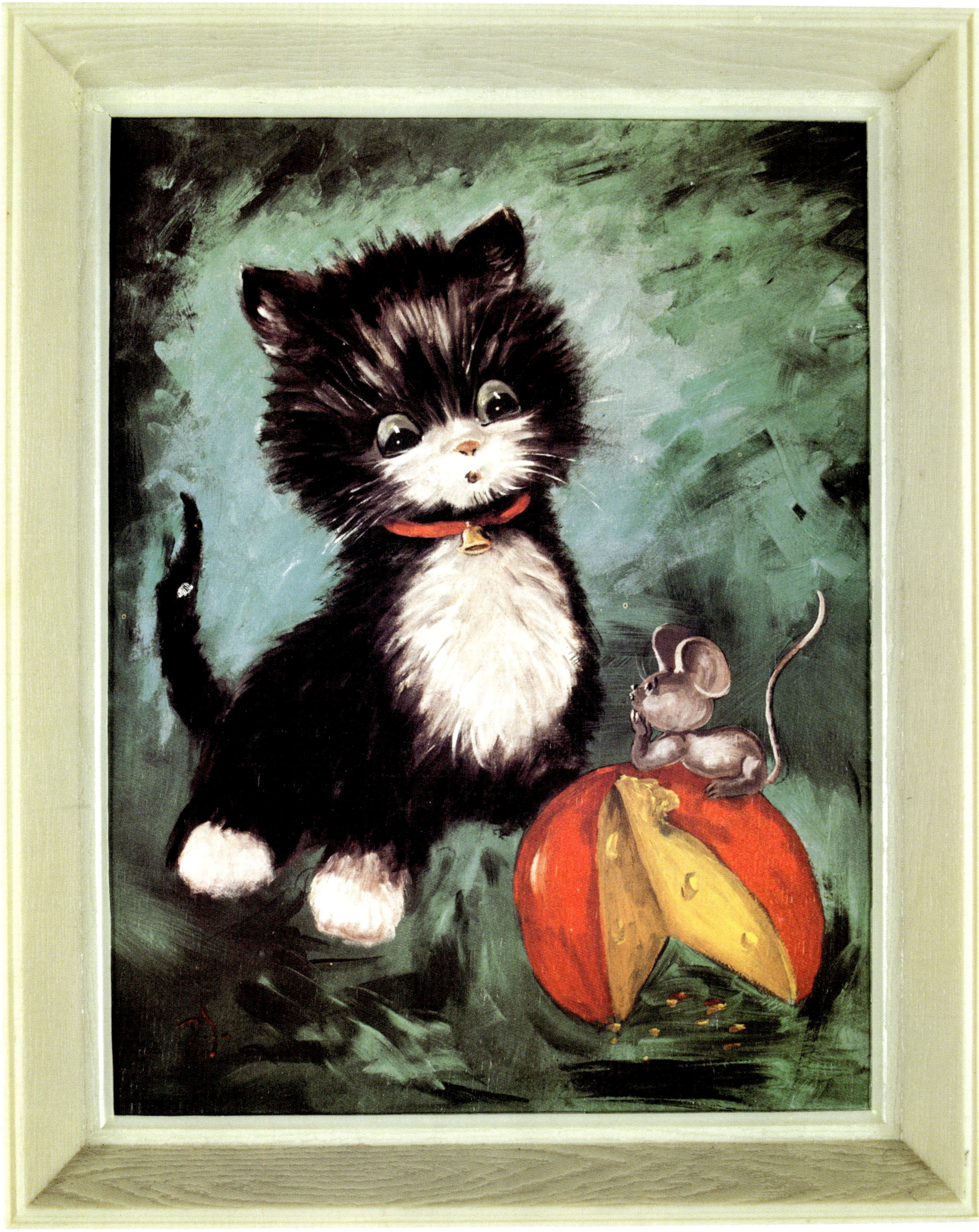

Mass-market art, like most movements, took time to find a true home. Woolworths, Boots and Freeman's sold the **Tretchikoff** and Big Eye genres, but there were no dedicated art retailers until **Athena** opened its first store in Hampstead, London, on 4 July 1964. Olé Christiansen conceived **Athena** to target art lovers who accepted prints but wanted a gallery style ambience rather than a hardware store or chemist's shop. **Athena** sold unknown artists next to licensed prints of Picasso, Van Gogh, Turner, Constable, Salvador Dali, Lowry et al. Prints sold in their tens of thousands for thirty-six shillings (£1.80) and framed or blockmounted (an Athena innovation) for fifty shillings (around £2.50).

Gradually weaning the public away from the classical artist, Athena seemed to succeed, given that photo-

Athena

realism and airbrushing had become buzz words in the art world. They sold 375,000 copies of the 'bare-buttocked lady tennis player'. Unicorns frolicked in the waves, birds of paradise sang on swaying palms. Naïve silhouettes of sophisticated Dior- and Chanel-clad Parisian ladies walking their poodles, impossibly ruby-lipped beauties sipping nuclear-coloured exotic cocktails from avant-garde glassware became the height of good taste at fledgling urban restaurant chains like Pizza Express.

Like many great concepts, when Olé Christiansen sold **Athena** to a big corporation in the mid 1980s the spark was lost and the chain slipped in and out of receivership, as well as out of favour.

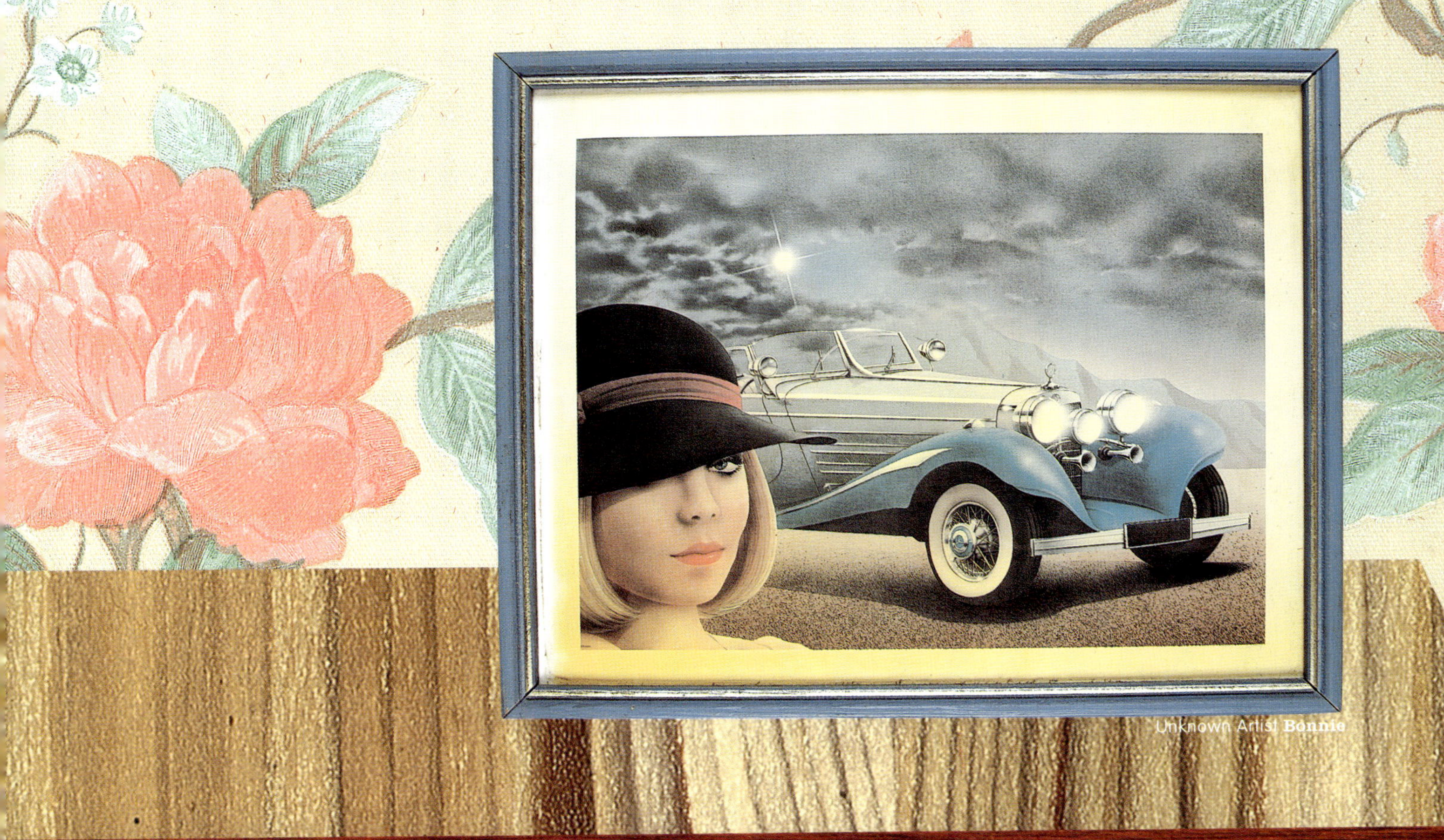

Unknown Artist **Bonnie**

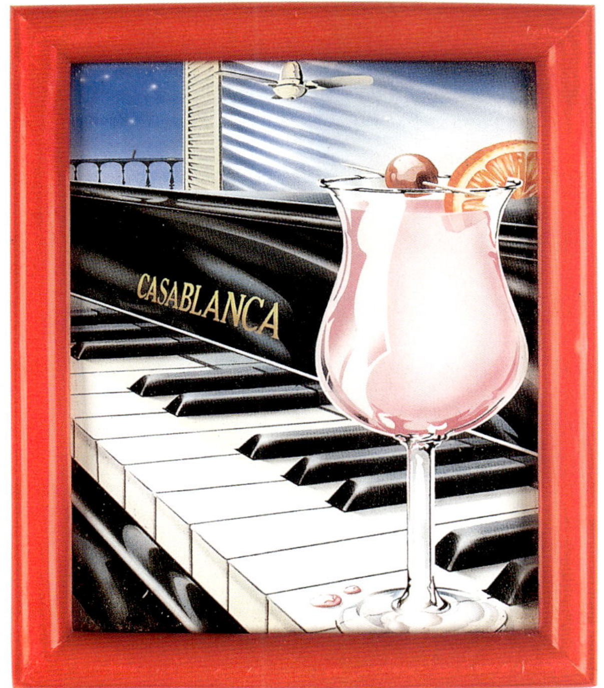

Unknown Artist **Casablanca**

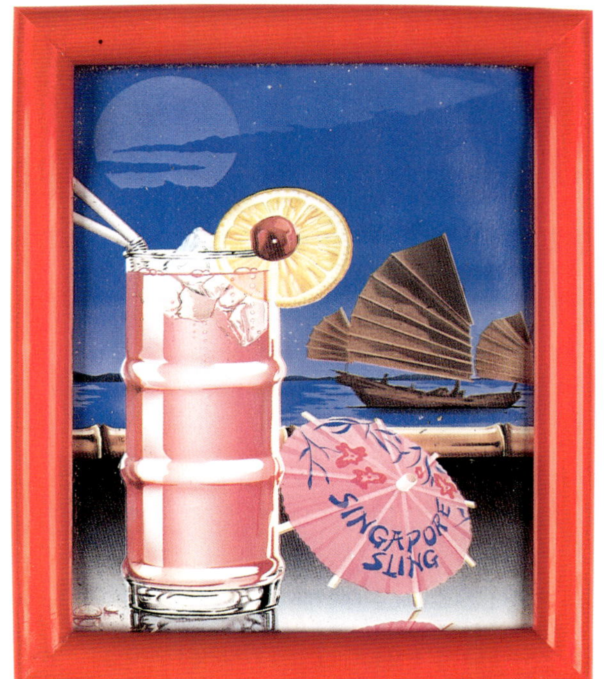

Unknown Artist **Singapore Sling No 2**

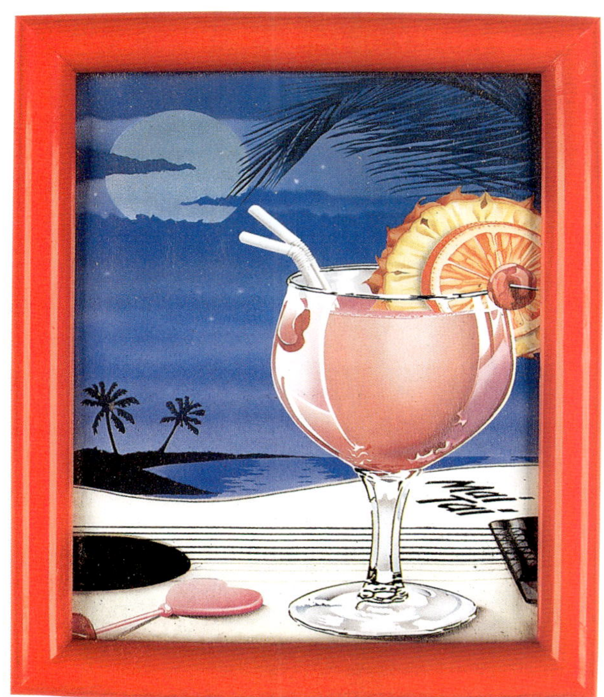

Unknown Artist **Mai Tai**

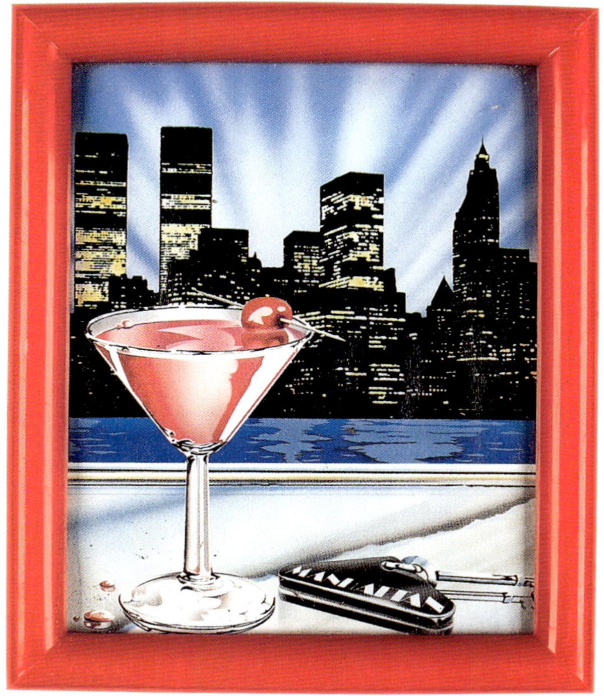

Unknown Artist **Manhattan**

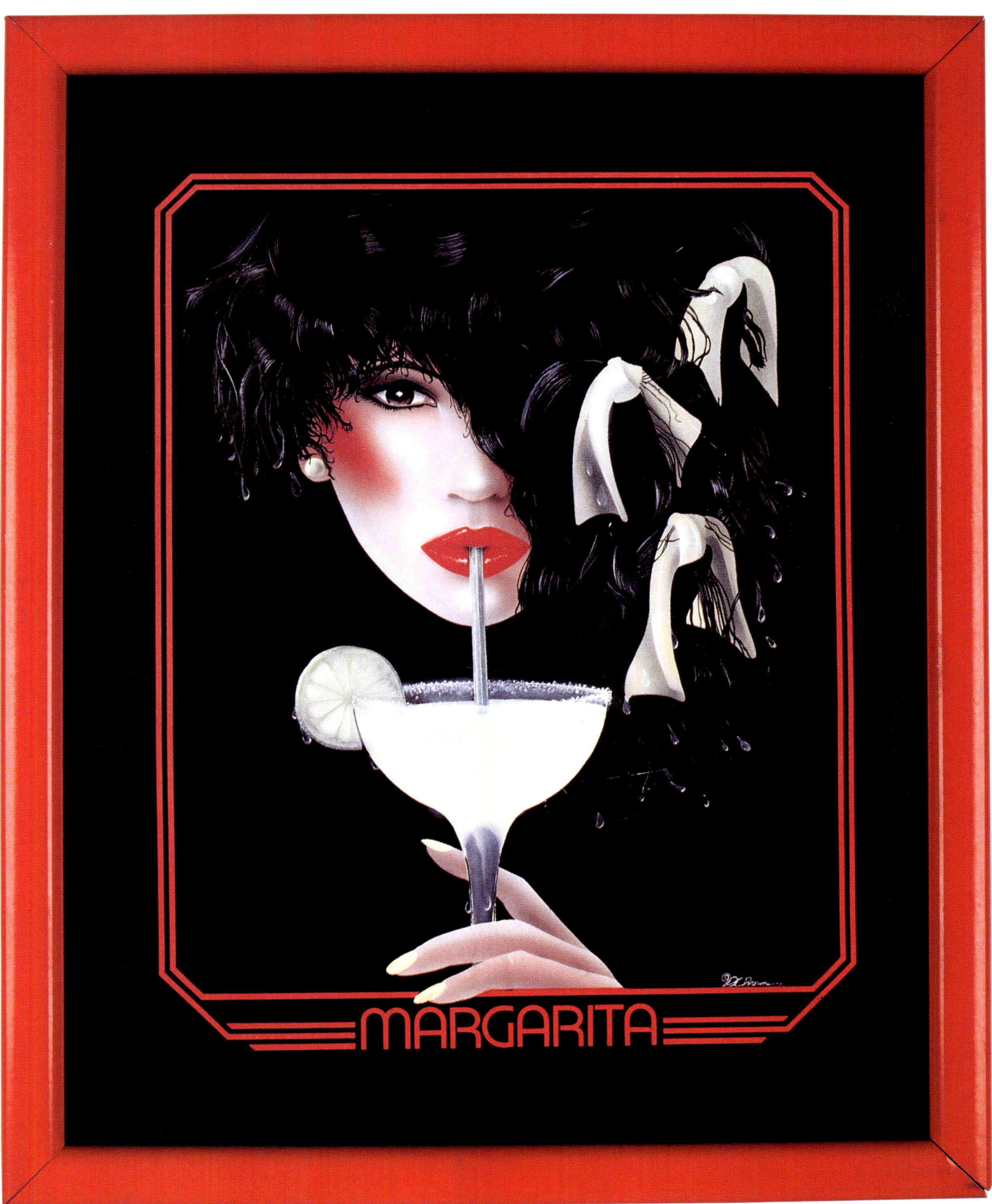

D C Brown **Margarita**

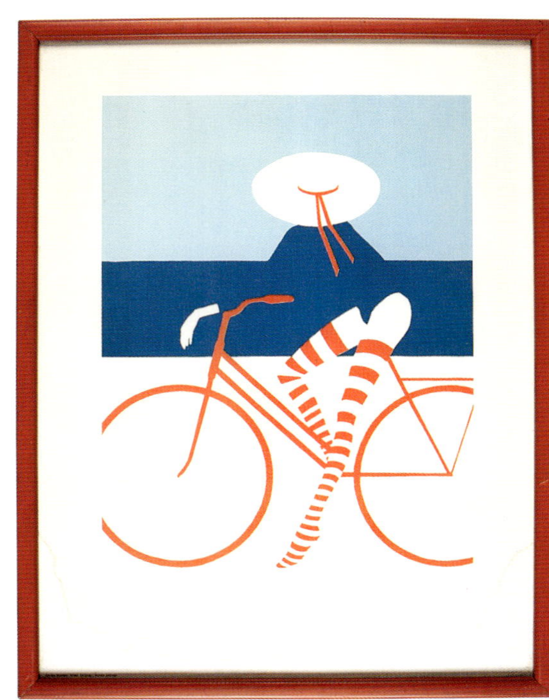
Unknown Artist **Lady on Bike**

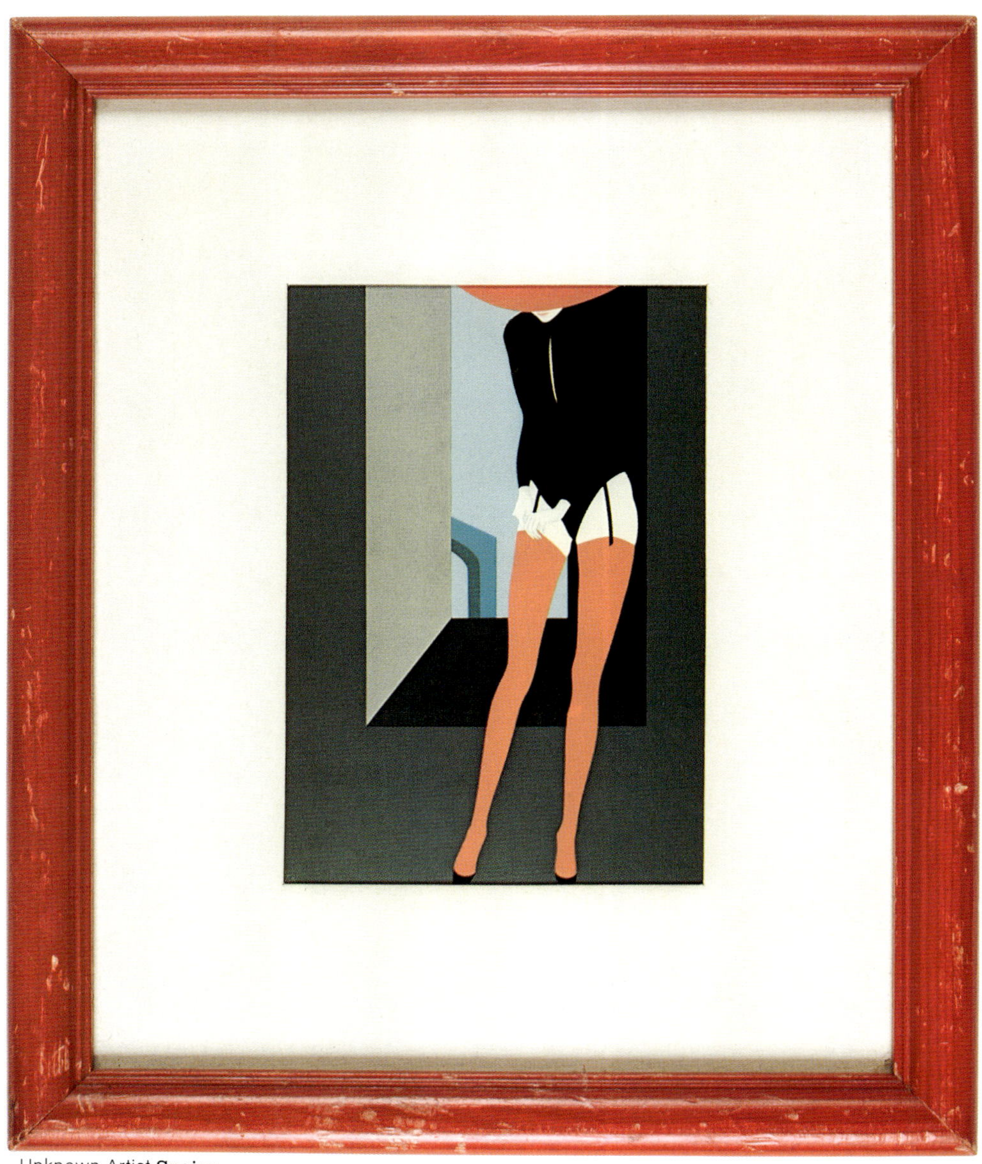
Unknown Artist **Susies**

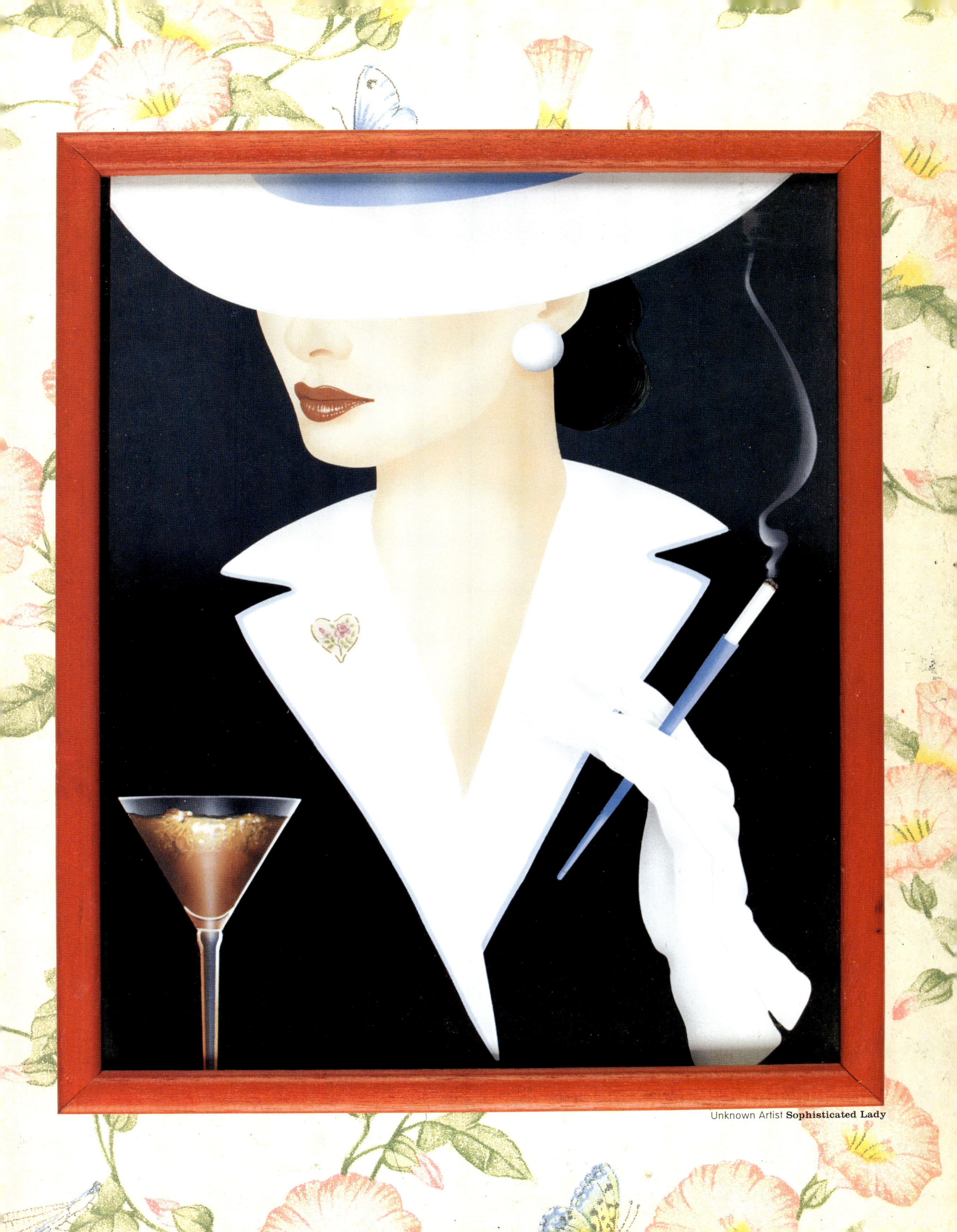

Unknown Artist **Sophisticated Lady**

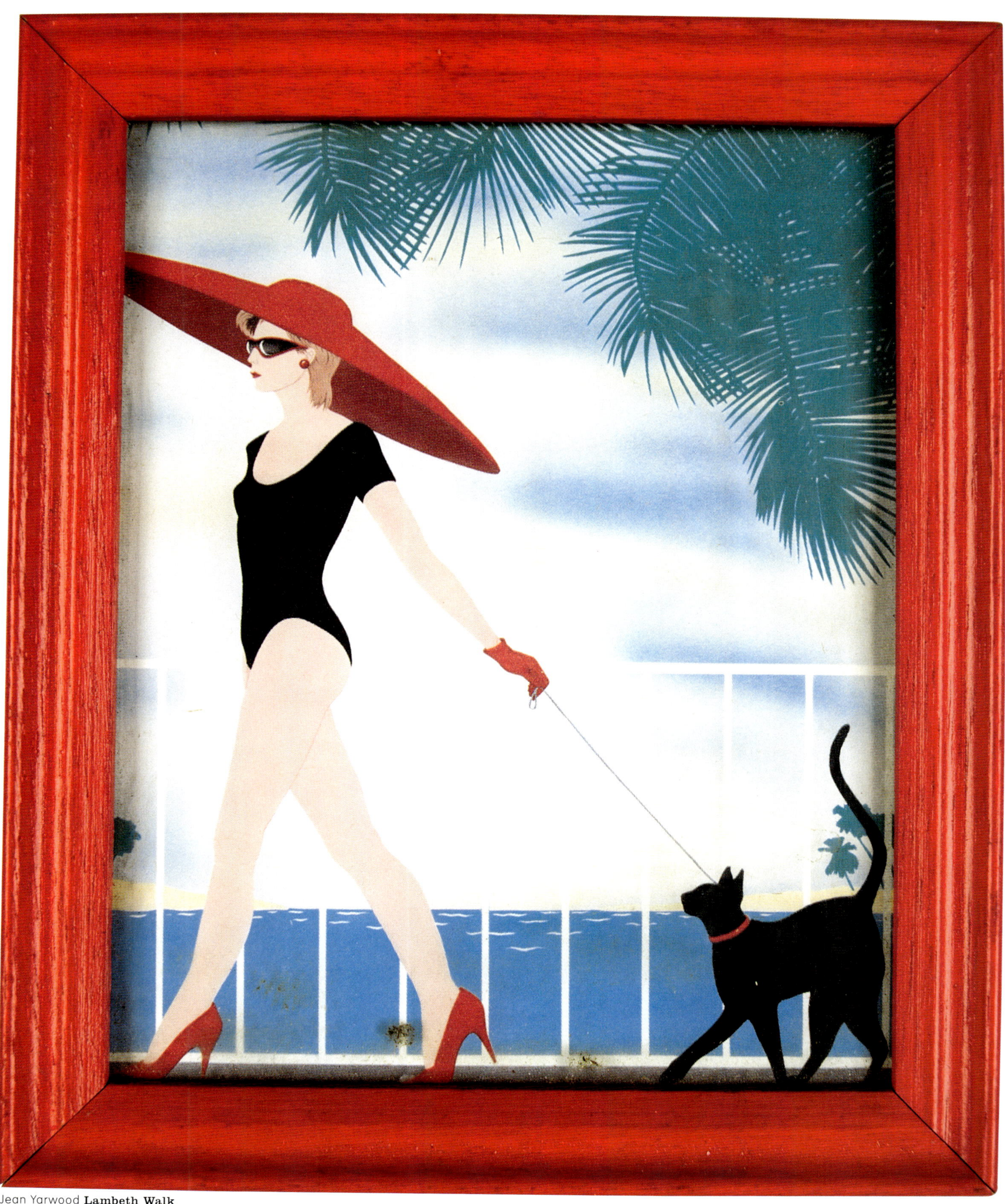

Jean Yarwood **Lambeth Walk**

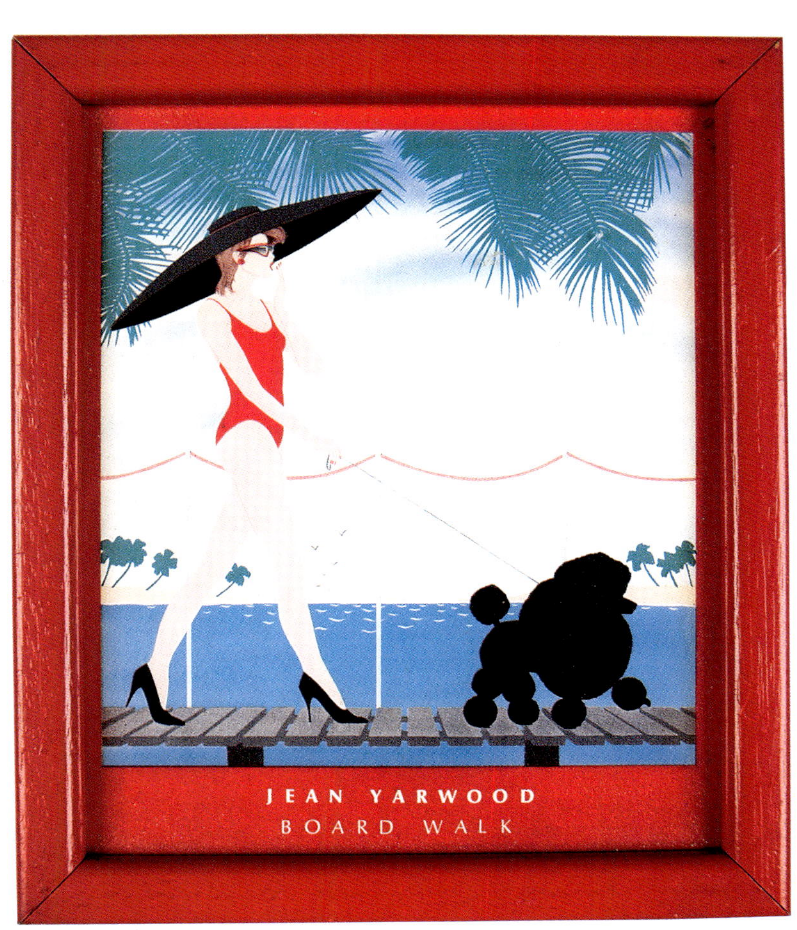

Jean Yarwood **Board Walk**

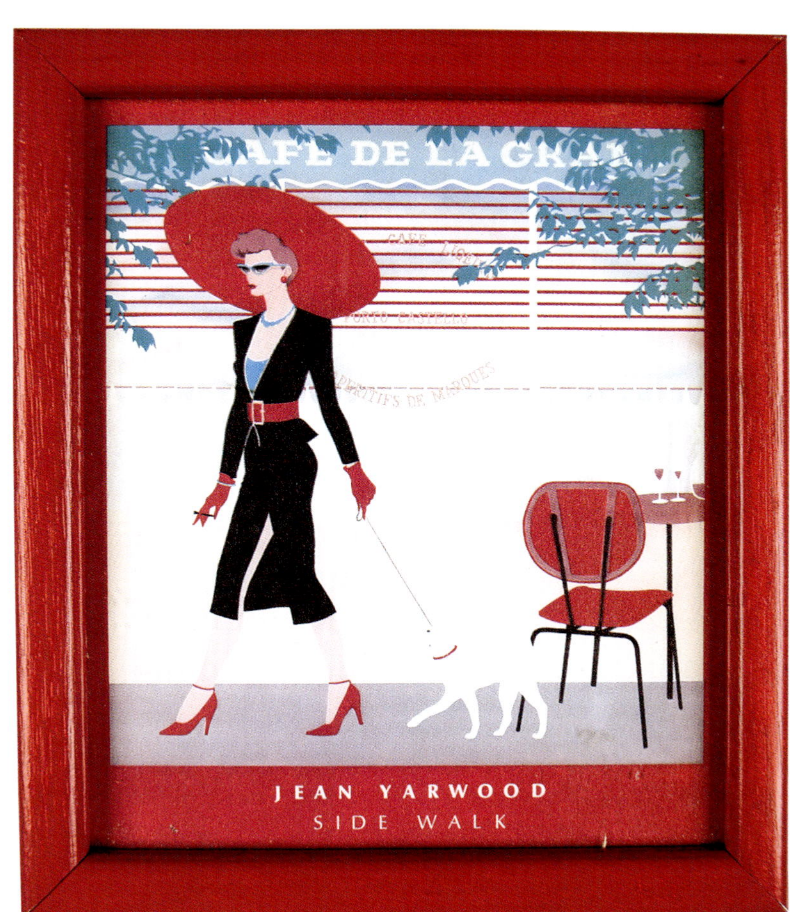

Jean Yarwood **Side Walk**

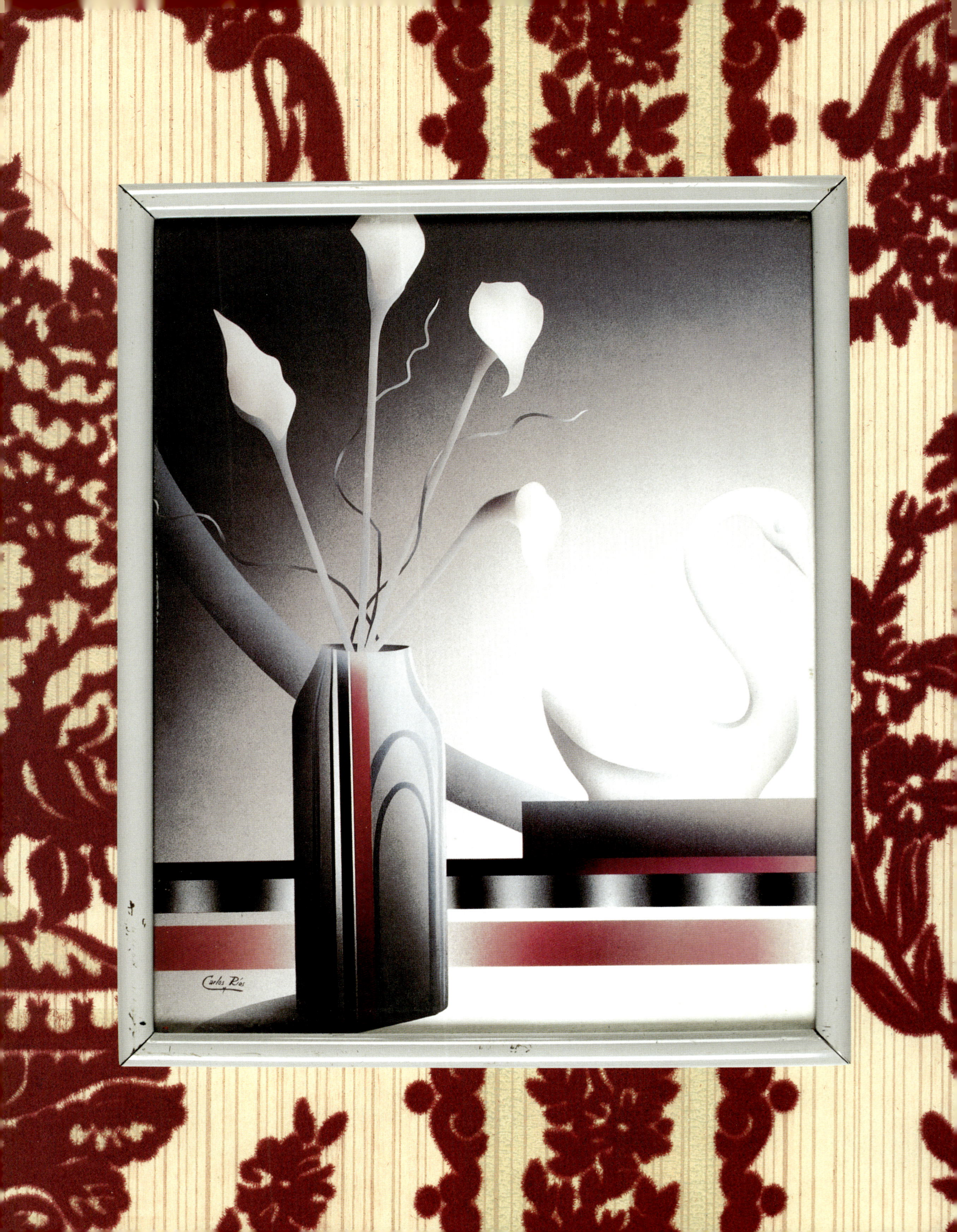
Carlos Ríos

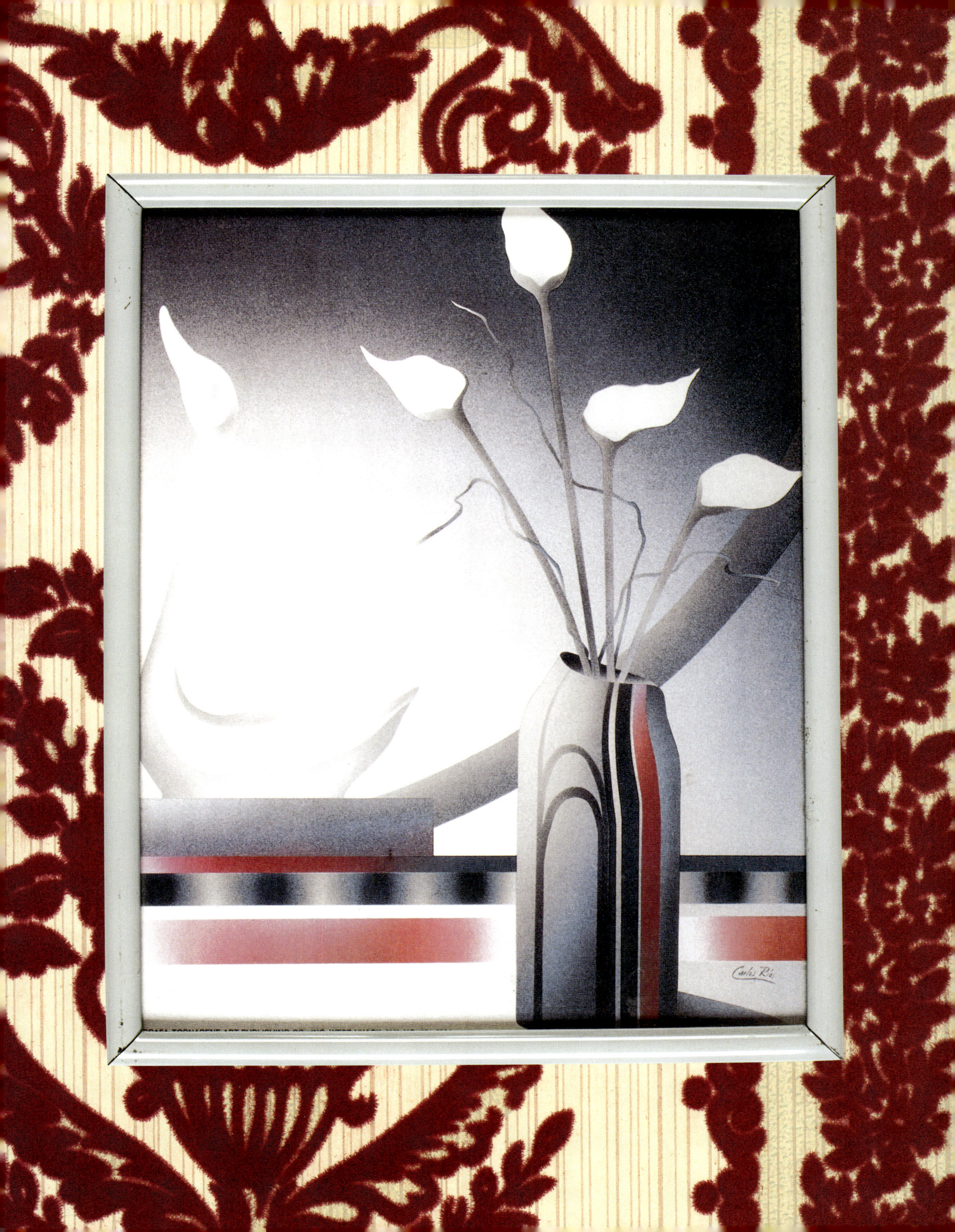

preceding pages: Carlos Rios **Swans**

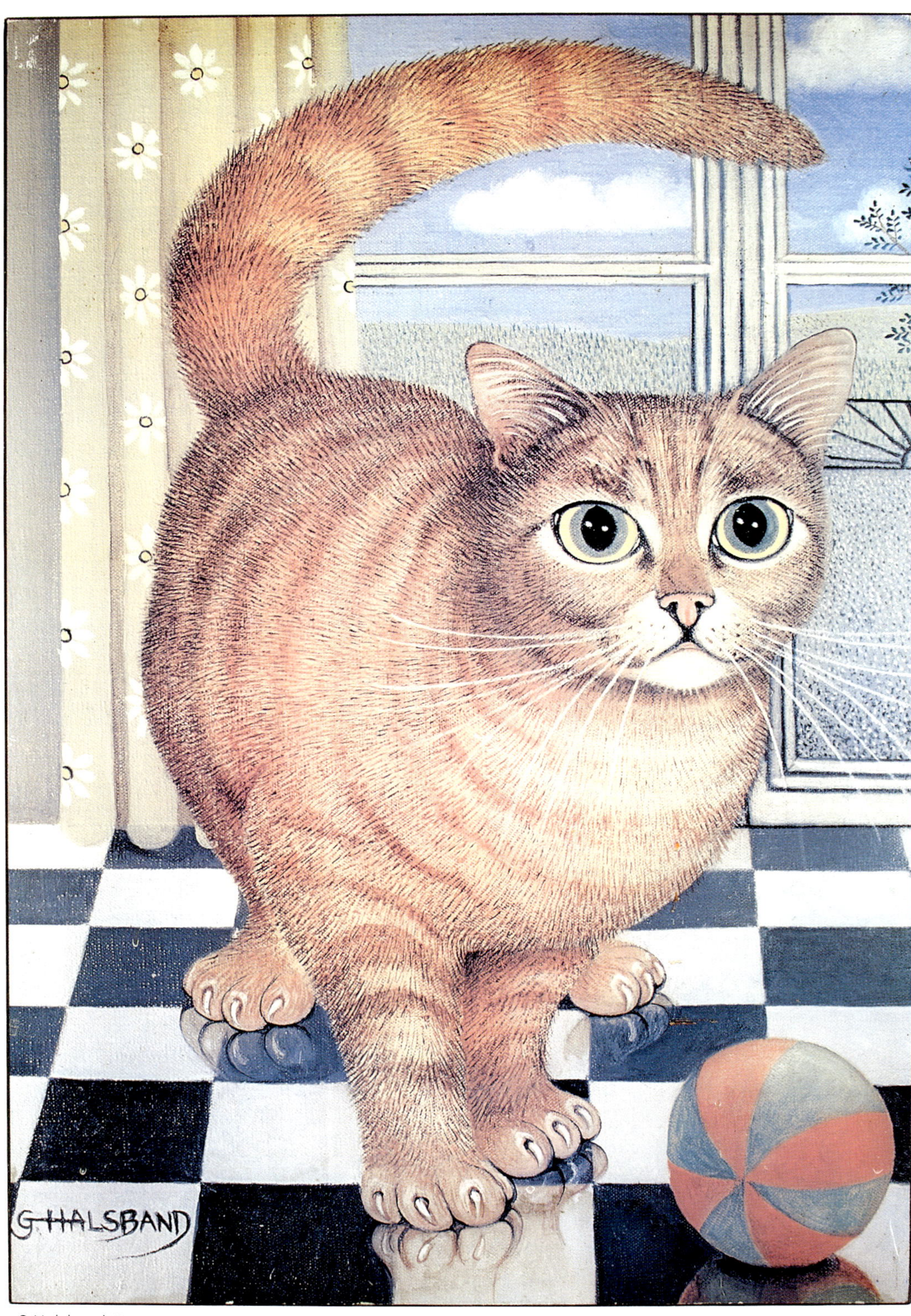

G Halsband **Cat on Tiles**

A Matthews **Scenic**

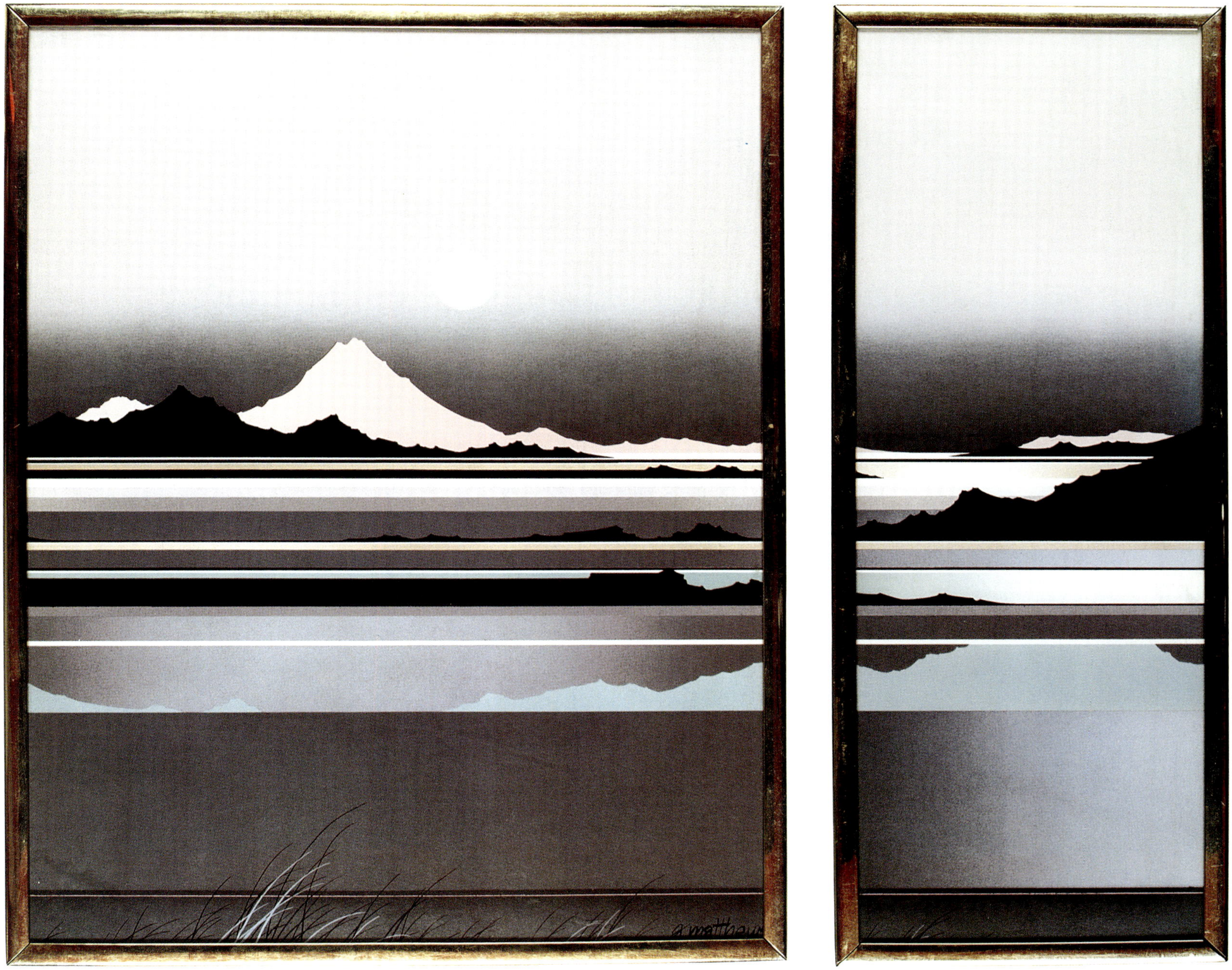

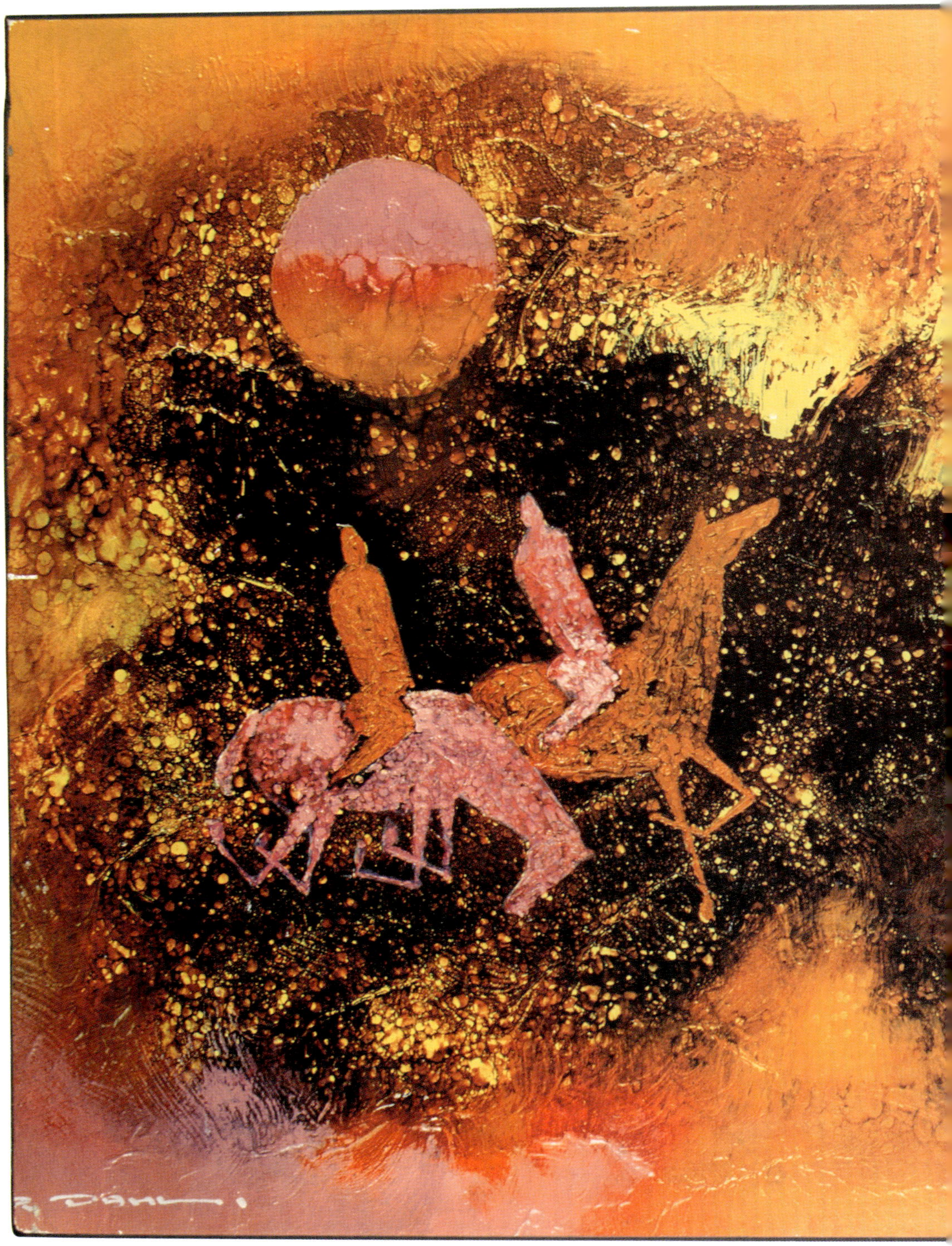

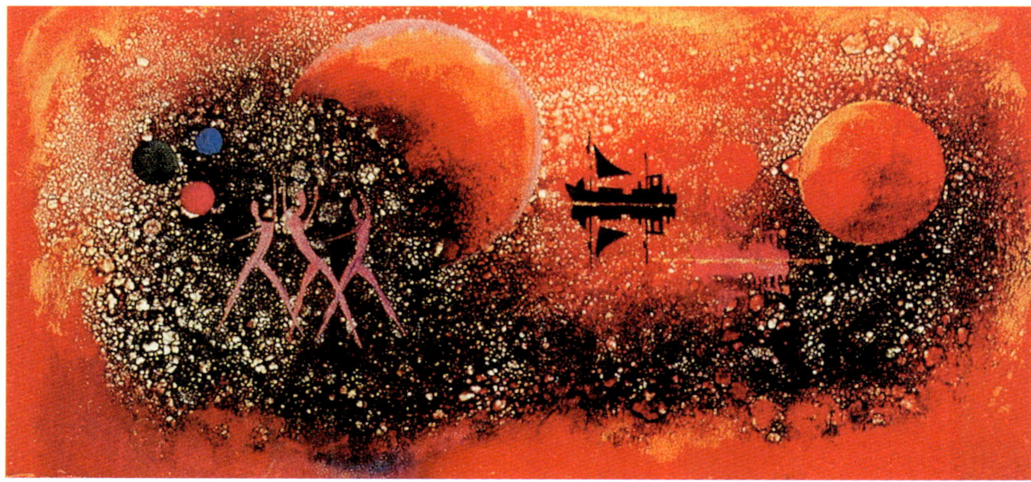

Per Dahl **Fisherman's Dream**

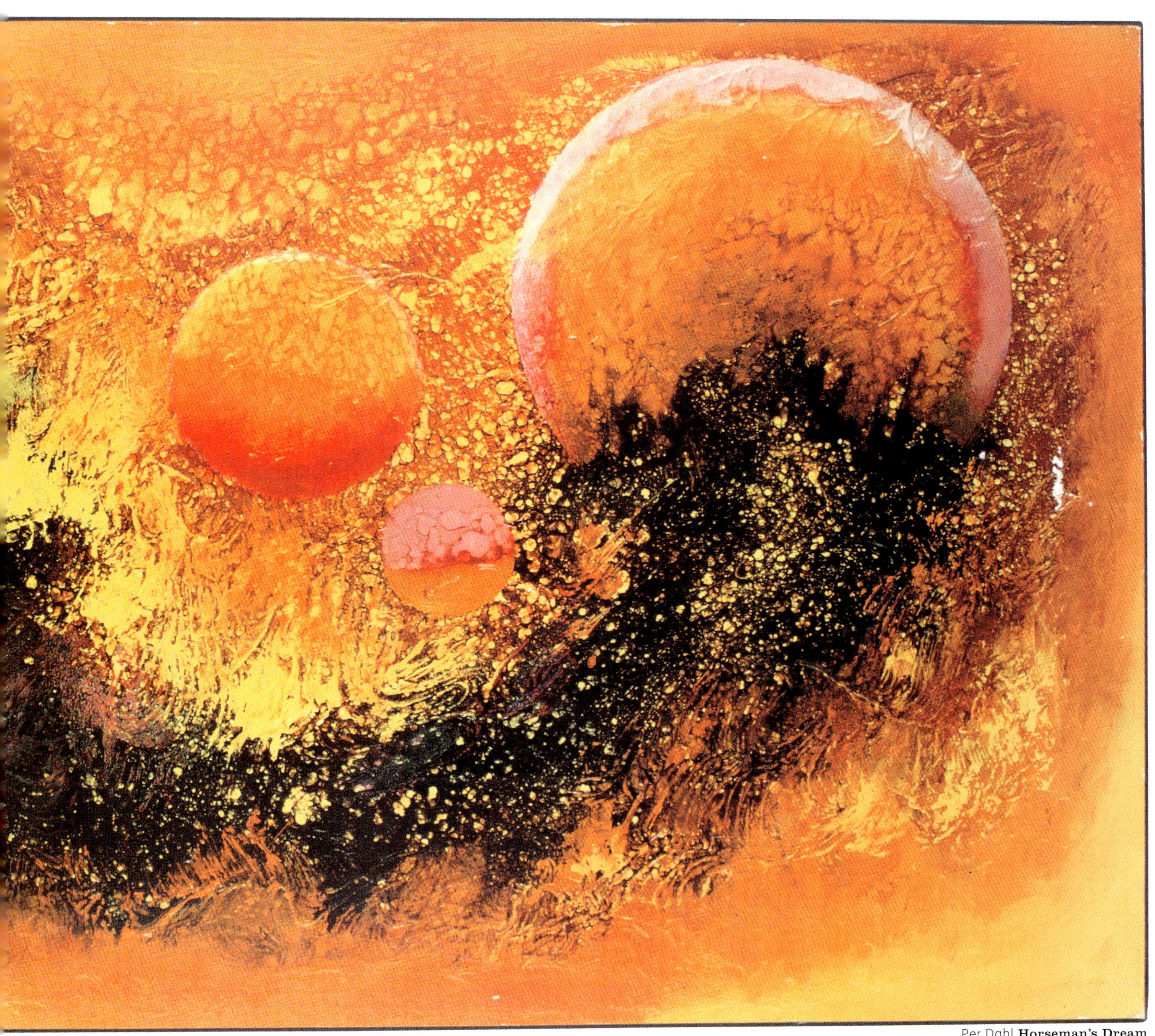

Per Dahl **Horseman's Dream**

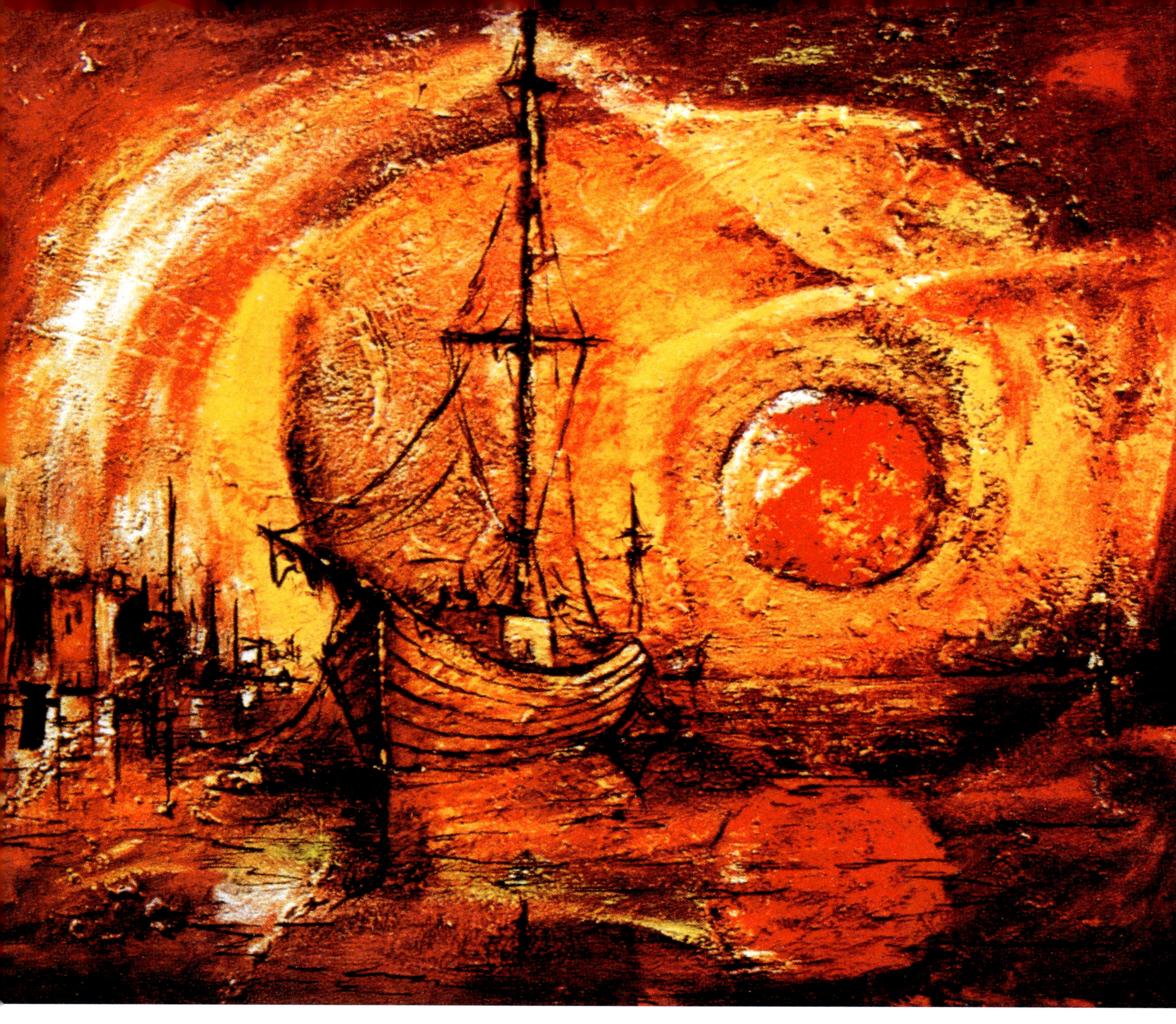

Bogie **Fishing Boats**

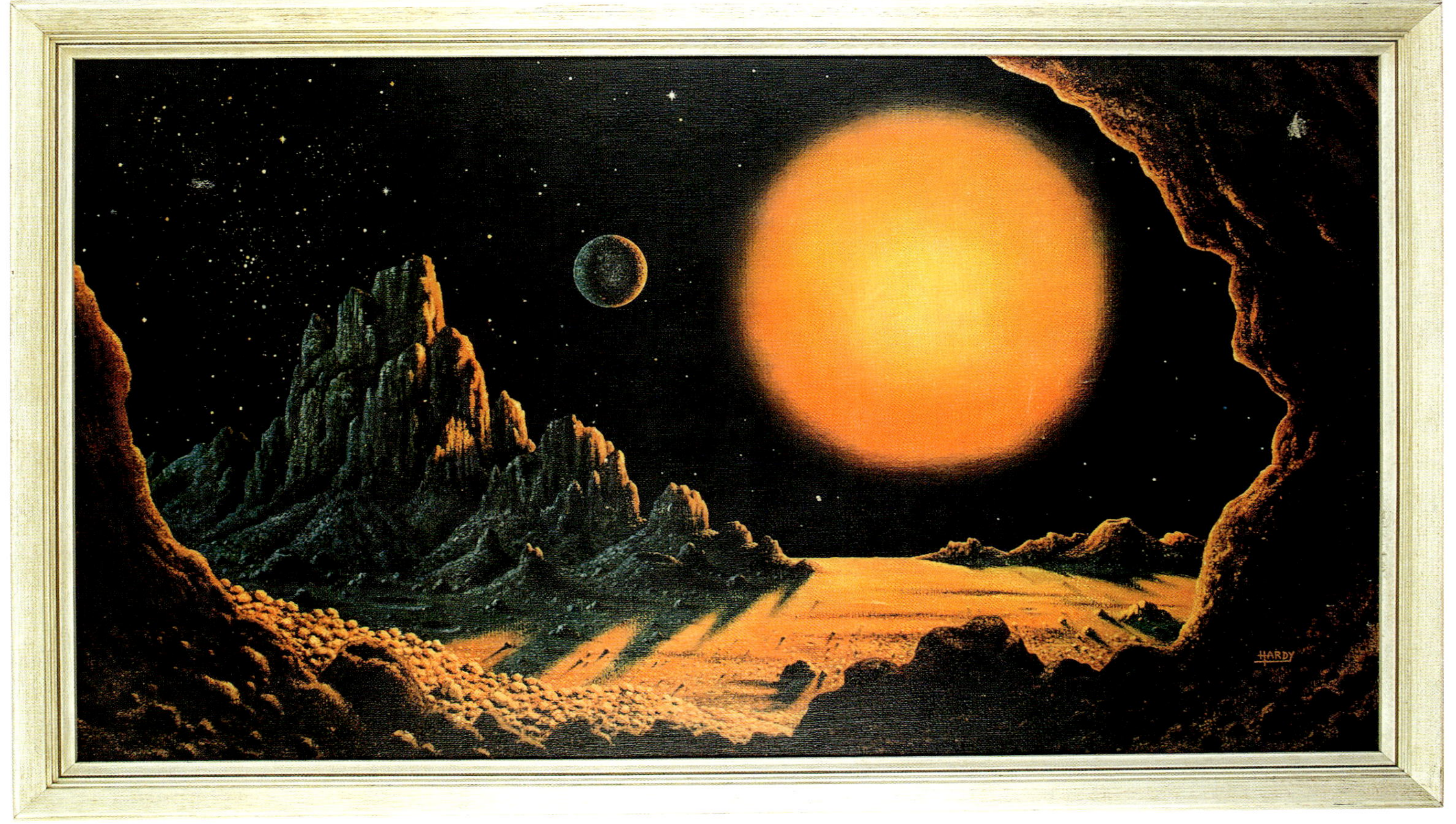

Hardy **Stellar Rockscape**

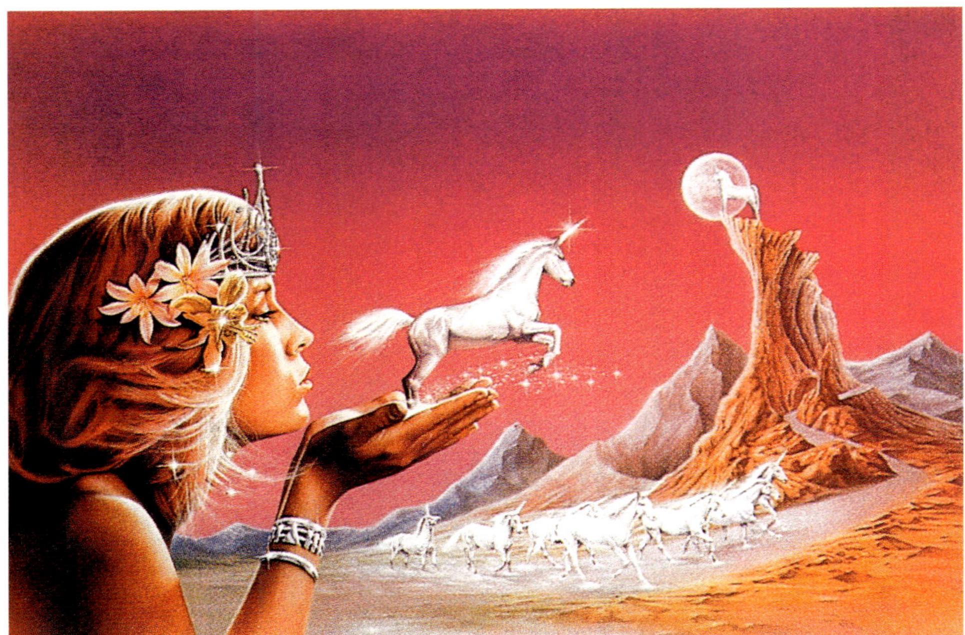

Unknown Artist **Unicorn Princess** 1989

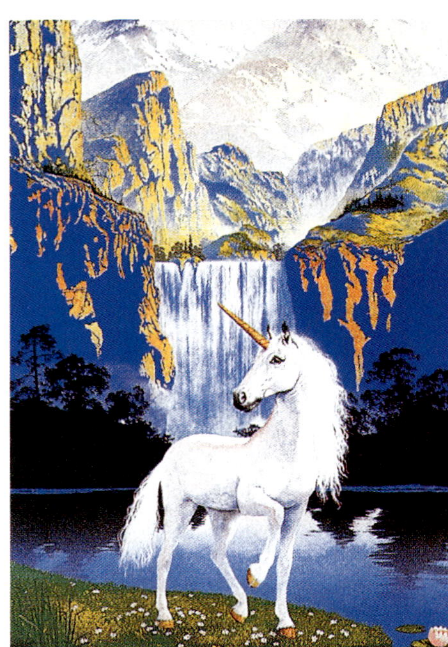

Unknown Artist **Unicorn Landscape** 1989

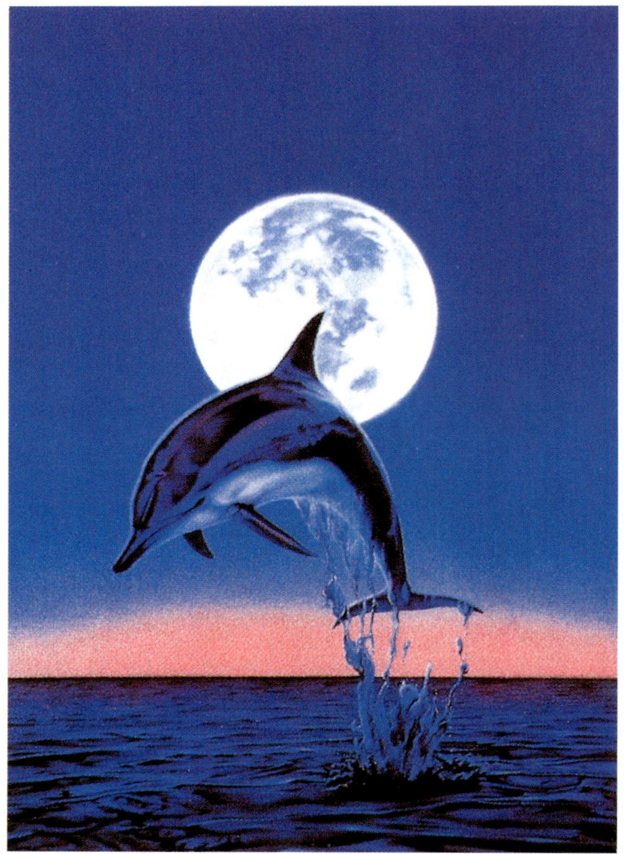

Unknown Artist **A Dolphin Moon** 1984

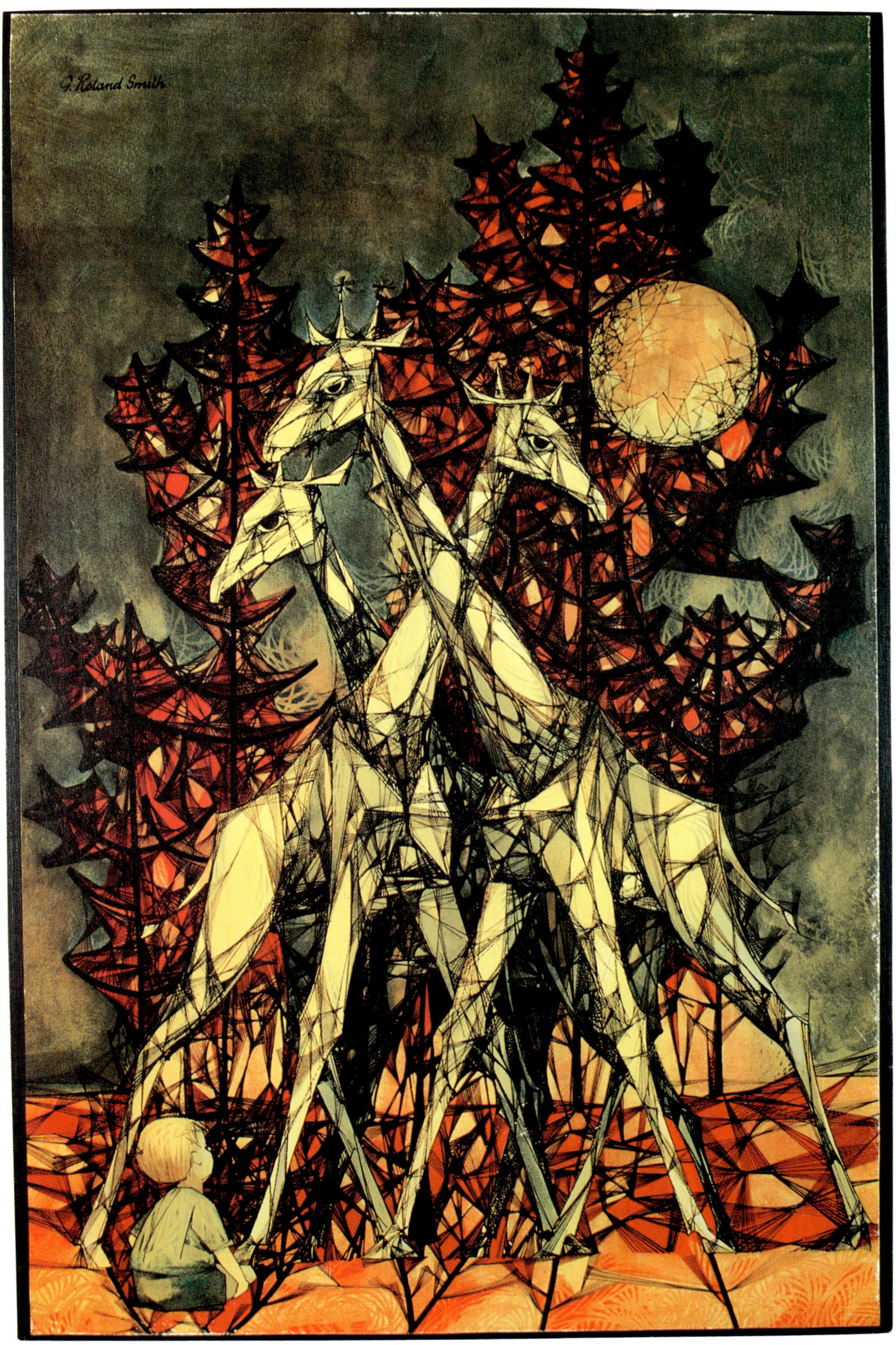

G Roland Smith **Boy With Giraffes**

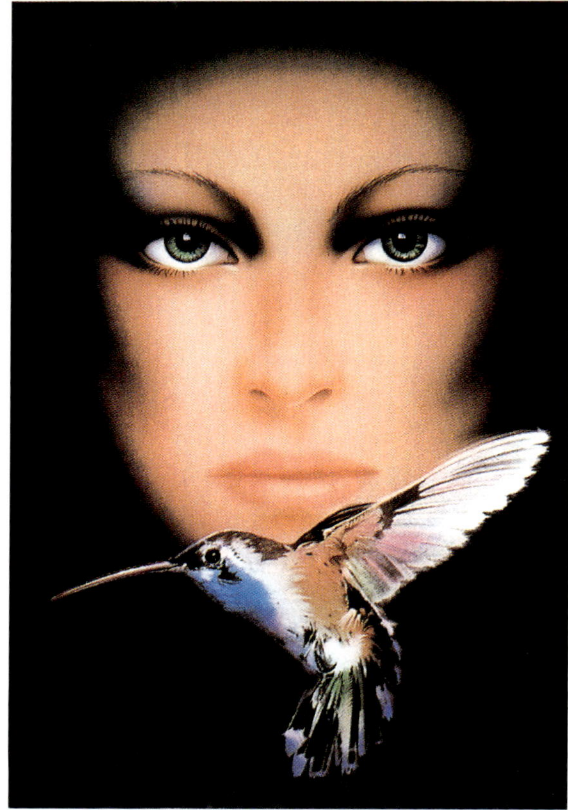

Owen **The Humming Bird** 1983

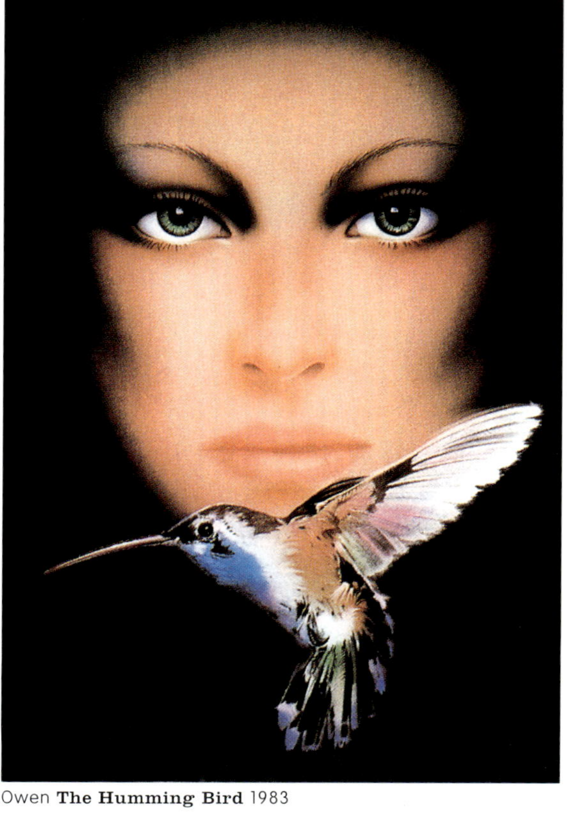

Kelly **Wildcat** 1983

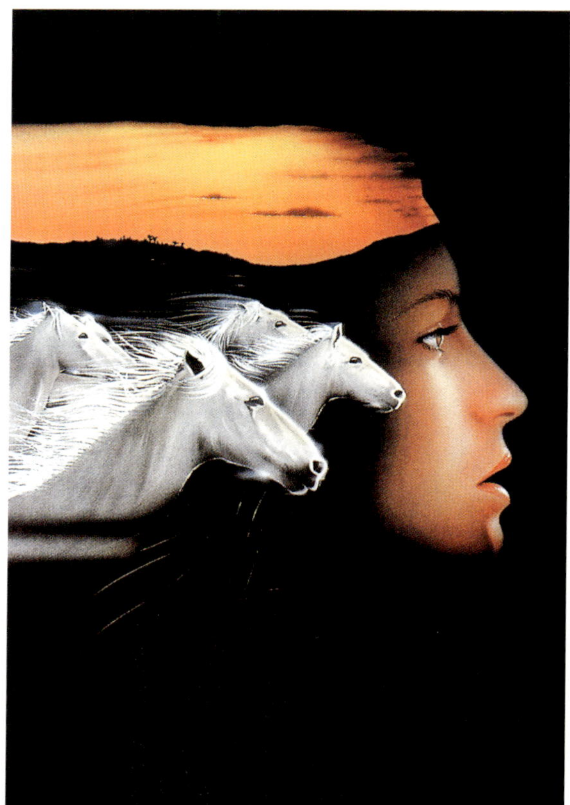

Kelly **Running Free** 1983

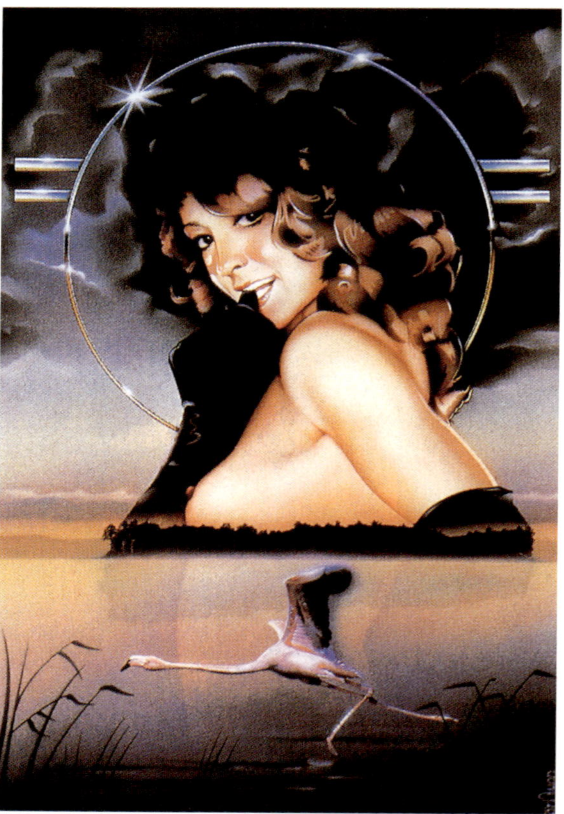

Kelly **The Flamingo Girl** 1983

Kelly **Cat Woman**

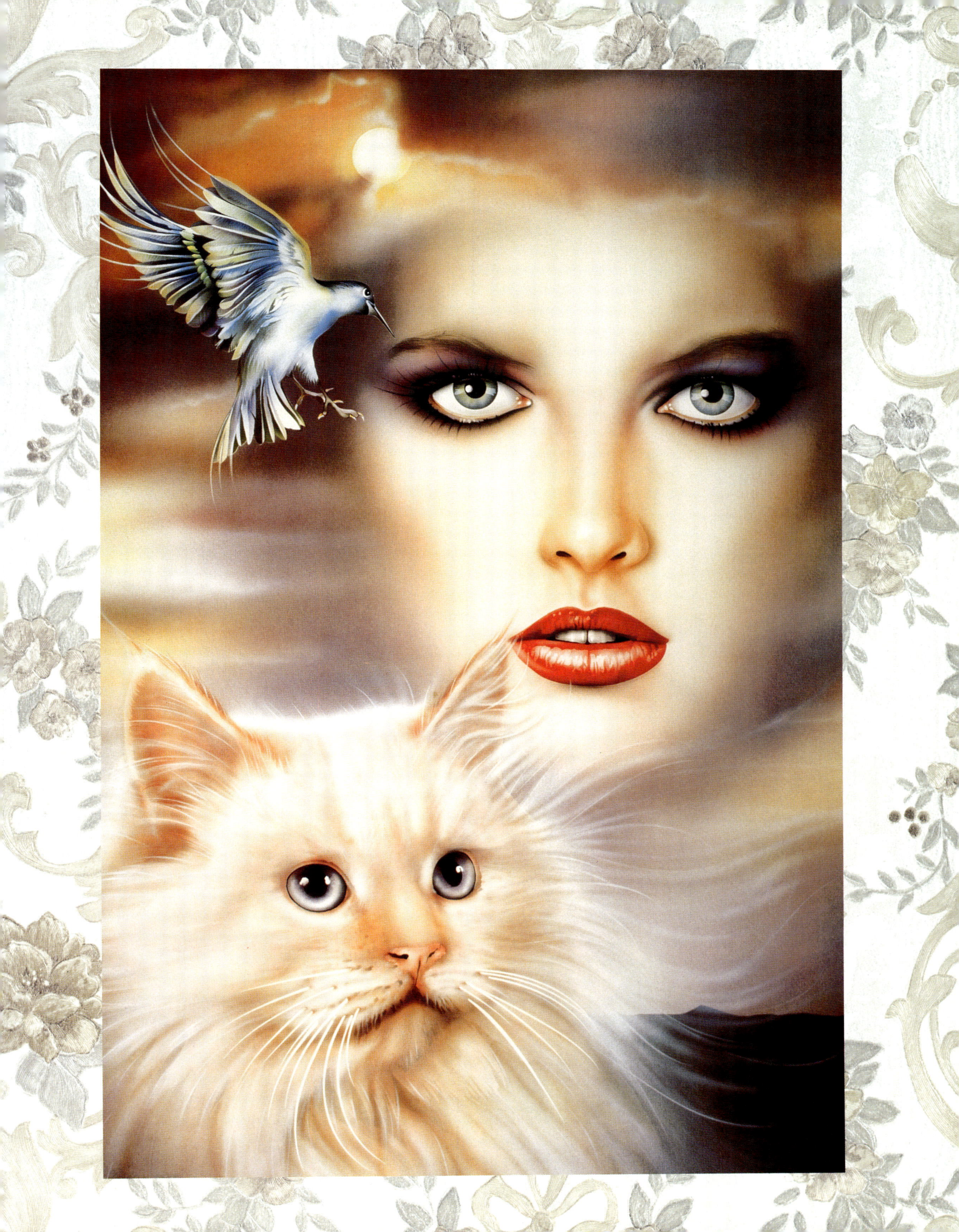

Alton **Peaches** 1983

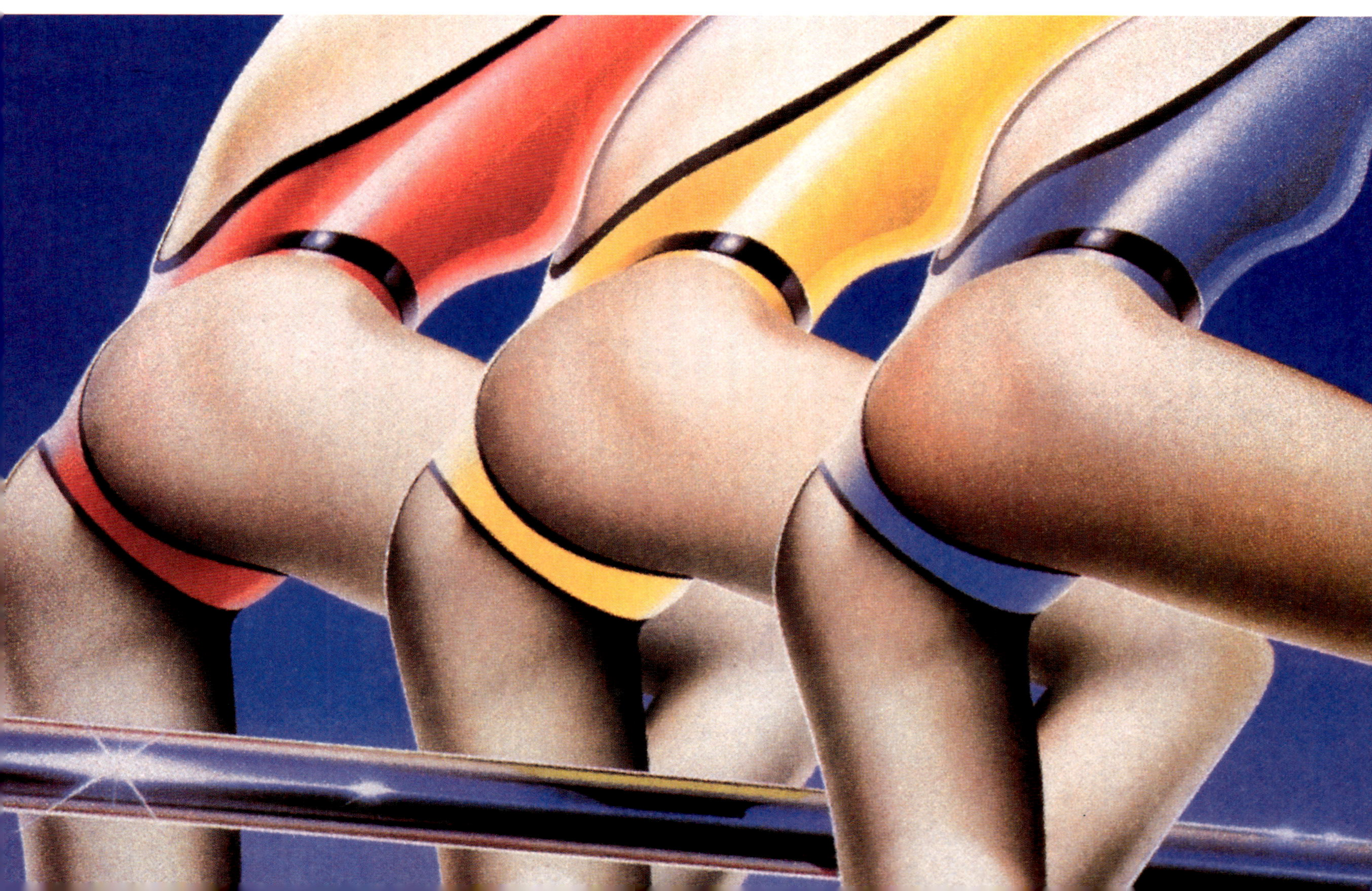

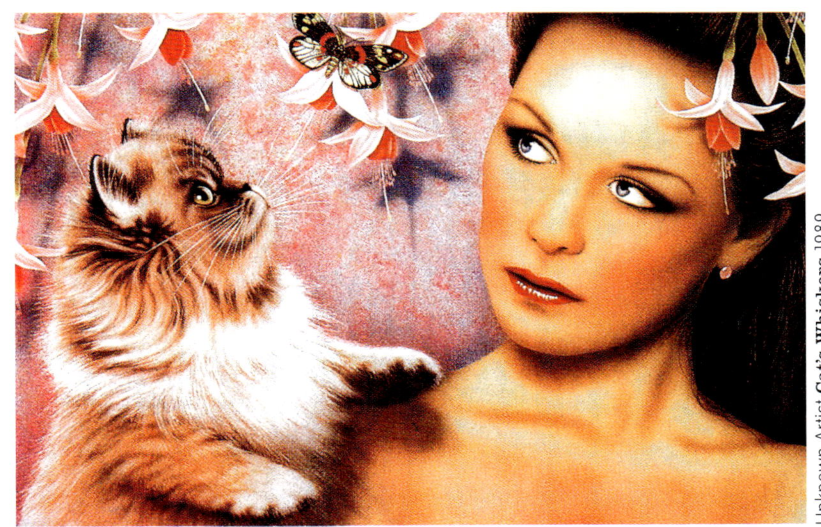

Unknown Artist **Cat's Whiskers** 1989

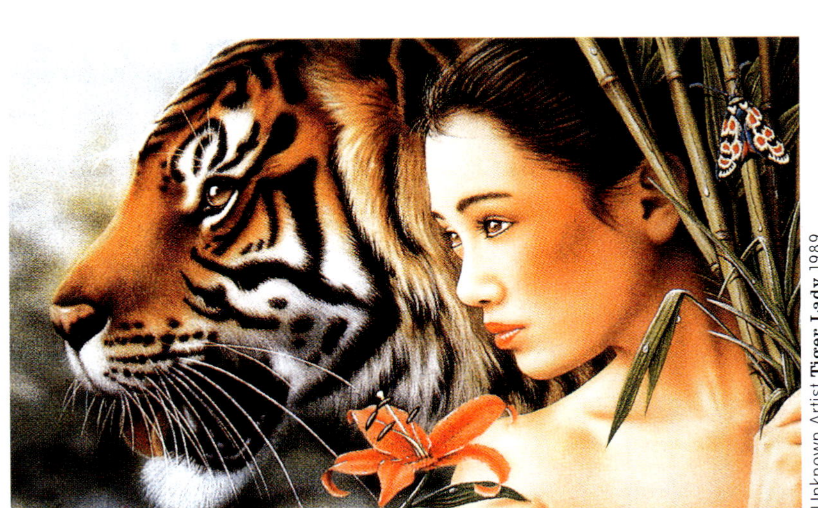

Unknown Artist **Tiger Lady** 1989

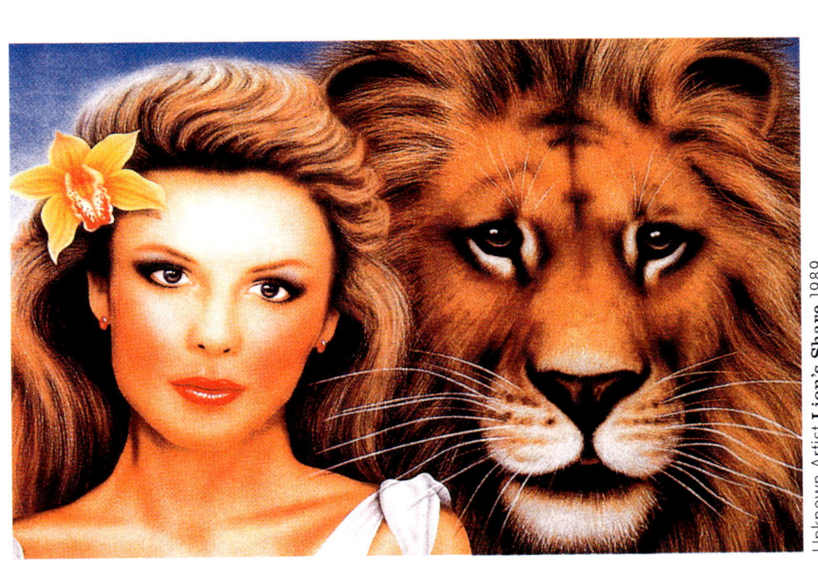

Unknown Artist **Lion's Share** 1989

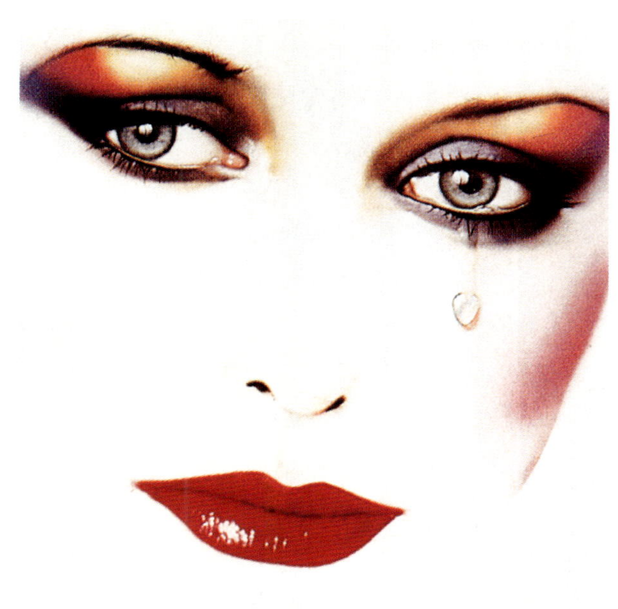

Unknown Artist **Lost Love** 1989

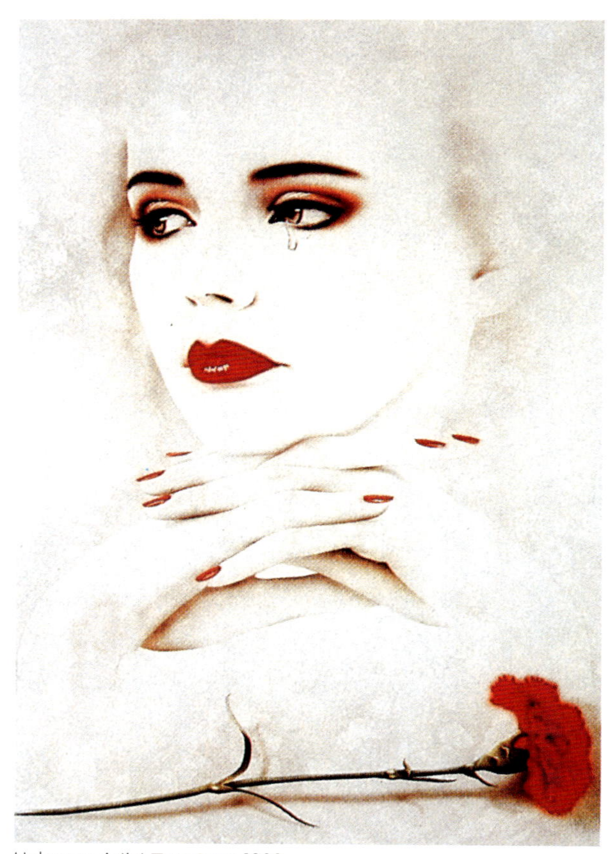

Unknown Artist **Teardrop** 1989

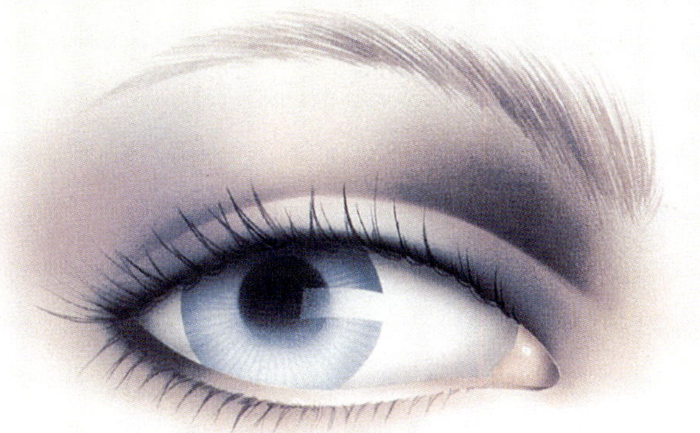

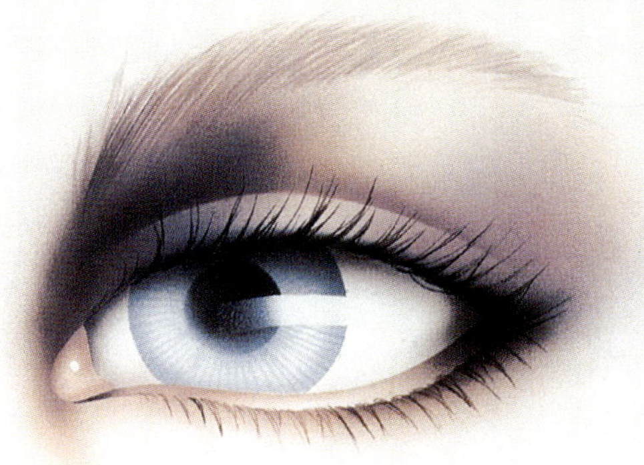

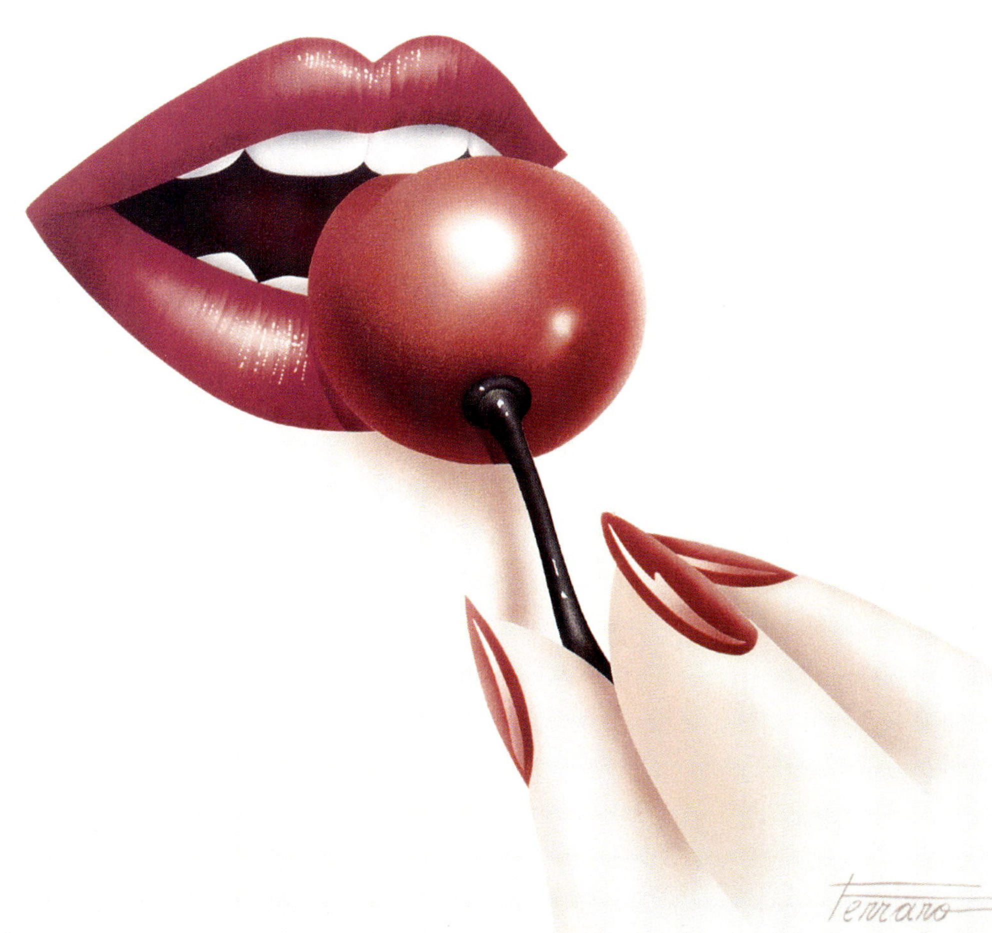
Ferraro

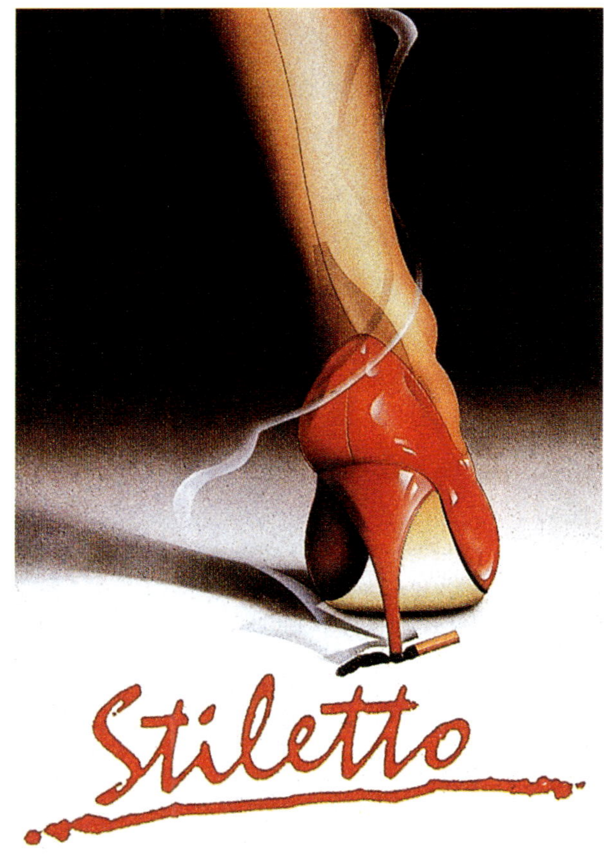

Unknown Artist **Stiletto** 1985

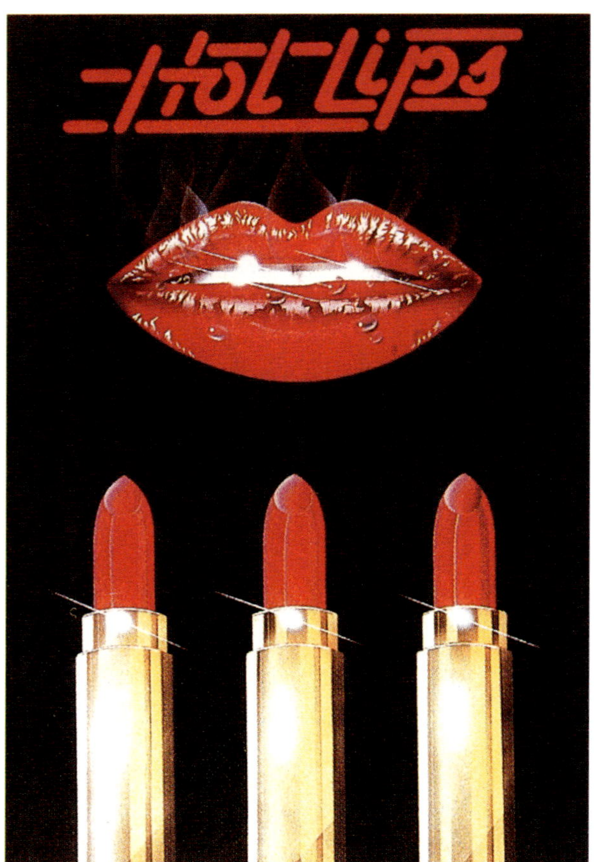

Unknown Artist **Hot Lips** 1985

Unknown Artist **Hot Line** 1985

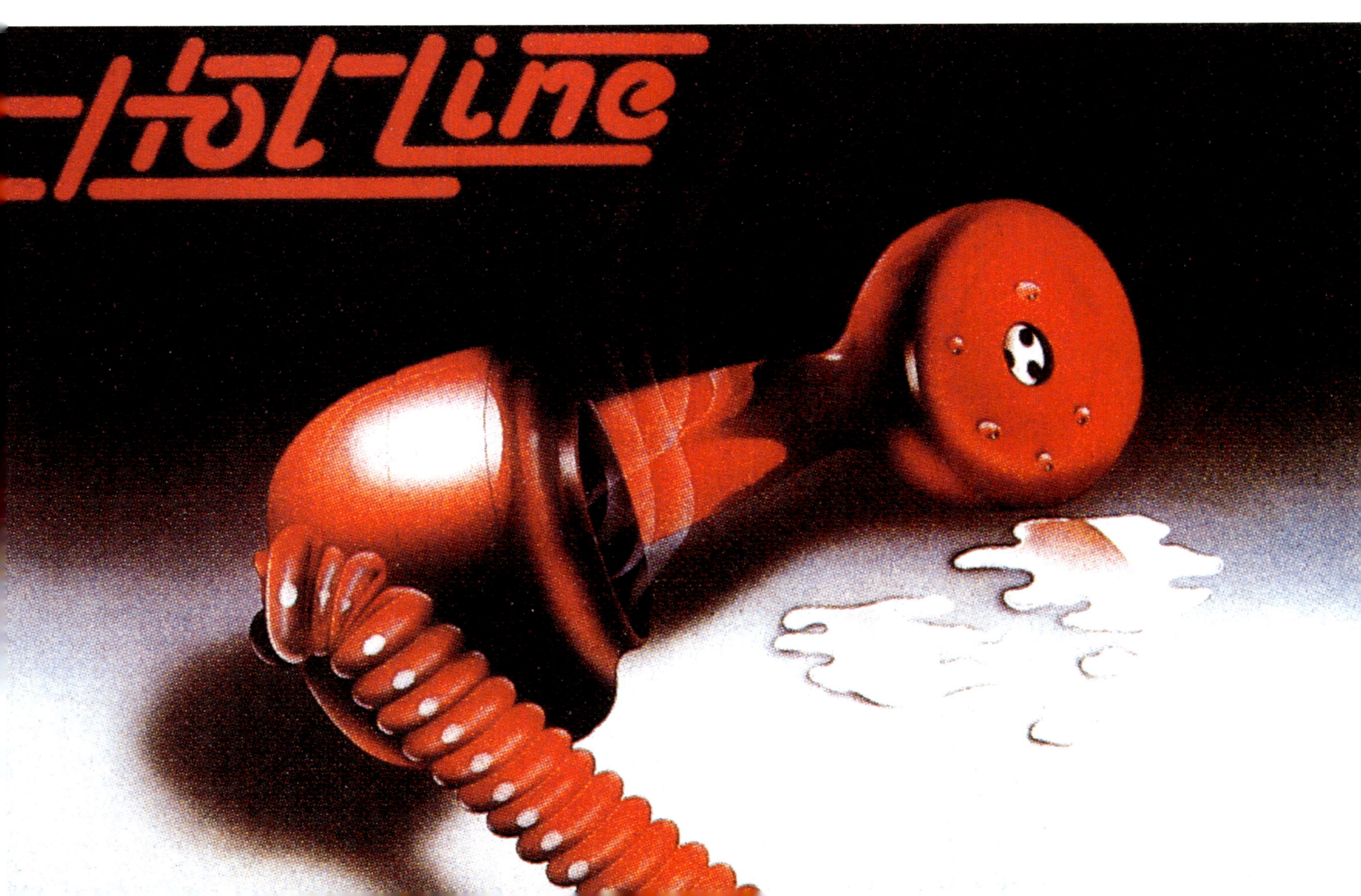

A

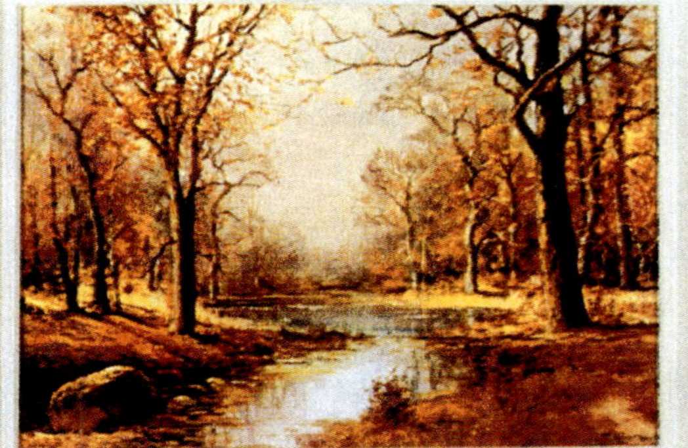

B

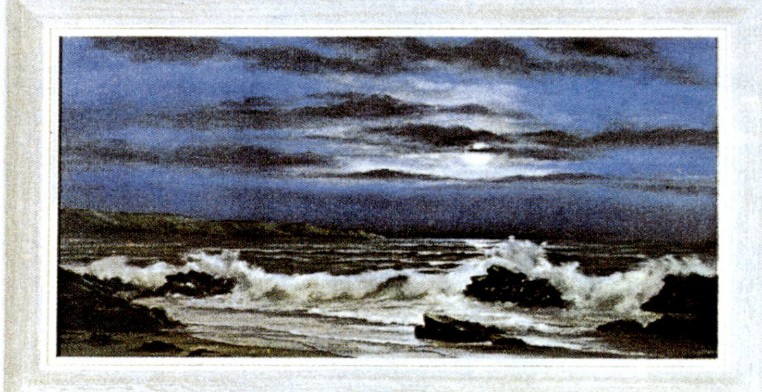

C

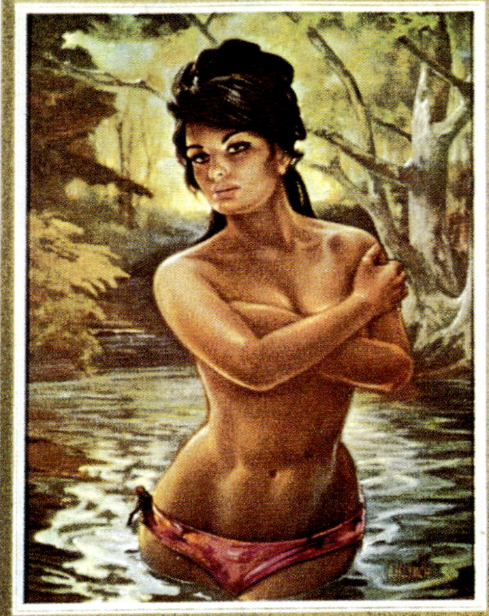

F

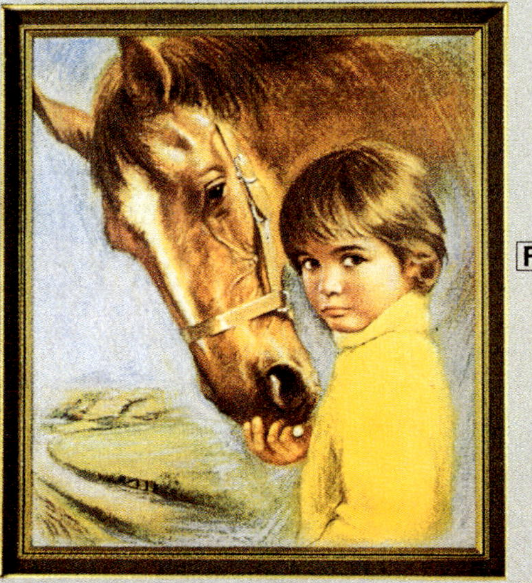

D

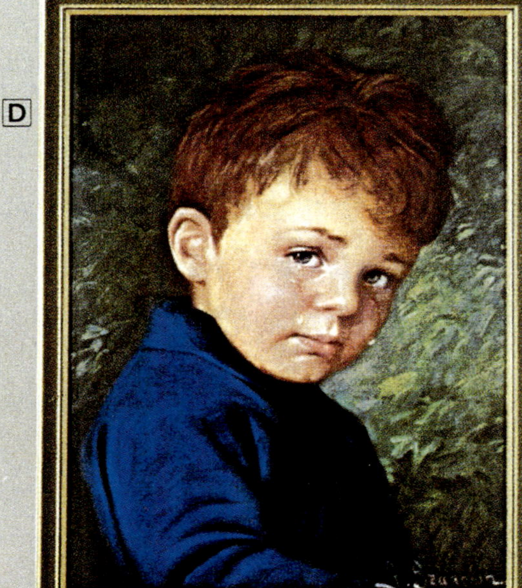

G

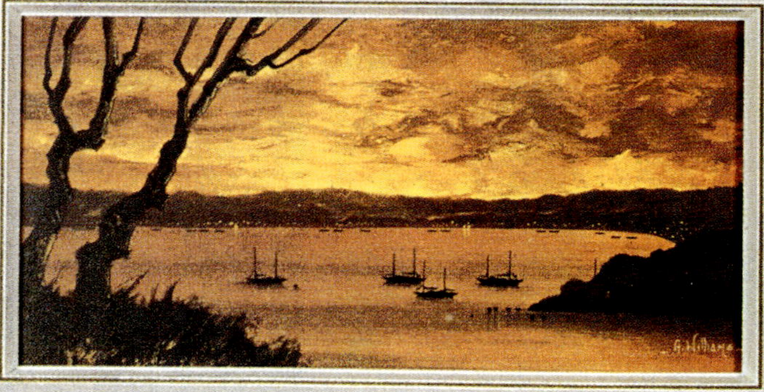

H

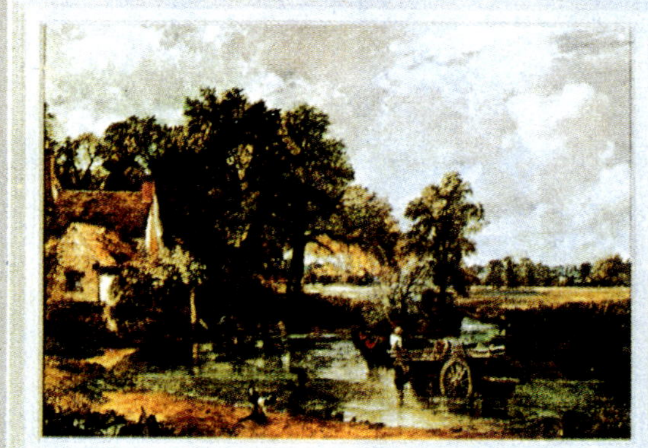

A "October Morn" by Wood. Reproduction print mounted on hardboard and framed in Melamine-coated wood fibre one-piece moulding. Fitted with hanging rings. *Size:* 24 in. x 18 in.
EAG 3683 **£3·95** (£3/19/–) **Picture**

B "Moonlight Surf" by D. Smythe. Reproduction print mounted on hardboard and framed in 3 in. white-painted wooden moulding with light wood-grain vinyl insert. Fitted with hanging rings. *Size:* 34 in. x 20 in.
EAM 3684 **£4·50** (£4/10/–) **Picture**

C "Nymph" by J. H. Lynch. Reproduction print mounted on hardboard and framed in 2 in. white-painted wooden moulding with green-coloured vinyl insert. Fitted with hanging rings. *Size:* 29¾ in. x 22 in.
EAX 3686 **£5·75** (£5/15/–) **Picture**

D "Alfie" by G. Bragolin. Reproduction print mounted on hardboard and framed in 2 in. gold-painted moulding with green-coloured vinyl insert. Fitted with hanging rings. *Size:* 29¾ in. x 22 in.
EAO 3687 **£5·75** (£5/15/–) **Picture**

F "Friends" by L. Shabner. Reproduction print mounted on hardboard and framed in 2 in. gold-painted moulding with green-coloured vinyl insert. Fitted with hanging rings. *Size:* 25½ in. x 21½ in.
EAK 3689 **£5·75** (£5/15/–) **Picture**

G "Evening Hue" by A. Williams. Reproduction print mounted on hardboard and framed in 1½ in. deep white-painted moulding with light green vinyl insert. Fitted with hanging rings. *Size:* 30¾ in. x 16¾ in.
EAD 3688 **£4·50** (£4/10/–) **Picture**

H "Haywain" by Constable. Reproduction print mounted on hardboard and framed in Melamine-coated wood fibre one-piece moulding. Fitted with hanging rings. *Size:* 24 in. x 18 in.
EAR 3685 **£3·95** (£3/19/–) **Picture**

When ordering item numbers beginning with 'E' please use 'E' order form XX0169

List of Works

References

Tretchikoff – Pigeon's Luck – Collins – 1973

Tretchikoff – Howard Trimmins – 1969

Tomorrow's Masters Series – Margaret and Walter Keane – Richard Nolan

MDH Margaret Keane – Johnson Meyers – 1964

Walter Keane – Johnson Meyers – 1964

Freeman's Catalogue – 1970

The Phoenix New Times – 15, 21 April 1999

New York Times Magazine – 23 May 1999

The Sun – 26 October 1985

News of the World Library

Success Story – The Green Lady – BBC – 1974

Red Jacket – SABC – 1997

Montmartre Gallery – www.icon.za/montmart/tretchikoff.htm

Keane Eyes Gallery – www.keane-eyes.com

Megan Besmirched – http://members.tripod.com/besmirched/eyes.html

Kim and Noel – http://members.xoom.xom/foofoo

Artlister – www.artlister.com

Ozz Manor – http://members.tripod.com ~ozz~manor

J & I Art Dealers – http://www.jandiart.com

Starbulletin.com

Photo Credits

Both Author and Publisher have made all reasonable efforts to trace artists and copyright owners of images used in this book and apologise for any unintentional omissions. They would be pleased to insert the appropriate acknowledgments in any subsequent edition. They are prepared to pay fair and reasonable fees for any usage made without compensation or agreement.

Please note: works reproduced courtesy of Felix Rosenstiel's Widow & Son Ltd are not to be removed from the book for display purposes.

Alton, courtesy of the artist, 232

Alvaro, courtesy of the artist, 193

Audrey, courtesy of the artist, 141

Bogie, courtesy of the artist, 226

Bragolin, G, courtesy of the artist, 85

Brown, D C, courtesy of the artist, 215

Bulanos, B, courtesy of the artist, 92

Clemente, F R S, © Felix Rosenstiel's Widow & Son Ltd, 52, 53, 54, 55

Cominoff, P, courtesy of the artist, 144

Collins, cover of Tretchikoff's Pigeon Lock, 15

Dahl, Per, © Per Dahl, 224, 225

D'Argent, A, courtesy of the artist, 90, 91

Degrum, courtesy of the artist, 77

Eden, courtesy of the artist, 192

Edwards, C, courtesy of the artist, 56

Eve, courtesy of the artist, 178, 179, 180

Ferrano, courtesy of the artist, 235

Franca, Ozz, courtesy of the artist, 184, 185, 186, 187, 188, 189

Freeman's catalogue, 238

Genet, courtesy of the artist, 115

Gig, courtesy of the artist, 201, 202, 203, 204, 205, 206, 207

Giusto, courtesy of the artist, 62, 63

Golding, D, courtesy of the artist, 142, 143

Granger, courtesy of the artist, 121

Halsband, G, courtesy of the artist, 222

Hardy, courtesy of the artist, 227

Hemingway, Wayne, courtesy of the author, 3, front and back endpapers, from the Hemingway family album

Idyll, F, courtesy of the artist, 129, 130, 131, 132, 133

Itaya, Foussa, © Felix Rosenstiel's Widow & Son Ltd, 51

J R, courtesy of the artist, 208

Johnson Meyers, covers of MDH Margaret Keane and Walter Keane, 97 (centre), 97 (right)

Kane, Margaret, courtesy of the artist, 195

Keane, Margaret © Margaret Keane, 99, 100, 101, 102, 103, 104-5, 106, 107, 108, 109

Kelly, courtesy of the artist, 230, 231

Kira, courtesy of the artist, 122

Kwatz, courtesy of the artist, 181

Lee, courtesy of the artist, 171 173, 175, 176, 172, 177

Leireiser, Doris, © Felix Rosenstiel's Widow & Son Ltd, 57

Lynch, J H, courtesy of the artist, 71, 72 , 73, 74, 75

Maio, courtesy of the artist, 194, 196, 197

Manes, courtesy of the artist, 134

Matthews, A, courtesy of the artist, 223

Meno, courtesy of the artist, 93

Michel, courtesy of the artist, 126

Nash, courtesy of the artist, 182, 183

Nolan, Richard, Tomorrow's Masters series, cover, 97 (left)

Owen, courtesy of the artist, 230

Pearson, Stephen © Felix Rosenstiel's Widow & Son Ltd, 64, 65, 66, 67, 68, 69, 81

Pouc, courtesy of the artist, 123

Raphael, Betty © Betty Raphael, 136, 137, 138, 139

Rios, Carlos, courtesy of the artist, 220, 221

Roland Smith, G, courtesy of the artist, 229

Shabney, Lou, courtesy of the artist, 78

Simpson, Dallas © Felix Rosenstiel's Widow & Son Ltd, 89, 111, 147, 148, 149, 150, 151, 152, 153, 154, 155, 156, 157, 158, 159, 160, 161, 162, 163, 164, 165, 166, 167

Skinner, Violet © Felix Rosenstiel's Widow & Son Ltd, 58, 59, 60, 61

Spencer, Irene © Felix Rosenstiel's Widow & Son Ltd, 87

Sun, The, p83

T, Michel, courtesy of the artist, 116, 117, 118, 119, 125 126 127

Tretchikoff, Vladimir © Felix Rosenstiel's Widow & Son Ltd, 18, 19, 20, 21, 22, 24, 25, 26, 27, 28, 29, 30, 31, 32, 33, 34, 35, 36, 37, 38, 39, 40, 41, 42, 43, 44, 45, 46, 47, 48, 49

Van der Syde, courtesy of the artist, 78

Yarwood, Jean, courtesy of the artist, 218, 219

Yeend, R T, courtesy of the artist, 23

Zinkeisen, Anna, courtesy of the artist, 88

Acknowledgements

Maureen at **Planet Bazaar**, 151 Drummond Street, London NW1 – a true lover of **Tretchikoff**.

David A. Roe of **Rosenstiel's**, 33 Markham Street, Chelsea Green, London SW3 3NR – the **Tretchikoff** Big Eye historian and 'guardian of the prints'.

Booth-Clibborn Editions.

Jason Beard at **Jonathan Barnbrook** – a great 'book layer outerer'.

Betty Raphael – for her time in telling me about her works.

Popcultaton – the Big Eye Community in the States.

Thank you, **Theda Antrican**, **Gina Garan**, **Megan Besmirched**, **Paul** and **Heather Packrats**, **Laurie Kiddlebit** and the rest of you.

Olé Christiansen – Founder of **Athena**.

Silvano Geraldi – General Manager of **Le Gavroche**.

In addition, the publisher would like to thank **Freeman's** and **Robert Brown** of the **Keane Eyes Gallery**, San Francisco.

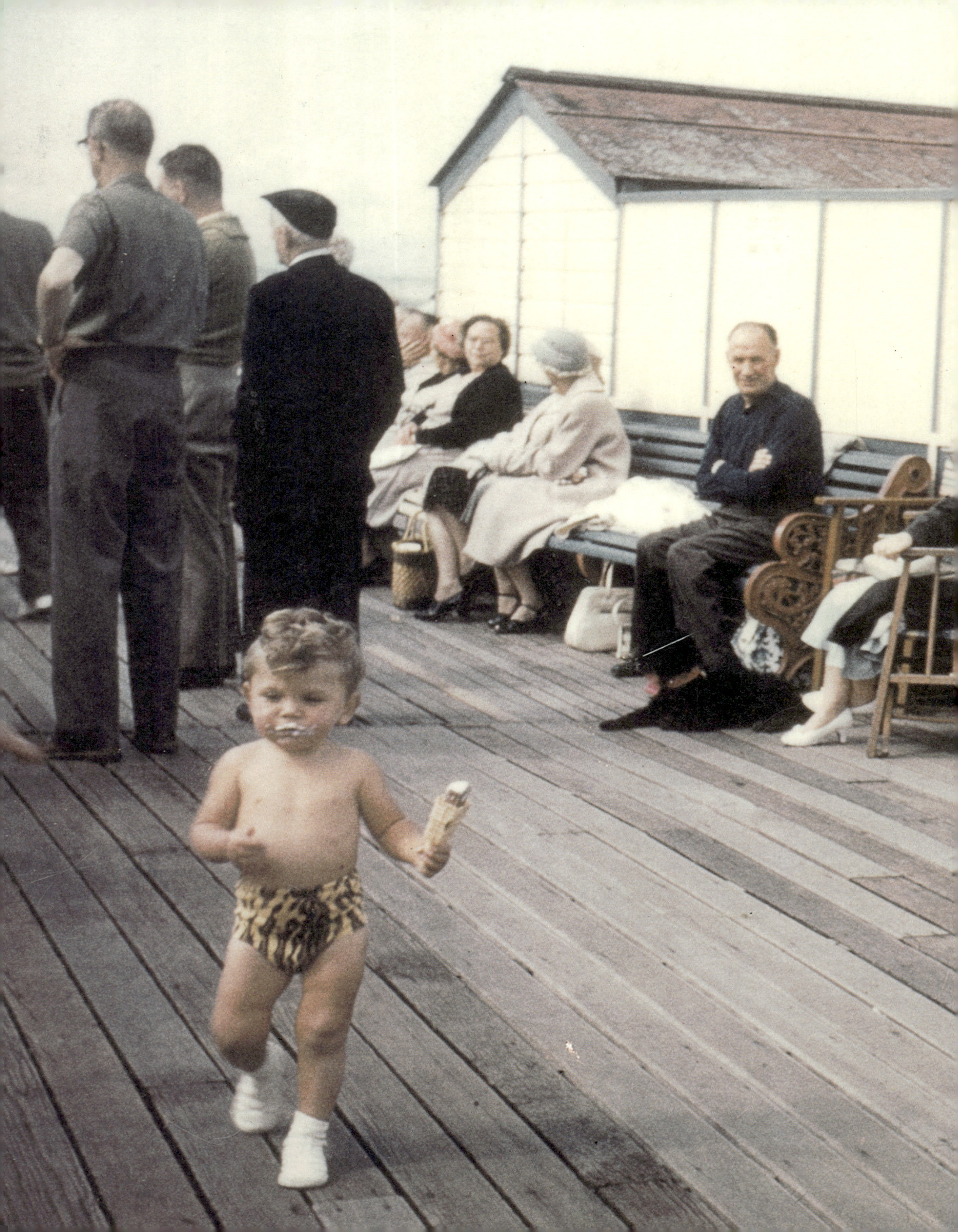